THE TRINITY FORUM

P9-APN-834

STEERING THROUGH CHAOS
Vice and Virtue in an Age of Moral Confusion

OS GUINNESS

Edited by Virginia Mooney
Reader's Guide by Karen Lee-Thorp

NAVPRESS
BRINGING TRUTH TO LIFE
P.O. Box 35001, Colorado Springs, Colorado 80935

OUR GUARANTEE TO YOU

We believe so strongly in the message of our books that we are making this quality guarantee to you. If for any reason you are disappointed with the content of this book, return the title page to us with your name and address and we will refund to you the list price of the book. To help us serve you better, please briefly describe why you were disappointed. Mail your refund request to: NavPress, P.O. Box 35002, Colorado Springs, CO 80935.

NavPress is the publishing ministry of The Navigators. NavPress publications help believers learn biblical truth and apply what they learn to their lives and ministries. Our mission is to stimulate spiritual formation among our readers.

Library of Congress Catalog Card Number: 00-027397
ISBN 1-57683-158-2

Cover illustration by FPG / Jill Sabella; FPG / Steve Hix
Cover design by Dan Jamison
Creative team: Steve Webb, Darla Hightower, Tim Howard, Melissa Munro

Unless otherwise identified, all Scripture quotations in this publication are taken from the *HOLY BIBLE: NEW INTERNATIONAL VERSION* (NIV). Copyright © 1973, 1978, 1984 by International Bible Society. Used by permission of Zondervan Publishing House. All rights reserved.

Steering through chaos: the vices and virtues in an age of moral confusion / compiled by Os Guinness; edited by Virginia Mooney; reader's guide by Karen Lee-Thorp.
    p. cm.
    Includes bibliographical references.
    ISBN 1-57683-158-2
    1. Deadly sins. 2. Christian ethics—Anglican authors. I. Guinness, Os. II. Mooney, Virginia.
III. Lee-Thorp, Karen.

BV4626 .S79 2000
241'.3—dc21   00-027397

Printed in the United States of America

1 2 3 4 5 6 7 8 9 10 11 12 13 14 15 / 01 00

FOR A FREE CATALOG OF
NAVPRESS BOOKS & BIBLE STUDIES,
CALL 1-800-366-7788 (USA)
OR 1-416-499-4615 (CANADA)

THE TRINITY FORUM and design is a registered service mark of The Trinity Forum, Inc.

THE TRINITY FORUM

Contents

THE *TRINITY FORUM STUDY SERIES*
    Not So Much a Book as a Way of Thinking 7

INTRODUCTION 13
    Kay Haugaard, "'The Lottery' Revisited" 25
    Robert Coles, "The Story of Ruby Bridges" 31

ONE: PRIDE 35
    Pride *(Superbia)* Versus Poverty of Spirit 35
        C. S. Lewis, "The Great Sin" 41
        John Milton, *Paradise Lost* 48
        Nancy Collins, "What Makes [Shirley] MacLaine Run?" . . . 51
        William Golding, *The Spire* 54
    The Counterpoint to Pride:
    Blessed Are Those Who Are Poor in Spirit 60
        Thomas à Kempis, "How Through Humility We Should Think
            Ourselves Mean and Abject in the Sight of God" 64
        Jeremy Taylor, "Acts or Offices of Humility" 67

TWO: ENVY 71
    Envy *(Invidia)* Versus Mourning 71
        Plutarch, *Aristides* 80
        William Langland, "Visions from Piers Plowman" 85
        Nathaniel Hawthorne, *The Scarlet Letter* 89
        Henry Fairlie, "Envy or Invidia" 92
        Peter Shaffer, *Amadeus* 98
    The Counterpoint to Envy:
    Blessed Are Those Who Mourn 105
        Victor Hugo, *Les Misérables* 107
        John Wesley & Charles Simeon, "Committed Body Rules,"
            "How to Cope with Evil-Speaking" 111

THREE: ANGER 115
    Anger *(Ira)* Versus Meekness 115
        Plutarch, "Alexander" 120
        Seneca, "On Anger" 125
        John Weir, "Rage, Rage" 128
        Mary Gordon, "The Fascination Begins in the Mouth" 132
    The Counterpoint to Anger:
    Blessed Are the Meek 137
        C. S. Lewis, "Forgiveness" 139
        Martin Luther King Jr., "Loving Your Enemies" 143

FOUR: SLOTH 149

Sloth (*Acedia*) Versus Hunger for Righteousness 149
    Blaise Pascal, *Pensées* 153
    Søren Kierkegaard, "On the Wickedness of the Age" 157
    Dorothy L. Sayers, *The Other Six Deadly Sins* 159
    Václav Havel, *Letters to Olga* 162
The Counterpoint to Sloth:
  Blessed Are Those Who Hunger for Righteousness 167
    John Donne, "Holy Sonnet" 168
    George Herbert, "Love (III)" 170

FIVE: AVARICE 173

Avarice (*Avaritia*) Versus Mercy 173
    Geoffrey Chaucer, "The Pardoner's Prologue" 177
    Leo Tolstoy, "How Much Land Does a Man Need?" 183
    Langdon Gilkey, *Shantung Compound* 198
The Counterpoint to Avarice:
  Blessed Are Those Who Are Merciful 205
    Victor Hugo, "The Bishop at Work" 206

SIX: GLUTTONY 211

Gluttony (*Gula*) Versus Courage Under Suffering and Persecution ... 211
    Petronius, *The Satyricon* 216
    Time magazine, "The Importance of Being Greedy" 217
    C. S. Lewis, *The Screwtape Letters* 219
    Henry Fairlie, "The Gluttony of Our Age" 222
    Frederick Buechner, "The Dwarves in the Stable" 227
The Counterpoint to Gluttony:
  Blessed Are Those Who Are Persecuted for Righteousness' Sake .. 234
    Thomas à Kempis, "Of Patient Suffering of Injuries and
        Wrongs and Who Is Truly Patient" 235
    John of the Cross, "On the Divine Light" 237

SEVEN: LUST 239

Lust (*Luxuria*) Versus Purity of Heart 239
    Molière, *Don Juan, or the Feast with the Statue* 245
    D. H. Lawrence, *The Rainbow* 248
    Ernesto Cardenal, "A Prayer for Marilyn Monroe" 256
The Counterpoint to Lust:
  Blessed Are the Pure in Heart 260
    Augustine, *Confessions* 261
    William F. May, "False Worship: Impurity of Heart" 266

CONCLUSION: FIVE REMINDERS 271

    Aristotle, "Moral Goodness" 273
    Samuel Johnson, "Self-Deception" 277
    Langdon Gilkey, *Shantung Compound* 282
    C. S. Lewis, "Christian Behaviour" and *The Weight of Glory* 289
    Maximilian Kolbe, *Orbit of Darkness*, by Ian MacMillan ... 294
    Corrie ten Boom, "Love Your Enemy" 301

FOR FURTHER READING 304

READER'S GUIDE 305

THE TRINITY FORUM

"Contributing to the transformation and renewal of society through the transformation and renewal of leaders."

The Trinity Forum would like to recognize the following people for
their work on this project:
Project Director: Os Guinness
Selections and Introductions: Os Guinness
Resource Scholar: Louise Cowan
Researchers: Nelson González, Margaret Gardner
Editor: Virginia Mooney
Copyeditors: Peter Edman, Amy Boucher, Ginger Koloszyc

NOT SO MUCH A BOOK
AS A WAY OF THINKING

The 'Why' and 'How' of The Trinity Forum Study Series

Thinkers from the time of Socrates to our own day have believed that the unexamined life is not worth living. Today's unique challenge is to lead an examined life in an unexamining age. The sheer pace and pressure of our modern lives can easily crowd out time for reflection. To make matters worse, we live in a war zone against independent thinking. Television jingles, advertising hype, political soundbites, and "dumbed down" discourse of all kinds assault an individual's ability to think for himself or herself. Carefully considered conclusions about life and the best way to live it are too often the casualties.

Into this challenging landscape The Trinity Forum launches its *Study Series,* inviting individuals to think through today's issues carefully and deliberately—in the context of faith—to reach deeper and more firmly established convictions.

About The Trinity Forum

The Trinity Forum was founded in 1991. Its aim: to contribute to the transformation and renewal of society through the transformation and renewal of leaders. Christian in commitment, but open to all who are interested in its vision, it has organized dozens of forums for leaders of all sectors of modern life—from business to education, from fashion to government and the media.

Hundreds of leaders from many faiths across the United States, Canada, and Europe have taken part in these forums.

A distinctive feature of The Trinity Forum is its format. There are no lectures, addresses, or talks of any kind. A curriculum of readings on a given topic is sent out in advance and then explored at the forum in a Socratic-style open discussion led by moderators. This give-and-take challenges the participants to wrestle with the issues themselves and—importantly—to reach their own thought-out conclusions.

By popular demand, The Trinity Forum now offers these curricula to a wider audience, enhanced as the *Trinity Forum Study Series* and designed for individual readers or study groups in homes, churches, and colleges. Each *Study* is intended to help thoughtful people examine the foundational issues through which faith acts upon the public good of modern society. A reader's guide at the back of each book will aid those who want to discuss the material with a group. Those reading the book on their own may also find that the reader's guide will help them focus on the *Study's* big ideas. The reader's guide contains basic principles of small group leadership, an overview of the *Study's* main ideas, and suggested selections for groups that don't have time to discuss every reading in the *Study*.

Adult in seriousness and tone, yet popular rather than scholarly in style, the *Trinity Forum Study Series* probes each topic through the milestone writings that have shaped its development. This approach will be fresh and exciting to many and, we trust, stimulating to all. It is worth laying out some of the assumptions and convictions that guide this approach, for what is presented here is not so much a book as it is a way of thinking.

Defining Features of the Trinity Forum Study Series

First, the Trinity Forum Study Series *explores the issues of our day in the context of faith.* As stated earlier, The Trinity Forum is Christ-centered in its commitment, but opens its programs to all who share its aims—whether believers, seekers, or skeptics. The same committed but open spirit marks this series of books.

For people of faith, it should be natural to take into account the place of faith when discussing the issues of life, both historically and presently. But it should also be natural for all citizens of Western society, of whatever faith. For no one can understand Western civilization without understanding the Christian faith that, for better or worse, has been its primary shaping force. Yet a striking feature of many of today's thought-leaders and opinion-shapers is their "tone deafness" toward faith of any kind—which means that, unwittingly or otherwise, they do not hear the music by which most people orchestrate their lives.

For example, a national media executive recently admitted his and his colleagues' befuddlement about Americans' deep reliance upon faith. Citing the outpouring of public prayer in response to a tragic school shooting in Kentucky, he confessed, "We simply don't get it." These readings aim to remedy that neglected dimension of understanding, and thereby reintroduce to the modern discussion the perspective of faith that is vital both for making sense of the past and dealing with the present.

Second, the Trinity Forum Study Series *presents the perspective of faith in the context of the sweep of Western civilization, recognizing the vital place of the past in the lives of nations as well as individuals.* A distinctive feature of the modern world is its passion for the present and fascination with the future at the expense of the past. Progress, choice, change, novelty, and the myth of newer-the-truer and latest-is-greatest reign unchallenged, while ideas and convictions from earlier times are boxed up in the cobwebbed attic of nostalgia and irrelevance. By contrast, Winston Churchill said, "The further backward you can look, the farther forward you can see." For him, as well as the American framers in the eighteenth century and the writers of the Bible before them, remembering is not foremost a matter of nostalgia or historical reverie, and it is far more than mental recall. For all of them, it is a vital key to identity, faith, wisdom, renewal, and the dynamism of a living tradition, for both nations and individuals.

By reintroducing important writings from the past, the *Trinity Forum Study Series* invites readers to a living conversation of ideas and imagination with the great minds of our heritage. Only when we know where we have come from do we know who we are and where we are going.

Third, the Trinity Forum Study Series *presents the perspective of faith in the context of the challenge of other faiths.* If the first feature of this series is likely to offend some unthinking secularists, this one may do the same to unthinking believers. But the truth is, some believers don't appear to know their own faith because they know *only* their own faith. Familiarity breeds inattention. It is true, as essayist Ronald Knox quipped, that comparative religion can make us "comparatively religious." But it is also true that contrast is the mother of clarity.

One important benefit of understanding one's own faith in distinction to others is the ability to communicate ideas and positions persuasively in the public square. Believers properly hold their beliefs on the basis of divine authority. Such beliefs, however, must be conveyed compellingly in a society that does not accept the same authority. An important part of meeting that challenge effectively is the ability to grasp and highlight the differences between faiths.

This series of books, therefore, sets out the perspectives of the Christian faith in the context of the challenge of other faiths. If "all truth is God's truth," and if differences truly make a difference, then such contrasts between one faith and another are not only challenging but illuminating and important for both individuals and society.

Fourth, the Trinity Forum Study Series *is unashamed about the necessity for tough-minded thinking.* Much has been made recently of Christian anti-intellectualism and the scandal of the lack of a Christian mind. As Bertrand Russell put it, "Most Christians would rather die than think—in fact, they do." But failure to think is not confined to any one community or group. Former Secretary of State Henry Kissinger is quoted as saying, "In Washington D.C. there is so little time to think that most people live forever off the intellectual capital from the day they arrive."

In contrast, Abraham Lincoln's greatness was fired in times of thoughtful reflection during the Civil War. Today's profound crises call for similar thoughtful reflection and courage by men and women prepared to break rank with a largely unthinking and conformist age. Just as an earlier generation broke with accepted practices of little exercise and bad eating, restoring a vogue for fitness, so our generation must shake off the lethargy of "dumbed down" discourse and recover the capacity to think tough-mindedly as the issues and our times require.

Fifth, the Trinity Forum Study Series *recognizes that many of the urgent public issues of our day are cultural rather than political.* Much recent discussion of public affairs oscillates uneasily between heavily moral issues (such as abortion) and more strongly political issues (such as campaign finance reform). Yet increasingly, many of the urgent concerns of our day lie in between. They are neither purely moral nor purely political, but integrate elements of both. In other words, many key issues are morally grounded "pre-political" issues, such as the role of "trust" in capitalism, "character" in leadership, "truth" in public discourse, "stewardship" in philanthropy and environmentalism, and "voluntarism" in civil society.

To be sure, it is a symptom of our present crisis that such foundational issues have to be debated at all. But the *Trinity Forum Study Series* addresses these often neglected issues, always presenting them in the context of faith and always addressing them in a nonpartisan manner that befits such cultural discussion.

Finally, the Trinity Forum Study Series *assumes the special need for, and the possibility of, a social and cultural renaissance in our time.* As we consider our present crises with clear-eyed realism, one of the great challenges is to be hopeful with a real basis for hope, while always being critical of what is wrong without collapsing into alarmism or despair. To be sure, no freedom, prosperity, or success lasts forever in this life, in either spiritual or secular affairs. But, equally, the grand cycle of birth, growth, and decline is never deterministic, and no source of renewal is more sure and powerful than spiritual revival. The *Study Series* is born of this conviction.

Giving up hope in the worthwhileness of the worthwhile—in God, the good, the true, the just, and the beautiful—is another name for the deadly sin of sloth. Venturing out, under God, to be entrepreneurs of life is another name for faith. Thus, while always uncertain of the outcome of our times, always modest about our own contribution, and always confident in God rather than ourselves, those who present the *Trinity Forum Study Series* desire to encourage people to move out into society with constructive answers and a sense of a confidence born of faith and seasoned by history. In so doing we seek to sow the seeds for a much-needed renaissance in our own time.

INTRODUCTION

Right up to the end of the nineteenth century, the most important course in a student's college career was moral philosophy, or what we today call ethics. The course was taken as the crowning unit in the senior year, usually taught by the college president himself.

Today a remarkable explosion of interest in ethics suggests to some people that we are going back to that morally robust era. A survey by the Hastings Center claims that the United States now offers more than eleven thousand courses in applied ethics. These courses tackle all manner of ethical problems in business, politics, medicine, science, engineering, and social work, and are backed by some staggeringly generous financial grants, dozens of journals, hundreds of textbooks, and thousands of experts. During the nineties, both MTV and The New York Times took up the topic of the seven deadly sins.

Yet this resurgent interest in ethics is hardly cause for celebration. For one thing, morality is like health—preoccupation with it is often a sign of illness, not vitality. For another thing, a closer look at the resurgence is not so reassuring.

First, part of the renewed interest is simply fashionable and transient. As one commentator put it, "In our low-fat, low-conscience culture, Sin-Lite has found shelf space alongside other low-guilt pleasures." Or in the words of MTV, "A little lust, pride, sloth, and gluttony—in moderation—are fun, and that's what keeps your heart beating."

For one thing, morality is like health—preoccupation with it is often a sign of illness, not vitality.

WHAT'S BECOME OF BECOMING?

"The question to be asked at the end of an educational step is not 'What has the student learned?' but 'What has the student become?'"

—President James Monroe

13

"My client pleads not guilty to the murder charges, Your Honor, on the grounds that you can't legislate morality."

From the WALL STREET JOURNAL. Permission, Cartoon Features Syndicate.

Second, a great deal more of the renewed interest is about "prevention ethics" rather than principled ethics. It is more concerned with "not being caught" (or sued or exposed in the press) than with doing right. What Oscar Wilde said cynically a century ago is uncomfortably apt in the climate of today's culture wars: "Morality is simply the attitude we adopt toward people we personally dislike."

Third, even where good ethics is taught in a good way, it is usually more social than personal—what matters for the politically correct is to hold the right views, not to practice them. The issues have to do with corporations, schools, courts, governments, and the treatment of the environment, not with the individual's virtue and responsibility that underlies these secondary issues.

Fourth, and worse still, the current ethics is often taught with a shallow view of human nature and an even shallower view of evil in human society. For example, topics such as hypocrisy, self-deception, selfishness, and cruelty rarely come up. And the place of envy in politics, greed in the economy, lust in the fashion industry, and violence in the entertainment business is rarely probed.

The fruit of the last two hundred years of elite thinking has been to destroy the possibility of any moral knowledge on which to pursue moral formation.

Fifth, and worst of all, the present preoccupation with ethics in elite intellectual centers has an element of absurdity. The fruit of the last two hundred years of elite thinking has been to destroy the possibility of any moral knowledge on which to pursue moral formation. Because there are no moral conclusions left, all that remains is evermore clever talk about ethics, and trying to navigate the moral confusion is like driving through New York City with all the traffic lights turned off.

NOT A SINGLE MORAL CONCLUSION?

"[W]here ethics is concerned, I hold that, so far as fundamentals are concerned, it is impossible to produce conclusive intellectual arguments. . . . In a fundamental question of ethics I do not think a theoretical argument is possible."

—Bertrand Russell

"Today's course in applied ethics does not seek to convey a set of moral truths but tries to encourage the student to think carefully about complex moral issues. . . . The principle aim of the course is not to impart 'right answers' but to make the student more perceptive in detecting ethical problems when they arise."

—Derek Bok, Harvard University's
"President's Report" 1986–1987

"Had [President Bok] strolled across Harvard Yard to Emerson Hall and consulted with some of the most influential thinkers in our nation, he would have discovered that there now is no recognized moral knowledge upon which projects of fostering moral development could be based.

"There is now not a single moral conclusion about behavior or character traits that a teacher could base a student's grade on—not even those most dear to educators, concerning fairness and diversity."

—Dallas Willard, *The Divine Conspiracy*

"A glance at a typical anthology of a college course in ethics reveals that most of what the student will read is directed toward analyzing and criticizing policies on such issues as punishment, recombinant DNA research, abortion, and euthanasia. . . . Inevitably the student gets the idea that applying ethics to modern life is mainly a matter of being for or against some social policy."

—Christina Sommers,
"Where Have All the Good Deeds Gone?"

"I've been taking all these philosophy courses, and we talk about what's true, what's important, what's good. Well, how do you teach people to be good? What's the point of knowing good if you don't keep trying to become a good person?"

—On dropping out of Harvard,
a student's comment to Professor Robert Cole

These shortcomings in the current discussion of ethics are reinforced by two blind spots. One is the lack of a serious analysis of why we have an ethics crisis in the first place. Most attention is directed at symptoms, not causes. For example, there is little understanding that, because of the convictions of its founders, the United States is a nation with a realistic view of evil embedded in its constitutional checks and balances. Yet, psychologist Karl Menninger's 1973 book Whatever

Became of Sin? *was not only a startling title, but a sobering benchmark to gauge the slippage from the position of the founders. The notion of evil, he argued, had slid from being "sin," defined theologically, to being "crime," defined legally, to being "sickness," defined only in psychological categories. In Senator Daniel Patrick Moynihan's more recent analysis, Americans have "defined deviancy down." What was "deviant" fifty years ago is today just "feeling one's oats."*

SIN OR BAD TASTE?

"An educated Chinese would simply refuse to be continually burdened with 'sin.' The concept of 'sin' is usually felt as shocking and lacking in dignity by genteel intellectuals everywhere. Usually it is replaced by conventional, or feudal, or aesthetically formulated variants such as 'indecent' or 'not in good taste.'"

—Max Weber, *The Religion of China*

The moral crisis in the West (similar problems exist in other modern countries) can be probed best with the help of three terms—"permissive," "transgressive," and "remissive." Dostoyevsky captured the first term a hundred years ago in his famous refrain in The Brothers Karamazov: If God is dead, and there is no future life, "nothing would be immoral any longer, everything would be permitted." The second term, transgressive, *found its classic expression in the slogan painted on a wall at the Sorbonne in Paris in 1968, "It is forbidden to forbid"—later popularized by basketball player Dennis Rodman as "bad as I wanna be."*

The third term, remissive, *comes up repeatedly when people try to describe the moral crisis and grope for terms that capture the overwhelming and snowballing nature of it. Society, they say, is "eroding," "unraveling," "fraying," and the like. Or, as one political leader expressed it during the scandals swirling around the Clinton presidency, "You can stop a flood by putting your finger in the dyke, but how do you stop a mudslide?"*

RULES ARE FOR BREAKING

"Man is the only animal that blushes. Or needs to."

—Mark Twain, *Pudd'nhead Wilson's New Calendar*

"It is not the repressions that trouble us now but the permissions."

—Philip Rieff, University of Pennsylvania

"Madonna told me to break every rule I could think of, and then when I was done to make up some new ones and break them."

—Madonna's choreographer, following her 1990 world tour

The other blind spot in the current ethics discussion is an ignorance of the tradition of "the virtues and the vices"—the most profound and influential ethical tradition in the West. As historian W. E. H. Lecky wrote, the teachings of Jesus are "an agency which all men must now admit to have been, for good or for evil, the most powerful moral lever that has ever been applied to the affairs of man." This tradition has both a high view of human nature and a deeply realistic view of the presence and power of evil. Before asking "What sort of action should I take?" it asks "What sort of person should I be?" From this perspective, being moral is not merely learning what is right. Even psychopaths may well know what is right and wrong, but because of their basic lack of human sympathy, they do not care enough to do it. In this tradition, being moral means translating the knowledge of right and wrong into character and consistent action. It is, once again, a matter of becoming a good person, *not just* knowing about good.

In this tradition, being moral means translating the knowledge of right and wrong into character and consistent action.

"GOOD DEED" PROFESSIONALS

"Good deeds have been given over to experts: the acts that constitute the social morality of our time are being performed by paid professionals in large public agencies. Helping the needy, the sick, and the aged has become an operation whose scale and character leave little room for the virtuous private person. Our ancestors in their idiosyncratic charitable endeavors look like moral amateurs. . . .

"Because morality has been sublimated into ideology, great numbers of people, the young and educated especially, feel they have an adequate moral identity merely because they hold the 'right' views on such matters as ecology, feminism, socialism, and nuclear energy. They may lead narrow, self-indulgent lives, obsessed with their physical health, material comforts, and personal growth, yet still feel a moral advantage over those who actively work to help the needy but who are, in their eyes, ideologically unsound."

— Christina Sommers,
"Where Have All the Good Deeds Gone?"

"Volunteers are there but you have to offer them something . . . career benefits and résumé experience."
— Greater Boston Red Cross

Ironically, the realistic view of human evil housed in this tradition is a statement of hope, not despair. Not only is sin the most verifiable of all biblical truths, it is the urgent precursor to the necessity and wonder of redemption. Those with a superficial view of sin, evil, and vice run the serious risk of intellectual hubris. As Washington journalist Henry Fairlie put it, "I have for a long time thought that the psychological explanations of the waywardness of our behavior and the sociological *explanations of the evils of our societies have come very nearly to a dead end. . . . They have come to this impasse because they shirk the problem of evil."*

If we don't need to take the human inclination to evil seriously, why has all our tinkering with ourselves and our societies over the centuries done so little good? Why was the most knowledgeable, enlightened, and advanced century of all—the twentieth—also the darkest and most brutal? Are we perhaps even regressing? How could a president who announced that his administration would be "the most ethical in American history" end up as the most corrupt and the most corrupting? To people steeped in the virtues-and-vices tradition, such questions are neither idle nor surprising.

Every generation has its own conscious or unconscious ranking of the sins—Victorians, for example, exaggerated sloth and lust while underestimating envy and avarice. But a defining feature of our generation is its minimizing of any notion of sin.

Today the concept of "virtue" is either stuntedly narrow (almost a synonym for chastity) or piously hollow, and the concept of "vice" has a dated and faintly ridiculous air—were it not for the growing number of people unable to master their physical and psychological impulses. As one psychologist says, the burgeoning self-help groups are not only evidence of the shunning of mainstream psychology but an unintended testimony to the prominence of "vices", as every conceivable "vice" has its respective Anonymous meetings to attend.

In contrast to the virtues-and-vices tradition, modern culture hands us a license to eat whatever we feel like eating, sleep with whomever is willing, rebel against whatever frustrates us, lash back at whoever has hurt us, and cross whatever legal and ethical lines are beyond detection. Yet the resulting loss of self-control is a critical part of the cultural crisis of the West. It is also an urgent reminder of why an understanding of the virtues and vices is important.

> *If we don't need to take the human inclination to evil seriously, why has all our tinkering with ourselves and our societies over the centuries done so little good?*

THE ROAD MORE TRAVELED

"The girl speaks eighteen languages and can't say 'no' in any of them."

—Dorothy Parker

"Lead me not into temptation; I can find the way myself."

—Rita Mae Brown, in the movie *Ghost*

"Here's a rule I recommend: Never practice two vices at once."

—Tallula Bankhead

"A man should not be without morals; it is better to have bad morals than none at all."

—Mark Twain, *Notebook*

Needless to say, a collection of readings on the virtues and vices has its own pitfalls. One is that there is more to ethics than simply knowing the cardinal virtues and avoiding the deadly vices. (The New York Times Book Review and an MTV special covered the seven deadly sins, but neither did so with depth or realism.) An ounce of virtue is worth more than tons of sophisticated talk about virtue.

A second pitfall is the lurking danger of legalism and moralism—"legalism" being the reduction of life to external rules of behavior and "moralism" being the removal of grace from an issue and the reduction of the many dimensions of life to the single dimension of morality.

A third pitfall is to reduce the virtuous life to what Dallas Willard aptly calls "sin management"—which for liberals means only the removal of social evils and for conservatives means only the forgiveness of individual's sins. The virtuous life, by contrast, is a matter of people enabled to be good, rather than simply talking about it.

Having said that, the forgotten classical tradition of the virtues and vices is fundamental to the renaissance of the "good society" of which so many people speak. (At the very least, the "good society" is a society that, on balance, is favorable to its citizens being good.) As such, wrestling with the dynamics of the virtues and vices is important for any society and a probing personal examination for each of us.

This book should perhaps carry a Surgeon General's warning: "The following material may prove injurious to personal complacency and self-satisfaction." But challenging as it is, the net effect can only be beneficial. Knowing the cardinal virtues and deadly vices provides essential moral compasses for us as modern people. In a day of extreme moral confusion, a clear grasp of the virtues and vices helps us steer through chaos. Moral exercise may be challenging, but as with physical exercise: No pain, no gain.

> *The virtuous life, by contrast, is a matter of people enabled to be good, rather than simply talking about it.*

> *In a day of extreme moral confusion, a clear grasp of the virtues and vices helps us steer through chaos.*

WHY "SINS" AND WHY "SEVEN"?

Restaurants have their soup du jour. Talk shows have their topic du jour. And Washington, D.C., says The Washington Post, has its "deadly sin du jour." One day it is illegal baby-sitters, another it is pot smoking, yet another it is club membership or check bouncing. In each case what was formerly considered a peccadillo suddenly becomes a capital offense, and then quickly goes back to barely raising an eyebrow.

This superficial and short-attention-span view of evil is light years from the classical tradition of the virtues and vices. The very notion that the virtues are "cardinal" and the vices "deadly," "capital," or "cardinal" expresses the conviction that these particular virtues and vices are the "head" (caput in Latin), "source," or "root" of all other forms of human goodness and evil.

ALMOST, BUT NOT QUITE

"Politics without principle, Wealth without work, Commerce without morality, Pleasure without conscience, Education without character, Science without humanity, Worship without sacrifice."

—Gandhi's version of the Seven Deadly Sins

The tradition of the virtues and vices comes from two main sources—the Greek and Roman philosophers and the Old and New Testaments. After these two streams of moral understanding converged, there was general agreement that the virtues and vices are the most important character traits, or universal human tendencies, from which all goodness and evil result. As such, the virtue-and-vice tradition contributed massively to the Western definition of what it means to be human, both in theory and practice.

The virtues and vices are the most important character traits, or universal human tendencies, from which all goodness and evil result.

REVELATIONS

"Prosperity unmasks the vices; adversity reveals the virtues."

—Diderot

The following readings attest to the vitality of this theme in literature and art as well as in philosophy. The literary portrayal of the vices reached its zenith in Dante's Divine Comedy. Far from dry legalism or moralism, Dante's work is great poetry and great drama, painting the vices with vivid, unsettling imagery. In the Inferno's journey through hell, sinners appear bobbing up and down in rivers of excrement or blood, are metamorphosed into trees, and float face up and swollen in the lake of ice. Naked and tormented, some are constricted by snakes, others dazed and disemboweled. As the Purgatory adds, following Augustine's famous observation that "sin is the punishment of sin" and therefore that judgment is the consequence of settled choice, Dante portrays them all receiving the specific punishment appropriate to their specific sin.

Contrary to what some people expect, the Greeks and Romans were stronger on the virtues and the Jews and Christians on the vices. Indeed, the latter saw "vices" and "sins" as one. The two words are interchangeable and radical. The vices are therefore never peccadilloes or lovably excusable flaws. They are truly deadly.

No modern formulation of humanness comes close to the virtue-and-vice tradition in capturing both the grandeur and the fatally flawed nature of human existence. Modern views, instead, tend to be flippant about vice and reduce its seriousness to a yawn or a snicker. This dismissal is illustrated in the following comment by Ian Fleming, the creator of James Bond, as he introduced the London Times *book on the seven deadly sins.*

No modern formulation of humanness comes close to the virtue-and-vice tradition in capturing both the grandeur and the fatally flawed nature of human existence.

NO DEADLY SEVEN FOR 007

"To be precise and truthful, the critical examination of these famous sins by some of the keenest brains of today has led me to the dreadful conclusion that in fact all these ancient sins . . . are in fact very close to virtues. . . . How drab and empty life would be without these sins, and what dull dogs we would all be without a healthy trace of many of them in our makeup!"

—Ian Fleming

For the Greeks, virtue was that excellence which causes something to perform its purpose well. Thus the virtue of the eye is seeing clearly, the virtue of the knife is cutting sharply, the virtue of the horse is running strongly, and so on. Vice was largely a matter of excess or deficit, missing the desired balance or "golden mean" that is the virtue. Aristotle, for example, worked out in detail the excesses, means (virtues), and deficiencies displayed in the most common and important life activities. These categories, which are typical of the Greek and Roman understanding, are summarized in the following table.

Activity	Vice (excess)	Virtue (mean)	Vice (deficit)
Facing death	Too much fear (cowardice)	Right amount of fear (courage)	Too little fear (foolhardiness)
Bodily actions (eating, drinking, sex)	Profligacy	Temperance	No name for this state; could be called "insensitivity"
Giving money	Prodigality	Liberality	Illiberality
Large-scale giving	Vulgarity	Magnificence	Meanness
Claiming honors	Vanity	Pride	Humility
Social intercourse	Obsequiousness	Friendliness	Sulkiness
According honors	Injustice	Justice	Injustice
Retribution for wrongdoing	Injustice	Justice	Injustice

The Christian classification of the seven deadly sins is deeper and more dynamic. Because it began in the Christian monastic movement in the Egyptian desert, it was originally a list of the vices besetting monastic communities. But even there it was given a dynamic vitality by its conviction that the Devil is the ultimate source of temptation.

In the fourth century, Evagrius, a monk, listed eight chief sins: gluttony, lust, avarice, sadness, anger, spiritual lethargy, vainglory, and pride. Evagrius's disciple John Cassian of Marseilles carried this list to the West where it received its classical formulation from Pope Gregory the Great in the sixth century. Gregory not only modified the list (which became the classical one followed in this curriculum), but he made pride a category by itself and redefined the very status of the vices.

From then on, the seven deadly sins were not restricted to monastic life. They were understood as the normal perils of the soul in the midst of everyday life—discovered by plumbing the human heart at its deepest. Augustine saw the sins as prideful attempts to mimic the attributes of God—avarice parodying God's possession of all things, anger parodying his wrath, and so on. Also, as Chaucer's Parson says in The Canterbury Tales, *the seven deadly sins are "all leashed together." They are "the trunk of the tree from which others branch." Far from being a comprehensive list of all countable sins, the seven deadly sins are the basic, interlocking capital sins that lie at the core of our human natures and from which others arise.*

Far from being a comprehensive list of all countable sins, the seven deadly sins are the basic, interlocking capital sins that lie at the core of our human natures and from which others arise.

ART IS NOT LIFE

"The vices that make good theater are intolerable in life, and the banality of goodness on the stage is no argument against the virtues."

—Simone Weil

A number of other introductory points are important. First, the Christian view regards the impulse to love as being at the very center of all the virtues and vices. Whereas the virtues stem from the proper ordering of love, the vices stem from a disordering of love. Anger, for example, is perverted love in the sense that love is directed toward a worthy object (oneself) but in a false manner (through anger at someone else). Similarly, sloth is a sin of defective love just as avarice and gluttony are sins of excessive love.

Second, there is widespread agreement about the overall categories of the seven vices. The first five vices (pride, envy, anger, sloth, and avarice) are different from the last two (gluttony and lust). The former are sins of the spirit, rather than of the flesh, and are often described as the "cold" but "respectable" sins. The latter are obviously sins of the flesh, and therefore "warm" but "disreputable."

Third, there is no exact parallelism—beyond the obvious one of number— between the seven deadly vices and the seven cardinal virtues (prudence, fortitude, temperance, justice, faith, hope, and charity). In most cases the virtues are not the opposite of the vices.

And so this curriculum follows a lesser-known path of interpretation. It focuses in-depth on the seven deadly vices and in so doing, contrasts them not with the traditional virtues, but with the Beatitudes of Jesus from the Sermon on the Mount. Though lesser-known, this path is nevertheless well-trodden. Classical commentators, such as Augustine, and modern commentators, such as Peter Kreeft, have argued that the Beatitudes are the "virtues of the kingdom" and superbly opposed to the vices. In some cases the contrast is obvious (pride versus poverty of spirit or humility). In other cases it is not so obvious, but on deeper examination is equally illuminating. Peter Kreeft, professor of philosophy at Boston College, lays out the contrasts in the following table.

VICES: Seven Deadly Sins	VIRTUES: Beatitudes
Pride self-absorption, self-assertion	**Poverty of Spirit** humility, selflessness
Envy resentment at the happiness of others	**Mourning** sharing the unhappiness of others
Anger the willing of harm and destruction to others	**Meekness** refusal to do harm to others and desire for peacemaking
Sloth lethargy toward God, the good, and the ideal	**Hunger and Thirst After Righteousness** passion for and pursuit of God, the good, and the ideal
Avarice the centrifugal reach to grasp and hang on to the world's goods	**Mercy** the centripetal reach to share with others, even the undeserving
Gluttony the drive to consume an inordinate amount of worldly goods	**Those Persecuted** the dedication that can surmount deprivation of even basic necessities
Lust the inordinate and dissipating desire for every attractive body	**Purity of Heart** the true desire for God that centers and unifies the soul

Finally, in line with the Surgeon General's warning earlier, it must be said that anyone who wrestles with the seven deadly sins may find himself or herself facing a moment of truth. Talk of the vices usually starts out as joking about particular sins, especially gluttony and lust, and ends up by confronting the idea

Evil comes into focus when we see it in others, but it comes into sharp and terrible focus when we see it in ourselves.

of sin itself—*a far more dangerous proposition. Evil comes into focus when we see it in others, but it comes into sharp and terrible focus when we see it in ourselves. If we really wish to understand evil, the hardest but best place to look is in our own hearts, as the following readings suggest.*

IN THE EYE OF THE BEHOLDER

"Nothing so needs reforming as other people's habits."

—Mark Twain, *Pudd'nhead Wilson's Calendar*

❧ *Kay Haugaard* ❧

Kay Haugaard is a teacher of creative writing in southern California whose essay "'The Lottery' Revisited" was first published in The Chronicle of Higher Education *in June 1997 under the title "Suspending Moral Judgment." This fascinating account of her years of teaching creative writing using such examples as Shirley Jackson's short story "The Lottery," struck a chord in many readers and sparked widespread discussion.*

"The Lottery" first appeared in The New Yorker *in 1948. Since then it has been read and discussed in countless high school and college classes. Fifty years ago the stunning climax of the story raised a storm of shocked outrage and* The New Yorker *was deluged with sacks full of mail in response. In the 1990s, by contrast, the rise of relativism, tolerance, cynicism, radical multiculturalism, and morally ungrounded morality poses the question, how is anyone to judge anything, let alone condemn?*

The shifting responses from different generations of Haugaard's students to "The Lottery" tell us more about our moral condition than endless public opinion surveys and presidential speeches.

It is a telling exercise to read Kay Haugaard's essay as a yardstick to measure where we stand today on several things earlier generations thought vital to a free society, including faith, character, truth, and right and wrong. The shifting responses from different generations of Haugaard's students to "The Lottery" tell us more about our moral condition than endless public opinion surveys and presidential speeches. We're left with the haunting questions: Has it truly become "forbidden to forbid"? Is our eleventh commandment, "Thou shalt not judge"?

The following excerpt from "The Lottery" picks up at the second stage of the lottery. All the townspeople have already drawn, and the lottery has been narrowed to the Hutchinson family: Bill and Tessie, Nancy, Bill, Jr., and little Dave. The family members have to draw again, with Mr. Graves helping little Dave open his paper.

"All right," Mr. Summers said. "Open the papers. Harry, you open little Dave's."

Mr. Graves opened the slip of paper and there was a general sigh through the crowd as he held it up and everyone could see that it was blank. Nancy and Bill, Jr., opened theirs at the same time, and both beamed and laughed, turning around to the crowd and holding their slips of paper above their heads. . . .

"Tessie," Mr. Summers said. There was a pause, and then Mr. Summers looked at Bill Hutchinson, and Bill unfolded his paper and showed it. It was blank.

"It's Tessie," Mr. Summers said, and his voice was hushed. "Show us her paper, Bill."

Bill Hutchinson went over to his wife and forced the slip of paper out of her hand. It had a black spot on it, the black spot Mr. Summers had made the night before with the heavy pencil in the coal-company office. Bill Hutchinson held it up, and there was a stir in the crowd.

"All right, folks," Mr. Summers said. "Let's finish quickly."

Although the villagers had forgotten the ritual and lost the original black box, they still remembered to use stones. The pile of stones the boys had made earlier was ready; there were stones on the ground with the blowing scraps of paper that had come out of the box. Mrs. Delacroix selected a stone so large she had to pick up with both hands and turned to Mrs. Dunbar. "Come on," she said. "Hurry up."

Mrs. Dunbar had small stones in both hands, and she said, gasping for breath, "I can't run at all. You'll have to go ahead and I'll catch up with you." The children had stones already, and someone gave little Davy Hutchinson a few pebbles.

Tessie Hutchinson was in the center of a cleared space by now, and she held her hands out desperately as the villagers moved in on her. "It isn't fair," she said. A stone hit her on the side of the head.

Old Man Warner was saying, "Come on, come on, everyone." Steve Adams was in the front of the crowd of villagers, with Mrs. Graves beside him.

"It isn't fair, it isn't right," Mrs. Hutchinson screamed, and then they were upon her.

'THE LOTTERY' REVISITED

Once again I was going to teach Shirley Jackson's short story "The Lottery." I sighed as I gathered my books to leave for my evening class in creative writing; I had taught this story so many times over the past two decades.

Throughout the twenty-four years that I had been teaching creative writing, I had found that the various anthologies that I had used, as well as the stories written by the students themselves during the semester, had reflected national changes in social mores and attitudes.

When I started teaching, in 1970, my students—ranging from an occasional 18-year-old to an occasional 80-year-old—were still shocked into giggles and frowns at the sound of naughty words, whether they appeared in the published stories we read or in students' work. The youngest students (mostly the males) wrote pieces calculated to shock and reveled in an abundant use of vulgar slang and details of drug parties and sexual encounters. Remembering my commitment to freedom of speech, I steeled myself and read all of the students' stories out loud to the class, even when I could feel my cheeks flaming.

A few years later, I started getting floods of powerful stories written by Vietnam veterans, who described killing, maiming, being wounded and crippled, having friends die in their laps, and sexual encounters with Vietnamese prostitutes.

As the years went by, the students seemed to become jaded by the obscenities. If a story contained a great deal of lewdness, they sighed and pointed out that it was boringly excessive. The Vietnam War began to fade and, for the first time, we began reading students' narratives of homosexual inclinations and encounters. At first these, too, startled the class. The students did not condemn the stories, but their eyes flew open in visible shock. A student would say, "Did I understand it right? The characters were two men, not a man and a woman?" Assured that that interpretation was correct, the student usually did not respond, but sat back with a serious, reflective expression . . .

Along with the students' stories, anthology after anthology mirrored the social concerns of the particular period in which it was published: free-speech issues, civil rights, sexual liberation, feminism, and, most recently, multiculturalism. But every anthology, without fail, included "The Lottery," and students often chose the story for discussion.

Students who had never read this story were always absolutely stunned by it—as though they personally had been struck with the first ritual stone.

Students who had never read this story were always absolutely stunned by it—as though they personally had been struck with the first ritual stone. I had vivid mental pictures of their faces as we discussed the story: wide-eyed, unsmiling, disturbed. They made comments such as, "I thought this was kind of an ordinary little story, and then wham! I never thought. . . ."

Students who had read the story before were calmer but admitted that it had shocked them the first time. Everyone thought it was scary because, as someone inevitably said, "The characters seem just like regular people—you know, like us!"

In spite of the changes that I had witnessed over the years in anthologies and in students' writing, Jackson's message about blind conformity always spoke to my students' sense of right and wrong. Jackson had made an important and powerful point. . . .

That evening, I thought to myself, it would be more fun if we had a story to discuss that I had not read before.

"So, what did you think of 'The Lottery'?" I asked as soon as I sat down in front of the class.

Beth, a slender, stylish woman in her mid-40s, pushed up the sleeves of her enormously baggy sweater as she spoke: "I was rather surprised that this seemed to be taking place in the United States and like it was right now."

"Yes, it does make it more shocking when the characters seem like people we might know, or even be, doesn't it?" I said. "How about you, Jeanette?" I asked the plump 19-year-old, whose dyed black ringlets framed an ivory, kewpie-doll face.

She replied: "It was pretty boring until the end. The end was neat!"

"Neat?" I asked. "How do you mean, neat?"

"Just neat! I liked it."

"I see. Kind of Stephen King 'neat,' I suppose." I turned to Edward, well dressed in the suit he had worn to his job as a high-school teacher that day. "What was your response to the story, Edward?"

He bounced the foot of his crossed leg and looked up with a kind of bored expression. "It was all right. It wasn't that great."

But, I pressed, "how about that ending, where the whole village turns on one of their neighbors and kills her with stones? Had you read it before?"

Edward furrowed his brow but refused to be impressed. "No, I hadn't read it before. It was all right."

I could not believe these responses. Everyone seemed so blasé. Giving up on Edward, who was never very vocal in discussions, I turned to Richard, a slightly graying elementary-school teacher. "Why do these people perform this ritual, Richard, this human sacrifice?"

He took a deep breath. "Well, I agree with Beth that it was pretty surprising to have it take place right today, as it were."

"But why do they do it?" I persisted.

"Uh, well, it isn't too clear."

Someone else spoke up. "For the crops. They do it so the crops will grow well."

"That's one of the reasons they give," I responded, pleased that someone had found a clue in the text. "Is that a sufficient justification? Any other reason?"

"They just always do it. It's a ritual," said Maria.

"That's right. They do it because they've always done it," I said.

"I was wondering if there was anything religious about it," said Beth. "If this were part of something of long standing. It doesn't seem to be religious."

"Would that make a difference, if it were part of a religious ritual?"

Beth furrowed her brows and gazed toward the ceiling.

"There isn't anything mentioned in the story about religion, but it does seem related to religious traditions of human sacrifice intended to make the crops grow better," I said. I took a few moments to talk about Sir James Frazer's *The Golden Bough*, which describes many cultures with such traditions.

"Oh, well, if it was something like that . . . ," Beth responded.

"How do you mean? That would make it all right?"

"Are you asking me if I believe in human sacrifice?" Beth responded thoughtfully, as though seriously considering all aspects of the question.

"Well, yes," I managed to say. "Do you think that the author approved or disapproved of this ritual?" I was stunned: This was the woman who wrote so passionately of saving the whales, of concern for the rain forests, of her rescue and tender care of a stray dog.

"I really don't know. If it was a religion of long standing. . . ."

For a moment I couldn't even respond. This woman actually couldn't seem to bring herself to say plainly that she was against human sacrifice. My classes of a few years before would have burst into nervous giggles at the suggestion. This class was calmly considering it.

This woman actually couldn't seem to bring herself to say plainly that she was against human sacrifice.

"There have been studies," said Richard, "about certain cultures, and they show that, when there aren't any killings for a long time, the people seem to . . . require it. . . ."

I listened in a state of shock as Richard went on to describe a psychological theory he had read that seemed to espouse the social function of a certain amount of bloodshed. "It almost seems a need," he concluded in cool, reasonable tones.

It was too much. I had always tried to keep my personal feelings out of class discussion and allow the students to discover a story's theme and significance as much as possible. But I had reached my limit.

"There certainly are precedents for it," I said, "but does a precedent necessarily make something right? I think the author strongly disapproves of this ritual and is attempting to shock us into re-examining our activities every now and then to see when they still seem justified and functional."

I went on, probably longer than I should have. "The Aztecs believed that the sun would not rise if they did not feed the hummingbird god Huichtlipochtli with human blood. This was their rationale for human sacrifice. But we know that the sun will rise on its own. Are these things justified on the basis of precedent?"

I turned to Patricia, a 50-something, redheaded nurse. She had always seemed an intelligent person of moderate views.

"Well, I teach a course for our hospital personnel in multicultural understanding, and if it is part of a person's culture, we are taught not to judge, and if it has worked for them . . ."

At this point I gave up. No one in the whole class of more than twenty ostensibly intelligent individuals would go out on a limb and take a stand against human sacrifice.

I wound up the discussion. "Frankly, I feel it's clear that the author was pointing out the dangers of being totally accepting followers, too cowardly to rebel against obvious cruelties and injustices." I was shaken, and I thought that the author, whose story had shocked so many, would have been shaken as well.

The class finally ended. It was a warm night when I walked out to my car after class that evening, but I felt shivery, chilled to the bone.

I was shaken, and I thought that the author, whose story had shocked so many, would have been shaken as well.

From Kay Haugaard, "Suspending Moral Judgment: Students Who Refuse to Condemn the Unthinkable—A Result of Too Much Tolerance?" *The Chronicle of Higher Education*, June 27, 1997. Reprinted by permission of the author.

NOT MY PROBLEM!

"I'm not going to get upset over somebody else's life. I just worry about myself first. I'm not going to lose sleep over somebody else's problems."

　　—David Cash, 18, when asked if he was appalled by his friend's murder of a seven-year-old girl in a casino restroom while he waited outside.

"When asked whether he felt worse for the dead girl or her murderer (his buddy), Cash replied, 'Because I know Jeremy, I feel worse for him. I know he had a lot going for him.'"

　　　　　　　　　—*The Washington Post*, September 1998

"Dear Mom,

"Gosh, can you believe it's 2023 already? I'm still writing '22' on nearly everything. Seems like just yesterday I was sitting in first grade celebrating the century change. I know we haven't really chatted since

Christmas. Sorry. Anyway, I have some difficult news and I really didn't want to call and talk face-to-face. Ted's had a promotion and I should be up for a hefty raise this year if I keep putting in those crazy hours. You know how I work at it. Yes, we're still struggling with the bills. Timmy's been 'okay' at kindergarten although he complains about going. But then, he wasn't happy about day care either, so what can I do?

"He's been a real problem, Mom. He's a good kid, but quite honestly, he's an unfair burden at this time in our lives. Ted and I have talked this through and through and finally made a choice. Plenty of other families have made it and are much better off. Our pastor is supportive and says hard decisions are necessary. The family is a 'system' and the demands of one member shouldn't be allowed to ruin the whole. He told us to be prayerful, consider all the factors, and do what is right to make the family work. He says that even though he probably wouldn't do it himself, the decision is really ours. He was kind enough to refer us to a children's clinic near here, so at least that part's easy. I'm not an uncaring mother. I do feel sorry for the little guy. I think he overheard Ted and me talking about 'it' the other night. I turned around and saw him standing at the bottom step in his PJ's with the little bear you gave him under his arm and his eyes sort of welling up. Mom, the way he looked at me just about broke my heart. But I honestly believe this is better for Timmy, too. It's not fair to force him to live in a family that can't give him the time and attention he deserves. And please don't give me the kind of grief Grandma gave you over your abortions. It is the same thing, you know. We've told him he'd be just going in for a vaccination. Anyway, they say it is painless. I guess it's just as well you haven't seen that much of him.
"Love to Dad,
"Jane."

—from a parish newsletter, quoted in *First Things*, January 1999

QUESTIONS FOR THOUGHT AND DISCUSSION

1. What response does Kay Haugaard expect from students who had never read "The Lottery" before? In the past, what had struck nearly all of Haugaard's students about the people in the story? What message about conformity had students gleaned from the story?

2. How did big public events, such as the Vietnam War and the rise of the gay movement, affect the way her students responded to the story?

3. This time, what are the first three student responses to the story? What shocks Haugaard about these opening reactions?

4. How does Beth react to the idea of human sacrifice in the story? What is particularly ironic about her response? What does Richard, the elementary school teacher, suggest about the ritual killing? What is Haugaard's

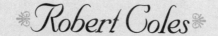
response? How would you have responded to the class had you been the teacher?

5. What is the final response of Patricia, the 50-something nurse? On what idea does she base her answer? Why do you agree or disagree with her underlying assumption?

6. As you see it, what factors have caused this massive change? What are the obvious dangers of being unwilling to judge or condemn? How can you tell when tolerance is taken too far?

Robert Coles

Robert Martin Coles (born 1929) is an eminent Harvard psychiatrist and the author of several best-selling books on children and their inner worlds. Born in Boston, he attended both Harvard and Columbia Universities and has taught and worked in the Cambridge area for forty years. Among his best-known books are Children of Crisis *(1967), which won the Pulitzer Prize, and* The Moral Life of Children *(1986).*

Coles is an unashamed Episcopalian. He not only tempers his science with a deep commitment to human beings, but blurs the line between "academic" and "popular" in his writing. He always allows his listeners to tell their own stories. As one reviewer wrote, Coles is to children's stories what Homer was to the Trojan War. The story of Ruby Bridges comes from Coles' formative journey to the deep South in the early 1960s. Ruby, he wrote later, "is one of the first children I met— a six-year-old child who was a mentor of mine. . . ." Nothing was more striking to Coles than the obvious place of character in his six-year-old mentor.

THE STORY OF RUBY BRIDGES

I was once helped in the effort at clarification by a black woman whom I sup-pose I'd have to call illiterate. She pointed out that "there's a lot of people who talk about doing good, and a lot of people who argue about what's good and what's not good." Then she added that "there are a lot of people who always worry about whether they're doing right or doing wrong." Finally, there are some other folks: "They just put their lives on the line for what's right, and they may not be the ones who talk a lot or argue a lot or worry a lot; they just *do* a lot!"

Her daughter happened to be Ruby Bridges, one of the black children, who, at age six, initiated school desegregation in New Orleans against terrible, fearful odds. For days that turned into weeks and weeks that turned into months, this child had to brave murderously heckling mobs, there in the morning and there in the evening, hurling threats and slurs and hysterical denunciations and accusations. Federal marshals took her to school and brought her home. She attended school all by herself for a good part of a school year, owing to a total boycott by white families. Her parents, of sharecropper background, had just recently arrived in the great, cosmopolitan port city — yet another poor black family of rural background trying to find a slightly better deal in an urban setting. They were unemployed, and, like Ruby, in jeopardy; mobs threatened them, too.

Still, Ruby persisted, and so did her parents. Ruby's teachers began to wonder *how come*—about the continuing ability of such a child to bear such adversity, and with few apparent assets in her family background. I reassured those teachers, I regret to say, with the notion that all was not as it seemed. Ruby appeared strong, but she would, soon enough, show signs of psychological wear and tear. Perhaps she was "denying" her fears and anxieties; perhaps her strange calm in the face of such obvious danger represented a "reaction formation." Then there was this bit of information: "I was standing in the classroom, looking out the window, and I saw Ruby coming down the street, with the federal marshals on both sides of her. The crowd was there, shouting, as usual. A woman spat at Ruby but missed; Ruby smiled at her. A man shook his fist at her; Ruby smiled at him. Then she walked up the stairs, and she stopped and turned and smiled one more time! You know what she told one of the marshals? She told him she prays for those people, the ones in that mob, every night before she goes to sleep!"

The words of a white schoolteacher—incredulous and, by that time, quite perplexed. As for me, I'd been interested in knowing how Ruby slept at night (an indicator of her state of apprehension, a measure of how well she was handling things mentally), but I hadn't thought to inquire about what she said or even thought each night before falling off. What to make of such a concern being addressed by such a child? I asked Ruby, after a while, about her prayers—first telling her what I'd heard from the teacher. Ruby was cheerful

Finally, there are some other folks: "They just put their lives on the line for what's right, and they may not be the ones who talk a lot or argue a lot or worry a lot; they just do a lot!"

She told him she prays for those people, the ones in that mob, every night before she goes to sleep!

and matter-of-fact, if terse, in her reply: "Yes, I do pray for them." I wondered why. She said only, "Because." I waited for more, but to no effect. I started over, told her I was curious about why she would want to pray for people who were being so unswervingly nasty to her. "I go to church," she told me, "every Sunday, and we're told to pray for everyone, even the bad people, and so I do." She had no more to say on that score.

From Robert Coles, *The Moral Life of Children* (Boston: Houghton Mifflin Company, 1986), pp. 20–23. Reprinted with permission from the author.

Questions for Thought and Discussion

1. What are Mrs. Bridges' four categories of moral response? What sort of people fit into each? What does it take for people to "just do a lot" of good rather than talking about it or arguing over what is good?

2. What was Ruby's school experience like? When have you or someone close to you experienced anything similar—severe criticism, harassment, ridicule, threats? What was your/their reaction?

3. What was Coles' explanation to Ruby's teachers of her seemingly undaunted strength? What story does Ruby's teacher tell Coles in response to his explanation? What does it say of these two professionals—a psychiatrist and a teacher—that they completely missed the point?

4. What was Ruby's answer to Coles' question as to why she prayed for the mob? What do you find most interesting or surprising about her answer? Why did Coles' academic and psychological training leave him unprepared to understand Ruby Bridges?

5. How do you understand Ruby's one-word answer "Because"? What sort of upbringing lies behind Ruby's moral strength?

Beware The Seven Deadly Sins!

This illustration is from a South German woodcut of 1414 and illustrates "The World"—personification of the Seven Deadly Sins. The figure offers a cup representing gluttony. Her diadem represents pride; the bodice—lust; the severed left hand—sloth; the belt—covetousness; the wolf's head (to the left)—anger, and the dog's head—envy. Her right leg represents life; her left leg with the snake's head represents death.

ONE:
PRIDE (SUPERBIA)
VERSUS POVERTY OF SPIRIT

Pride is the first, worst, and most prevalent of the seven deadly sins. It is either the source or the chief component of all other sin. Pride is also the first of the sins of the spirit, which are "cold" but highly "respectable." Its source is neither the world nor the flesh, but the Devil. This first vice is unique in that it is the one vice of which its perpetrator is frequently unaware.

This classical view of pride is shared by Jews, Christians, and Greeks (for example, the Greek notion of hubris, or overweening arrogance), but it flies in the face of modern attitudes. The contemporary world has transformed this vice into a virtue in two important ways. The common way is to change the definition by confusing pride with self-respect—so that to be opposed to pride is to be seen as unhealthy. After all, isn't it right to be proud of ourselves? Isn't it damaging not to appreciate our self-worth? Why is pride counted a sin at all?

This first vice is unique in that it is the one vice of which its perpetrator is frequently unaware.

PRIDE OR SELF-RESPECT?

"Self-respect is faith in the idea that God had, when he made us."

—Isak Dinesen, *Out of Africa* and *Shadows on the Grass*

But the deadly sin of pride is not pride in the sense of self-respect, a justifiable sense of one's own worth. Certainly there are problems with our modern preoccupation with self-esteem, especially when it leads to such practices as inflating school grades or rewriting history to boost the esteem of an individual or a group.

35

There are also dangers in such current maxims as "feeling good about oneself," "boosting one's self-esteem," or "building a positive self-image," for they are often used to cover all sorts of conditions about which one ought not to feel good. But that is not the real problem of pride.

VICE OR VIRTUE?

"Pride has always been one of my favorite virtues. I have never regarded it, except in certain cases, as a major sin. . . . I despise anything which reduces the pride of Man."

—Dame Edith Sitwell

The rarer way to transform vice into a virtue is to impugn its motivation.

The rarer way to transform vice into a virtue is to impugn its motivation. Seen this way, as advocated by Friedrich Nietzsche and his followers, the attack on pride is a mask to cover the resentment of the weak. Calls for "love" and "compassion" are therefore bogus—the grand rationalization by which the slave class can curtail the power of the master class, with its nobility, excellence, and "pride."

THE VIRTUE OF THE SUPERMAN

"'Man is evil'—all the wisest men have told me that to comfort me. Oh, if only this were true today! For evil is man's strength.

"'Man must grow better and more evil'—this is what I teach. The greatest evil is necessary for the superman's greatest achievement.

"Perhaps it was good the poor peoples' sage took upon himself and suffered the sins of humanity. I, on the other hand, rejoice in great sins as my consolation."

—Friedrich Nietzsche, *Thus Spake Zarathustra, IV*

Against both these changes, the Christian, classical view is that the sin of pride is wrong and deadly because it is inordinate and overweening. As the Oxford English Dictionary defines it, pride is "an unreasonable conceit of superiority," an "overweening opinion of one's own qualities." Consider its synonyms: egotism, arrogance, hubris, selfishness, vanity, haughtiness, presumption, boastfulness, bigheadedness, self-satisfaction, self-centeredness, and the like. None of them is admirable.

SELF-DEFINITION

"—Self, n. The most important person in the universe.

—Selfish, adj. Devoid of consideration for the selfishness of others.

—Self-Esteem, n. An erroneous appraisement."

—Ambrose Bierce, *The Devil's Dictionary*

Seen this way, nothing divides Jewish, Christian, and classical ethics more sharply from modern secular ethics than their contrasting attitudes toward pride.

In most other views, pride is rarely a major problem. The Greeks, however, warned of hubris, the overreaching arrogance that creates the illusion of invulnerability, and in the biblical view, pride is the fundamental violation and disordering of love because it puts the love of the human self before the love of God. It begins by breaking the first great commandment, "You shall love the Lord your God with all your heart, soul, strength, and mind," and inevitably goes on to break the second, "You shall love your neighbor as yourself." Even the differences between these two great commandments are instructive. We are to love our neighbors as ourselves, and a low sense of self-worth will often lead to a poor love of our neighbors. But the same is not said of God. We are not to love God "as ourselves," but for Himself, and love of God and love of self are often pitted against each other.

Seen this way, nothing divides Jewish, Christian, and classical ethics more sharply from modern secular ethics than their contrasting attitudes toward pride.

FOR THE LOVE OF SELF

"Ach! what things people are capable of doing for love—of themselves!"

—Jewish saying

"Egotist, n. A person of low taste, more interested in himself than in me."

—Ambrose Bierce, *The Devil's Dictionary*

"Good breeding consists of concealing how much we think of ourselves and how little we think of the other person."

—Mark Twain

"A walking personal pronoun."

—description of Victor Hugo

"Every man would like to be God, if it were possible; some few find it difficult to admit the impossibility."

—Bertrand Russell

PICTURES AND METAPHORS

Throughout history, each of the seven vices has been portrayed by association with different parts of the body, different animals, and different colors. Pride is characteristically described with images suggesting loftiness, aloofness, and inaccessibility. Angus Wilson calls pride "camel-nosed," while journalist Henry Fairlie calls it "high-blown, puffed-up, stuck-up, stiff-necked." For medieval poets and artists, pride was the king or queen of the vices. It was often portrayed as a lion, an eagle, a strutting peacock, or a vain man or woman.

PRACTICAL APPLICATIONS

Because pride is the fountainhead of all other sins, the list of possible examples of pride is endless.

Because pride is the fountainhead of all other sins, the list of possible examples of pride is endless. Rooted in the very essence of sin—"the claim to the right to myself"—pride is linked inevitably with hypocrisy and denial—"the claim to the right to my view of things whatever the reality." As such, it is also linked to hubris—"the arrogance of the illusion of invulnerability"—and thus to history's march of folly, sweeping up nations as well as individuals.

FOR EVER AND EVER . . . AMEN

"America's destiny is to be the richest, freest, most powerful nation on earth, and to remain so forever."

—Irving Kristol, 1998

"The U.S. economy likely will not see a recession for many years to come. We don't want one, we don't need one, and as we have the tools to keep the current expansion going, we won't have one. This expansion will run forever."

—Dr. Rudl Dornbusch, M.I.T. professor

"The promise of our future is limitless."

—President Clinton, 1999 State of the Union Address

But this is only the beginning. Pride is found in individual form, such as in common neuroses and the narcissists' complete preoccupation with themselves. It is also found in collective form, such as the group pride of nationalism, tribalism, jingoism, and racism. It also shows in the great criminal acts of history, which in one form or another pivot on a prideful lack of sympathy and fellow-feeling for other human beings (as a following reading illustrates). But often it creeps into our noblest and most enterprising ventures.

In short, pride can run through everything we do. And the worst of it, as Dorothy Sayers warned, is that "the devilish strategy of Pride is that it attacks us, not in our weakest points, but in our strongest. It is preeminently the sin of the noble mind."

STRONG POISON

"Pride is the fortress of evil in a man."

—Victor Hugo

"Pride is a poison so very poisonous that it not only poisons the virtues; it even poisons the other vices. This is what is felt by the poor men in the public tavern, when they tolerate the tippler or the tipster or even the thief, but feel something fiendishly wrong with the man who bears so close a resemblance to God Almighty. And we all do in fact know that the primary sin of pride has this curiously freezing and hardening effect upon the other sins."

—G. K. Chesterton, "If I Had Only One Sermon to Preach"

One other theme should not be missed. Pride is linked to restlessness and discontent. The reason lies in the self-absorption and pretended self-sufficiency of pride. Because the individual human being is too small and too frail, genuine self-sufficiency is impossible and so, for pride, discontent is inevitable. There is always more that is needed beyond the self, and more to be desired, so contentment proves a mirage. Just as Narcissus fell in love with his own reflection in a spring and eventually died of frustration because his self-love could never be consummated, so are proud people enamored with themselves to the point of inevitable frustration.

The antidote is offered in the famous prayer of Augustine, "You have made us for yourself and our hearts are restless until they find their rest in you." The counterpoint to pride, considered in more depth later, is the beatitude, "Blessed are those who are poor in spirit."

Because the individual human being is too small and too frail, genuine self-sufficiency is impossible and so, for pride, discontent is inevitable.

Calvin and Hobbes by Bill Watterson

CALVIN AND HOBBES copyright © 1992 Watterson. Reprinted with permission of UNIVERSAL PRESS SYNDICATE. All rights reserved.

C. S. Lewis

Clive Staples Lewis (1898–1963) was a scholar and writer, and a celebrated and much-loved Christian apologist. Born in Belfast, Northern Ireland, he was educated at University College, Oxford. After brief service in World War I, he resumed his studies at Oxford where he became a fellow in English Language and Literature at Magdalen College. For the last seven years of his life, he was a professor at Cambridge University but insisted on living at Oxford.

Lewis was an excellent scholar in his field, but his enormous reputation rests on his popular writings. Three dozen of his titles are still available with well over 50 million in print—making Lewis the best-selling Christian author of all time. His scholarly study The Allegory of Love *was awarded the Hawthornden Prize in 1936, but he became known popularly through such books as* The Screwtape Letters *and* Mere Christianity, *and later through his children's stories* The Chronicles of Narnia *and his science fiction trilogy. Lewis, known to friends as Jack, was the leading light of the Inklings, a discussion group that met regularly in his rooms or in the Oxford pub called the Eagle and Child. Other accomplished writers such as J. R. R. Tolkien, Charles Williams, and Dorothy Sayers were part of the Inklings. Lewis died on November 22, 1963, the same day that John F. Kennedy and Aldous Huxley died.*

An almost endless number of people have come to faith or have been aided in faith by Lewis's writings, and all have their favorite passages. The one that follows comes from Mere Christianity, *the book through which more thinking people have come to faith than any other in the twentieth century. In contrast to most celebrated writings on the seven deadly sins, Lewis's works come to us not from the ancient world, but from a time close to our own. Yet his essay that follows, though modern and not in historical sequence here, is perhaps the single best summary of the Christian position on pride.*

MY FAIR MAN

"Cycling and showing off."

     —George Bernard Shaw's list of his hobbies in *Who's Who*

"With the single exception of Homer, there is no eminent writer, not even Sir Walter Scott, whom I can despise so entirely as I despise Shakespeare, when I measure my mind against his."

     —George Bernard Shaw

> "The longer I live the more I see that I am never wrong about anything, and that all the pains I have so humbly taken to verify my notions have only wasted my time."
>
> —George Bernard Shaw
>
> "Bernard Shaw discovered himself, and gave ungrudgingly of his discovery to the world."
>
> —Saki

THE GREAT SIN

Today I come to that part of Christian morals where they differ most sharply from all other morals. There is one vice of which no man in the world is free; which every one in the world loathes when he sees it in someone else; and of which hardly any people, except Christians, ever imagine that they are guilty themselves. I have heard people admit that they are bad-tempered, or that they cannot keep their heads about girls or drink, or even that they are cowards. I do not think I have ever heard anyone who was not a Christian accuse himself of this vice. And at the same time I have very seldom met anyone, who was not a Christian, who showed the slightest mercy to it in others. There is no fault which makes a man more unpopular, and no fault which we are more unconscious of in ourselves. And the more we have it ourselves, the more we dislike it in others.

The vice I am talking of is Pride or Self-Conceit: and the virtue opposite to it, in Christian morals, is called Humility. You may remember, when I was talking about sexual morality, I warned you that the center of Christian morals did not lie there. Well, now, we have come to the center. According to Christian teachers, the essential vice, the utmost evil, is Pride. Unchastity, anger, greed, drunkenness, and all that, are mere fleabites in comparison: it was through Pride that the devil became the devil: Pride leads to every other vice: it is the complete anti-God state of mind.

Does this seem to you exaggerated? If so, think it over. I pointed out a moment ago that the more pride one had, the more one disliked pride in others. In fact, if you want to find out how proud you are the easiest way is to ask yourself, "How much do I dislike it when other people snub me, or refuse to take any notice of me, or shove their oar in, or patronize me, or show off?" The point is that each person's pride is in competition with every one else's pride. It is because I wanted to be the big noise at the party that I am so annoyed at someone else being the big noise. Two of a trade never agree.

I have heard people admit that they are bad-tempered, or that they cannot keep their heads about girls or drink, or even that they are cowards. I do not think I have ever heard anyone who was not a Christian accuse himself of this vice.

Now what you want to get clear is that Pride is *essentially* competitive — is competitive by its very nature — while the other vices are competitive only, so to speak, by accident. Pride gets no pleasure out of having something, only out of having more of it than the next man. We say that people are proud of being rich, or clever, or good-looking, but they are not. They are proud of being richer, or cleverer, or better-looking than others. If every one else became equally rich, or clever, or good-looking there would be nothing to be proud about. It is the comparison that makes you proud: the pleasure of being above the rest. Once the element of competition has gone, pride has gone. That is why I say that Pride is essentially competitive in a way the other vices are not. The sexual impulse may drive two men into competition if they both want the same girl. But that is only by accident; they might just as likely have wanted two different girls. But a proud man will take your girl from you, not because he wants her, but just to prove to himself that he is a better man than you. Greed may drive men into competition if there is not enough to go round; but the proud man, even when he has got more than he can possibly want, will try to get still more just to assert his power. Nearly all those evils in the world which people put down to greed or selfishness are really far more the result of Pride. . . .

Nearly all those evils in the world which people put down to greed or selfishness are really far more the result of Pride.

The Christians are right: it is Pride which has been the chief cause of misery in every nation and every family since the world began. Other vices may sometimes bring people together: you may find good fellowship and jokes and friendliness among drunken people or unchaste people. But Pride always means enmity — it is enmity. And not only enmity between man and man, but enmity to God.

In God you come up against something which is in every respect immeasurably superior to yourself. Unless you know God as that — and, therefore, know yourself as nothing in comparison — you do not know God at all. As long as you are proud you cannot know God. A proud man is always looking down on things and people: and, of course, as long as you are looking down, you cannot see something that is above you.

That raises a terrible question. How is it that people who are quite obviously eaten up with Pride can say they believe in God and appear to themselves very religious? I am afraid it means they are worshipping an imaginary God. They theoretically admit themselves to be nothing in the presence of this phantom God, but are really all the time imagining how He approves of them and thinks them far better than ordinary people: that is, they pay a pennyworth of imaginary humility to Him and get out of it a pound's worth of Pride towards their fellow-men. I suppose it was of those people Christ was thinking when He said that some would preach about Him and cast out devils in His name, only to be told at the end of the world that He had never known them. And any of us may at any moment be in this deathtrap. Luckily, we have a test. Whenever we find that our religious life is making us feel that we are good—above all, that we are better than someone else—I think we may be sure that we are being acted on, not by God, but by the devil. The real test of being in the presence of God is that you either forget about yourself altogether or see yourself as a small, dirty object. It is better to forget about yourself altogether.

It is a terrible thing that the worst of all the vices can smuggle itself into the very center of our religious life. But you can see why. The other, and less bad, vices come from the devil working on us through our animal nature. But this does not come through our animal nature at all. It comes direct from Hell. It is purely spiritual: consequently it is far more subtle and deadly. For the same reason, Pride can often be used to beat down the simpler vices. Teachers, in fact, often appeal to a boy's Pride, or, as they call it, his self-respect, to make him behave decently: many a man has overcome cowardice, or lust, or ill-temper by learning to think that they are beneath his dignity—that is, by Pride. The devil laughs. He is perfectly content to see you becoming chaste and brave and self-controlled provided, all the time, he is setting up in you the Dictatorship of Pride—just as he would be quite content to see your chilblains [corns on the foot] cured if he was allowed, in return, to give you cancer. For Pride is spiritual cancer: it eats up the very possibility of love, or contentment, or even common sense.

Before leaving this subject I must guard against some possible misunderstandings:

(1) Pleasure in being praised is not Pride. The child who is patted on the back for doing a lesson well, the woman whose beauty is praised by her lover, the saved soul to whom Christ says "Well done," are pleased and ought to be. For here the pleasure lies not in what you are but in the fact that you have pleased someone you wanted (and rightly wanted) to please. The trouble begins when you pass from thinking, "I have pleased him; all is well," to thinking, "What a fine person I must be to have done it." The more you delight in yourself and the less you delight in the praise, the worse you are becoming. When you delight wholly in yourself and do not care about the praise at all, you have reached the bottom. That is why vanity, though it is the sort of Pride which shows most on the surface, is really the least bad and most pardonable

The real test of being in the presence of God is that you either forget about yourself altogether or see yourself as a small, dirty object. It is better to forget about yourself altogether.

sort. The vain person wants praise, applause, admiration, too much and is always angling for it. It is a fault, but a childlike and even (in an odd way) a humble fault. It shows that you are not yet completely contented with your own admiration. You value other people enough to want them to look at you. You are, in fact, still human. The real black, diabolical Pride comes when you look down on others so much that you do not care what they think of you. Of course, it is very right, and often our duty, not to care what people think of us, if we do so for the right reason; namely, because we care so incomparably more what God thinks. But the Proud man has a different reason for not caring. He says "Why should I care for the applause of that rabble as if their opinion were worth anything? And even if their opinions were of value, am I the sort of man to blush with pleasure at a compliment like some chit of a girl at her first dance? No, I am an integrated, adult personality. All I have done has been done to satisfy my own ideals — or my artistic conscience — or the traditions of my family — or, in a word, because I'm That Kind of Chap. If the mob like it, let them. They're nothing to me." In this way real thoroughgoing Pride may act as a check on vanity; for, as I said a moment ago, the devil loves "curing" a small fault by giving you a great one. We must try not to be vain, but we must never call in our Pride to cure our vanity; better the frying-pan than the fire.

(2) We say in English that a man is "proud" of his son, or his father, or his school, or regiment, and it may be asked whether "pride" in this sense is a sin. I think it depends on what, exactly, we mean by "proud of." Very often, in such sentences, the phrase "is proud of" means "has a warm-hearted admiration for." Such an admiration is, of course, very far from being a sin. But it might, perhaps, mean that the person in question gives himself airs on the ground of his distinguished father, or because he belongs to a famous regiment. This would, clearly, be a fault; but even then, it would be better than being proud simply of himself. To love and admire anything outside yourself is to take one step away from utter spiritual ruin; though we shall not be well so long as we love and admire anything more than we love and admire God.

(3) We must not think Pride is something God forbids because He is offended at it, or that Humility is something He demands as due to His own dignity — as if God Himself was proud. He is not in the least worried about His dignity. The point is, He wants you to know Him: wants to give you Himself. And He and you are two things of such a kind that if you really get into any kind of touch with Him you will, in fact, be humble — delightedly humble,

feeling the infinite relief of having for once got rid of all the silly nonsense about your own dignity which has made you restless and unhappy all your life. He is trying to make you humble in order to make this moment possible: trying to take off a lot of silly, ugly, fancy-dress in which we have all got ourselves up and are strutting about like the little idiots we are. I wish I had got a bit further with humility myself: if I had, I could probably tell you more about the relief, the comfort, of taking the fancy-dress off—getting rid of the false self, with all its "Look at me" and "Aren't I a good boy?" and all its posing and posturing. To get even near it, even for a moment, is like a drink of cold water to a man in a desert. . . .

If anyone would like to acquire humility, I can, I think, tell him the first step. The first step is to realize that one is proud. And a biggish step, too. At least, nothing whatever can be done before it. If you think you are not conceited, it means you are very conceited indeed.

If you think you are not conceited, it means you are very conceited indeed.

NEVER OUTDONE

"As Majority Leader, [Lyndon B. Johnson] was thrilled to be the first legislator in Washington with a car phone. When Everett Dirksen, Republican Minority Leader and a friendly rival, also acquired one, he telephoned Johnson's limo to say that he was calling from his new car phone. 'Can you hold on a minute, Ev?' Johnson asked. 'My other phone is ringing.'"

—Robert Dallek, Johnson's biographer

"I am extraordinarily patient—provided that I get my own way in the end."

—Margaret Thatcher

QUESTIONS FOR THOUGHT AND DISCUSSION

1. Lewis's opening paragraph is packed with striking observations on pride. What part of this description strikes you most deeply? Is Lewis right when he says of pride, "And the more we have it in ourselves, the more we dislike it in others"? If so, why do you think this is the case?

2. Lewis describes pride as "the complete anti-God state of mind." What does he mean by this? Why, according to Lewis, are the more visible

vices of anger, greed, and drunkenness "mere fleabites" by comparison to pride? Why do you agree or disagree?

3. From the world of business to the world of sport, modern life thrives on competition, yet Lewis says, "Pride is *essentially* competitive." What examples does he give? What other examples can you think of? Is all competition wrong? If not, why is this characteristic of pride so destructive? How can you encourage a child, spouse, or employee to excel other than by appealing to pride?

4. According to Lewis, what does pride do to a man or woman's relation to other men and women? To God? What test does Lewis suggest for determining our pride regarding our religious life? How does he say we can tell when we're truly in God's presence?

5. How does pride become a component of temptation to "beat down the simpler vices"? Why is this strategy so successful? What is its danger? Can you recall an example in your life of someone appealing to pride to get you to change your behavior? What do you think of Lewis's description of pride as "spiritual cancer"?

6. What is the first misunderstanding of pride Lewis mentions? At what point does the joy of pleasing someone become pride? What do you think of Lewis's distinction between the lesser sin of vanity and "the real black, diabolical Pride" that is so proud it doesn't care what others think?

7. What second misunderstanding of pride does Lewis address? Why is that not pride? "To love and admire anything outside yourself is" what, according to Lewis? If this is true, what then does "spiritual ruin" consist of?

8. What is the final misunderstanding about pride? What does Lewis say is the real reason God forbids pride? What shift takes place in one's attitude when one becomes truly humble before God?

9. What do you think of Lewis's final line, "If you think you are not conceited, it means you are very conceited indeed?" Is this a catch-22 or simply true? In light of your character and work, what are your main temptations to pride?

THERE BUT FOR THE GRACE OF GOD GOES GOD

"I fear that would be impossible. I have written only five."

—Oscar Wilde, when asked to compile a list of the world's 100 best books

"There but for the grace of God goes God."

—Winston Churchill, commenting on a fellow Cabinet member, Stafford Cripps

"Ellison insisted that his recruiters hire only the finest, and cockiest, new college graduates. 'When they were recruiting from universities, they'd ask people, "Are you the smartest person you know?" And then if they said yes, they'd hire them. If they said no, they'd say, "Who is?" And they'd go hire that guy instead,' Oracle engineer Roger Bamford said. 'I don't know if you got the smartest people that way, but you definitely got the most arrogant.'"

—Mike Wilson, *The Difference Between God and Larry Ellison*

"Q. What's the difference between God and Larry Ellison?
A. God doesn't think he's Larry Ellison."

—Joke circulating around Oracle about CEO Larry Ellison

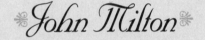

John Milton

John Milton (1608–1674) is one of the best-known and most respected English poets and prose writers. The son of a London notary who was a convert to Anglicanism, Milton was well educated at St. Paul's School and Cambridge University. After graduating he toured Europe for two years, during which he wrote some of his best poetry. He returned to England just before the outbreak of the English Civil War.

His brilliance as a controversialist earned him the position of Latin Secretary to Oliver Cromwell the Revolutionary, but the grueling work cost him his eyesight. The restoration of the monarchy found him aged, blind, unemployed, and with his hopes for a godly, republican England collapsed. He therefore returned to poetry and his plan of a great epic, Paradise Lost and Paradise Regained.

Milton was a noble but difficult man. He was not only an austere Puritan but also a humanist—committed to the highest possibilities of human nature—and a lover of music and literature. His own character combined pride, passion, sensuality, and ambition with idealism, discipline, and self-sacrifice.

Temptation is a recurring theme in Milton's writing, which he always traces to the Devil. The following excerpt from Book I of Paradise Lost *is a celebrated depiction of the raw, undiluted pride that Milton sees as constituting the very being of Satan.*

DEADLY LOVE

"Often it has struck me as a curious thing (yet it is not perhaps curious) that suicides are occasioned nearly always by a mortified self love."

—Elizabeth Barrett Browning

PARADISE LOST

Say first, for Heav'n hides nothing from thy view
Nor the deep tract of hell—say first, what cause
Mov'd our grand Parents in that happy state,
Favour'd of heav'n so highly, to fall off
From their Creator, and transgress his will
For one restraint, lords of the world besides?
Who first seduced them to that foul revolt?
Th' infernal serpent; he it was, whose guile
Stirr'd up with envy and revenge, deceiv'd
The mother of mankind, what time his pride
Had cast him out from heav'n, with all his host
Of rebel Angels, by whose aid aspiring
To set himself in glory above his peers,
He trusted to have equall'd the Most High,
If he opposed; and with ambitious aim
Against the throne and monarchy of God
Raised impious war in heav'n, and battle proud,
With vain attempt. Him the almighty Power
Hurl'd headlong flaming from th' ethereal sky
With hideous ruin and combustion, down
To bottomless perdition, there to dwell
In adamantine chains and penal fire,
Who durst defy th' Omnipotent to arms.

Is this the region, this the soil, the clime,
Said then the lost Arch-Angel, this the seat
That we must change for heav'n, this mournful gloom
For that celestial light? be it so, since he,
Who now is Sov'reign, can dispose and bid
What shall be right: farthest from him is best,
Whom reason hath equall'd, force hath made supreme
Above his equals. Farewell happy fields
Where joy for ever dwells: hail horrors; hail
Infernal world, and thou profoundest hell
Receive thy new possessor; one who brings
A mind not to be changed by place or time.
The mind is its own place, and in itself
Can make a heav'n of hell, a hell of heav'n.
What matter where, if I be still the same,
And what I should be, all but less then he
Whom thunder hath made greater? here at least
We shall be free; th' Almighty hath not built
Here for his envy, will not drive us hence:
Here we may reign secure, and in my choice
To reign is worth ambition, though in hell:
Better to reign in hell, than serve in heav'n.
But wherefore let we then our faithful friends,
Th' associates and copartners of our loss
Lie thus astonish'd on th' oblivious pool,
And call them not to share with us their part
In this unhappy mansion; or once more
With rallied arms to try what may be yet
Regain'd in heav'n, or what more lost in hell?

From John Milton, *Paradise Lost*, Book I (1669).

GOD'S RIVAL

"Johnson's grandiosity had a large impact on what he did as President. One can easily take offense at LBJ's impulse to make himself a larger-than-life character. 'I understand you were born in a log cabin,' German chancellor Ludwig Erhard said during a visit to the President's ranch. 'No, no,' Johnson replied. 'You have me confused with Abe Lincoln; I was born in a manger.'"

—Robert Dallek, biographer of Lyndon B. Johnson

QUESTIONS FOR THOUGHT AND DISCUSSION

1. On what does John Milton lay the blame for the fall of "our grand Parents"? According to the poem, what motivated Satan in deceiving "the mother of mankind"?
2. For what was Satan grasping prior to his outcast from heaven? How does Milton describe the vice of pride in Satan?
3. Satan describes himself as having "a mind not to be changed by place or time." Do you see such a trait as strength or arrogance? What makes the difference?
4. What do you think of the often-quoted line spoken by Satan, "Better to reign in hell than serve in heaven"? Why is this statement different from the equally passionate declaration of independence by Patrick Henry at the time of the American Revolution, "Give me liberty or give me death!"?
5. At the end of the passage, has Satan yet given up? Do you find Milton's Satan horrifyingly negative or rather heroic and attractive?

Shirley MacLaine

Shirley MacLaine Beaty (born 1934) is an Oscar-winning stage and screen actress. Born in Richmond, Virginia, she attended high school in Washington, D.C., and took ballet lessons to prepare her for her career in film. Her breakthrough came in the 1954 Broadway production of Pajama Game, *which led immediately to an Alfred Hitchcock film and then a whole slew of Hollywood successes, including* Around the World in Eighty Days, Irma La douce, The Turning Point, *and* Terms of Endearment, *which won her an Oscar in 1984.*

In the 1960s MacLaine championed many liberal causes, including the Vietnam protest, but she became even more controversial in the 1980s with her New Age books and television programs promoting such ideas as reincarnation and trance channeling. The following passage comes from the late 1970s when MacLaine launched a series of consciousness-raising seminars ("Tune in to your higher self or else"). It captures an important side of modern pride—the fatuousness of self-absorption. It also fits in with other expressions of self-absorption (for example, Woody Allen: "Don't knock masturbation—it's sex with someone I love").

It captures an important side of modern pride— the fatuousness of self-absorption.

YOU SAY, "I AM A GOD" . . .

"This is what the Sovereign LORD says: 'In the pride of your heart you say, "I am a god; I sit on the throne of a god in the heart of the seas." But you are a man and not a god, though you think you are as wise as a god.'"

—Ezekiel 28:2

"Me, me alone, and that's enough."

—Corneille, *Medea*

"We are as gods and might as well get good at it."

—Stewart Brand, founder of the *Whole Earth Catalog*

WHAT MAKES MACLAINE RUN?

Picking at one of the six small meals she eats a day—grilled-cheese sandwich, potato salad, and a cup of walnuts, in this case—Shirley MacLaine sat in her Watergate Hotel suite Saturday explaining why somewhere on her way to turning 40 a few years ago her life suddenly became the pits.

It was, she says, about five years ago—about the time she had worked a year for McGovern and he lost . . . about the time she had all but "no'd" herself out of the movie business by turning down scripts . . . about the time she lost her sense of humor, got dissatisfied, gained twenty-five pounds . . . about the time she had a mid-30s crisis.

It was, she says, worse than her teens. The moment in her life when she had to decide whether to "go on living positively" or, well, keep on eating.

So she stopped eating. And started jogging, exercising, dancing—and now, at 43, has danced her way back into a successful nightclub act whose performances she sandwiched in between finishing her third book and the movie

The Turning Point—a marvelous MacLaine/Anne Bancroft tour de force whose world premiere has brought her to Washington. A movie she likes a lot. A movie she'd pay to see if she weren't in it. . . .

For MacLaine, identity is a big number. The only number. The thing she is always onto—racing for it, jogging for it, acting for it, campaigning for it—attacking whatever urge she must in order to fulfill the sum parts of her whole.

And when she talks about it—and she does a lot—when she tells you that "the most pleasurable journey you take is through yourself . . ." it comes out okay, isn't gooey, doesn't sound like a chapter out of *Your Erroneous Zones,* because MacLaine is careful to qualify herself . . . admit that for her at least it is the partial battle cry of the "compulsive overachiever"—the decathlon competitor competing only with herself.

"When you look back on your life and try to figure out where you've been and where you are going," she will tell you, "when you look at your work, your love affairs, your marriages, your children, your pain, your happiness—when you examine all that closely, what you really find out is that the only person you really go to bed with is yourself. The only person you really eat with is yourself. So in the end life must be what you do with yourself.

"And all the wonderful surroundings, like people you live with, your friends, your co-workers, are all extensions but they're not you. The only thing you have is working to the consummation of your own identity. And that's what I've been trying to do all my life. People always want to know where my drive comes from. Well, all I can say is my drive is what I have to do. See, what always finally happens to me is that the not trying is harder than the anticipation of failure if I do try. That's why I started writing. It was harder not to write than to write, and as you know, there's nothing harder than writing."

From Nancy Collins, "What Makes MacLaine Run?" *The Washington Post,* November 14, 1977, p. C1. Copyright © 1977 *The Washington Post.* Reprinted with permission.

QUESTIONS FOR THOUGHT AND DISCUSSION

1. What, according to the author, drives Shirley MacLaine? What is she willing to do to get it?
2. What do you think of MacLaine's theme statement, "The most pleasurable journey you take is through yourself . . ."? How does this statement measure against modern culture? Against the teachings of Jesus?

3. Do you agree with MacLaine that, "The only person you really go to bed with is yourself. . . . In the end life must be what you do with yourself"? What factors in our culture have helped to produce this kind of thinking?

4. What sort of pride, if any, do you see exhibited in this interview? What are the logical consequences of MacLaine's thinking for individuals? Families? Communities?

❦ *William Golding* ❦

William Gerald Golding (1911–1993) is a celebrated modern English novelist who won the Nobel Prize in Literature in 1983. His most famous book was his first, Lord of the Flies. When it was published in 1955 it became an instant success in Britain and the United States, attaining the status of "contemporary classic" enjoyed by such books as J. D. Salinger's The Catcher in the Rye. Lord of the Flies is a powerful combination of a children's adventure story, an anthropological insight, and a Christian conception of Eden and original sin.

Golding called his books fables. He was a highly original writer of moral allegories that expressed his deeply realistic view of human nature—shaped in part, it is said, by his years of teaching small boys in a boarding school.

The Spire (1964) is just such a moral fable, but one based on historical fact. When Salisbury Cathedral was built, it had neither a spire nor the necessary foundations on which to build one. A spire was added, however, as a monument to the maniacal egotism of the Dean—who built it against all the architectural wisdom of the time. Visitors to the cathedral today can see the severe buckling in the pillars with the naked eye.

Proud, powerful, and relentlessly driven, Golding's Dean Jocelin represents human vision and energy raised to the level of hubris, or overweening arrogance. In fact, the odds were defied and the spire was built, but the architectural and human costs were enormous. This reading describes the point in the story where Jocelin overpowers the reluctance of his master builder, Roger, and forces the project onward and upward to its logic-defying success. It speaks directly to the

As the story shows, religion does not solve the problem; it makes it worse. Spiritual pride at its full-blown is literally demonic pride.

thrusting compulsion with which many strong leaders tackle great projects and the danger of slipping over the invisible line between calling and drivenness, vision and hubris, enterprise and egotism. As the story shows, religion does not solve the problem; it makes it worse. Spiritual pride at its full-blown is literally demonic pride.

DRIVING OR DRIVEN?

"Do nothing out of selfish ambition or vain conceit, but in humility consider others better than yourselves. Each of you should look not only to your own interests, but also to the interests of others."

—Philippians 2:3-4

"Basically the man who, given the chance to measure himself by his own standards, justifies his life through his creative works, turns into a very demanding sort of person: I mean he no longer thinks about pleasing people. He is too serious and they sense it; there is a devilish seriousness behind someone who wants respect from his work."

—Friedrich Nietzsche

"My sense of reality was just altered. I started out being excited working for the president. Then I became arrogant, then I became grandiose, and then I became self-destructive. . . . Man, everybody who turns 40 should read the Greek tragedies. They all have within them the same idea: The thing that may have helped you move up then destroys you. And I'm a living example of that."

—Dick Morris, President Clinton's political advisor, in an interview with the Associated Press after his resignation following a scandal

THE SPIRE

Roger was watching him closely, tongue licking at his lips.

"No. I don't know what you mean. But I know how much the spire will weigh, and I don't know how strong it'll be. Look down, Father—right over the parapet, all the way down, past the lights, the buttresses, all the way down to the cedar top in the cloister."

"I see it."

"Let your eye crawl down like an insect, foot by foot. You think these walls are strong because they're stone; but I know better. We've nothing but a skin of glass and stone stretched between four stone rods, one at each corner. D'you understand that? The stone is no stronger than the glass between the verticals because every inch of the way I have to save weight, bartering strength for weight or weight for strength, guessing how much, how far, how little, how near, until my very heart stops when I think of it. Look down, Father. Don't look at me—look down! See how the columns at each corner are tacked together. I've clamped the stones together but still I can't make them stronger than stone. Stone snaps, crumbles, tears. Yet even now, when the pillars sing, perhaps this much may stand. I can give you a roof over it, and perhaps a weather vane that men will see for miles."

Jocelin was suddenly very still, very wary.

"Go on, my son."

"The sheer impossibility of the spire! You need to be thrust this high, Father, to understand it, don't you see? It'll be a stone skin with stone members. Inside there'll be a series of those octagons, each a little smaller than the one below it. But the wind, Father! I should have to pin those octagons together, and hang them from the capstone so that they hold the skin down by their weight. Weight, weight, weight, weight! All added to this; all boring down on the columns, on the skin of the wall, down on the singing pillars."

Now his hand was on Jocelin's sleeve.

"And even that isn't the end of it. However I contrive, the spire won't thrust perpendicularly. It'll thrust at the tops of these four columns and it'll thrust—*out!* I could put pinnacles on each to bear down—should have to—but there'd be a limit to the height I could make them, because of the weight. At what point should I have to give up the one for the other? Oh yes; we could put in the first octagon and the second and perhaps the third—" his hand clenched on Jocelin's arm—"but sooner or later there'd be a new noise in the building. Look down again, Father. Sooner or later there'd be a bang, a shudder, a roar. Those four columns would open apart like a flower, and everything else up here, stone, wood, iron, glass, men, would slide down into the church like the fall of a mountain."

He was silent again for a moment. Then his voice came, no more than a whisper.

"I tell you—whatever else is uncertain in my mystery—this is certain. I know. I've seen a building fall."

Jocelin's eyes were shut. Inside his head, a series of octagons, each made of oak beams a foot thick, had built themselves up and up. For a moment, as he stood with gritted teeth, he felt the solid stone under him move—swinging sideways and out. The dunce's cap a hundred and fifty feet tall began to rip down and tear and burst, sliding with dust and smoke and thunder, faster and faster, breaking and sheering with spark and flame and explosion, crashing down to strike the nave so that the paving stones danced like wood chips till the ruin buried them. So clear was this that he fell with the southwest column that swung out over the cloister bent in the middle like a leg and destroyed the library like the blow of a flail. He opened his eyes, sick with falling through the air. He was clutching the parapet and the cloisters were moving below him.

"What must we do?"

"Stop building."

For a moment, as he stood with gritted teeth, he felt the solid stone under him move—swinging sideways and out.

The answer came pat; and even before his sickness had sunk away and the cloisters steadied, some deep center of awareness understood how the master builder had led up to this answer.

"No, no, no, no."

He was muttering and understanding and shaking his head. He understood the plea refused, the final resource, building talk, a mystery not displayed down there on the solid earth, but pondered on, brought up the tower in privacy, used at last like a lever on a fulcrum of vertigo; all so contrived as to bring the will within a single moment of defeat.

"No."

At last the reply was assured. It was the reply of one blade to another, clash, slither, clash.

"Roger, I tell you the thing can be done."

The master builder flung away furiously, stood in the southwest corner with his back to Jocelin. He faced the rain and looked at nothing.

"Listen, Roger."

What can I tell him? I talked about mayfly, but ten minutes later and I can't remember what. Let the will talk to him.

"You tried to frighten me as you might frighten a child with a ghost story. You thought it out carefully, didn't you? And yet you know you can't go. Can't go. Can't get away. And all that time, your curious, valuable mind was finding a way round the impossible. You found it too, because that's what you're for. You don't know if it's the right answer but it's the best one you've got. But you're frightened. The best part of you would like to try, but the rest snivels and whimpers."

He stood next to the broad back and spoke into the rain and the nothingness.

"Now I'll tell you what no one else knows. They think I'm mad perhaps; but what does that matter? They'll know about it one day when I—but you shall hear it now, as man to man, on this very stump of a tower, up here with no one else to listen. My son. The building is a diagram of prayer; and our spire will be a diagram of the highest prayer of all. God revealed it to me in a vision, his unprofitable servant. He chose me. He chooses you, to fill the diagram with glass and iron and stone, since the children of men require a thing to look at. D'you think you can escape? You're not in my net—oh yes, Roger, I understand a number of things, how you are drawn, and twisted, and tormented—but it isn't my net. It's His. We can neither of us avoid this work. And there's another thing. I've begun to see how we can't understand it either, since each new foot reveals a new effect, a new purpose. It's senseless, you think. It frightens us, and it's unreasonable. But then—since when did God ask the chosen ones to be reasonable? They call this Jocelin's Folly, don't they?"

"I've heard it called so."

"The net isn't mine, Roger, and the folly isn't mine. It's God's Folly. Even in the old days He never asked men to do what was reasonable. Men can do that for themselves. They can buy and sell, heal and govern. But then out of some deep place comes the command to do what makes no sense at all—to build a ship on dry land; to sit among the dunghills; to marry a whore; to set their son on the altar of sacrifice. Then, if men have faith, a new thing comes."

He was silent for a while, in the prickling rain, looking at Roger Mason's back. It was my voice that spoke the words, he thought. No. Not my voice. Voice of the devouring Will, my master.

"Roger?"

"Well?"

"You'll build it to the top. You think those are your own hands, but they aren't. You think it's your own mind that's been working, nagging at the problem, and now sits in secret pride of having solved it. But it isn't. Any more than my mind speaks the words that are using my voice."

Then they were silent again; and he was aware of the third with them, the angel that stood in the cold and rain, warming him at his back.

At last the master builder spoke, toneless and resigned.

"Steel. Or perhaps steel. I can't tell. We can pass a great band of it round the whole tower up here and bind the stones together. I don't know. No one has ever used as much steel as that before. I still don't know. And it'll cost more money, much more."

"I'll find it."

He reached out, timidly almost, and touched the master builder's shoulder.

"Roger—He isn't needlessly cruel, you know. Why, to those who need it because they're weak, perhaps, He even sends a comforter to stand at their back! He warms them in the rain and the wind. And you're necessary. Think how the chisel must feel, ground, forced against the hard wood, hour after hour! But then it's oiled and wrapped in rag and put away. A good workman never uses a tool for something it can't do; never ignores it; takes care of it."

He paused, thinking. I speak of myself, perhaps, as much as of him. It was joy once; but strangely, no longer joy. Only a longing for peace.

"And Roger—when you have done and it stands here for all to see—the net may break."

The master builder muttered.

"I don't know what you mean."

"But build quickly—quickly! Before you consent to the major evil and the net never break—"

The master builder swung round, head down and lowering.

"Keep your sermons to yourself!"

"Because you have all become precious to me—you and all the rest—and I begin to live by you."

"What d'you mean?"

What did I mean, he thought. I meant something about Goody and Rachel—I must speak to her as I spoke to him, or as the Will spoke to him.

He nodded seriously at the master builder.

"I must go down now, Roger. There's something I have to do."

So he began to climb down the ladders with his angel; and before he was out of sight, he heard Roger Mason speaking softly.

"I believe you're the devil. The devil himself."

Excerpt from *The Spire*. © 1964 and renewed 1992 by William Golding, reprinted by permission of Harcourt Inc.

QUESTIONS FOR THOUGHT AND DISCUSSION

1. With what specific arguments does the master builder try to persuade Jocelin to abandon his plans for a spire? What is the meaning of his plea, "Don't look at me—look down!"? To what do all of these arguments appeal?

2. During the master builder's warnings, Jocelin shuts his eyes. What does he see? What purpose might this nightmarish vision have served?

3. What is Jocelin's immediate response to the vision? How does the master builder answer his question? At this moment, Jocelin suddenly sees the master builder's answer in a different light. How does he view the entire lead-up to this moment? Why the change?

4. Golding writes, "It was the reply of one blade to another." When have you been caught in such a "will against will" battle? Have you ever been

so determined to do something that any amount of reason against it won't budge your resolve? What is the strength and what is the danger of such an immovable stance?

5. Jocelin now turns his mind to persuading Roger to build the spire. He first says, "Your curious, valuable mind was finding a way round the impossible. . . . The best part of you would like to try." To what does this argument appeal? What makes it such a strong pull? What is the fear of saying "no" to such an approach?

6. Jocelin next wraps his argument in spiritual clothes. Specifically, how does he do this? Are his examples of God's "unreasonable demands" in history true and used rightly, or true but used in the wrong context? What makes the "spiritual" spin so potentially pernicious?

7. At what point does Jocelin recognize the power of his own will? How does he react to this knowledge? What does Roger's voice "toneless and resigned" tell you about his view of the Dean's resolve? What does the Dean's private thought reveal: "It was joy once; but strangely, no longer joy. Only a longing for peace"?

8. What is Jocelin's strategy in his final appeal, ". . . You have all become precious to me—you and all the rest—"? Does it work or not work? Read the final line spoken by the master builder. He sees Jocelin's ambition not as a response to God's call, but as a proud diabolical drivenness. How do you see it? What marks the difference?

9. Hundreds of years later, Salisbury Cathedral is still standing, defying the odds. With this in mind, do you agree with the Dean or the master builder's view of the spire project? Why?

10. Do you know examples today of ambition toppling over into pride and drivenness—in business? Politics? Society? Religious empire building? Where does someone cross the line? What are realistic checks against such dangers?

THE COUNTERPOINT TO PRIDE:
Blessed Are Those Who Are Poor in Spirit

What are traditionally understood as the seven classical virtues are actually a blend of pagan and Christian thought. The four Cardinal Virtues (justice, wisdom, courage, and moderation) of the ancient, pre-Christian world, and the three Theological Virtues (faith, hope, and love) of Christendom were joined to make up a set of seven—as counterpoints to the seven deadly sins. Yet, in addition to their artificial construction, the classical virtues also fall short of being true counterpoints to the vices.

The Beatitudes of Jesus, in contrast, are mirror images of the vices, clear counterpoints as outlined in the table in the introduction to this book. As such, they are neither antidotes to the vices nor curatives, but rather superb opposites. If the seven deadly sins summarize the misery of human evil, the Beatitudes summarize the bliss of the supernatural virtue of the kingdom of God. They are, in fact, the "virtues of the kingdom." Though space does not permit a full treatment of the Beatitudes here, they will be touched upon as the opposing virtue to each vice, offering clarity by contrast.

If the seven deadly sins summarize the misery of human evil, the Beatitudes summarize the bliss of the supernatural virtue of the kingdom of God.

Acquiring the virtues, it is important to remember, is not the automatic outcome of eliminating the vices. In the same way that a garden must be weeded before flowers can be planted, so eliminating the vices prepares the soil of our lives for the cultivation of virtue, but in no way guarantees it.

BLESSED ARE THOSE WHO ARE POOR IN SPIRIT

"Poverty of spirit," or humility, is the direct counterpoint to pride. The word Jesus uses in the beatitude is clear. Of two common Greek words for "poor," Jesus uses the strongest, meaning poverty that is destitute and bankrupt. Sophocles uses this word to describe the aged Oedipus in exile as a beggar; Aeschylus applies it to the prophetess Cassandra as a gypsy vagrant. Coupled with the words "of spirit," the meaning is clear. "Blessed are those who are so aware of their own bankruptcy, in and of themselves, that they have nothing to count on in this world except God, for his bliss will be theirs."

Two misconceptions of humility are to be guarded against. The first, more superficial error is that of the "self as doormat." The mealy-mouthed, passive, I-have-no-important-needs-or-desires attitude is not the humility represented in the Beatitudes, as evidenced by Jesus' own life and teaching. False humility is actually self-driven and self-absorbed. A person who is falsely humble is a person who is truly proud.

A person who is falsely humble is a person who is truly proud.

PROUDLY HUMBLE

"It is always the humble man who talks too much; the proud man watches himself too closely."

—G. K. Chesterton

"A man is never so proud as when striking an attitude of humility."

—C. S. Lewis

"My list of virtues contain'd at first but twelve; but a Quaker friend having kindly informed me that I was generally thought proud; that my pride show'd itself frequently in conversation; that I was not content with being in the right when discussing any point, but was overbearing, and rather insolent, of which he convinc'd me by mentioning several instances; I determined endeavoring to cure myself, if I could, of this vice or folly among the rest, and I added Humility to my list, giving an extensive meaning to the word. I cannot boast of much success in acquiring the reality of this virtue, but I had a good deal with regard to the appearance of it. . . . In reality, there is, perhaps, no one of our natural passions so hard to subdue as pride. Disguise it, struggle with it, beat it down, stifle it, mortify it as much as one pleases, it is still alive, and will every now and then peep out and show itself; you will see it, perhaps, often in this history; for, even if I could conceive that I had completely overcome it, I should probably be proud of my humility."

—Benjamin Franklin, *Autobiography*

"Yes, pride is a perpetual nagging temptation. Keep on knocking it on the head, but don't be too worried about it. As long as one knows one is proud, one is safe from the worst form of pride."

—C. S. Lewis

"Don't be humble, you're not that great."

—Golda Meir, former Prime Minister of Israel

"Those who travel the high road of humility are not troubled by the traffic."

—Alan Simpson, former U.S. Senator from Wyoming

The second misconception is deeper and more dangerous. Humility, Nietzsche believed, was the unconscious expression of resentment, an inversion of aggression by the weak. Because Christianity was first the religion of slaves under oppression by the Roman Empire, Nietzsche argued that these believers turned their unchangeable powerlessness into a virtue (humility), but inwardly resented the power of those in charge.

This too is a gross misunderstanding of the beatitude of humility. Christ commands "poverty of spirit" of the ruler as well as the servant. Humility, in the biblical understanding, is not masked resentment, but rather a form of clear-sightedness. It is realism about ourselves plus trust in God.

Most world religions deal with the overcoming of self-love. But the exalted view of humility in the beatitude is uniquely Jewish and Christian, not shared by pagan philosophers. From the biblical perspective, it is simply an acknowledgment of the truth of the human condition. Pride, in thinking we are finally ever anything other than dependent on God, is simply presumptuous folly.

Pride, in thinking we are finally ever anything other than dependent on God, is simply presumptuous folly.

THE GRAND INVERSION

"When Nebuchadnezzar, the mighty King of Babylonia, wanted to sing praises to God, an angel came and slapped him in the face. When asked about this story, Rabbi Mendl of Kotzk answered, 'Why did he deserve to be slapped, if his intention was to sing God's praises? You want to sing praises while you are wearing your crown? Let me hear how you praise me after having been slapped in the face.'"

—The Talmud

"It was the Jews who, with awe-inspiring consistency, dared to invert the aristocratic value-equation (good=noble=powerful=beautiful=happy=beloved of God) and to hang onto this inversion with their teeth, the teeth of the most abysmal hatred (the hatred of impotence), saying 'the wretched alone are the good; the suffering, deprived, sick, ugly alone are pious, alone are blessed by God . . . and you, the powerful and noble, are on the contrary the evil, the cruel, the lustful, the insatiable, the godless to all eternity, and you shall be in all eternity the unblessed, the accursed, and damned!'"

—Friedrich Nietzsche, *On the Genealogy of Morals*

When Hapsburg emperor Franz Joseph died, the cortège arrived at the closed doors of the monastery and a herald knocked at the gate. Then one could hear the voice of the abbot: "Who are you?" "I am Franz Joseph, Emperor of Austria, King of Hungary," the herald replied. "I don't know you. Who are you?" "I am Franz Joseph, Emperor of Austria, King of Hungary, Bohemia, Galicia, Lodomeria, and Dalmatia, Grand Duke of Transylvania, Margrave of Moravia, Duke of Styria and Carinthia. . . ." "We don't know you. Who are you?" the sepulchral voice reiterated. Thereupon the messenger knelt down and said: "I am Franz Joseph, a poor sinner humbly begging for God's mercy." "Thou mayest enter, then," the abbot said, and the gates were flung open.

—Comte de Saint-Aulaire, remarking on how the church historically checked kings' royal pride, 1945

"In America you know you have lost power when your limousine is yellow and your driver speaks no English."

—James A. Baker, former Secretary of State

Thomas à Kempis

Thomas à Kempis (about 1380–1471) is a leading Christian devotional writer most widely known for his best-selling classic The Imitation of Christ. *French-born to poor parents in Kempen, near Cologne, his real name was Thomas Hemerker. He was educated at the school of the Brethren of the Common Life, and in 1399 entered a monastery of which his elder brother was cofounder and prior. There he lived nearly all the rest of his life, preaching, writing, copying manuscripts, and offering spiritual counsel.*

    The Imitation of Christ *is a manual of spiritual devotion that instructs Christians on how to reach maturity by following Christ as their model. It was first put into circulation in 1418. The first two parts contain general counsel for the spiritual life while the third deals with the inner attitudes of the soul, and the fourth with the sacrament of Holy Communion.*

    Thomas à Kempis's stance on pride and humility is strenuous and unrelenting, almost ascetic. It does not sit comfortably with modern views. But many of our modern views, rather than that of Kempis, would be the odd man out among Christian views through the centuries. It is worth asking, however, how such tough-minded views as those of Thomas à Kempis can be heard constructively today without being dangerously distorted within the context of our modern misconceptions and crises of identity.

SELF: SERVED OR SERVANT?

"When fortune favors us, what need of friends?"

—Euripides

"Your attitude should be the same as that of Christ Jesus: Who, being in very nature God, did not consider equality with God something to be grasped, but made himself nothing, taking the very nature of a servant, being made in human likeness. And being found in appearance as a man, he humbled himself and became obedient to death—even death on a cross! Therefore God exalted him to the highest place and gave him the name that is above every name, that at the name of Jesus every knee should bow, in heaven and on earth and under the earth, and every tongue confess that Jesus Christ is Lord, to the glory of God the Father."

—Philippians 2:5-11

"The most preposterous falsehood is the most common, most cherished one: self-centeredness. Man tends to act as if his ego were the hub of the world, the source and purpose of existence. What a shameless affront to deny that God is that source and purpose, the sap and the meaning."

—Rabbi Mendl of Kotzk

HOW THROUGH HUMILITY WE SHOULD THINK OURSELVES MEAN AND ABJECT IN THE SIGHT OF GOD

Shall I, Lord Jesus, dare speak to You, I who am but dust and ashes? Truly, if I think myself any better than ashes and dust, You stand against me, and my own sins also bear witness against me. That I cannot deny. But if I despise myself and set myself at naught and think myself but ashes and dust, as I am, then Your grace will be close to me and the light of true understanding will enter into my heart, so that all presumption and pride in me will be drowned in the valley of meekness, through perfect knowledge of my wretchedness.

Through humility You will show me what I am, what I have been, and from whence I came, for I am nothing, and did not know. If I am left to myself, then I am nothing, and all is frailty and imperfection; but if You vouchsafe a little to regard me, soon I am made strong and am filled with a new joy. It is a marvel that I, a wretch, am so soon lifted up from my instability into the contemplation of heavenly things, and that I am so lovingly supported by You, who of myself always fall before worldly attractions. But Your love, Lord, causes all this, Your love which goes before me, and helps me in all my necessities, and keeps me carefully from all perils and dangers into which I am daily likely to fall. I have lost You, and myself as well, by the inordinate love I have had for myself, in seeking You again, I have found both You and myself. Therefore, I will from now on more deeply set myself at naught and more diligently seek You than I have done in times past. You, Lord Jesus, You deal with me above all my merits, and above all that I can possibly ask or desire.

PROGRESSIVE IGNORANCE

"If I have seen a little farther than others, it is because I have stood on the shoulders of giants."

—Sir Isaac Newton

"I do not know what I may appear to the world but to myself I seem to have been only a boy playing on the sea-shore, and diverting myself in now and then finding a smoother pebble or a prettier shell than ordinary, whilst the great ocean of truth lay all undiscovered before me."

—Sir Isaac Newton

"Does it mean that we, today, for instance, everyone sitting in this hall, have a greater knowledge of the conditions of life under which we exist than has an American Indian or a Hottentot? Hardly. Unless he is a physicist, one who rides on a streetcar has no idea how the car happened to get into motion. And he does not need to know. He is satisfied that he may 'count' on the behavior of the streetcar, and he orients his conduct according to this expectation; but he knows nothing about what it takes to produce such a car so that it can move. The savage knows incomparably more about his tools."

—Max Weber, warning students that progress humbles pride

QUESTIONS FOR THOUGHT AND DISCUSSION

1. In the first paragraph, how does Kempis strive to see himself? What does he believe is the positive outcome of maintaining such a view? What link does he make between humility and "true understanding"? Explain this link in your own words.

2. What, to Kempis, is the road to strength and joy? What does he see as the dangerous consequence of inordinate self-love? How does one truly "find himself or herself" according to the author? Contrast his position on the closeness of sin and self-love to the modern view of self-love and "finding oneself."

3. Does Kempis's view of humility apply to everyone—even those in positions of secular leadership? Do you see a conflict between humility and some styles of leadership? Which ones?

4. How can such a self-deprecating understanding of humility be distinguished from false humility and the unhealthy idea of the self-as-doormat?

Jeremy Taylor

Jeremy Taylor (1613–1667) was an Anglican bishop, theologian, and writer in the seventeenth century. A native and graduate of Cambridge, he caught the eye of Archbishop William Laud who appointed him chaplain to the ill-fated Charles I (and later to the royalist army in the English Civil War). He was briefly imprisoned following the king's defeat, and later went to live in Wales and eventually Ireland, where he became Vice Chancellor of Dublin University.

Taylor was a somewhat undistinguished theologian whose works managed to rile the Presbyterians on one side and the Roman Catholics on the other. His claim to fame rests on his preaching and his devotional writings, especially The Rule and Exercise of Holy Living *(1650). The book has become a minor classic, praised for its elegant prose and its balanced, practical spirituality. These qualities are apparent in Taylor's very helpful guidelines for practicing humility.*

RIGHTEOUSLY UNRIGHTEOUS

To some who were confident of their own righteousness and looked down on everybody else, Jesus told this parable:

"Two men went up to the temple to pray, one a Pharisee and the other a tax collector. The Pharisee stood up and prayed about himself: 'God, I thank you that I am not like other men—robbers, evildoers, adulterers—or even like this tax collector. I fast twice a week and give a tenth of all I get.' But the tax collector stood at a distance. He would not even look up to heaven, but beat his breast and said, 'God, have mercy on me, a sinner.' I tell you that this man, rather than the other, went home justified before God. For everyone who exalts himself will be humbled, and he who humbles himself will be exalted."

—Luke 18:9-14

"God creates everything out of nothing—and everything which God is to use he first reduces to nothing."

—Søren Kierkegaard

"A saint is long past any desire for distinction; he is the only sort of superior man who has never been a superior person."

—G. K. Chesterton

ACTS OR OFFICES OF HUMILITY

The grace of humility is exercised by these following rules.

1. Think not thyself better for any thing that happens to thee from without. . . .

2. Humility consists not in railing against thyself, or wearing mean clothes, or going softly and submissively: but in hearty and real evil or mean opinion of thyself. . . .

3. Whatsoever evil thou sayest of thyself, be content that others should think to be true: and if thou callest thyself fool, be not angry if another say so of thee. . . .

4. Love to be concealed, and little esteemed: be content to want praise, never being troubled when thou art slighted or undervalued; for thou canst not undervalue thyself, and if thou thinkest so meanly as there is reason, no contempt will seem unreasonable, and therefore it will be very tolerable.

5. Never be ashamed of thy birth, or thy parents, or thy trade, or thy present employment. . . .

6. Never speak any thing directly tending to thy praise or glory; that is, with a purpose to be commended, and for no other end. If other ends be mingled with thy honour, as if the glory of God, or charity, or necessity, or any thing of prudence be thy end, you are not tied to omit your discourse or your design that you may avoid praise, but pursue your end, though praise come along in the company. Only let not praise be the design.

7. When thou hast said or done any thing for which thou receivest praise or estimation, take it indifferently, and return it to God; reflecting upon him as the giver of the gift, or the blesser of the action, or the aid of the design: and give God thanks for making thee an instrument of his glory, or the benefit of others.

8. Secure a good name to thyself by living virtuously and humbly: But let this good name be nursed abroad: and never be brought home to look upon it: let others use it for their own advantage; let them speak of it if they please; but do not thou at all use it, but as an instrument to do God glory, and thy neighbour more advantage. Let thy face like Moses's shine to others, but make no looking-glasses for thyself.

9. Take no content in praise when it is offered thee: but let thy rejoicing in God's gift be allayed with fear, lest this good bring thee to evil. Use the praise as you use your pleasure in eating and drinking: if it comes, make it do drudgery, let it serve other ends, and minister to necessities, and to caution, lest

Humility consists not in railing against thyself, or wearing mean clothes, or going softly and submissively: but in hearty and real evil or mean opinion of thyself.

by pride you lose your just praise which you have deserved; or else by being praised unjustly, you receive shame into yourself with God and wise men.

10. Use no stratagems and devices to get praise. Some use to enquire into the faults of their own actions or discourses on purpose to hear that it was well done or spoken, and without fault: others bring the matter into talk, or thrust themselves into company, and intimate and give occasion to be thought or spoke of. These men make a bait to persuade themselves to swallow the hook, till by drinking the waters of vanity they swell and burst.

11. Make no suppletories [excuses for deficiencies] to thyself, when thou art disgraced or slighted, by pleasing thyself with supposing thou didst deserve praise, though they understood thee not, or enviously detracted from thee: neither do thou get to thyself a private theatre and flatterers, in whose vain noises and fantastic praises thou mayest keep up thine own good opinion of thyself.

12. Entertain no fancies of vanity and private whispers of this devil of pride; such as was that of Nebuchadnezzar; Is not this great Babylon which I have built for the honour of my name, and the might of my majesty, and the power of my kingdom? Some fantastic spirits will walk alone, and dream waking of greatnesses, of palaces, of excellent orations, full theatres, loud applauses, sudden advancement, great fortunes, and so will spend an hour with imaginative pleasure; all their employment being nothing but fumes of pride, and secret indefinite desires and significations of what their heart wishes. In this although there is nothing of its own nature directly vicious, yet it is either an ill mother or an ill daughter, an ill sign or an ill effect, and therefore at no hand consisting with the safety and interest of humility.

13. Suffer others to be praised in thy presence, and entertain their good and glory with delight; but at no hand disparage them, or lessen the report, or make an objection; and think not the advancement of thy brother is a lessening of thy worth. But this act is also to extend farther.

14. Be content that he should be employed, and thou laid by as unprofitable; his sentence approved, thine rejected; he be preferred, and thou fixed in a low employment.

15. Never compare thyself with others, unless it be to advance them and to depress thyself. To which purpose we must be sure in some sense or other to think ourselves the worst in every company where we come: one is more learned than I am, another is more prudent, a third honourable, a fourth more chaste, or he is more charitable, or less proud. For the humble man observes their good, and reflects only upon his own vileness; or considers the many evils of himself certainly known to himself, and the ill of others but by uncertain

Suffer others to be praised in thy presence, and entertain their good and glory with delight; but at no hand disparage them, or lessen the report, or make an objection; and think not the advancement of thy brother is a lessening of thy worth.

report: or he considers that the evils done by another are out of much infirmity or ignorance, but his own sins are against a clearer light; and if the other had so great helps, he would have done more good and less evil: or he remembers that his old sins before his conversion were greater in the nature of the thing, or in certain circumstances, than the sins of other men. . . .

16. Be not always ready to excuse every oversight, or indiscretion, or ill action: but if thou beest guilty of it, confess it plainly; for virtue scorns a lie for its cover: but to hide a sin with it, is like a crust of leprosy drawn upon an ulcer. If thou beest not guilty, (unless it be scandalous) be not over-earnest to remove it; but rather use it as an argument to chastise all greatness of fancy and opinion in thyself; and accustom thyself to bear reproof patiently and contentedly, and the harsh words of thy enemies, as knowing that the anger of an enemy is a better monitor, and represents our faults or admonishes us of our duty with more heartiness, than the kindness does, or precious balms of a friend.

17. Give God thanks for every weakness, deformity, and imperfection, and accept it as a favour and grace of God, and an instrument to resist pride and nurse humility; ever remembering, that when God, by giving thee a crooked back, hath also made thy spirit stoop or less vain, thou art more ready to enter the narrow gate of heaven, than by being straight, and standing upright, and thinking highly. Thus the apostles rejoiced in their infirmities not moral, but natural and accidental, in their being beaten and whipt like slaves, in their nakedness and poverty.

18. Upbraid no man's weakness to him to discomfort him, neither report it to disparage him, neither delight to remember it to lessen him, or to set thyself above him. Be sure never to praise thyself, or to dispraise any man else, unless God's glory or some holy end do hallow it. And it was noted to the praise of Cyrus, that amongst his equals in age he would never play at any sport, or use any exercise in which he knew himself more excellent than they: but in such in which he was unskillful he would make his challenges, lest he should shame them by his victory, and that himself might learn something of their skill and do them civilities.

19. Besides the foregoing parts and actions, humility teaches us to submit ourselves and all our faculties to God. *To believe all things, to do all things, to suffer all things* which his will enjoins us: to be content in every estate or change, knowing we have deserved worse than the worst we feel; and (as Anytus said to Alcibiades) he hath taken but half, when he might have taken all: to adore his goodness, to fear his greatness, to worship his eternal and infinite excellencies, and to submit ourselves to all our superiors in all things according to godliness, and to be meek and gentle in our conversation towards others.

Besides the foregoing parts and actions, humility teaches us to submit ourselves and all our faculties to God.

Now although according to the nature of every grace, this begins as a gift, and is increased like a habit, that is, best by its own acts; yet besides the former acts and offices of humility, there are certain other exercises and considerations, which are good helps and instruments for the procuring and increasing this grace, and the curing of pride.

From Jeremy Taylor, *The Rule and Exercise of Holy Living* (London: Bell and Daldy, 1857), pp. 79–84.

THE ARSE-SITTER
"On the highest throne in the world man sits on his arse."

—Montaigne

QUESTIONS FOR THOUGHT AND DISCUSSION

1. One at a time, reread Taylor's practical tips on combating pride: numbers 1, 3, 4, 6, 7, 10, 11, 13, and 15. For each tip, ask yourself these questions: What is being said? Why does it work? How is it practically helpful?
2. Of the other tips, find the two that stand out to you the most. Ask the above questions of each.
3. Of all the nineteen tips, which one hits closest to home? Which do you find the most helpful? Why? How can you practically put it into practice in your life?
4. What factors in our modern society make such an attitude toward humility difficult? What changes do you think would take place in your circles if such humility were seriously practiced?

TWO
ENVY (INVIDIA) VERSUS MOURNING

Envy is the second of the seven deadly sins, commonly reckoned the second worst and second most prevalent. It has been called "the rabies of the heart" (Herman Melville) and "cancer of the psyche" (Richard Condon). Envy is a major source and component of other sins. Like pride, it is also a sin of the spirit and a child of the Devil, thus a "cold" and "respectable" sin. Its uniqueness lies in the fact that it is the one vice that its perpetrators never enjoy and rarely ever confess. As Henry Fairlie wrote, "The face of envy is never lovely. It is never even faintly pleasant." Because envy is congenitally incapable of enjoyment, the more its appetite increases, the more it drives its perpetrator toward torment.

Because envy is congenitally incapable of enjoyment, the more its appetite increases, the more it drives its perpetrator toward torment.

THE INADMISSIBLE VICE

"No vice more pernicious than envy is implanted in the souls of men. This passion is first and foremost a personal detriment to the one guilty of it and does not harm others in the least. . . . Now envy is pain caused by our neighbor's prosperity. Hence, an envious man is never without cause for grief and despondency. . . . The worst feature of this malady, however, is that its victim cannot reveal it to anyone."

—St. Basil the Great

"Is envy then such a monster? Well, though many an arraigned mortal has in hopes of mitigated penalty pleaded guilty to horrible actions, did ever anybody seriously confess to envy? Something there is in it

71

universally felt to be more shameful than even felonious crime. And not only does everybody disown it but the better sort are inclined to incredulity when it is in earnest imputed to an intelligent man. But since its lodgement is in the heart not the brain, no degree of intellect supplies a guarantee against it."

—Herman Melville, *Billy Budd*

"Our envy of others devours us most of all. Rub your eyes and purify your heart and prize above all else in the world those who love you and who wish you well."

—Aleksandr Solzhenitsyn

As with pride, certain popular misunderstandings of envy numb the sting of the classical view. First, envy is not emulation. It is not simply a question of seeing that someone else possesses something that we desire and wishing that we possessed it too. Such a desire can become a positive aspiration that leads in turn to positive emulation, positive ambition, and higher success—as in the rising mobility of the American dream.

WHAT ENVY ISN'T

"This passion, while it is simply a desire to excel another, by fair industry in the search of truth and the practice of virtue is properly called *Emulation*. When it aims at power as a means of distinction, it is *Ambition*. . . . When it is in a state of mortification at the superiority of another and desires to bring him down to our level or to depress him below us, it is properly called *Envy*. . . . These observations alone would be sufficient to show that this propensity in all its branches is a principal source of the virtues and vices, the happiness and misery of human life, and that the history of mankind is little more than a simple narration of its operation and effects."

—John Adams, *Discourses on Davila*

Envy, by contrast, is "sorrow at another's good" (Thomas Aquinas). Envy enters when, seeing someone's happiness or success, we first compare and find ourselves or our condition lacking, then—out of the hurt of our wounded self-esteem—seek to bring the other person down to our level by word or deed. Envy, in short, moves from dejection to disparagement on to destruction. It is not so much the looking up as the bringing down. If anyone's possession or success belittles me, says envy, I must bring him or her down to where I am. Wishing that I might have what others have topples over into wishing that they would not have it and, finally, into working to make sure they don't. What is decisive is the feeling that the envied person's fortune is to blame for the envier's feeling of *inferiority. Thus, if emulation (as in the American dream) can be pictured as an escalator moving individuals upward in society, envy throws the gear into reverse and moves the escalator downward.*

Envy, in short, moves from dejection to disparagement on to destruction. It is not so much the looking up as the bringing down.

IF NOT I, THEN NO ONE

"Few are able to suppress in themselves a secret satisfaction at the misfortune of their friends."

—La Rochefoucauld

"Happiness, n. An agreeable sensation arising from contemplating the misery of another."

—Ambrose Bierce, *The Devil's Dictionary*

"Envy begins by asking plausibly: 'Why should I not enjoy what others enjoy?' and it ends by demanding: 'Why should others enjoy what I may not?'"

—Dorothy Sayers

"Envy always brings the truest charge, or the charge most nearest to the truth, that she can think up; it hurts more."

—C. S. Lewis

"When Sir Laurence Olivier played Hamlet in 1948, and the critics raved, I wept."

—Sir John Gielgud

Second, envy is different from jealousy *because envy rises from an aggrieved sense of inferiority and jealousy from an aggrieved sense of one's due. The words envy and jealousy commonly overlap in ordinary usage, but jealousy was once distinctive—the passionate effort to keep what is one's own by right. In this sense God is properly described in the Bible as jealous, but never as envious. For example, God is "jealous for his name," but being infinite, he is never rivaled or threatened. Such proper jealousy goes wrong in human experience—not God's— when it is threatened. Thus when the suspicion arises that someone is seeking to take what is ours by right, mistrust and hatred mount too, and proper jealousy degenerates into a vice.*

This clear distinction between envy and jealousy does not apply to those whose gods are finite, such as the Greeks, because such gods—being only finite—can be rivaled. Therefore the Greeks warned again and again: whatever excels, the gods disable. The lightning of the gods strikes the tallest trees, the largest animals, and the highest buildings. Ancient ways of avoiding this "envy of the gods," which still survive in the contemporary world, include such attitudes as English and Japanese self-effacing modesty or the superstitious custom of "knocking on wood" after an optimistic or boastful remark.

The deadly sin of envy has several common characteristics. First, envy is a vice of proximity. We are always prone to envy people close to us in temperament, gifts, or position. Thus mothers are more likely to envy other mothers, writers other writers, lawyers other lawyers, politicians other politicians, golfers other golfers, ministers other ministers, and so on.

TOO CLOSE FOR COMFORT

"Malice is created by low garden fences, or in narrow streets, where men unceasingly rub shoulders, and this man's orchard casts a blighting shade over that man's vineyard. It is an elixir brewed by close contact. . . . Indifference yields no malice."

—George Steiner, *Malice*

Second, envy is highly subjective. It is "in the eye of the beholder." It is not the objective difference between people that feeds envy but the subjective perception. As a Russian proverb says, "Envy looks at a juniper bush and sees a pine forest."

Third, the temptation to envy does not lessen with age. It gets worse, as we run into more and more people of happiness and success, offering more fodder for envy.

Fourth, envy is often petty but always insatiable and all-consuming. However small the occasion that gives rise to it, envy becomes central to the envier's whole being. The envier "stews in his own juice." At its worst, envy begins from the highest of the seven deadly sins—pride—and plunges into the lowest sin of all—hatred, or lovelessness. (Hatred is not included in the seven deadly sins because it is not capital in the sense of being fertile soil for other sins. It is terminal, the full-grown tree, the last stage of sin, when envy or anger becomes pure hatred and thus truly satanic—for as Peter Kreeft points out, "Satan is pure hatred, as God is pure love.")

However small the occasion that gives rise to it, envy becomes central to the envier's whole being.

WHEN PRAISE IS POISON

"Whatever Saul sent him to do, David did it so successfully that Saul gave him a high rank in the army. This pleased all the people, and Saul's officers as well.

"When the men were returning home after David had killed the Philistine, the women came out from all the towns of Israel to meet King Saul with singing and dancing, with joyful songs and with tambourines and lutes. As they danced, they sang:

"'Saul has slain his thousands, and David his tens of thousands.'

"Saul was very angry; this refrain galled him. 'They have credited David with tens of thousands,' he thought, 'but me with only thousands. What more can he get but the kingdom?' And from that time on Saul kept a jealous eye on David."

—1 Samuel 18:5-9

Lastly, envy is always self-destructive. What the envier cannot enjoy, no one should enjoy, and thus the envier loses every enjoyment. As an eighth-century Jewish teacher put it, "The one who envies gains nothing for himself and deprives the one he envies of nothing. He only loses thereby."

The essential masochism of envy is illustrated by a Jewish parable of an envious man and a greedy man who met a king:

"One of you," said the king, "may ask something of me and I will grant it, provided that I give twice as much to the other."

This put the two men in a quandary. The envious man did not want to ask first for he was envious of his companion who would receive twice as much. But nor did the greedy man since he wanted everything there was to be had.

Finally the greedy man prevailed on the envious man to be the first to make his request. So the envious man asked the king to pluck out one of his eyes, knowing that his companion would then have them both plucked out.

Those consumed by envy, the teaching concluded, are willing to suffer great injury so long as those they envy suffer even more.

What the envier cannot enjoy, no one should enjoy, and thus the envier loses every enjoyment.

PICTURES AND METAPHORS

If pride's characteristic stance is "looking down," envy's is "looking up," and eyes are the first main metaphor for the vice. Indeed, throughout history protecting oneself from the envious has always been "warding off the evil eye." Envy's color, of course, is green. But "green with envy" is always a picture of eyes—"slit eyes" that are turned up or aside to whatever is thought superior. Dante's terrible picture in Canto 13 of the Purgatory is a good example of his recurring theme that specific sins are punished with specific punishment. The envious in purgatory are described as having eyes closed by iron threads drawn through the eyelids—just as silk threads were sewn through the eyelids of hawks to blind and tame them. Having lived on earth unable to look on joy, their punishment is to have their eyes closed, so that they cannot see either the sun or the human happiness of any who look them in the eye and greet them.

The other main metaphor for envy is fire. Envy is a raging fire, a spreading poison, a red hot coal, a poison-tipped arrow. Whenever it hits, it hurts and spreads. It scorches and devours. It burns up the envier until he or she is consumed by the vindictive, inward torment. Though a more secret vice than most of the others, it rages more freely. Small wonder that, as Angus Wilson wrote, envy wears "an uglier face than Lust's bloodshot eyes, or Gluttony's paunch, or Pride's camel nose, or Avarice's thin lips."

Envy is a raging fire, a spreading poison, a red hot coal, a poison-tipped arrow.

PRACTICAL APPLICATIONS

As with pride, the potential harvests sown by envy are incalculable. Significantly, neither popular wisdom nor any traditional system of ethics has ever made a virtue of envy—though Western advertising occasionally does and twentieth-century Marxism made proletarian envy legitimate on a grand scale.

INCLUDED IN THE ROOM RATE

"If you've never been a Waldorf guest, you could unthinkingly believe it to be expensive. The admiration (if not envy) of the folks at home is included in the room rate."

—Advertisement in *The New York Times*, December 1961

"You will be envied for sitting in this seat."

—Advertisement for a German truck, 1966

"Suite Obsession? Living Room Lust? Kitchen Envy? Dining Room Desire? . . . Become the envy of your neighborhood while enhancing the comfort and value of your home."

—Advertisement for a Washington, D.C., home remodeling company, 1999

Many of the characterizations of envy in literature and art are legendary—such as William Shakespeare's Iago in Othello, Charles Dickens' Uriah Heep in David Copperfield, Herman Melville's Billy Budd, and Peter Shaffer's Antonio Salieri in Amadeus. But envy also works in everyday life, at almost every level and sphere of society, creating neighborhood tensions, ethnic and racial hostility, gender rivalries, and national and international strife.

TAKIN' IT TO THE STREET

"I shut the works down on several occasions because it was a nice day and I wanted to go fishing. I did not want the other fellows to have more money in their pay packets than I did."

—English trade-unionist, when called to account for habitually starting wildcat strikes in his factory

"I couldn't afford to own an automobile . . . and I didn't want anyone else to have one."

—A vandal's confession to the police after setting fire to eight cars in Bridgeport, Connecticut

Among problems directly linked to envy are arson (as opposed to theft), assassination, and vandalism. Resentment and hatred at the individual level are obvious and unsurprising, though still quite sobering. But envy is less often traced at the public level where it has enormous consequences in many areas—for example, the excessive egalitarianism of all socialism and some forms of modern democracy, the excesses of affirmative action, the barely concealed appeal of progressive taxation and much advertising, the twisted motivation of therapeutic victim playing, the rage for rights and entitlement, the destructive tearing down by gossip columns and television "gawk shows," and the fact that many Western societies are becoming increasingly angry, fueling a disturbing culture of rage, while Western elites commonly display signs of extreme guilt said to serve as ways to avoid envy.

ENVY AS SOCIAL JUSTICE?

"Equality is the political translation of the word envy."

—Victor Hugo, Journal 1830-1848

"Social justice means that we deny ourselves many things so that others may have to do without them as well, or, what is the same thing, may not be able to ask for them."

—Sigmund Freud, "Group Psychology and the Analysis of the Ego"

"Political antagonism should not degenerate into social envy."

—Motto of England's Liberal Party

In sum, envy is an enduring menace to human success at both the individual and national levels. The successful person can never be sure that there is not someone, somewhere lurking to avenge the fact of his success or superiority. The fact of human envy also raises a supreme challenge to Western capitalist democracies: How can a nation empower the inequality that results from opportunity and competition without also triggering the social harm that is produced by envy of others?

The following readings examine the destructive power of envy and its consequences both for individuals, groups, and society as a whole.

In sum, envy is an enduring menace to human success at both the individual and national levels.

CANCER OF THE PSYCHE

"President Kennedy was Lee Harvey Oswald's victim, because the young prince of the White House was and had everything that Oswald, the perpetual failure, never could be or have."

—*Newsweek,* December 1963

"The resenters, those men with cancer of the psyche, make the great assassins."

—Psychiatrist in Richard Gordon's *The Manchurian Candidate*

"I was not meant for the job or the spotlight of public life in Washington. Here ruining people is considered sport."

—Vincent Foster, Jr., White House aide, in his 1993 suicide note

"There is a lot of jealousy here of the rich and successful. If you have something nice, you are resented. The Americans say, 'I'm going to have one of those one day'; over here, it's 'Who does he think he is?' It's because here the gap between the haves and the have-nots is wider than ever. And so much hypocrisy has been exposed that the British public is much more aware of it. Twenty years ago, when a politician talked about family values and care in the community, you believed him; now you think he's taking backhanders as well as having a string of mistresses and he's laughing all the way to his country house."

—Max Clifford, 1995, Britain's leading agent for "kiss and tell" stories exposing the sexual offenses of the rich and famous

❊ *Plutarch* ❊

Plutarch (A.D. *46–120*) *is one of the most famous historians of the ancient world, best known for his book,* The Lives of the Noble Grecians and Romans. *Born in Boeotia, he studied in Athens and traveled extensively, including trips to Rome where his lectures attracted great attention. He lived most of his life in Greece, serving as a leader in his hometown and a priest to the god Apollo.*

Though Plutarch is best known for his historic work in The Lives of the Noble Grecians and Romans, *he was not a historian in the modern sense. For a start, he was notoriously careless about his accuracy with numbers. Also, he was more of a moralist than he was a historian, having a passion for stories that taught lessons, whether true or fabled. It is significant, however, that character, virtues, and vices* mattered more to him than politics, laws, and wars. His mind seemed to return continually to the great theories and ethics of his fellow Greeks, Plato and Aristotle.

The following passage is from his chapter on the Athenian leader Aristides "the Just." Aristides was an outstanding statesman and general who fell victim to popular envy. He had fought bravely at the battle of Marathon and was conspicuous in defending Athens against the Persian invasion of 480 B.C. But he was known above all for his fairness and integrity—when the Delian league was formed after the Persian War, he was called on to determine the contribution each of the nearly two hundred states should make. Not a single one questioned his assessment or accused him of unfairness.

It was therefore all the more astonishing that Aristides became the victim of Athenian ostracism. Ostracism, a ten-year exile, had been intended as a constitutional safeguard, the Athenian equivalent of "term limits." But Plutarch describes it here as an unfair way of venting popular envy on a leading citizen who stood out from the crowd.

Also, he was more of a moralist than he was a historian, having a passion for stories that taught lessons, whether true or fabled. It is significant, however, that character, virtues, and vices mattered more to him than politics, laws, and wars.

NATIONAL ENVY TAX

"Whenever there is great property, there is great inequality. For one very rich man, there must be at least five hundred poor. The affluence of the few supposes the indigence of the many, who are often both driven by want, and prompted by envy, to invade his possessions. It is only under the shelter of the civil magistrate that the owner of that valuable property, which is acquired by the labour of many years, or perhaps of many successive generations, can sleep a single night in security. He is at all times surrounded by unknown enemies, whom, though he never provoked, he can never appease, and from whose injustice he can be protected only by the powerful arm of the civil magistrate continually held up to chastise it."

—Adam Smith, *Wealth of Nations*

"In a passionless and strongly reflective age *envy is the negative unifying principle*. . . . The envy which establishes itself is the process of levelling and while a passionate age spurs on, lifts and casts down, raises and lowers, a reflective, passionless age does the opposite, it strangles and inhibits and levels. Levelling is a silent mathematical abstract activity that avoids all sensation."

—Søren Kierkegaard, *The Present Age*

"Government of the duds, by the duds, and for the duds."

—Winston Churchill, defining socialism

"The Socialist dream is no longer Utopia but Queue-topia!"

—Winston Churchill

"Socialism is the philosophy of failure, the creed of ignorance, and the gospel of envy."

—Winston Churchill

"'All men are created equal' says the American Declaration of Independence. 'All men shall be kept equal' say the Socialists."

—Winston Churchill

"I hate these socialists and their 'what you have got that I haven't got I'll take from you although I can't have it.'"

—David Lean, film director, *Lawrence of Arabia*

ARISTIDES

Aristides, the son of Lysimachus, was of the tribe Antiochis, and township of Alopece. As to wealth, statements differ; some say he passed his life in extreme poverty, and left behind him two daughters whose indigence long kept them unmarried; but Demetrius, the Phalerian, in opposition to this general report, professes in his Socrates to know a farm at Phalerum going by Aristides's name, where he was interred; and, as marks of his opulence, adduces first, the office of archon eponymus, which he obtained by the lot of the bean; which was confined to the highest assessed families, called the Pentacosiomedimni; second, the ostracism, which was not usually inflicted on the poorer citizens, but on those of great houses, whose station exposed them to envy; third and last, that he left certain tripods in the temple of Bacchus, offerings for his victory in conducting the representation of dramatic performances, which were even in our age still to be seen, retaining this inscription upon them, "The tribe Antiochis obtained the victory: Aristides defrayed the charges: Archestratus's play was acted." . . .

Of all his virtues, the common people were most affected with his justice, because of its continual and common use; and thus, although of mean fortune and ordinary birth, he possessed himself of the most kingly and divine appellation of Just: which kings, however, and tyrants have never sought after; but have taken delight to be surnamed besiegers of cities, thunderers, conquerors, or eagles again, and hawks; affecting, it seems, the reputation which proceeds from power and violence, rather than that of virtue. Although the divinity, to whom they desire to compare and assimilate themselves, excels, it is supposed, in three things, immortality, power, and virtue; of which three the noblest and divinest is virtue. For the elements and vacuum have an everlasting existence; earthquakes, thunders, storms, and torrents have great power; but in justice and equity nothing participates except by means of reason and the knowledge of that which is divine.

And thus, taking the three varieties of feeling commonly entertained towards the deity, the sense of his happiness, fear, and honour of him, people would seem to think him blest and happy for his exemption from death and corruption, to fear and dread him for his power and dominion, but to love, honour, and adore him for his justice. Yet though thus disposed, they covet that immortality which our nature is not capable of, and that power the greatest part of which is at the disposal of fortune; but give virtue, the only divine good really in our reach, the last place, most unwisely; since justice makes the life of such as are in prosperity, power, and authority the life of a god, and injustice turns it to that of a beast.

Aristides, therefore, had at first the fortune to be beloved for this surname, but at length envied. Especially when Themistocles spread a rumour amongst the people that, by determining and judging all matters privately, he had destroyed the courts of judicature, and was secretly making way for a monarchy in his own person, without the assistance of guards. Moreover the spirit of the people, now grown high, and confident with their late victory, naturally entertained feelings of dislike to all of more than common fame and reputation. Coming together, therefore, from all parts into the city, they banished Aristides by the ostracism, giving their jealousy of his reputation the name of fear of tyranny. For ostracism was not the punishment of any criminal act, but was speciously said to be the mere depression and humiliation of excessive greatness and power; and was in fact a gentle relief and mitigation of envious feeling, which was thus allowed to vent itself in inflicting no intolerable injury, only a ten years' banishment. . . .

Although the divinity, to whom they desire to compare and assimilate themselves, excels, it is supposed, in three things, immortality, power, and virtue; of which three the noblest and divinest is virtue.

Moreover the spirit of the people, now grown high, and confident with their late victory, naturally entertained feelings of dislike to all of more than common fame and reputation.

OSTRACISM

Ostracism was a procedure introduced into Athens by Cleisthenes, the founder of democracy. It was designed to deter factions and act as a safeguard against the rise of tyranny. Each year, probably in January, the Athenian assembly voted on whether there should be an ostracism that year. If the majority voted no, there was none. But if they voted yes, another vote took place in March. Each citizen could write the name of one person to be exiled from the city. The names were written on an ostracon, a broken piece *of pottery, which was the scrap of paper of the day—hence "ostracize." If as many as 6,000 voted, the required majority, then the one who received the most ballots was sent into exile for a period of ten years.*

"The original sense of this peculiar institution however is not that of a safety-valve but that of a stimulant. The all-exciting individual was to be removed in order that the contest of forces might reawaken. . . ."

—Friedrich Nietzsche, *Collected Works*

It was performed, to be short, in this manner. Every one taking an *ostracon*, a sherd, that is, or piece of earthenware, wrote upon it the citizen's name he would have banished, and carried it to a certain part of the marketplace surrounded with wooden rails. First, the magistrates numbered all the sherds in gross (for if there were less than six thousand, the ostracism was imperfect); then, laying every name by itself, they pronounced him whose name was written by the larger number banished for ten years, with the enjoyment of his estate.

As therefore, they were writing the names on the sherds, it is reported that an illiterate clownish fellow, giving Aristides his sherd, supposing him a common citizen, begged him to write *Aristides* upon it; and he being surprised and asking if Aristides had ever done him any injury, "None at all," said he, "neither know I the man; but I am tired of hearing him everywhere called the Just." Aristides, hearing this, is said to have made no reply, but returned the sherd with his own name inscribed. At his departure from the city, lifting up his hands to heaven, he made a prayer (the reverse, it would seem, of that of Achilles), that the Athenians might never have any occasion which should constrain them to remember Aristides.

Excerpt from Plutarch, *The Lives of the Noble Grecians and Romans*, trans. John Dryden, rev. Arthur Hugh Clough (New York: Modern Library, 1864).

EQUALLY UNEQUAL

"The danger is not that a particular class is unfit to govern. Every class is unfit to govern."

—Lord Acton

"That all men are born to equal rights is true. Every being has a right to his own, as clear, as moral, as sacred as any other being has. This is as indubitable as a moral government in the universe. But to teach that all men are born with equal powers and faculties, to equal influence in society, to equal property and advantages through life, is as gross a fraud, as glaring an imposition on the credulity of the people as ever was practised by monks, by Druids, by Brahmins, by priests of the immortal Lama, or by the self-styled philosophers of the French revolution."

—John Adams, Letters to John Taylor

"The envious man is susceptible to every sign of individual superiority to the common herd, and wishes to depress everyone once more to the level—or raise himself to the superior place."

—Friedrich Nietzsche, *Collected Works*

"Not, of course, that at the age of ten I had any pronounced political views or emotions, although one of my most vivid experiences had occurred earlier. I think it must have been during the General Election of 1924. Some new drains were being put in through the garden near the front of the house. I grew very friendly with the young workman, and when the election came I asked him if he was going to vote Conservative. His narrow face, which I had previously known as kindly and friendly, darkened and scowled.

"'What?' he said. 'Vote for people like your father who live in big houses like that while I'm digging this drain? Why the hell should I vote for him?'

"He was wrong in assuming that because we lived in a large house—and a school could hardly have been in a small house—that we had any money, but I took his point and ran back into the house scared and shaken.

"I often used to think about that conversation afterwards. It grew to represent in my mind what I imagined to be the atmosphere of the French Revolution. I can remember thinking again and again, 'There are so many more of them than there are of us.' This was quite realistic."

—Woodrow Wyatt, English Member of Parliament (Labour Party),
Into the Dangerous World
(From *Into the Dangerous World* by Woodrow Wyatt, © 1952 by Woodrow Wyatt. By permission of Weidenfield and Nic, division of Orion Publishing Group.)

Questions for Thought and Discussion

1. In the opening paragraph, what does Plutarch say exposed certain people to envy? How are the causes of envy the same or different in our time?
2. What are Plutarch's thoughts on Aristides being called "the Just," a rare tribute for rulers? What tributes do most rulers, according to Plutarch, seek after instead of virtue? Why is virtue, rather than immortality or power, the divine trait most noble to be sought after?
3. In the fourth paragraph, what two specific reasons does Plutarch give for the growing envy of Aristides? How is it that the same surname brought him first love, and then envy? What name did the Athenians give to

their "jealousy of his reputation"? When have you encountered situations in which envy was given another, more respectable name to accomplish its purpose?

4. What was the stated purpose of ostracism? Do you think ostracism was a healthy or unhealthy way of dealing with the sin of envy? Why?

5. Why did the "illiterate, clownish fellow" wish the name of Aristides to be inscribed on his sherd? What does his dialogue with Aristides reveal about the cause of the widespread envy that led to the ostracism?

6. What is Aristides' prayer for Athens as he leaves the city? Why do you think he says what he says?

7. What factors in our own society encourage the rise of destructive envy? What modern equivalents to ostracism do we practice as a result?

❧ *William Langland* ❧

William Langland—or perhaps Langley—(about 1332–about 1400) is the name given to the author of the Middle English poem, The Vision of William Concerning Piers Plowman. *(There are actually three different versions of the poem, written by at least two and perhaps even five different writers.) Although contemporary with Geoffrey Chaucer, the poem is written in a rustic, older style. A struggling clerk himself, Langland's poem held special appeal for those of the working class in England—more like an episode of* The Simpsons *today than an obscure literary work.*

A struggling clerk himself, Langland's poem held special appeal for those of the working class in England—more like an episode of The Simpsons *today than an obscure literary work.*

Piers Plowman is a moral and social satire, and perhaps the most vigorous account of the seven deadly sins in medieval English literature. Each sin is portrayed as an individual character whose particular moral weakness finds vivid physical description through Langland's pen.

The poet falls asleep in the Malvern Hills and dreams that in a wilderness he comes upon a tower of Truth (God) set on a hill, with the dungeon of Wrong (the Devil) in the deep valley below. Between them is a "fair field full of folk" (the world). He describes all the people he sees, including abstract personifications such as Conscience (who persuades people to turn away from the Seven Deadly Sins and go in search of St. Truth). A simple plowman named Piers (Peter) appears and offers to guide anyone who would go on the journey toward Truth.

This short excerpt is a vivid example of the medieval understanding of envy. It also illustrates how deep ethical teaching was translated from theology into artistic media, such as poetry, theater, and sculpture (including gargoyles), to provide powerful popular teaching-cum-entertainment.

CHOP-LICKING ENVY

"It (envy) is a disease in a state like to infection. For as infection spreadeth upon that which is sound, and tainteth it; so when envy is gotten once into a state, it traduceth even the best actions thereof, and turneth them into an ill-odour."

—Francis Bacon, *The Essays of Counsels, Civil and Moral*

"Envy (livor) is a tendency to perceive with displeasure the good of others, although it in no way detracts from one's own, and which, when it leads to action (in order to diminish that good) is called qualified envy, but otherwise only ill-will (invidentia)."

—Immanuel Kant, *The Metaphysics of Morals*

"Malicious joy arises when a man consciously finds himself in evil plight and feels anxiety of remorse or pain. The misfortune that overtakes B. makes him equal to A., and A. is reconciled and no longer envious. If A. is prosperous, he still hoards up in his memory B.'s misfortune as a capital, so as to throw it in the scale as a counter-weight when he himself suffers adversity."

—Friedrich Nietzsche, *Collected Works*

VISIONS FROM PIERS PLOWMAN

LANGLAND
Envy, with a heavy heart, asked to be shriven;
He was as pale as a pebble; he seemed in a palsy.
And like a leek that had lain a long time in the sun,
So he looked, lean of cheek, and louring foully.
His body bulged with anger, and he bit his lips,
And wrung his fist for wrath, to revenge himself.
Every word he uttered was adder-tongued,
Scolding and scoffing and scandal were his livelihood,
Bile and back-biting, and bearing false witness.

That was all his courtesy, wherever he came.

ENVY

'I would be shriven,' said this shrew, 'If I durst, for shame.
By God, I am gladder, if Gilbert is unlucky
Than though I had won, this week, a weight of Essex cheese!
I have a next-door neighbor, and have often annoyed him,
Making his friends his foes, by my false-speaking.
When I meet at market my most-hated man
I hail him as happily as my firmest friend;
But when I come to church, and creep to the cross
I cry as I crouch there "Christ give him sorrow!"
Away from the altar as I turn my eyes
I notice that Nancy has a new coat
And I wish it were my own, in envy of the weaving;
I laugh at men's losses, they lick about my heart,
And I weep at their winnings, and bewail hard times.
And thus I live, loveless, like a lying dog,
And all my body boils, for bitterness of gall.
May no sugar sweeten or assuage the swelling,
No drug or *diapendion* drive it from my heart,
No shame or shrift, unless you scrape my belly!'

REPENTANCE

'Yes, indeed,' said Repentance, reaching out help,
'Sorrow for sin is the salvation of souls.'

ENVY

'Sorry I am,' he said, 'and very seldom other.
What makes me look so meager is missing my revenges.
I will amend if I may, through the might of God Almighty!'

And thus I live, loveless, like a lying dog, And all my body boils, for bitterness of gall.

'I will amend if I may, through the might of God Almighty!'

From William Langland, *Visions from Piers Plowman,* translated by Nevill Coghill (New York: Oxford University Press, 1950), pp. 38–39.

A REAL BARN-BURNER

"An Englishman and a Frenchman and a Russian are captured by a cannibal king. Condemned to death on Monday, they are allowed a free weekend to do whatever they would wish. The Frenchman wishes for a weekend in Paris with his mistress, no questions asked, no promises made. The Englishman wishes for a weekend walking in the fields of Oxfordshire with his setter, reciting Wordsworth and Shelley. The Russian wishes that his neighbor's barn will burn down."

—A Russian tale

QUESTIONS FOR THOUGHT AND DISCUSSION

1. In Langland's first stanza, what trait or behavior of Envy jumps out at you? What is the benefit of describing Envy as a person with particular, vivid characteristics?

2. Langland uses the words "scoffing," "scandal," and "back-biting" to describe Envy. What modern forms of media or entertainment would fit into this category? Does the portrait of Envy bring any other modern institutions to your mind? Which ones?

3. In Envy's first stanza, find three examples of the way Envy perceives and behaves toward others. Envy says, "And thus I live, loveless. . . ." Why are envy and genuine love incompatible?

4. What's the difference between the sorrow that Repentance describes and the sorrow of Envy? What are the characteristics of each?

5. What does William Langland's depiction of Envy add to your previous understanding?

6. Think about our modern equivalents of medieval teaching-cum-enter-tainment (such as cartoons, television sitcoms, movies). Are they a plus or a minus in terms of ethical instruction, or are they completely irrelevant?

❧ *Nathaniel Hawthorne* ❧

Nathaniel Hawthorne (1804–1864) was an eminent American novelist, short-story writer, and diplomat. The son of a New England sea captain, he was educated at Bowdoin College, where he knew both Franklin Pierce (later president) and the poet Henry Wadsworth Longfellow. He always carried a deep sense of guilt for his ancestors' part in both the Puritan persecution of the Quakers and the Salem witch trials, and wove this theme into his work.

He always carried a deep sense of guilt for his ancestors' part in both the Puritan persecution of the Quakers and the Salem witch trials, and wove this theme into his work.

Hawthorne was briefly attracted to the Transcendentalist experiment at Brook Farm, but found communal living unattractive. He then moved to Concord and later back to Salem where in 1849 he wrote his great masterpiece The Scarlet Letter. *The book brought him fame and financial independence, allowing him to focus on novels instead of short stories. When Franklin Pierce became president, he appointed Hawthorne American Consul to Liverpool, England. Hawthorne's precise, classic prose style and his use of symbol and allegory made a great impression on his contemporary Herman Melville, and on later American writers such as Henry James and William Faulkner.*

The following passage from The Scarlet Letter *displays the final phase of envy's deforming power, when it grows into resentment and revenge. Hester, having committed adultery and borne a child out of wedlock, had endured her punishment—wearing the scarlet letter A (for adulterer)—but emerged from the tragedy with a dignified maturity. Rev. Arthur Dimmesdale, her lover, though late in coming forward to confess his responsibility, had eventually done so. The story's real victim, then, turns out to be Hester's husband, the physician Roger Chillingworth. Refusing to forgive, he is ultimately destroyed by his own resentment.*

THE OLD, LONG ROAD TO REVENGE

"Now Abel kept flocks, and Cain worked the soil. In the course of time Cain brought some of the fruits of the soil as an offering to the LORD. But Abel brought fat portions from some of the firstborn of his flock. The LORD looked with favor on Abel and his offering, but on Cain and his offering he did not look with favor. So Cain was very angry, and his face was downcast.

"Then the LORD said to Cain, 'Why are you angry? Why is your face downcast? If you do what is right, will you not be accepted? But if you do not do what is right, sin is crouching at your door; it desires to have you, but you must master it.'

"Now Cain said to his brother Abel, 'Let's go out to the field.' And while they were in the field, Cain attacked his brother Abel and killed him."

—Genesis 4:2-8

"[Envy and jealousy], the private parts of the human psyche, [adopt the strangest disguises. Whereas ordinary envy clucks as soon as the envied hen lays an egg, and so is mitigated, there is another and deeper form of envy:] . . . envy that in such a case becomes dead silent, desiring every mouth shall be sealed and always more and more angry because the desire is not gratified. Silent envy grows in silence."

—Friedrich Nietzsche, *Collected Works*

"Revenge is, of all satisfactions, the most costly and long drawn out; retroactive persecution is . . . the most pernicious."

—Winston Churchill

THE SCARLET LETTER

All this while Hester had been looking steadily at the old man, and was shocked, as well as wonder-smitten, to discern what a change had been wrought upon him within the past seven years. It was not so much that he had grown older; for though the traces of advancing life were visible he bore his age well, and seemed to retain a wiry vigour and alertness. But the former aspect of an intellectual and studious man, calm and quiet, which was what she best remembered in him, had altogether vanished, and been succeeded by a eager, searching, almost fierce, yet carefully guarded look. It seemed to be his wish and purpose to mask this expression with a smile, but the latter played him false, and flickered over his visage so derisively that the spectator could see his blackness all the better for it. Ever and anon, too, there came a glare of red light out of his eyes, as if the old man's soul were on fire and kept on smoldering duskily within his breast, until by some casual puff of passion it was blown into a momentary flame. This he repressed as speedily as possible, and strove to look as if nothing of the kind had happened.

In a word, old Roger Chillingworth was a striking evidence of man's faculty of transforming himself into a devil, if he will only, for a reasonable space of time, undertake a devil's office. This unhappy person had effected such a transformation by devoting himself for seven years to the constant analysis of a heart full of torture, and deriving his enjoyment thence, and adding fuel to those fiery tortures which he analyzed and gloated over.

The scarlet letter burned on Hester Prynne's bosom. Here was another ruin, the responsibility of which came partly home to her.

"What see you in my face," asked the physician, "that you look at it so earnestly?"

"Something that would make me weep, if there were any tears bitter enough for it," answered she. "But let it pass!" . . .

Nothing was more remarkable than the change which took place, almost immediately after Mr. Dimmesdale's death, in the appearance and demeanor of the old man known as Roger Chillingworth. All his strength and energy— all his vital and intellectual force—seemed at once to desert him, insomuch that he positively withered up, shrivelled away and almost vanished from mortal sight, like an uprooted weed that lies wilting in the sun. This unhappy man had made the very principle of his life to consist in the pursuit and systematic exercise of revenge; and when, by its completest triumph consummation that evil principle was left with no further material to support it—when, in short,

But the former aspect of an intellectual and studious man, calm and quiet, which was what she best remembered in him, had altogether vanished, and been succeeded by a eager, searching, almost fierce, yet carefully guarded look.

there was no more Devil's work on earth for him to do, it only remained for the unhumanized mortal to betake himself whither his master would find him tasks enough, and pay him his wages duly. But, to all these shadowy beings, so long our near acquaintances—as well Roger Chillingworth as his companions we would fain be merciful.

This unhappy man had made the very principle of his life to consist in the pursuit and systematic exercise of revenge.

From Nathaniel Hawthorne, *The Scarlet Letter* (1859), chapters 14, 24.

RESENTMENT'S RAVAGES

"Impotent envy is also the most terrible kind of envy. Hence the form of envy which gives rise to the greatest amount of resentment is directed against the individual and essential being of an unknown person: existential envy. For this envy, as it were, is forever muttering: 'I could forgive anything, except that you are, and what you are; except that I am not what you are; that "I," in fact am not "you."' This 'envy' from the start, denies the other person his very existence."

—Social scientist Max Scheler

"All men of resentment are these physiologically distorted and worm-riddled persons, a whole quivering kingdom of burrowing revenge, indefatigable and insatiable in its outbursts against the happy, and equally so in disguises for revenge, in pretexts for revenge: when will they really reach their final, fondest, most sublime triumph of revenge? At that time, doubtless, when they succeed in pushing their own misery, indeed all misery there is, into the consciousness of the happy; so that the latter begin one day to be ashamed of their happiness, and perchance say to themselves when they meet, 'It is a shame to be happy! *There is too much misery!*'"

—Friedrich Nietzsche, *Genealogy of Morals*

QUESTIONS FOR THOUGHT AND DISCUSSION

1. How does Hawthorne describe Chillingworth's face? How does the physician attempt to mask his envy? Why does this effort fail? In your experience, in what ways are envy, resentment, and anger visible on the face?

2. Considering the distinction made in the introduction, is Chillingworth *envious* or *jealous*? Or, has one grown into the other? If so, describe the progression that may have taken place.

3. What does Hawthorne mean when he says that Chillingworth undertook "a devil's office"? What is the result? Why do you think Chillingworth, even seven years later, refused to let go of his bitterness?
4. What effect does Chillingworth's envy have on his wife Hester? Why might a person devoured by envy evoke sympathy from others?
5. What happens to Chillingworth when the target of his revenge, Mr. Dimmesdale, dies? What is the explanation for the drastic change in him? Do you know people whose energy and intellect are consumed by envy? What would happen if the target of their envy suddenly disappeared?
6. Chillingworth, who was truly the victim of Hester Prynne's and Arthur Dimmesdale's adultery, ends up the most ruined. Had he forgiven, how might the story's outcome have been different?

Henry Fairlie

Henry Fairlie (1924–1990) was a journalist and author. Born in London and educated at Oxford, he wrote for both The Observer *and* The Times of London *before moving to Washington, D.C., in 1966. He lived in the United States for the remainder of his life and was a regular contributor to* The New Republic *and* The Washington Post. *A stylish but sometimes acerbic writer, Fairlie was the author of several acclaimed books, including* The Kennedy Promise *and* The Spoiled Child of the Western World.

Fairlie's book The Seven Deadly Sins Today *is highly original. For one thing, he looks at the implications of the seven sins not just for the individual, but for society at large. Further, he writes as a "reluctant unbeliever" in an accent of "reverent disbelief." Far from mocking or indifferent to matters of faith, he described his own writing as coming from "the conviction that, both as individuals and societies, we are trifling with the fact that sin exists, and that its power to destroy is as great as ever."*

Envy, Fairlie argues, is the one deadly sin to which no one readily confesses because it is the one sin with no gratification at all (unlike pride, greed, and gluttony). Envy is the antithesis of enjoyment. Interestingly, modern developments have

Far from mocking or indifferent to matters of faith, he described his own writing as coming from "the conviction that, both as individuals and societies, we are trifling with the fact that sin exists, and that its power to destroy is as great as ever."

produced an environment in which envy has run rampant in Western society at the same time that it has become invisible—invisible because we have lost the category of "sin" required to name the sin of envy.

Fairlie's argument is even more striking today because our age has seen the heyday of gossip shows and "tabloid TV" with their unspoken motto, "What goes up must be cut down"—in other words, anyone of status or position must be "brought down to size." The result is a massive, further contribution to the erosion of character at the hands of envy.

WORLD DESTROYERS

"Admiration is happy self-abandon, envy, unhappy, self-assertion."

—Søren Kierkegaard, *The Sickness unto Death*

"When some men fail to accomplish what they desire to do they exclaim angrily, 'May the whole world perish!' This repulsive emotion is the pinnacle of envy, whose implication is 'If I cannot have something, no one is to have anything, no one is to be anything.'"

—Friedrich Nietzsche, *Dawn of Day*

ENVY OR INVIDIA

The legend of our times, it has been suggested, might be "The Revenge of Failure." This is what Envy has done for us. If we cannot paint well, we will destroy the canons of painting and pass ourselves off as painters. If we will not take the trouble to write poetry, we will destroy the rules of prosody and pass ourselves off as poets. If we are not inclined to the rigors of an academic discipline, we will destroy the standards of that discipline and pass ourselves off as graduates. If we cannot or will not read, we will say that "linear thought" is now irrelevant and so dispense with reading. If we cannot make music, we will simply make a noise and persuade others that it is music. If we can do nothing at all, why! we will strum a guitar all day, and call it self-expression. As long as no talent is required, no apprenticeship to a skill, everyone can do it, and we are all magically made equal. Envy has at least momentarily been appeased, and failure has had its revenge.

If we cannot make music, we will simply make a noise and persuade others that it is music.

Envy grows naturally, said Aristotle, in relationships between equals. "We live in a society that perhaps as much as any other has pitted equals against equals," writes William F. May, but I think that he misstates his point. The United States and other Western societies are not pitting equals against equals, but unequals against unequals as if they are equals. This is a distortion of the idea of equality, and it is this distortion, as much as anything else, that has enabled the enemies of genuine equality to move to the offensive. To pit unequals against unequals as if they are equals is to make a breeding ground for Envy. The idea that we are equal has been perverted into the idea that we are identical; and when we then find that we cannot all do and experience and enjoy the things that others do and experience and enjoy, we take our revenge and deny that they were worth doing and experiencing and enjoying in the first place. What we are unable to achieve, we will bring low. What requires talent and training and hard work, we will show can be accomplished without them.

W. H. Auden once said that he could not understand the point of writing poetry if one did not obey at least the basic rules of prosody. It was like doing a crossword puzzle and, on being unable to find the correct word of seven letters, writing in one of nine letters that spills over the margin. Where is the point and satisfaction in that? The same can be asked of much of the revenge that Envy is taking today to conceal the sense of failure that gnaws at it. We are giving the name of art to what is not art, of poetry to what is not poetry, of education to what is not education, of achievement to what is not achievement, of morality to what is not morality, and of love to what is not love. We trivialize our concepts of them all, to make it seem as if we may all attain them. None of us is wholly exempt from the corruption. We find no place for the unique, for what is rare and cannot be imitated, since we would then not be able to achieve it. We seem no longer able to admire, respect, or be grateful for what is nobler or lovelier or greater than ourselves. We must pull down — or put down — what is exceptional. . . .

One of the evils into which Envy leads us is that of backbiting. Spite, malignity, accusation. It is well understood that to take away someone's good name is second only to murder as an offense against that person; it is itself a way of destroying him. The gossip column is the symbol of an envious age, and so is the contemporary form of the interview, which seems designed to ensure, in the same manner as the gossip column, that virtue and talent and achievement will be reduced to the level at which we can feel that we are their equals. They are "just like us," even a little lower than us. Nothing is allowed to seem out of the ordinary, beyond our own abilities, and even beyond our understanding. "Is nothing sacred any more?" is a cry of our age and, even allowing for the secularization of the sacred, it reaches to a particular sinfulness of Envy.

The sacred is what we cannot entirely know or master as human beings, and when we allowed a place to it in earlier ages, we did not feel the need to humble

We are giving the name of art to what is not art, of poetry to what is not poetry, of education to what is not education, of achievement to what is not achievement, of morality to what is not morality, and of love to what is not love.

the things that we were unable to understand or control. We even realized that some things are as they are, simply as a result of fate or fortune or accident, and that they might no less deserve our respect and admiration. We can hardly expect the gossip columnists and the interviewers to put off their shoes and consider that they may be walking on holy ground. That is not what one is asking of them. But there is something sinful in an age that has spawned them and seems able only to smirk with them at whatever surpasses our own achievements.

Envy cannot bear to think that mere accident or fortune—or some other unknowable Power, fate, or destiny, or perhaps even God—has conferred a good on someone else. There has to be a reason, and if only it could find that reason, it persuades itself from day to day, it could also enjoy that good. This is what whets its appetite for self-torment. It will not allow for chance or admit the unknowable, so it bites its nails, believing that there is a secret that it has only to discover to succeed as another succeeds, experience as another experiences, enjoy as another enjoys. This is what is profane in Envy. It will not embrace what is fate-given, chance-given, or God-given. It will not let into its heart the notion that those of us who are only mediocre are not therefore necessarily to be counted as failures; and so it equally will not let into its heart the notion that those who excel can ungrudgingly be given our admiration and respect with no diminishing of ourselves. The envious person is moved, first and last, by his own lack of self-esteem, which is all the more tormenting because it springs from an inordinate self-love.

Envy cannot bear to think that mere accident or fortune—or some other unknowable Power, fate, or destiny, or perhaps even God—has conferred a good on someone else.

To criticize a public figure from deeply held political or religious, moral or aesthetic, convictions is one thing. To chip away at his or her reputation from no public belief at all is another. But our society is riddled with this kind of Envy. "The dullard's envy of brilliant men," said Max Beerbohm in *Zuleika Dobson*, "is always assuaged by the suspicion that they will come to a bad end." We feel cheated by our newspapers and magazines if no one is leveled in the dust in them. We wait in ambush for the novel that fails, for the poet who commits suicide, for the financier who is a crook, for the politician who slips, for the priest who is discovered to be an adulterer. We lie in ambush for them all, so that we may gloat at their misfortunes. It has long been recognized that *schadenfreude*—joy at the suffering of another—is peculiarly a mark of our age; but Envy makes us no less despicable—in the face of the good fortune of another, by making us capable only of despising what is admirable. There is little now that we honor.

QUESTIONS FOR THOUGHT AND DISCUSSION

1. In the opening paragraph, what point is Fairlie making about the impact of envy? Is it true to your experience of the modern world? Explain in your own words what the author means by the phrase, "failure has had its revenge."

2. According to Fairlie, how has the democratic ideal of equality been perverted? How does this perversion contribute to envy? What, if any, is the parallel to the idea of "sour grapes" taught in *Aesop's Fables*?

3. In the illustration of the crossword puzzle (getting the "right" answer by breaking the rules), Fairlie asks, "Where is the point and satisfaction in that?" How would you answer that question? Can there be some satisfaction in "giving the name of art to what is not art, of poetry to what is not poetry"? How is this satisfaction linked to envy? What are the dangers of this type of leveling through the erosion of standards?

4. In a culture of envy, what is the role of the gossip column? Tabloid TV? What lies behind our fascination with such things? Can you think of other ways our society "cuts down to size" those of great virtue, talent, or achievement? Institutions that make envy "respectable"? How do we do it on a more personal level?

5. What connection does Fairlie make between the loss of the "sacred" and the increase of envy? Do you agree? Why can envy not tolerate the idea that "fate, or destiny, or perhaps even God" has conferred an exceptional gift or talent on an individual? What are the devastating consequences of such thinking?

6. Can you relate to the "nail-biting" image Fairlie uses? How so? What influences in our culture feed the idea that there is a "secret" to the success, experiences, and joy others have? Have you ever been "burned" by such messages?

7. Read again the final two sentences of the second-to-last paragraph—a summation of the cause of envy. What is your response? What, according to Fairlie, moves the envious person? Does this seem like a contradiction? Why or why not?

8. In the final paragraph, Fairlie distinguishes between legitimate criticism, based on conviction, and envious slander. Why does this distinction matter? How can we teach this difference to our children?

9. How do you feel when you read Fairlie's final line? With these words in mind, why do you think earlier thinkers such as James Madison viewed envy as so corrupting to a free society?

THE PENALTY OF LEADERSHIP

"In every field of human endeavor, he that is first must perpetually live in the white light of publicity. Whether the leadership be vested in a man or in a manufactured product, emulation and envy are ever at work. In art, in literature, in music, in industry, the reward and the punishment are always the same. The reward is widespread recognition; the punishment, fierce denial and detraction. When a man's work becomes a standard for the whole world, it also becomes a target for the shafts of the envious few. If his work be merely mediocre, he will be left severely alone—if he achieves a masterpiece, it will set a million tongues a-wagging. Jealousy does not protrude its forked tongue at the artist who produces a commonplace painting. Whatsoever you write, or paint, or play, or sing, or build, no one will strive to surpass or to slander you, unless your work be stamped with the seal of genius. Long, long after a great work or a good work has been done, those who are disappointed or envious continue to cry out that it cannot be done. Spiteful little voices in the domain of art were raised against our own Whistler as a mountebank, long after the big world had acclaimed him its greatest artistic genius. Multitudes flocked to Bayreuth to worship at the musical shrine of Wagner, while the little group of those whom he had dethroned and displaced argued angrily that he was no musician at all. The little world continued to protest that Fulton could never build a steamboat, while the big world flocked to the river banks to see his boat steam by.

"The leader is assailed because he is a leader, and the effort to equal him is merely added proof of that leadership. Failing to equal or to excel, the follower seeks to depreciate and to destroy—but only confirms once more the superiority of that which he strives to supplant. There is nothing new in this. It is as old as the world and as old as the human passions—envy, fear, greed, ambition, and the desire to surpass. And it all avails nothing. If the leader truly leads, he remains—the leader. Master-poet, master-painter, master-workman, each in his turn is assailed, and each holds his laurels through the ages. That which is good or great makes itself known, no matter how loud the clamor of denial. That which deserves to live—lives."

—Theodore Francis MacManus, 1915, text of the famous "Penalty of Leadership" image advertisement for Cadillac, sometimes called the greatest ad of all time

Peter Shaffer

Peter Levin Shaffer (born 1926) is a modern British playwright. His diverse plays persistently return to two themes: deception of the self or others and the place of worship in the modern world. The last theme is dominant in his two most celebrated plays, Equus (1973) and Amadeus (1980), which were both made into highly successful films. (Equus, for example, has the famous line: "Without worship you shrink. It's as brutal as that.")

The following scenes are from Amadeus. They deal with Wolfgang Amadeus Mozart's nemesis—Antonio Salieri—and his struggle to reconcile his own aspirations to be great with Mozart's real greatness. Although gripping drama, the play—it should be said—is closer to legend than to history. Rumors persisted after Mozart's death that Salieri had poisoned him. But though Salieri definitely obstructed Mozart's career, especially at the court of Joseph II in Vienna, he was probably no more a rival than many musicians in Mozart's day. Salieri in fact conducted Mozart's memorial service. Even before that, Mozart was known to be grateful for Salieri's kindnesses. But the play is still riveting because Salieri's purported envy of Mozart is inflated to transcendental proportions by Shaffer as he ties it to theological questions about the justice of God's gifting.

But the play is still riveting because Salieri's purported envy of Mozart is inflated to transcendental proportions by Shaffer as he ties it to theological questions about the justice of God's gifting.

TURF WARS FOR THE TALENTED

"Salieri is an insufferable egoist. He wants successes in my thetre only for his own operas and his own woman. He is not only your enemy. He is an enemy of all composers, all singers, all Italians."
    —Emperor Leopold II, in H. C. Robbins Landon, *1791: Mozart's Last Year*

"Of course it's too bad about such a great genius, but it's good for us that he's dead. Because if he'd lived any longer, really the world would not have given a single piece of bread for our compositions."
    —a fellow composer, in H. C. Robbins Landon, *1791: Mozart's Last Year*

"Your Majesty, everybody has enemies, ... but nobody has been more strenuously and continuously attacked and slandered by his enemies than my husband, merely because he had such great talent."
    —Constanze Mozart, in H. C. Robbins Landon, *1791: Mozart's Last Year*

"I, who for the time have staked my all on being a psychologist, am mortified if others know much more psychology than I. But I am contented to wallow in the grossest ignorance of Greek. My deficiencies there give me no sense of personal humiliations at all. Had I 'pretensions' to be a linguist, it would have been just the reverse. So we have the paradox of a man shamed to death because he is only the second pugilist or the second oarsman in the world. That he is able to beat the whole population of the globe minus one is nothing; he has 'pitted' himself to beat that one; and as long as he doesn't do that nothing else counts."

—William James, *The Principles of Psychology,* 1890

"'Does one live when others live?' I have read that question somewhere, I am not sure precisely where, but in some prominent place. Privately or publicly you all ask it; only out of good manners and for appearance's sake do you take notice of each other—if you do take notice of each other. Wolf, Brahms, and Bruckner lived for years in the same town—Vienna, that is—but avoided each other the whole time and none of them, so far as I know, ever met the others. It would have been penible, too, considering their opinions of each other. They did not judge or criticize like colleagues; their comments were meant to annihilate, to leave their author alone in the field. Brahms thought as little as possible of Bruckner's symphonies; he called them huge, shapeless serpents. And Bruckner's opinion of Brahms was very low. He found the first theme of the D-minor Concerto very good, but asserted that Brahms never came near inventing anything so good a second time."

—Thomas Mann, *Doctor Faustus*

"Puritanism is represented as a lofty sort of obedience to God's law. Democracy is depicted as brotherhood, even as altruism. All such notions are in error. There is only one honest impulse at the bottom of Puritanism, and that is the impulse to punish the man with a superior capacity for happiness—to bring him down to the miserable level of 'good' men, i.e., of stupid, cowardly, and chronically unhappy men. And there is only one sound argument for democracy, and that is the argument that it is a crime for any man to hold himself out as better than other men, and, above all, a most heinous offence for him to prove it."

—H. L. Mencken, "A Blind Spot"

AMADEUS

[SALIERI *turns in a ferment to the audience.*]

SALIERI: Fiasco! . . . Fiasco! . . . The sordidness of it! The sheer sweating sordidness! . . . Worse than if I'd actually done it! . . . To be that much in sin and feel so *ridiculous* as well! [*Crying out*] Nobile, nobile Salieri! . . . What had he done to me, this Mozart? Before he came, did I behave like this? Did I? Toy with adultery? Blackmail women? It was all going— slipping—growing rotten . . . because of *him!*

[*He moves upstage in a fever—reaches out to take the portfolio on the chair—but as if fearful of what he might find inside it, he withdraws his hand and sits instead. A pause. He contemplates the music lying there as if it were a great confection he is dying to eat, but dare not. Then suddenly he snatches at it—tears the ribbon—opens the case and stares greedily at the manuscripts within. Music sounds instantly, faintly, in the theater, as his eye falls on the first page. It is the opening of the Twenty-ninth Symphony, in A major. Over the music, reading it.]*

She had said that these were his original scores. First and only drafts of the music. Yet they looked like fair copies. They showed no corrections of any kind. It was puzzling—then suddenly alarming.

[He looks up from the manuscript at the audience: the music abruptly stops.]

What was evident was that Mozart was simply transcribing music completely finished in his head. And finished as most music is never finished.

[He resumes looking at the music. Immediately the Sinfonia Concertante for Violin and Viola sounds.]

Displace one note and there would be diminishment. Displace one phrase and the structure would fall.

[He looks up again: the music breaks off.]

Here again—only now in abundance—were the same sounds I'd heard in the library.

[He resumes reading, and the music also resumes: a ravishing phrase from the slow movement of the Concerto for Flute and Harp.]

The same crushed harmonies—glancing collisions—agonizing delights.

[He looks up again. The music stops.]

The truth was clear. That Serenade had been no accident.

[Very low, in the theater, a faint thundery sound is heard accumulating, like a distant sea.]

I was staring through the cage of those meticulous ink strokes at—an Absolute Beauty!

[And out of the thundery roar writhes and rises the clear sound of a soprano, singing the Kyrie from the C Minor Mass. The accretion of noise around her voice falls away—it is suddenly clear and bright—then clearer and brighter. The light grows bright: too bright: burning white, then scalding white!

What was evident was that Mozart was simply transcribing music completely finished in his head. And finished as most music is never finished.

SALIERI *rises in the downpour of it, and in the flood of the music, which is grow-ing ever louder—filling the theater—as the soprano yields to the full chorus, fortissimo, singing its massive counterpoint.*

This is by far the loudest sound the audience has yet heard. SALIERI *staggers toward us, holding the manuscripts in his hand, like a man caught in a tum-bling and violent sea.*

Finally the drums crash in below: SALIERI *drops the portfolio of manu-scripts—and falls senseless to the ground. At the same second the music explodes into a long, echoing, distorted boom, signifying some dreadful annihilation.*

The sound remains suspended over the prone figure in a menacing continuum—no longer music at all. Then it dies away, and there is only silence.

The light fades again.

A long pause.

SALIERI *is quite still, his head by the pile of manuscripts. Finally the clock sounds: nine times.* SALIERI *stirs as it does. Slowly he raises his head and looks up. And now—quietly at first—he addresses his God.]*

SALIERI: *Capisco!* I know my fate. Now for the first time I feel my emptiness as Adam felt his nakedness. . . . *[Slowly he rises to his feet.]* Tonight at an inn somewhere in this city stands a giggling child who can put on paper, without actually setting down his billiard cue, casual notes which turn my most considered ones into lifeless scratches. *Grazie, Signore!* You gave me the desire to serve You—which most men do not have—then saw to it the service was shameful in the ears of the server. *Grazie!* You gave me the desire to praise You—which most men do not feel—then made me mute. *Grazie tanti!* You put into me perception of the Incomparable—which most men never know!—then ensured that I would know myself forever mediocre. *[His voice gains power.]* Why? . . . What is my fault? . . . Until this day I have pursued virtue with rigor. I have labored long hours to relieve my fellow men. I have worked and worked the tal-ent You allowed me. *[Calling up]* You know how hard I've worked! Solely that in the end, in the practice of the art which alone makes the world comprehensible to me, I might hear Your Voice! And now I do hear it—and it says only one name: MOZART! . . . Spiteful, sniggering, conceited, infantine Mozart—who has never worked one minute to help another man! Shit-talking Mozart, with his botty-smacking wife! *Him* You have chosen to be Your sole conduit! And *my* only reward—my sublime privilege—is to be the sole man alive in this time who shall clearly recognize Your Incarnation! *[Savagely]* *Grazie e grazie ancora!* *[Pause]* So be it! From this time we are enemies, You and I! I'll not accept it from You—*do you hear?* . . . They say God is not mocked. I tell You, *Man* is not mocked! . . . *I am not mocked!* . . . *They say the spirit bloweth where it listeth: I tell You NO! It must list to virtue or not blow at all!* *[Yelling]* *Dio ingiusto*—You are the Enemy! I name Thee now—*Nemico Eterno!* And this I swear: To my last breath I shall *block* You on earth, as far as I am able! *[He glares up at God. To audience]* What use, after all, is man, if not to teach God His lessons?

[Pause. Suddenly he speaks again to us in the voice of an old man. He slips off his powdered wig, crosses to the fortepiano and takes from its lid where they lie the old dressing gown and cap which he discarded when he conducted us back to the eighteenth century. He slips these on. It is again 1823.]

Before I tell you what happened next—God's answer to me—and indeed Constanze's—and all the horrors that followed—let me stop. The bladder, being a human appendage, is not something you need concern yourselves with yet. I, being alive, though barely, am at its constant call. It is now one hour before dawn—when I must dismiss us both. When I return, I'll tell you about the war I fought with God through His preferred Creature—Mozart, named *Amadeus.* In the waging of which, of course, the Creature had to be destroyed.

[He bows to the audience with malignant slyness—snatches a pastry from the stand—and leaves the stage, chewing at it voraciously. The manuscripts lie where he spilled them in his fall. The lights in the theater come up as he goes.] . . .

[A SERVANT *comes in quickly with the wheelchair.* SALIERI *speaks again in the voice of an old man.]*

SALIERI: *[To audience]* Dawn has come. I must release you—and myself. One moment's violence and it's done. You see, I cannot accept this. I did not live on earth to be His joke for eternity. I will be remembered! *I will be remembered!*—if not in fame, then infamy. One moment more and I win my battle with Him. Watch and see! . . . All this month I've been shouting about murder. "Have mercy, Mozart! Pardon your Assassin! . . ."And now my last move. A false confession—short and convincing!

[He pulls it out of his pocket.]

How I really did murder Mozart—with arsenic—out of envy! And how I cannot live another day under the knowledge! By tonight they'll hear out there how I died—and they'll believe it's true! . . . Let them forget me then. For the rest of time whenever men say Mozart with love, they will say Salieri with loathing! . . . *I am going to be immortal after all!* And He is powerless to prevent it.

[To God] So, *Signore*—see now if man is mocked!

[The VALET *comes in with a tray, bearing a bowl of hot shaving water, soap, and a razor. He sets this on the table.* SALIERI *hands him the confession.]*

[To VALET*]* Good morning. Lay this on the desk in the cabinet. Append your name to it in witness that this is my hand. *Via—subito!*

[The man takes the paper and goes, bewildered, upstage right. SALIERI *picks up the razor, and rises. He addresses the audience most simply and directly.]*

SALIERI: *Amici cari.* I was born a pair of ears and nothing else. It is only through hearing music that I know God exists. Only through writing music that I could worship . . . All around me men seek liberty for mankind. I sought only slavery for myself. To be owned—ordered—exhausted by an *Absolute*. Music. This was denied me, and with it all meaning.
[He opens the razor.]

Now I go to become a ghost myself. I will stand in the shadows when you come here to this earth in your turns. And when you feel the dreadful bite of your failures—and hear the taunting of unachievable, uncaring God—I will whisper my name to you: "Salieri: Patron Saint of Mediocrities!" And in the depth of your downcastness you can pray to me. And I will forgive you. *Vi saluto.*

[He cuts his throat, and falls backwards into the wheelchair. The COOK— *who has just come in, carrying a plate of fresh buns for breakfast, sees this and screams. The* VALET *rushes in at the same time from the other side. Together they pull the wheelchair, with its slumped body, backward upstage, and anchor it in the center. The* VENTICELLI *APPEAR AGAIN, IN THE COSTUME OF 1823.]*

Act I, Scene 12 and Act II, Scene 18 from *Amadeus* by Peter Shaffer. Copyright © 1980, 1981 by Peter Shaffer. Reprinted by permission of HarperCollins Publishers, Inc.

CRUELTY'S COUSIN

"The worst trait in human nature, however, is Schadenfreude [envy], for it is closely related to cruelty."

—Arthur Schopenhauer

"It could justly be said that life envies the distinguished man, mockingly intimating to him that he is a man like any other, like the least of men, that the human element demands its rights."

—Søren Kierkegaard, *Four Edifying Discourses*

"Yea, my friend, the bad conscience art thou of thy neighbours; for they are unworthy of thee. Therefore they hate thee, and would fain suck thy blood. . . . Thy neighbours will always be venomous insects; whatever is great in thee,—that very thing must make them more venomous."

—Friedrich Nietzsche, *Thus Spake Zarathustra*

"There is no vice of which a man can be guilty, no meanness, no shabbiness, no unkindness, which excites so much indignation among his contemporaries, friends, and neighbours, as his success. This is the one unpardonable crime, which reason cannot defend, nor humility mitigate. . . . The man who writes as we cannot write, who speaks as we cannot speak, labours as we cannot labour, thrives as we cannot thrive, has accumulated on his own person all the offences of which man can be guilty. Down with him! Why cumbereth he the ground?"

—*London Times*, October 9, 1858

"I do wish I were more creative—it is such a miserable trickle. A man like Mozart makes one feel such a worm."

—Bertrand Russell

QUESTIONS FOR THOUGHT AND DISCUSSION

1. In the opening monologue, on what does Salieri blame his own sin? On what basis do you think he makes such a claim?

2. What sudden revelation does Salieri have when he examines Mozart's scores? How do you think he felt at that moment? What kinds of thoughts likely ran through his head? When have you ever experienced such a moment? What was your response?

3. What traits of Mozart make his musical brilliance especially hard for Salieri to accept? Why do those traits even enter into the equation?

4. In your own words, describe Salieri's desperate appeal to God. What are the chief components of his attack? What phrases make it particularly heart-wrenching? How do you feel toward the agonizing man at this moment of his grief?

5. What words in particular tell you that Salieri feels he's been cheated of "his due"? How else might he have viewed Mozart's phenomenal gifts in light of his own mediocre talents?

6. How does God, whom Salieri claims he has always yearned to serve, suddenly become his archenemy? What do you think of the line, "What use, after all, is man, if not to teach God His lessons?"

7. When Salieri speaks after the break, how has his envy altered him? What is he plotting to do? Why the false confession? What is the real reason he's decided to take his own life?

8. In his final expression of angst, what does Salieri say he's been "denied"? Is it true? What do you think of the name he gives himself, "Patron Saint of Mediocrity"? Is this self-pity? Resentment? Or just an expression of the truth? Why is the idea of being "average" difficult?

9. If envy is a vice always driven by closeness (from "sibling rivalry" on), where are your temptations to envy likely to come from? Is there a rival in your life whose success has stirred deep envy in you? How have you handled it?

THE COUNTERPOINT TO ENVY:
Blessed Are Those Who Mourn

The second beatitude, "Blessed are those who mourn," is the direct counterpoint to the second deadly sin of envy. The word Jesus uses for "mourn" is one of the strongest in the Greek language, used especially for mourning the dead. It speaks of an intense, heart-crushing sorrow. "Blessed are the mourning ones who see the true nature of things in a broken, fallen world so that, broken-hearted, they are open to the comfort only God can give." A defining characteristic of such "mourning" is sympathy and solidarity—the suffering of others is mourned as deeply as one's own.

Thus, if envy is "sorrow at another's good," its counterpoint is sorrow at another's evil, grieving with others in their affliction or loss. Whereas envy weeps at those who celebrate and celebrates at those who weep, mourning weeps with those who weep and rejoices with those who rejoice.

Notice three features of this very positive virtue of mourning. First, it is a positive virtue, not simply a preventative, or defensive attitude toward the vice. As stressed earlier, mechanisms to avoid the "evil eye" of envy are common—from "knock on wood" and taboos against boasting to characteristic national styles of speaking, such as English understatement and Chinese self-effacement. Mourning with those who mourn and rejoicing with those who rejoice, by contrast, is entirely positive, not defensive.

Thus, if envy is "sorrow at another's good," its counterpoint is sorrow at another's evil, grieving with others in their affliction or loss.

Mourning with those who mourn and rejoicing with those who rejoice, by contrast, is entirely positive, not defensive.

ENVY'S ANTIBIOTIC?

"The virtue of modesty was only discovered as a protection against envy."

—Arthur Schopenhauer

"Only scoundrels are modest."

—Johann Wolfgang von Goethe

Second, this virtue is characteristically sympathetic rather than stand-offish. In the second paragraph above, envy's characteristic preposition is "at." Envy stands apart from others, aware only of differences that rankle. Its typical movement is from self-centeredness to self-sufficiency to solitariness. Mourning, on the other hand, pivots on the preposition "with." It stands beside others. Its movement *is from suffering to sympathy to solidarity. Where envy is competitive, mourning is compassionate. Envy never sees people but only comparisons between itself and others; it treats giving as a matter of diminishing returns for itself. Mourning, however, ignores comparisons and sees people. It treats giving as a matter of compound interest and multiplying dividends.*

Third, the virtue of mourning and rejoicing with those who mourn and rejoice is expressly non-utopian. It does not pretend to seek a society completely freed from envy. Such a society would be both impossible and evil, given the fallen state of the world, for it would require the eradication of anything that could produce envy. The effort to create a society in which there is nothing enviable left leads directly to a grand leveling of everything—except envy. The history of communism shows that. The only entity that escapes leveling is envy itself, for it persists even if the only things left to envy are the imagined inner feelings and thoughts of others.

The effort to create a society in which there is nothing enviable left leads directly to a grand leveling of everything— except envy. The history of communism shows that.

Of course, the practice of mourning and rejoicing is not the only counterpoint to envy. History shows that there are other antidotes—for example, the social condition of mobility and the spiritual truth of calling—but nothing is more essentially human in every possible kind of society than the virtue of mourning with those who mourn and rejoicing with those who rejoice.

This non-utopian character of the virtue requires emphasis, for without it we can misuse Christian virtue to create a catch-22 situation: Faith attacks envy, thereby attempting to keep the envier within bounds, but at the same time, if carried out in the blind hope of an envy-free utopia, faith's pursuit of the ideal of social justice and equality can reinforce envy rather than remove it, as in the case of communism. *In sum, the virtue of mourning appears simple and modest, but it has the power to short-circuit the dangerous political maneuver of attempting to attack the enviable by appealing to the envious.*

The following readings explore true mourning (weeping with those who weep and rejoicing with those who rejoice) as the powerful, life-giving opposite of envy.

Victor Hugo

Victor Marie Hugo (1802–1885) was a French poet, novelist, dramatist, and a leader of the Romantic movement. Born at Besançon and educated in Paris and Madrid, he wrote his first play at the age of fourteen and went on to become the most prolific French writer of the nineteenth century. Hugo was elected to the Legislative Assembly, but a coup caused him to flee into exile in Brussels and then the Channel Islands. After eighteen years, he returned to Paris and became a senator. At his death he was given a national funeral.

Hugo's two best-known novels are The Hunchback of Notre Dame *(1831) and* Les Misérables *(1862). Both novels display Hugo's deep humanitarian interest as well as his colorful style and panoramic sense of history.*

The following passage from Les Misérables *tells the story of how Jean Valjean's resentment dissolved into penitence. Having been surprised by the bishop's forgiveness of him after stealing his candlesticks, Valjean is shocked to discover that he would then turn around and steal forty sous from Petit Gervais, a small boy. This contradiction between his own meanness to the boy and the undeserved grace he had been shown by the bishop reduces him to a life-transforming mourning, the antidote to envy.*

LES MISÉRABLES

One thing was certain, though he did not suspect it, that he was no longer the same man, that all was changed in him, that it was no longer in his power to prevent the bishop from having talked to him and having touched him.

In this frame of mind, he had met Petit Gervais and stolen his coin. Why? He certainly could not have explained it. Was it the final effect, the final effort of the evil thought he had brought from prison, a remaining impulse, a result of what is called in physics "acquired force"? It was that, and perhaps it was also even less than that. To put it plainly, it was not he who had stolen, it was not the man, it was the beast that, from habit and instinct, had stupidly set its foot on that money, while the intellect was struggling in the midst of so many new and unknown influences. When the intellect awoke and saw this act of the brute, Jean Valjean recoiled in anguish and cried out in horror.

It was a strange phenomenon, possible only in his current condition, but the fact is that in stealing this money from the child, he had done a thing of which he was no longer capable.

It was a strange phenomenon, possible only in his current condition, but the fact is that in stealing this money from the child, he had done a thing of which he was no longer capable.

However that may be, this last offense had a decisive effect upon him; it rushed across the chaos of his intellect and dissipated it, set the light on one side and the dark clouds on the other, and acted on his soul, in the state it was in, as certain chemical reagents act on a murky mixture, by precipitating one element and producing a clear solution of the other.

At first, even before self-examination and reflection, distractedly, like someone trying to escape, he sought the boy to give him his money back; then, when he found this was futile, he stopped in despair. At the very moment when he exclaimed, "I'm such a miserable man!" he saw himself as he was, and was already so far separated from himself that he felt he was no more than a phantom and that he had there before him, in flesh and bone, stick in hand, a shirt on his back, a knapsack filled with stolen articles on his shoulders, with his set and gloomy face and his thoughts full of abominable projects, the hideous convict Jean Valjean.

Excessive misfortune, as we have noted, had made him somehow a visionary. This then was like a vision. He truly saw this Jean Valjean, this ominous face, in front of him. He was on the point of asking himself who the man was, and he was horrified at the idea of asking himself such a question.

His brain was in one of those violent, yet frighteningly calm, states where reverie is so profound it swallows up reality. We no longer see the objects before us, but we see, as if outside of ourselves, the forms we have in our minds.

He saw himself then, so to speak, face to face, and at the same time through that hallucination he saw, at a mysterious distance, a sort of light, which he took at first to be a torch.

He saw himself then, so to speak, face to face, and at the same time through that hallucination he saw, at a mysterious distance, a sort of light, which he took at first to be a torch. Looking more closely at this light dawning on his conscience, he recognized it had a human form, that it was the bishop.

His conscience considered in turn these two men placed before it, the bishop and Jean Valjean. Anything less than the first would have failed to soften the second. By one of those singular effects peculiar to this kind of ecstasy, as his reverie continued, the bishop grew larger and more resplendent to his eyes; Jean Valjean shrank and faded away. For one instant he was no more than a shadow. Suddenly he disappeared. The bishop alone remained.

He filled the whole soul of this miserable man with a magnificent radiance.

Jean Valjean wept for a long time. He shed hot tears, he wept bitterly, more powerless than a woman, more terrified than a child.

While he wept, the light grew brighter and brighter in his mind—an extraordinary light, a light at once entrancing and terrible. His past life, his first offense, his long expiation, his exterior degradation, his interior hardening, his release made sweet by so many schemes of vengeance, what had happened to him at the bishop's, his recent act, this theft of forty sous from a child, a crime all the meaner and more monstrous in that it came after the bishop's pardon—all this returned and appeared to him clearly, but in a light he had never seen before. He could see his life, and it seemed horrible; his soul, and it seemed frightful. There was, however, a gentler light shining on that life and soul. It seemed to him that he was looking at Satan by the light of Paradise.

How long did he weep? What did he do after weeping? Where did he go? Nobody ever knew. It was simply established that, that very night, the stage driver who at that hour rode the Grenoble route and arrived at Digne about three in the morning, on his way through the bishop's street saw a man kneeling in prayer, on the pavement in the dark, before the door of Monseigneur Bienvenu.

He could see his life, and it seemed horrible; his soul, and it seemed frightful. There was, however, a gentler light shining on that life and soul. It seemed to him that he was looking at Satan by the light of Paradise.

QUESTIONS FOR THOUGHT AND DISCUSSION

1. What was Valjean's reaction to having stolen the coin when his "intellect awoke"? To what is this act attributed in the first paragraph?

2. What does Valjean mean when he reflects that he had done a thing "of which he was no longer capable"? (If he had done it, wasn't he "capable" of it?)

3. After a futile attempt to return the boy's money, Valjean exclaims, "I'm such a miserable man!" How does he see himself in that moment? What is the significance of the "phantom" sensation?

4. What form does the bishop take to Valjean's conscience? What's the meaning of the line, "Anything less than the first would have failed to soften the second"? When has your heart been "softened" by undeserved mercy?

5. Why does Valjean weep? What, if anything, is he losing? What is he gaining? What thoughts and emotions do you think he experienced in those moments of tears?

6. In your own words, describe what happens next. Have you ever suddenly seen your life from an entirely new perspective? What was the effect?

7. What ultimately drove Valjean to his knees? What might the content of his prayer have been? How do penitence and mourning act as a solvent to the bitterness of resentment?

8. Have you ever been able to give grace to someone poisoned by resentment and see him or her changed? If so, how did the experience affect you?

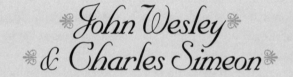

John Wesley (1703–1791) and Charles Simeon (1759–1836) were ministers of the Church of England and leaders of the great eighteenth-century revival known in the United States as the first Great Awakening. Wesley, a powerful preacher and evangelist, was one of the pioneers of the revival and, along with his brother Charles and his friend George Whitefield, was influential and well-known on both sides of the Atlantic. He was also the founder of the Methodist Church.

Charles Simeon, by contrast, lived mostly in Cambridge, England, and was a leader during the second stage of the revival. But because of his long and powerful ministry at Great St. Mary's Church (more than fifty years), he too was influential on generations of leaders.

Both Wesley and Simeon were deeply concerned about the practical implications of faith, especially as it is lived out by Christians in real life. The following two passages show their determination to short-circuit the power of the bastard child of envy—gossip. Their points are worth pondering in our own time, in a society where envy is rampant in a thousand different guises.

The following two passages show their determination to short-circuit the power of the bastard child of envy— gossip. Their points are worth pondering in our own time, in a society where envy is rampant in a thousand different guises.

THE FINAL WORD

"Who is this one condemning me, when set beside that One who does not condemn me?"

—Dallas Willard, *The Divine Conspiracy*

COMMITTED BODY RULES

It is agreed by us whose names are underwritten:
1. That we will not listen or willingly inquire after any Ill concerning each other.
2. That if we do hear any Ill of each other, we will not be forward to believe it.
3. That, as soon as possible, we will communicate what we hear, by speaking or writing, to the person concerned.
4. That till we have done this, we will not write or speak a syllable of it to any other person whatever.
5. That neither will we mention it, after we have done this, to any other person.
6. That we will not make any Exception to any of these Rules unless we think ourselves absolutely obliged in conference to do so.

John Wesley, 1752.

HOW TO COPE WITH EVIL-SPEAKING

The longer I live, the more I feel the importance of adhering to the rules which I have laid down for myself in relation to such matters.

1. To hear as little as possible what is to the prejudice of others.
2. To believe nothing of the kind till I am absolutely forced to it.
3. Never to drink into the spirit of one who circulates an ill report.
4. Always to moderate, as far as I can, the unkindness which is expressed toward others.
5. Always to believe, that if the other side were heard, a very different account would be given of the matter.

I consider love as wealth; and as I would resist a man who should come to rob my house, so would I a man who would weaken my regard for any human being. . . . I think religious people are too little attentive to these considerations; and that it is not in reference to the ungodly world only that that passage is true, "He that departeth from evil maketh himself a prey"; but even in reference to

I consider love as wealth; and as I would resist a man who should come to rob my house, so would I a man who would weaken my regard for any human being.

professors also, amongst whom there is a sad proneness to listen to evil reports, and to believe the representations they hear, without giving the injured person any opportunity of rectifying their views and of defending his own character.

The more prominent any person's character is, the more likely he is to suffer in this way; there being in the heart of every man, unless greatly subdued by grace, a pleasure in hearing anything which may sink others to his level, or lower them in the estimation of the world. We seem to ourselves elevated in proportion as others are depressed. Under such circumstances I derive consolation from the following reflections:

1. My enemy, whatever evil he says of me, does not reduce me so low as he would if he knew all concerning me that God knows.
2. In drawing the balance, as between Debtor and Creditor, I find that if I have been robbed of pence, there are pounds and talents placed to my account to which I have no just title.
3. If man has his day, God will have His.

Charles Simeon, from Hugh Evan Hopkins, *Charles Simeon of Cambridge* (Hodder and Stoughton), pp. 134–135.

QUESTIONS FOR THOUGHT AND DISCUSSION

1. Read the "Committed Body Rules." What undercurrents do you sense beneath the rules? Which of the six stands out to you most powerfully? Which do you think would be the most difficult to follow?
2. What does the phrase "in conference" in Rule 6 imply about accountability? How can this be an antidote to gossip or any kind of envy? How would your circle be different if each person committed to following these six rules? How would the quality of your relationships be changed?
3. How does the old saying, "Bad news travels fast" relate to envy? Why does "good news" not travel as quickly?
4. In the reading, "How to Cope with Evil-Speaking," which of the five rules would make the most difference in your own life if implemented immediately?
5. What do you think of the comparison Simeon makes between love and wealth? Why do you agree or disagree with him about religious people's

"sad proneness to listen to evil reports"? If true, in what way is this tendency at odds with the teachings of Jesus?

6. What does Simeon say is the real motive behind pleasurably hearing "anything which may sink others"? How does this "lowering" and "elevating" game demonstrate the sin of envy?

7. What do you think of the three reflections for dealing with others who speak evil against you? How do you view the last reflection—as an urge for revenge or a plea for ultimate justice? What makes the difference?

8. Do you have other specific and practical ways of standing against the spread of envy?

THREE
ANGER *(IRA)*
VERSUS MEEKNESS

Anger is the third of the seven deadly sins. Like pride and envy, it is also a sin of the spirit, and thus "cold" and "respectable" in its motivation, though obviously less so in its expression. Its uniqueness lies in the fact that it stems from one of the most common, natural, and powerful emotions, which when allowed to degenerate into a deadly sin, becomes the sin most harmful to oneself and others, as well as the most destructive to human happiness and harmony.

Expressed by such terms as rage, wrath, ire, and indignation, the deadly sin of anger is the most widely acknowledged of the vices. But even anger must be distinguished from two easily confused notions. First, the sin of anger is more than simply an emotion; it includes the added element of the will. Emotions—as emotions—rise and fall in us, often involuntarily. But they are not considered sin because no element of the will incites or directs the emotion. Anger becomes a deadly sin, however, when the will is directly responsible for the rise and expression of the emotion.

Expressed by such terms as rage, wrath, ire, and indignation, the deadly sin of anger is the most widely acknowledged of the vices.

TEMPORARY INSANITY

"Anger is a short madness."

—Horace, *Epistles*

115

Second, the deadly sin of anger is different from justifiable outrage. In the Bible, God is often described as angry in the sense of being justifiably outraged. And so is Jesus—for example, at the tomb of Lazarus when He was face-to-face with death. Here, the strongest Greek word for anger is used to convey Jesus' outrage at death itself. Thus it is right, not wrong, to be outraged in the presence of evil. Indeed, John Chrysostom, the early church father, wrote: "He who is not angry when he has cause to be, sins."

THE OUTRAGE OF DEATH

"When Jesus saw her weeping, and the Jews who had come along with her also weeping, he was deeply moved in spirit [or furiously indignant] and troubled. 'Where have you laid him?' he asked.

"'Come and see, Lord,' they replied.

"Jesus wept.

"Then the Jews said, 'See how he loved him!'

"But some of them said, 'Could not he who opened the eyes of the blind man have kept this man from dying?'

"Jesus, once more deeply moved [furiously angry], came to the tomb. It was a cave with a stone laid across the entrance. 'Take away the stone,' he said.

"'But, Lord,' said Martha, the sister of the dead man, 'by this time there is a bad odor, for he has been there four days.'

"Then Jesus said, 'Did I not tell you that if you believed, you would see the glory of God?'

"So they took away the stone. Then Jesus looked up and said, 'Father, I thank you that you have heard me. I knew that you always hear me, but I said this for the benefit of the people standing here, that they may believe that you sent me.'

"When he had said this, Jesus called in a loud voice, 'Lazarus, come out!' The dead man came out, his hands and feet wrapped with strips of linen, and a cloth around his face. Jesus said to them, 'Take off the grave clothes and let him go.'"

—John 11:33-44

Anger, however, becomes a deadly sin when the motive is awry, when the expression of the emotion is inordinate, or when outrage against evil becomes a hatred of evil that outweighs love for God or for our neighbor.

Anger, however, becomes a deadly sin when the motive is awry, when the expression of the emotion is inordinate, or when outrage against evil becomes a hatred of evil that outweighs love for God or for our neighbor. Such anger is wrong because it is too strong for the person or the occasion at which we are angry.

Thus John Chrysostom also wrote: "He that is angry without cause shall be in danger, but he that is angry with cause shall not" (Homily 10). Or as Psalm 4 puts it simply, "Be angry, and do not sin."

THE FEATURES OF ANGER

There are therefore five typical features of the sin of anger: the contribution of the will (discussed previously), the wrongness of the motive, the excess and disorderliness of the expression, the desire for revenge, and the easy descent into contempt.

The motives for anger are varied, but often are tied to a sense of impotence in the face of entitlement, or self-pity. Entitlement-provoked anger rehearses to itself, consciously or unconsciously: "I deserve thus-and-such. It is owed me. If I cannot have it, I will become angry and, in my anger, find a way to get it." Self-pity, in contrast, mulls over and over: "This should not be happening to me. I don't deserve it. I'm angry and I'm not going to take it." In either case, a purely self-consumed motive leads beyond the self to inflict its anger on others.

The third feature of anger—its uncontrollability—is central to understanding the deadly sin. As Henry Fairlie wrote in the 1970s, the reason why extremists and revolutionaries always corrupt and betray their own faith is "the wrath that they will not check." In contrast, George Washington, who was described by Gouverneur Morris as having those "tumultuous passions that accompany greatness" and a "wrath" that could be "terrible," did not leave his temper unchecked. Rather, at a very young age, Washington began taming his anger and other passions by repeatedly copying a translated version of a French book of etiquette, containing 110 rules of civility.

The fourth feature, the desire for revenge, is also central to anger, either as an incitement or an outcome. However an insult or injury is perceived, anger simply wants to "get back" at the perpetrator. As a result, prolonged anger becomes a perverted desire for justice that grows into an obsessive rage and finally into hatred. No longer a thunderclap, it becomes a stoked furnace of potentially terrible destruction.

The motives for anger are varied, but often are tied to a sense of impotence in the face of entitlement, or self-pity.

SWEET REVENGE

"Sweeter by far than the honeycomb is wrath."

—Homer

"Hatred is holy."

—Emile Zola

The final feature of anger is that, at its very worst, anger becomes contempt. Unlike the "quick trigger" of a hot temper, contempt is a kind of studied degradation of another. It is a complete denial of his or her worth. In anger, there is a

Unlike the "quick trigger" of a hot temper, contempt is a kind of studied degradation of another. It is a complete denial of his or her worth.

desire to hurt; in contempt, the perpetrator doesn't care whether the other is hurt or not—he or she is not worth such a moment's consideration. When Jesus said "Whoever says 'Raca' (fool) to his brother shall stand condemned," he used the Aramaic term for contempt— "raca" —possibly originating from the sound made in collecting spittle from the throat in order to spit. It is possible to be angry at someone without denying his or her worth. Holding others in contempt, however, makes it easier to hurt or degrade them again and again.

ANGER'S EVIL TWIN

"When we trace wrongdoing back to its roots in the human heart, we find that in the overwhelming number of cases it involves some form of anger. Close behind anger you will find its twin brother, contempt."

—Dallas Willard, *The Divine Conspiracy*

"Recently cultural observers have noted the overwhelming rise in the use of filthy language, especially among young people. Curiously, few have been able to find any grounds for condemning it other than personal taste. How strange! Can it be that they actually find contempt acceptable, or are unable to recognize it? Filthy language and name calling is always an expression of contempt. The current swarm of filthy language floats upon the sea of contempt in which our society is now adrift."

—Dallas Willard, *The Divine Conspiracy*

PICTURES AND METAPHORS

Whereas the characteristic color of envy is green, that of anger is red. Its dominant image is fire. Anger typically simmers, boils, sparks, smokes, smolders, explodes, blazes, scorches, and devours. It is "the Devil's furnace," the sin that stokes the other sins and inflames their potency—the deadly sins in a scorched earth mode.

THE MIND'S FURNACE

"Never speak of it, always think of it!"

—Madame Adam, after France was crushed by the 1870 German invasion and forced to sign a humiliating peace treaty

PRACTICAL APPLICATIONS

"The Wrath of Achilles is my theme, that fatal wrath which, in fulfillment of the will of Zeus, brought the Acheans so much suffering and sent the gallant sons of many noblemen to Hades, heaving their bodies as carrion for the dogs and passing birds." These are the celebrated opening lines of Homer's Iliad in which the theme of anger is terrifyingly central. Anger may start early with the temper tantrums of small children, but its flames lick high and far into history's worst ethnic and international conflicts.

In between, anger plays a fiery role in child abuse, assault, rape, and murder. As one psychologist remarked, the main sound associated with the British family is that of doors banged inside the home; the main sound associated with the American family is that of cars driven away from outside the home. "No plague," wrote the Roman Stoic Seneca, "has cost the human race more dear."

How much truer the words of Seneca in our own day. From domestic violence, road rage, and workplace shootings to blood baths such as the Rwanda massacre, the havoc and devastation caused by anger is truly sobering.

> *Anger may start early with the temper tantrums of small children, but its flames lick high and far into history's worst ethnic and international conflicts.*

MURDER MADNESS

"In the United States there are around 25,000 murders each year. There are 1,000 murders in the workplace, and a million people are injured in the workplace by violent attacks from co-workers. . . . It is a simple fact that none of the 25,000 murders, or only a negligible number of them, would have occurred but for an anger that the killers chose to embrace and indulge."

—Dallas Willard, *The Divine Conspiracy*

Jesus gives similar place to the sin of anger. He devotes more of His Sermon on the Mount to the problem of anger and hostility than to any other matter He takes up, suggesting perhaps anger's fundamental place in the propagation of human woes. If you pull contempt and unrestrained anger out of the human equation, you will have eliminated by far the greater part of the pain and destructiveness of life, both ancient and modern.

> *Jesus gives similar place to the sin of anger. He devotes more of His Sermon on the Mount to the problem of anger and hostility than to any other matter He takes up, suggesting perhaps anger's fundamental place in the propagation of human woes.*

Calvin and Hobbes by Bill Watterson

❊ *Plutarch* ❊

Plutarch was introduced earlier, in part 2 on envy. The compelling passage that follows is also from his classic Lives of the Noble Grecians and Romans. *It describes a fateful incident that was a key turning point in the degeneration of Alexander the Great.*

It is the spring of 328 B.C., exactly halfway into Alexander's Persian campaign—five years after its start and five years before Alexander's death in 323 B.C. The easy, glory days of the campaign are over. Opposition is stiffening as they go further east, and Alexander is growing more arrogant as the days pass. He has begun to introduce Persian practices into his ranks, such as prostration (subjects falling facedown in homage to their leader). Such a practice would have been unthinkable to Greeks, who bowed to the gods but to no human being.

Some of the veteran Greek officers, such as Clitus, are disgruntled and uneasy. Clitus, nicknamed Clitus the Black, was called the "Alexander Savior"—the hero who rescued Alexander from death in an earlier battle. Yet he has recently been demoted. Now Clitus is seeking to work his way back into Alexander's good graces.

The ensuing event, whatever the motives, is a vivid indication that Alexander's explosive anger is a fatal flaw that, left unchecked, will deepen his path to tyranny and prove to have dire consequences for the future of his empire.

DOUBLE-CROSSED

"Indeed, anger is in its own right—quite apart from 'acting it out' and further consequences—an injury to others. When I discover your anger at me, I am *already* wounded. Your anger alone will very likely be enough to stop me or make me change my course, and it will also raise the stress level of everyone around us. It may also evoke my anger in return. Usually it does, precisely because your anger places a restraint on me. It crosses my will. Thus anger feeds on anger. The primary function of anger in life is to alert me to an obstruction to my will, and immediately raise alarm and resistance, before I even have time to think about it."

—Dallas Willard, *The Divine Conspiracy*

ALEXANDER

It being my purpose to write the lives of Alexander the king, and of Caesar, by whom Pompey was destroyed, the multitude of their great actions affords so large a field that I were to blame if I should not by way of apology forewarn my reader that I have chosen rather to epitomise the most celebrated parts of their story, than to insist at large on every particular circumstance of it. It must be borne in mind that my design is not to write histories, but lives. And the most glorious exploits do not always furnish us with the clearest discoveries of virtue or vice in men; sometimes a matter of less moment, an expression or a jest, informs us better of their characters and inclinations, than the most famous sieges, the greatest armaments, or the bloodiest battles whatsoever. Therefore as portrait-painters are more exact in the lines and features of the face, in which the character is seen, than in the other parts of the body, so I must be allowed to give my more particular attention to the marks and indications of the souls of men, and while I endeavour by these to portray their lives, may be free to leave more weighty matters and great battles to be treated of by others.

Therefore as portrait-painters are more exact in the lines and features of the face, in which the character is seen, than in the other parts of the body, so I must be allowed to give my more particular attention to the marks and indications of the souls of men.

. . . Not long after this happened, the deplorable end of Clitus, which, to those who barely hear the matter, may seem more inhuman than that of Philotas; but if we consider the story with its circumstance of time, and weigh the cause, we shall find it to have occurred rather through a sort of mischance of the king's, whose anger and over-drinking offered an occasion to the evil genius of Clitus. The king had a present of Grecian fruit brought him from the sea-coast, which was so fresh and beautiful that he was surprised at it, and called Clitus to him to see it, and to give him a share of it. Clitus was then sacrificing, but he immediately left off and came, followed by three sheep, on whom the drink-offering had been already poured preparatory to sacrificing them. Alexander, being informed of this, told his diviners, Aristander and Cleomantis the Lacedæmonian, and asked them what it meant; on whose assuring him it was an ill omen, he commanded them in all haste to offer sacrifices for Clitus's safety, for as much as three days before he himself had seen a strange vision in his sleep, of Clitus all in mourning, sitting by Parmenio's sons who were dead.

Clitus, however, stayed not to finish his devotions, but came straight to supper with the king, who had sacrificed to Castor and Pollux. And when they had drunk pretty hard, some of the company fell a-singing the verses of one Pranichus, or as others say of Pierion, which were made upon those captains who had been lately worsted by the barbarians, on purpose to disgrace and turn them to ridicule. This gave offense to the older men who were there, and they upbraided both the author and the singer of the verses, though Alexander and the younger men about him were much amused to hear them, and encouraged them to go on, till at last Clitus, who had drunk too much, and was besides of a forward and willful temper, was so nettled that he could hold no longer, saying it was not well done to expose the Macedonians before the barbarians and their enemies, since though it was their unhappiness to be over-come, yet they were much better men than those who laughed at them.

And when Alexander remarked, that Clitus was pleading his own cause, giving cowardice the name of misfortune, Clitus started up:

"This cowardice, as you are pleased to term it," said he to him, "saved the life of a son of the gods, when in flight from Spithridates's sword; it is by the expense of Macedonian blood, and by these wounds, that you are now raised to such a height as to be able to disown your father Philip, and call yourself the son of Ammon."

"Thou base fellow," said Alexander, who was now thoroughly exasperated, "dost thou think to utter these things everywhere of me, and stir up the Macedonians to sedition, and not be punished for it?"

"We are sufficiently punished already," answered Clitus, "if this be the rec-ompense of our toils, and we must esteem theirs a happy lot who have not lived to see their countrymen scourged with Median rods and forced to sue to the Persians to have access to their king."

While he talked thus at random, and those near Alexander got up from their seats and began to revile him in turn, the elder men did what they could to compose the disorder. Alexander, in the meantime turning about to Xenodochus, the Pardian, and Artemius, the Colophonian, asked him if they were not of opinion that the Greeks, in comparison with the Macedonians, behaved themselves like so many demigods among wild beasts.

But Clitus for all this would not give over, desiring Alexander to speak out if he had anything more to say, or else why did he invite men who were free-born and accustomed to speak their minds openly without restraint to sup with him. He had better live and converse with barbarians and slaves who would not scruple to bow the knee to his Persian girdle and his white tunic. Which words so provoked Alexander that, not able to suppress his anger any longer, he threw one of the apples that lay upon the table at him, and hit him, and then looked about for his sword.

Which words so provoked Alexander that, not able to suppress his anger any longer, he threw one of the apples that lay upon the table at him, and hit him, and then looked about for his sword.

But Aristophanes, one of his life-guards, had hid that out of the way, and others came about him and besought him, but in vain; for, breaking from them, he called out aloud to his guards in the Macedonian language, which was a cer-tain sign of some great disturbance in him, and commanded a trumpeter to sound, giving him a blow with his clenched fist for not instantly obeying him; though afterwards the same man was commended for disobeying an order which would have put the whole army into tumult and confusion. Clitus still refusing to yield, was with much trouble forced by his friends out of the room.

But he came in again immediately at another door, very irreverently and confidently singing the verses out of Euripides's *Andromache*, —

"In Greece, alas! how ill things ordered are!"

Upon this, at last, Alexander, snatching a spear from one of the soldiers, met Clitus as he was coming forward and was putting by the curtain that hung before the door, and ran him through the body. He fell at once with a cry and a groan. Upon which the king's anger immediately vanishing, he came perfectly to himself, and when he saw his friends about him all in a profound silence, he pulled the spear out of the dead body, and would have thrust it into his own throat, if the guards had not held his hands, and by main force carried him away into his chamber, where all that night and the next day he wept bitterly, still being quite spent with lamenting and exclaiming, he lay as it were speechless, only fetching deep sighs.

His friends apprehending some harm from his silence, broke into the room, but he took no notice of what any of them said, till Aristander putting him in mind of the vision he had seen concerning Clitus, and the prodigy that followed, as if all had come to pass by an unavoidable fatality, he then seemed to moderate his grief. They now brought Callisthenes, the philosopher, who was the near friend of Aristotle, and Anaxarchus of Abdera, to him. Callisthenes used moral language, and gentle and soothing means, hoping to find access for words of reason, and get a hold upon the passion.

But Anaxarchus, who had always taken a course of his own in philosophy, and had a name for despising and slighting his contemporaries, as soon as he came in, cried aloud, "Is this the Alexander whom the whole world looks to, lying here weeping like a slave, for fear of the censure and reproach of men, to whom he himself ought to be a law and measure of equity, if he would use the right his conquests have given him as supreme lord and governor of all, and not be the victim of a vain and idle opinion? Do not you know," said he, "that Jupiter is represented to have Justice and Law on each hand of him, to signify that all the actions of a conqueror are lawful and just?"

With these and the like speeches, Anaxarchus indeed allayed the king's grief, but withal corrupted his character, rendering him more audacious and lawless than he had been. Nor did he fail these means to insinuate himself into his favour, and to make Callisthenes's company, which at all times, because of his austerity, was not very acceptable; more uneasy and disagreeable to him.

Excerpt from Plutarch, *The Lives of the Noble Grecians and Romans,* trans. John Dryden, rev. Arthur Hugh Clough (New York: Modern Library, 1864).

QUESTIONS FOR THOUGHT AND DISCUSSION

1. In the opening paragraphs, what rationale does Plutarch give for writing "lives" rather than "histories"? What is he aiming to expose or record for future generations? How does his approach differ from typical methods of recording history?

2. In the following paragraphs, consider some of the factors that led to the build up of the murder. What is the significance of the Grecian fruit incident for both Alexander and Clitus? What is the role of superstition? Of the hard drinking following the evil omens? Of the ridicule between the "young Turks" and the "old guard"? What part does anger play in this build up?

3. To what is Clitus referring when he speaks of those who "would not scruple to bow the knee" to Alexander? Why does this comment incite Alexander to anger? In his anger, what does he do? How often is your anger tied to feelings of guilt or the need to defend yourself?

4. Aristophanes, one of Alexander's guards, had already hidden his sword out of the way. What does this gesture imply about Alexander's past handling of anger? What does Aristophanes' treatment of his trumpeter indicate about his own anger? In general, how did anger contribute to the chaos of the situation?

5. Left without his sword, how does Alexander finally kill Clitus? Why didn't the guard's hiding of Alexander's sword prevent the murder? When have you seen anger's "inventiveness" displayed in your own life or in your circle?

6. What happens to the king's anger once he has killed Clitus? For how long does he experience the satisfaction of having "avenged" himself? What do you think lay behind the king's subsequent desire to kill himself? His weeping through the night?

7. How do Aristander, Callisthenes, and Anaxarchus each try to rationalize Alexander's explosive anger? Why is Anarchus the most successful? What factors make acts of anger particularly easy to justify?

8. Why might such rage as Alexander's be called "blind"? What consequences of his behavior did he not foresee?

Seneca

Lucius Annaeus Seneca the Younger (4 B.C.–A.D. 65) was a Roman statesman, philosopher, and author. Born in Spain the son of a Roman rhetorician, he was later chosen to be the tutor of the future emperor Nero. An advocate of Stoic philosophy, he spent most of his life studying, writing, and in the thankless task of instructing Nero in the art of government and the virtues of the Stoic philosopher-king. Seneca remained a most trusted advisor when Nero became emperor, but lost favor and withdrew from the court in A.D. 62. Three years later he was implicated in a plot to kill the cruel and tyrannical Nero. As a punishment, his one-time pupil commanded Seneca to kill himself. With typical Stoic composure, Seneca had his veins opened and bled to death.

Seneca is second only to Cicero as a Roman philosopher, and his writings have been influential primarily in three areas—drama, physics, and ethics. This passage gives us the Stoic view of anger. It is a good example of the high-minded classical approach to the flaws of human emotions.

ON ANGER

Moreover, if you choose to view its results and the harm of it, no plague has cost the human race more dear. You will see bloodshed and poisoning, the vile countercharges of criminals, the downfall of cities and whole nations given to destruction, princely persons sold at public auction, houses put to the torch, and conflagration that halts not within the city-walls, but makes great stretches of the country glow with hostile flame.

Behold the most glorious cities whose foundations can scarcely be traced—anger cast them down. Behold solitudes stretching lonely for many miles without a single dweller—anger laid them waste. Behold all the leaders who have been handed down to posterity as instances of an evil fate—anger stabbed this one in his bed, struck down this one amid the sanctities of the feast, tore this one to pieces in the very home of the law and in full view of the crowded forum, forced this one to have his blood spilled by the murderous act of his son, another to have his royal throat cut by the hand of a slave, another to have his limbs stretched upon the cross.

Seneca is second only to Cicero as a Roman philosopher, and his writings have been influential primarily in three areas—drama, physics, and ethics.

Behold the most glorious cities whose foundations can scarcely be traced—anger cast them down. Behold solitudes stretching lonely for many miles without a single dweller—anger laid them waste.

And hitherto I have mentioned the sufferings of individual persons only; what if, leaving aside these who singly felt the force of anger's flame, you should choose to view the gatherings cut down by the sword, the populace butchered by soldiery let loose upon them, and whole peoples condemned to death in common ruin? . . .

Whether the life is worth the price we shall see; that is another question. We shall not condole with such a chain-gang of prisoners so wretched, we shall not urge them to submit to the commands of their butchers; we shall show that in any kind of servitude the way lies open to liberty. If the soul is sick and because of its own imperfection unhappy, a man may end its sorrows and at the same time himself.

To him to whom chance has given a king that aims his shafts at the breasts of his friends, to him who has a master that gorges fathers with the flesh of their children, I would say: "Madman, why do you moan? Why do you wait for some enemy to avenge you by the destruction of your nation, or for a mighty king from afar to fly to your rescue? In whatever direction you may turn your eyes, there lies the means to end your woes. See you that precipice? Down that is the way to liberty. See you that sea, that river, that well? There sits liberty—at the bottom. See you that tree, stunted, blighted, and barren? Yet from its branches hangs liberty. See you that throat of yours, your gullet, your heart? They are ways of escape from servitude. Are the ways of egress I show you too toilsome, do they require too much courage and strength? Do you ask what is the highway to liberty? Any vein in your body!"

So long indeed as there shall be no hardship so intolerable in our opinion as to force us to abandon life, let us, no matter what our station in life may be, keep ourselves from anger. It is harmful for all who serve.

Reprinted by permission of the publishers and the Loeb Classical Library from *Seneca, Volume I*, translated by John W. Basore, Cambridge, MA: Harvard University Press, 1928.

QUESTIONS FOR THOUGHT AND DISCUSSION

1. Seneca is lamenting the baleful consequences of anger in human history from the perspective of nearly two thousand years ago. How has the situation changed since his time? What do you think he would add or subtract if he were writing his reflection today?

2. To what examples can you point of the large-scale destructiveness of anger (globally or nationally) since Seneca's time? On a narrower scale,

how has anger disrupted or destroyed groups or communities in your part of the world? How could the destruction have been avoided?

3. What do you think are the most harmful consequences of uncontrolled anger between parents and children? In friendships? In romantic or marital relationships?

4. What do you think of the stoic resort to suicide as an escape from one's own anger or the anger of others?

5. Read Seneca's last appeal (final paragraph) to "keep ourselves from anger" no matter our station in life. How would Seneca have responded to modern "anger politics," in which anger is the fuel for seeking redresses for grievances through the political system?

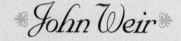

John Weir is a contemporary writer living in New York who has also been an AIDS activist. The following reading is an essay from The New Republic *that Weir wrote after the death, through AIDS, of his friend and fellow-activist, David Feinberg. It is both poignant and searing, a telling analysis of the place of anger in the homosexual movement.*

LICENSE FOR TERROR

"We understand that there are angry people, who seem simply to be angry, within themselves, at anything and everything: angry at life, angry at their lot, angry at the world, angry at everyone else, and angry at themselves, although this they do not see. It is hardly worth asking them the cause, because they will always be angry at something. . . . We live in an age of Wrath. It is to be found in the terrorist, the kidnapper, the hijacker, the looter, and in the clenched fist of the demonstrator. One mentions these at the beginning only because they are the most obvious symbolic figures. They are not alone. When we ask what is their justification, they hardly have to give an answer, because our age finds it for them. They are angry. That is apparently enough. We justify their Wrath, so we justify their violence. If someone thinks that he has cause to be angry, he may act from his Anger as destructively as he sees fit. In fact, we have come close to the point of giving to Wrath an incontestable license to terrorize our societies."

—Henry Fairlie, "An Age of Wrath" in *The Seven Deadly Sins Today*

"There is nothing that can be done with anger that cannot be done better without it."

—Dallas Willard, *The Divine Conspiracy*

RAGE, RAGE

My friend David Feinberg, the novelist and essayist who died of AIDS last November, has been memorialized as a kind of alternative North American martyr. He was not just homosexual, he was self-consciously "queer." His novel *Eighty-Sixed* was not just a brilliant monologue about male horniness, Jewish guilt, and AIDS anxiety, it was "transgressive." He was not merely a regular ACT UP member who was routinely arrested at demonstrations, he was "countercultural." He did not die, he was "killed by government neglect."

In short, David has emerged postmortem as the kind of outsider who is sentimentalized by the left and demonized by the right. He is noted for being difficult because we expect difficulty from antagonists and sufferers. Mourners celebrate his jokiness, his irritability, his honesty about how much of his life he spent wanting, having, or not getting sex. If David was popular among heterosexual readers, I suspect it was in part because his writing satisfied certain preconceptions about homosexual men. Of course, gay men like to believe clichés about themselves, too.

In short, David has emerged postmortem as the kind of outsider who is sentimentalized by the left and demonized by the right.

David's writing is not clichéd. Rather, it is profoundly superficial. It works not because it goes deeply into any subject, but because it skirts so quickly and so hectically over the surface of things, accumulating so many details, fact upon fact, that it gives the effect of deep feeling. It has virtual depth. There is no comfort in his writing, only anxiety, humor, sentimentality, rage, and despair, as well as a lot of silliness. His genius was in being silly; he could make it feel like a meaningful connection. He was also an artful complainer. His last book, *Queer and Loathing: Rants and Raves of a Raging AIDS Clone*, which was published the week he died, is the least wisecracking, and the hardest to read of all his work because it is the most unmitigated by irony. He used irony to distance himself from pain, but irony failed him in the end, and all that was left was his devastating fear and rage.

He used irony to distance himself from pain, but irony failed him in the end, and all that was left was his devastating fear and rage.

He was my closest friend for the past five years. As death approached, I was asked, "How do you feel about David's dying?" and I would answer, "If AIDS doesn't kill him, I will." People would laugh as if I were making a kind of Feinbergian joke, as an homage to him. What I didn't say is that shortly before he died, I stopped liking him. I stopped liking him not just then, but always. It was retroactive. He was so mean to me and to all of his devoted friends, so relentlessly and mindlessly and destructively angry, that I forgot, for a time, what I ever liked about him.

Yet he is being honored for his anger. Anger is the orthodoxy of the self-proclaimed AIDS activist community. It is the authority invested in the individual as well as the group. "Where is your anger?" people still ask, over and over, at ACT UP meetings, as if checking other people for I.D. Rage bestows authenticity. Anger is seen as wholly reliable because it is so intensely felt. The fundamental sentimentality of ACT UP is the belief that emotions always tell the truth. The group's miscalculation is that feelings alone, directly and powerfully expressed, can change things.

I am speaking now as someone who has laid across pavement in subzero temperature in February, my arm hooked to David's arm through steel tubing, blocking the entrance to Hoffman-LaRoche, a big pharmaceutical company in New Jersey. For three hours we chanted, "Arrest the real criminal," while the four local police officers who bothered to show up watched us with bemused contempt. In Albany, in New Hampshire during primary season, in Washington, D.C., inside Grand Central Station, marching through the financial district in Manhattan, I held David's hand, or clenched my fists with his and raised them high to shout, "We'll never be silent again." When I ran across the set of the "CBS Evening News" during the height of the Gulf War, chanting, "Fight AIDS, not Arabs," I was doing it for David.

Like David, I thought that if I got angry enough, he would not have to die. I was wrong, and so was he. ACT UP was wrong. Anger is a useful strategy— so is foolishness—if it remains a strategy, and does not become a faith. David was angry for a living. Not only did it not keep him alive, it kept him from whatever comfort he might fleetingly have felt when he was dying. I learned a lot about anger, watching David die. The New Age premise that "finding your anger" is the key to health and strength turns out to be wishful thinking. Anger generates nothing but anger. It doesn't express truth, it glorifies ego.

The limitations of anger as a public cry to action were clear to me when I went with David last October to help him deliver what he called his "scathing diatribe" to ACT UP. He weighed 106 pounds that night, down from 150. He was three weeks from death. His body, which he was always careful to maintain in perfect shape, as if he might be called upon to use it as a weapon, had disintegrated. His

The group's miscalculation is that feelings alone, directly and powerfully expressed, can change things.

Like David, I thought that if I got angry enough, he would not have to die. I was wrong, and so was he.

skeleton showed everywhere. He clutched his trousers in an angry fist to keep them from sliding halfway down his thighs. Like King Lear back from the heath, he looked and sounded furious, raving, and crazy. There was, however, no catharsis in his rage. It was wasted on him, and it was wasted on the room.

There ought to be a sign hanging over New York's Gay and Lesbian Community Center on Monday nights—ACT UP nights—that says, "ABANDON HOPE, ALL WHO ENTER HERE." The night David showed up, he was addressing an organization that no longer exists. So much anger was spent by so many people so quickly, to so little effect, that the residue of bitterness left most of New York's AIDS activist community burned out. A lot of people died. But many more were exhausted by the group's ineffectual ethos of collective, unquestioned rage.

It isn't poetry that makes nothing happen, it's anger. I don't remember much of David's speech. I remember he said "f___" a lot. Like many ACT UP members, he had an adolescent's faith in the totemic power of the word "f___." He also used the word "anger." He was angry about dying. He was angry ACT UP was not going to keep him alive. He was angry at everyone in the room, and everyone who had ever attended a meeting, living or dead. It was the kind of speech that has a long tradition in ACT UP, a purging cry of rage, meant to renew activist fervor. I couldn't listen. I thought the point was not that David wanted a cure for AIDS, but that he wanted a cure for him. For the past five years, he put all his faith and energy into a group that was supposed to be a community. In the end, however, David didn't care that his friends were dying, he cared that he was dying.

Many people in the room that night, and others who heard about what went on there, feel he had a perfect right to his self-interest. I don't. His death wasn't something that happened only to him. I was losing something, too. So were a lot of people. Apart from anger, one of the implicit faiths of ACT UP is selfishness. What ACT UP wants as a group is to provide an outlet for the personal gratification of each individual soul. The HIV-negative members want to be affirmed. The HIV-positive members want to be cured. David's speech was not courageous or inspiring, it was egotistical. What he finally said to the AIDS activist community was, "This is about *me*. Nothing matters now except saving *me*."

I would have done anything to help him, but finally, what David wanted rescuing from wasn't AIDS. He hated AIDS, but more than that, he hated being human. Like a lot of AIDS activists, he thought that he alone was too special to die.

John Weir, "Rage, Rage," *The New Republic*, February 13, 1995, pp. 11–12. © 1995, The New Republic, Inc. Reprinted by permission of *The New Republic*.

GOING THE GAY WAY?

"Our childlessness, our minimal responsibilities, the fact that our unions are not consecrated, even our very retreat into gay ghettoes for protection and freedom . . . have fostered a style in which we may be exploring, even in spite of our conscious intentions, things that will some day be for the heterosexual majority."

—Michel Foucault

QUESTIONS FOR THOUGHT AND DISCUSSION

1. Read the box, *License for Terror*. In the years since Henry Fairlie wrote these words in 1978, what examples can you find to support his tenet, "We justify their Wrath, so we justify their violence"? What might Fairlie write about the role of anger in today's society?

2. In John Weir's article, what is the link he suggests between Feinberg's anger and his purposeful use of such phrases as "transgressive," "countercultural," and "killed by government neglect"? What was the intended impact of such words on the public? What other emotive words or phrases are commonly used in "anger politics"?

3. Weir describes Feinberg's writing as having "virtual depth," skirting "over the surface of things." Is there a connection between this style of writing and the anger behind it? If so, what? Can you think of other examples of superficial writing driven by anger?

4. Why did Weir stop liking Feinberg? How does Weir view the place of rage in the psychology of homosexual activists? Why does anger "bestow authenticity" in such groups? In what other group activism have you seen anger play a similar defining role?

5. What constructive part can justifiable outrage play in fighting injustice? Can you think of examples? When does it cross the line and become the deadly sin of anger?

6. What did Weir and Feinberg mistakenly believe anger could accomplish? What is Weir's critique of the psychobabble/New Age sentiment that "finding your anger" is the key to health? How does anger "glorify ego"?

7. Why couldn't Weir listen to his friend's speech at ACT UP? How did anger eventually destroy the organization?

8. What does Weir conclude that Feinberg was *really* angry about? What similarities do you see between Feinberg's rage and that of other perpetually angry people in modern society?

❦ *Mary Gordon* ❦

Mary Catherine Gordon (born 1949) is an accomplished contemporary novelist and writer of short stories. Born in Long Island, New York, she was educated at Barnard College and Syracuse University. Currently she teaches English at Amherst College.

Gordon made a name for herself after only two novels, Final Payments *(1978) and* The Company of Women *(1981). A confident writer with a brilliant gift for words, Gordon is frequently compared with Jane Austen. As a devout Catholic, she is penetrating in her description of religious believers and their world. This short essay on anger written for* The New York Times *highlights both her descriptive powers and her refreshing honesty.*

THE FASCINATION BEGINS IN THE MOUTH

If the word sin has any useful meaning at all in a time when there is no possibility of redemption, it must speak about a distortion so severe that the recognizable self is blotted out or lost. Many current thinkers wish to abandon the idea of a continuous self; novelists have always known that selves are fleeting, malleable, porous. Nevertheless some recognizable thing, something constant enough to have a name sensibly fixed to it, seems to endure from birth to death. Sin makes the sinner unrecognizable.

I experienced this once myself, and I remember it because it frightened me. I became an animal. This sinful experience occurred—as so many do—around the occasion of a dinner party. It was a hot August afternoon. I was having ten people for dinner that evening. No one was giving me a bit of help. I was, of course, feeling like a victim, as everyone does in a hot kitchen on an August day. (It is important to remember that the angry person's habit of self-justification is often connected to his habit of seeing himself as a victim.) I had been chopping, stirring, bending over a low flame, and all alone, alone! The oven's heat was my Purgatory, my crucible.

My mother and my children thought this was a good time for civil disobedience. They positioned themselves in the car and refused to move until

If the word sin has any useful meaning at all in a time when there is no possibility of redemption, it must speak about a distortion so severe that the recognizable self is blotted out or lost.

I took them swimming. Now my children were at tender ages at that time, seven and four. My mother was seventy-eight and, except for her daily habit of verbal iron-pumping, properly described as infirm. They leaned on the horn and shouted my name out the window, well within hearing of the neighbors, reminding me of my promise to take them to the pond.

There are certain times when a popular cliché disgorges itself from the dulled setting of overuse and comes to life, and this was one of them. *I lost it.* I lost myself. I jumped on the hood of the car. I pounded on the windshield. I told my mother and my children that I was never, ever going to take any of them anywhere and none of them were ever going to have one friend in any house of mine until the hour of their death, which, I said, I hoped was soon. I couldn't stop pounding on the windshield. Then the frightening thing happened. I became a huge bird. A carrion crow. My legs became hard stalks; my eyes were sharp and vicious. I developed a murderous beak. Greasy black feathers took the place of arms. I flapped and flapped. I blotted out the sun's light with my flapping. Each time my beak landed near my victims (it seemed to be my fists on the windshield, but it was really my beak on their necks) I went back for more. The taste of blood entranced me. I wanted to peck and peck forever. I wanted to carry them all off in my bloody beak and drop them on a rock where I would feed on their battered corpses till my bird stomach swelled.

I don't mean this figuratively. I became that bird. I had to be forced to get off the car and stop pounding the windshield. Even then I didn't come back to myself. When I did, I was appalled. I realized I had genuinely frightened my children. Mostly because they could no longer recognize me. My son said to me: "I was scared because I didn't know who you were."

I understand that this is not sin of a serious nature. I know this to be true because it has its comic aspects and deadly sin is characterized by the absence of humor which always brings life. But because of that experience and others I won't tell you about, I understand the deadly sin of anger. I was unrecognizable to myself and, for a time, to my son, but I think I still would have been recognizable to most of the rest of the world as human. Deadly sin causes the rest of the human community to say: "How can this person do this thing and still be human?"

The events in the former Yugoslavia seem to me to characterize perfectly the results of deadly anger. We outsiders are tormented and bedeviled by unimaginable behavior from people who seemed so very like ourselves. They didn't look like our standard idea of the *other:* they read the same philosophers as we, and we vacationed among them, enjoying their food, their music, their

There are certain times when a popular cliché disgorges itself from the dulled setting of overuse and comes to life, and this was one of them. I lost it.

ordinary pleasantries. And yet, a kind of incomprehensible horror has grown up precisely because of an anger that has gone out of control and has fed on itself until all human eyes are blinded by the bloated flesh of overgorged anger. People who five years ago ate together, studied together, even married, have sworn to exterminate one another in the most bloody and horrifying ways. Hundreds of years of mutual injustices, treasured like sacred texts, have been gone over, resurrected, nurtured, so that a wholly new creature has been brought to life, a creature bred on anger to the exclusion of vision. Hypnotic, addictive vengeance, action without reflection has taken over like a disease. Thousands upon thousands of women have been raped; impregnation has become a curse, a punishment. The old are starved, beautiful ancient cities destroyed. The original cause of the anger is less important now than the momentum that has built up.

This is the deadly power of anger: It rolls and rolls like a flaming boulder down a hill, gathering mass and speed until any thought of cessation is so far beside the point as to seem hopeless.

This is the deadly power of anger: It rolls and rolls like a flaming boulder down a hill, gathering mass and speed until any thought of cessation is so far beside the point as to seem hopeless. It is not that there is no cause for the anger; the heavy topsoil of repressed injustice breeds anger better than any other medium. But the causes are lost in the momentum of the anger itself, and in the insatiable compulsion to destroy everything so that the open maw of rage may be fed.

GRAPES OF WRATH

"That fuse kept burning though, through the next two years of simmering tensions and sometimes open conflict. Then one day in November 1965, all the Mondavis assembled at one of our big family gatherings at the winery for what was supposed to be a happy, festive occasion. It turned out to be anything but. I don't remember exactly how it started, but at some point, Peter and I started to squabble. Tempers flared and Peter accused me of spending too much company money on travel and promotion. Then he really lost his temper and accused me of taking money from the winery. How else could I afford to buy that mink coat? In essence, I felt my own brother was accusing me of being a thief and a swindler.

"'Say that again and I'll hit you,' I warned him.

"He said it again.

"Then I gave him a third chance: 'Take it back.'

"'No.'

"So I smacked him, hard. Twice.

"Growing up, Peter and I rarely fought. I do recall going at it once as teenagers, in one of our bedrooms, and we really tore the place up. But after that, never. So here we were, two men in our early fifties, acting like kids in a school yard—with terrible consequences. When it was all over, there were no apologies and no handshake. Quite the contrary. Like a cleaver, the fight split our family in two, and there was no repairing the damage. It broke my mother's heart, divided our sisters, and left our children hurt and confused. The Mondavis, up to then a close-knit Italian family, were now deeply—and very publicly—split.

"The fight and its aftermath soon became notorious across the Napa Valley and throughout the American wine industry. Some evil-tongued gossips spoke of it as a modern-day version of Cain and Abel. My father might have been able to impose a peace in the family, but by then he had been dead for several years and it was just too much for my mother to handle. Lawyers and mediators were brought in."

—Robert Mondavi, *Harvest of Joy*
(Excerpt from *Harvest of Joy*. © 1998
by Robert Mondavi, reprinted by permission of Harcourt Inc.)

QUESTIONS FOR THOUGHT AND DISCUSSION

1. What do you think Mary Gordon means when she describes sin as "a distortion so severe that the recognizable self is blotted out"? Where have you seen such sin? Can you think of examples of such "distortion" in groups, such as political alliances, communities, or even nations?

2. According to Gordon, what view of oneself is key to the habit of justifying one's anger? Why does this rationale work so well? What mistaken thinking lies behind it?

3. Can you relate to Mary Gordon's experience of "losing herself" in anger? What part of the description of her rage hits closest to home? What other metaphors (other than the bird) would you use to describe the experience of rage, either in yourself or others?

4. What do you think of Gordon's test for deadly sin: "How can this person do this thing and still be human?" Are there cases that have received media attention in recent years that have caused you to ask that question? Which ones?

5. What is the connection, perceived or real, between anger and power? Why is the power achieved through anger ultimately weak?

6. Gordon writes that the original cause of anger is often diminished or completely lost in the momentum that builds from it. When have you been angry but unable to remember the first cause of your anger? What is it about anger that allows it to detach from its original source and feed upon itself?

7. What is the implication of the popular phrase "blind rage"? Why can rage and vision not coexist?

8. What should be our reaction when such explosions of anger take on a collective form, as in the Los Angeles riots of the 1980s or the killings in Rwanda in the 1990s?

THE COUNTERPOINT TO ANGER:
Blessed Are the Meek

The counterpoint to the deadly sin of anger is found in two beatitudes: "Blessed are the meek" and "Blessed are the peacemakers." Both have been neutered by confusion. Meekness has been confused with weakness and peacemaking with pacifism and passivism.

Meekness has been confused with weakness and peacemaking with pacifism and passivism.

IS MEEK WEAK?

"The meek shall inherit the earth, but not the mineral rights."

—John Paul Getty

"Those who beat their guns into plows will plow for those who don't."
—Bumper sticker on the truck of Francisco M. Duran, who shot at the White House with an assault rifle, November 1994

But far from being weak, both meekness and peacemaking pivot on strength. It is precisely when the capacity to use force is the greatest that the strength not to do so is the clearest and most constructive. The image of peace in the Hebrew Scriptures is not two lambs laying down together, but the lion laying beside the lamb, an otherwise easy prey.

Whereas the sin of anger commonly stems from feelings of inferiority and impotence, meekness stems from the accurate knowledge of one's strength. That strength, when submitted to God and thus under control, becomes true gentleness. Because meekness has no sense of inferiority to try to pacify or powerlessness to try to prove wrong, it can forego causing injury to others and instead work for peace and justice.

THE VIEW OF OTHERS

Both meekness and peacemaking are rooted in an appreciation of the infinite value of human life. Jesus' teachings in both beatitudes center on the preciousness of human beings and their intrinsic value as reflections of God's image. Therefore, the command not to kill others or take what is theirs is not sufficient. Meekness and

Whereas the sin of anger commonly stems from feelings of inferiority and impotence, meekness stems from the accurate knowledge of one's strength. That strength, when submitted to God and thus under control, becomes true gentleness.

peacemaking move beyond the negative (not killing, not stealing) to the positive—exhibiting gentleness and forbearance, and actively seeking reconciliation. As such, they fall under the umbrella of love, as the apostle Paul says in his summation of Jesus' teaching: "He that loves has fulfilled the law."

PEACEMAKING FOR A "FOOL"

"Then David moved down into the Desert of Maon. A certain man in Maon, who had property there at Carmel, was very wealthy. He had a thousand goats and three thousand sheep, which he was shearing in Carmel. His name was Nabal and his wife's name was Abigail. She was an intelligent and beautiful woman, but her husband, a Calebite, was surly and mean in his dealings.

"While David was in the desert, he heard that Nabal was shearing sheep. So he sent ten young men and said to them, 'Go up to Nabal at Carmel and greet him in my name. Say to him: "Long life to you! Good health to you and your household! And good health to all that is yours!

"'"Now I hear that it is sheep-shearing time. When your shepherds were with us, we did not mistreat them, and the whole time they were at Carmel nothing of theirs was missing. Ask your own servants and they will tell you. Therefore be favorable toward my young men, since we come at a festive time. Please give your servants and your son David whatever you can find for them."'

"When David's men arrived, they gave Nabal this message in David's name. Then they waited. Nabal answered David's servants, 'Who is this David? Who is this son of Jesse? Many servants are breaking away from their masters these days. Why should I take my bread and water, and the meat I have slaughtered for my shearers, and give it to men coming from who knows where?'

"David's men turned around and went back. When they arrived, they reported every word. David said to his men, 'Put on your swords!' . . . About four hundred men went up with David, while two hundred stayed with the supplies.

"One of the servants told Nabal's wife Abigail: 'David sent messengers from the desert to give our master his greetings, but he hurled insults at them. Yet these men were very good to us. They did not mistreat us, and the whole time we were out in the fields near them nothing was missing. Night and day they were a wall around us all the time we were herding our sheep near them. Now think it over and see what you can do, because disaster is hanging over our master and his whole household. He is such a wicked man that no one can talk to him.'

"Abigail lost no time. She took two hundred loaves of bread, two skins of wine, five dressed sheep, five seahs of roasted grain, a hundred cakes of raisins and two hundred cakes of pressed figs, and loaded them on donkeys. . . . But she did not tell her husband Nabal. . . .

"When Abigail saw David, she quickly got off her donkey and bowed down before David with her face to the ground. She fell at his feet and said: 'My lord, let the blame be on me alone. Please let your servant speak to you. . . . May my lord pay no attention to that wicked man Nabal. He is just like his name—his name is Fool, and folly goes with him. But as for me, your servant, I did not see the men my master sent. . . . [L]et this gift, which your servant has brought to my master, be given to the men who follow you. Please forgive your servant's offense, for the LORD will certainly make a lasting dynasty for my master, because he fights the LORD's battles. Let no wrongdoing be found in you as long as you live. . . . When the LORD has done for my master every good thing he promised concerning him and has appointed him leader over Israel, my master will not have on his conscience the staggering burden of needless bloodshed or of having avenged himself. And when the LORD has brought my master success, remember your servant.'

"David said to Abigail, 'Praise be to the LORD, the God of Israel, who has sent you today to meet me. May you be blessed for your good judgment and for keeping me from bloodshed this day and from avenging myself with my own hands. Otherwise, as surely as the LORD, the God of Israel, lives, who has kept me from harming you, if you had not come quickly to meet me, not one male belonging to Nabal would have been left alive by daybreak.'

"Then David accepted from her hand what she had brought to him and said, 'Go home in peace. I have heard your words and granted your request.'

"When Abigail went to Nabal, he was in the house holding a banquet like that of a king. He was in high spirits and very drunk. So she told him nothing until daybreak. Then in the morning, when Nabal was sober, his wife told him all these things, and his heart failed him and he became like a stone. About ten days later, the LORD struck Nabal and he died.

"When David heard that Nabal was dead, he said, 'Praise be to the LORD, who has upheld my cause against Nabal for treating me with contempt. He has kept his servant from doing wrong and has brought Nabal's wrongdoing down on his own head.' Then David sent word to Abigail, asking her to become his wife."

—1 Samuel 25:1-39

C. S. Lewis

C. S. Lewis (1898–1963) was introduced earlier in part 1 on pride. The following excerpt on forgiveness also comes from Mere Christianity.

FORGIVENESS

I said in a previous chapter that chastity was the most unpopular of the Christian virtues. But I am not sure I was right. I believe the one I have to talk of today is even more unpopular: the Christian rule, "Thou shalt love thy neighbor as thyself." Because in Christian morals "thy neighbor" includes "thy enemy," and so we come up against this terrible duty of forgiving our enemies.

Every one says forgiveness is a lovely idea, until they have something to forgive, as we had during the war. And then, to mention the subject at all is to be greeted with howls of anger. It is not that people think this too high and difficult a virtue: it is that they think it hateful and contemptible. "That sort of talk makes them sick," they say. And half of you already want to ask me, "I wonder how you'd feel about forgiving the Gestapo if you were a Pole or a Jew?"

Every one says forgiveness is a lovely idea, until they have something to forgive, as we had during the war.

So do I. I wonder very much. Just as when Christianity tells me that I must not deny my religion even to save myself from death by torture, I wonder very much what I should do when it came to the point. I am not trying to tell you in this book what I could do—I can do precious little—I am telling you what Christianity is. I did not invent it. And there, right in the middle of it, I find "Forgive us our sins as we forgive those that sin against us." There is no slightest suggestion that we are offered forgiveness on any other terms. It is made perfectly clear that if we do not forgive we shall not be forgiven. There are no two ways about it. What are we to do?

It is going to be hard enough, anyway, but I think there are two things we can do to make it easier. When you start mathematics you do not begin with the calculus; you begin with simple addition. In the same way, if we really want (but all depends on really wanting) to learn how to forgive, perhaps we had better start with something easier than the Gestapo. One might start with forgiving one's husband or wife, or parents or children, or the nearest N.C.O., for something they have done or said in the last week. That will probably keep us busy for the moment. And secondly, we might try to understand exactly what loving your neighbor as yourself means. I have to love him as I love myself. Well, how exactly do I love myself?

One might start with forgiving one's husband or wife, or parents or children, or the nearest N.C.O., for something they have done or said in the last week.

Now that I come to think of it, I have not exactly got a feeling of fondness or affection for myself, and I do not even always enjoy my own society. So apparently "Love your neighbor" does not mean "feel fond of him" or "find him attractive." I ought to have seen that before, because, of course, you cannot feel fond of a person by trying. Do I think well of myself, think myself a nice chap? Well, I am afraid I sometimes do (and those are, no doubt, my worst moments) but that is not why I love myself. In fact it is the other way round: my self-love makes me think myself nice, but thinking myself nice is not why I love myself. So loving my enemies does not apparently mean thinking them nice either.

That is an enormous relief. For a good many people imagine that forgiving your enemies means making out that they are really not such bad fellows after all, when it is quite plain that they are. Go a step further. In my most clear-sighted moments not only do I not think myself a nice man, but I know that I am a very nasty one. I can look at some of the things I have done with horror and loathing. So apparently I am allowed to loathe and hate some of the things my enemies do. Now that I come to think of it, I remember Christian teachers telling me long ago that I must hate a bad man's actions, but not hate the bad man: or, as they would say, hate the sin but not the sinner.

For a long time I used to think this a silly, straw-splitting distinction: how could you hate what a man did and not hate the man? But years later it occurred to me that there was one man to whom I had been doing this all my life—namely myself. However much I might dislike my own cowardice or conceit or greed, I went on loving myself. There had never been the slightest difficulty about it. In fact the very reason why I hated the things was that I loved the man. Just because I loved myself, I was sorry to find that I was the sort of man who did those things. Consequently, Christianity does not want us to reduce by one atom the hatred we feel for cruelty and treachery. We ought to hate them. Not one word of what we have said about them needs to be unsaid. But it does want us to hate them in the same way in which we hate things in ourselves: being sorry that the man should have done such things, and hoping, if it is anyway possible, that somehow, some-time, somewhere, he can be cured and made human again.

The real test is this. Suppose one reads a story of filthy atrocities in the paper. Then suppose that something turns up suggesting that the story might not be quite true, or not quite so bad as it was made out. Is one's first feeling, "Thank God, even they aren't quite so bad as that," or is it a feeling of disappointment, and even a determination to cling to the first story for the sheer pleasure of thinking your enemies as bad as possible? If it is the second then it is, I am afraid, the first step in a process which, if followed to the end, will make us into devils. You see, one is beginning to wish that black was a little blacker. If we give that wish its head, later on we shall wish to see gray as black, and then to see white itself as black. Finally, we shall insist on seeing everything—God and our friends and ourselves included—as bad, and not be able to stop doing it: we shall be fixed for ever in a universe of pure hatred.

For a long time I used to think this a silly, straw-splitting distinction: how could you hate what a man did and not hate the man? But years later it occurred to me that there was one man to whom I had been doing this all my life—namely myself.

QUESTIONS FOR THOUGHT AND DISCUSSION

1. According to Lewis, what happens to the "lovely idea" of forgiveness when the enemy to be forgiven takes on flesh and blood? What responses did he hear to the suggestion that a wartime enemy be forgiven?

2. What does learning to forgive ultimately depend upon? With this prerequisite in place, what is Lewis's first suggestion for making forgiveness easier? What do you think of this gradual "addition before calculus" approach? In what situations would it be particularly helpful?

3. How does the way Lewis defines "loving yourself" vary from the version of modern popular psychology? What is the implicit connection between "loving your neighbor as yourself" and forgiveness?

4. What does "loving your neighbor" not mean? What convinces Lewis that the maxim "hate the sin but not the sinner" is not just a hair-splitting distinction? Why do you agree or disagree?

5. What is the sentiment toward others that should lie behind our hatred of sinful behavior, according to the author? What is the real test of whether or not we hold this generous attitude?

6. What does Lewis believe that, if left unchecked, can turn us into devils? Where have you seen this corrosive process in action?

7. Lewis describes here what forgiveness is not, but not what it is. How would you go on to describe the essence of forgiveness? Do you see forgiveness as something idealistic and airy-fairy or practical and down-to-earth? What makes it "work"?

8. Who are the hardest people or groups for you to forgive? What arguments have you heard—or made yourself—for not forgiving? How might Lewis answer them?

✺ Martin Luther King Jr. ✺

Martin Luther King Jr. (1929–1968) was a civil rights leader, pastor, writer, and Nobel Laureate. The son and grandson of Baptist ministers, King was born in Atlanta and later graduated from Morehouse College in 1951. He earned a Ph.D. from Boston University in 1955. King was fundamentally shaped by his faith in Jesus Christ and his church background, but he was also helped by the life and teaching of Mahatma Gandhi.

In 1955 King led a historic black boycott of Montgomery's bus system. In 1957 he organized the Southern Christian Leadership Conference as the basis of a new civil rights movement based on nonviolence. Over the next eleven years, he led many protests throughout the South. He was arrested and jailed frequently, his house was burned three times, and he was stabbed once.

King's historic speech, "I Have a Dream," at the civil rights rally on August 28, 1963 in Washington, D.C., has come to epitomize the civil rights movement at its crescendo. He was given the Nobel Peace Prize the next year, at age thirty-five—the youngest person to receive it. In 1968 he was murdered in Memphis, Tennessee, most likely by a white man.

King's message grows in large part from the substance and style of traditional black preaching. The following passage, from a different speech, is therefore not a rhetorical, religious flourish to grace an otherwise secular, political message. It is the very heart of his call to justice and reconciliation.

LOVING YOUR ENEMIES

Probably no admonition of Jesus has been more difficult to follow than the command to "love your enemies." Some men have sincerely felt that its actual practice is not possible. It is easy, they say, to love those who love you, but how can one love those who openly and insidiously seek to defeat you? Others, like the philosopher Nietzsche, contend that Jesus' exhortation to love one's enemies is testimony to the fact that the Christian ethic is designed for the weak and cowardly, and not for the strong and courageous. Jesus, they say, was an impractical idealist.

Probably no admonition of Jesus has been more difficult to follow than the command to "love your enemies." Some men have sincerely felt that its actual practice is not possible.

In spite of these insistent questions and persistent objections, this command of Jesus challenges us with new urgency. Upheaval after upheaval has reminded us that modern man is traveling along a road called hate, in a journey that will bring us to destruction and damnation. Far from being the pious injunction of a Utopian dreamer, the command to love one's enemy is an absolute necessity for our survival. Love even for enemies is the key to the solution of the problems of our world. Jesus is not an impractical idealist: he is the practical realist.

I am certain that Jesus understood the difficulty inherent in the act of loving one's enemy. He never joined the ranks of those who talk glibly about the easiness of the moral life. He realized that every genuine expression of love grows out of a consistent and total surrender to God. So when Jesus said "Love your enemy," he was not unmindful of its stringent qualities. Yet he meant every word of it. Our responsibility as Christians is to discover the meaning of this command and seek passionately to live it out in our daily lives. . . .

Let us move now from the practical *how* to the theoretical *why: Why should we love our enemies?* The first reason is fairly obvious. Returning hate for hate multiplies hate, adding deeper darkness to a night already devoid of stars. . . .

Another reason why we must love our enemies is that hate scars the soul and distorts the personality. . . .

A third reason why we should love our enemies is that love is the only force capable of transforming an enemy into a friend. We never get rid of an enemy by meeting hate with hate; we get rid of an enemy by getting rid of enmity. By its very nature, hate destroys and tears down; by its very nature, love creates and builds up. Love transforms with redemptive power.

Lincoln tried love and left for all history a magnificent drama of reconciliation. When he was campaigning for the presidency one of his arch-enemies was a man named Stanton. For some reason Stanton hated Lincoln. He used every ounce of his energy to degrade him in the eyes of the public. So deep rooted was Stanton's hate for Lincoln that he uttered unkind words about his physical appearance, and sought to embarrass him at every point with the bitterest diatribes. But in spite of this Lincoln was elected President of the United States.

Then came the period when he had to select his cabinet which would consist of the persons who would be his most intimate associates in implementing his program. He started choosing men here and there for the various secretaryships. The day finally came for Lincoln to select a man to fill the all-important post of Secretary of War. Can you imagine whom Lincoln chose to fill this post? None other than the man named Stanton. There was an imme-

Love even for enemies is the key to the solution of the problems of our world. Jesus is not an impractical idealist: he is the practical realist.

We never get rid of an enemy by meeting hate with hate; we get rid of an enemy by getting rid of enmity. By its very nature, hate destroys and tears down; by its very nature, love creates and builds up. Love transforms with redemptive power.

diate uproar in the inner circle when the news began to spread. Adviser after adviser was heard saying, "Mr. President, you are making a mistake. Do you know this man Stanton? Are you familiar with all of the ugly things he said about you? He is your enemy. He will seek to sabotage your program. Have you thought this through, Mr. President?" Mr. Lincoln's answer was terse and to the point: "Yes, I know Mr. Stanton. I am aware of all the terrible things he has said about me. But after looking over the nation, I find he is the best man for the job."

So Stanton became Abraham Lincoln's Secretary of War and rendered an invaluable service to his nation and his President. Not many years later Lincoln was assassinated. Many laudable things were said about him. Even today millions of people still adore him as the greatest of all Americans. H. G. Wells selected him as one of the six great men of history. But of all the great statements made about Abraham Lincoln, the words of Stanton remain among the greatest. Standing near the dead body of the man he once hated, Stanton referred to him as one of the greatest men that ever lived and said "he now belongs to the ages."

If Lincoln had hated Stanton both men would have gone to their graves as bitter enemies. But through the power of love Lincoln transformed an enemy into a friend. It was this same attitude that made it possible for Lincoln to speak a kind word about the South during the Civil War, when feeling was most bitter. Asked by a shocked bystander how he could do this, Lincoln said, "Madam, do I not destroy my enemies when I make them my friends?" This is the power of redemptive love.

We must hasten to say that these are not the ultimate reasons why we should love our enemies. An even more basic reason why we are commanded to love is expressed explicitly in Jesus' words, "Love your enemies . . . *that ye may be children of your Father which is in heaven*." We are called to this difficult task in order to realize a unique relationship with God. We are potential sons of God. Through love that potentiality becomes actuality. We must love our enemies, because only by loving them can we know God and experience the beauty of his holiness. . . .

Of course, this is not *practical*. Life is a matter of getting even, of hitting back, of dog eat dog. Am I saying that Jesus commands us to love those who hurt and oppress us? Do I sound like most preachers—idealistic and impractical? Maybe in some distant Utopia, you say, that idea will work, but not in the hard, cold world in which we live.

We must love our enemies, because only by loving them can we know God and experience the beauty of his holiness. . . .

My friends, we have followed the so-called practical way for too long a time now, and it has led inexorably to deeper confusion and chaos. Time is cluttered with the wreckage of communities which surrendered to hatred and violence. For the salvation of our nation and the salvation of mankind, we must follow another way. This does not mean that we abandon our righteous efforts. With every ounce of our energy we must continue to rid this nation of the incubus of segregation. But we shall not in the process relinquish our privilege and our obligation to love. While abhorring segregation, we shall love the segregationist. This is the only way to create the beloved community.

To our most bitter opponents we say: "We shall match your capacity to inflict suffering by our capacity to endure suffering. We shall meet your physical force with soul force. Do to us what you will, and we shall continue to love you. We cannot in all good conscience obey your unjust laws, because non-co-operation with evil is as much a moral obligation as is co-operation with good. Throw us in jail, and we shall still love you. Send your hooded perpetrators of violence into our community at the midnight hour and beat us and leave us half dead, and we shall still love you. But be ye assured that we will wear you down by our capacity to suffer. One day we shall win freedom, but not only for ourselves. We shall so appeal to your heart and conscience that we shall win you in the process, and our victory will be a double victory."

Love is the most durable power in the world. This creative force, so beautifully exemplified in the life of our Christ, is the most potent instrument available in mankind's quest for peace and security. Napoleon Bonaparte, the great military genius, looking back over his years of conquest, is reported to have said: "Alexander, Caesar, Charlemagne, and I have built great empires. But upon what did they depend? They depended on force. But centuries ago Jesus started an empire that was built on love, and even to this day millions will die for him." Who can doubt the veracity of these words. The great military leaders of the past have gone, and their empires have crumbled and burned to ashes. But the empire of Jesus, built solidly and majestically on the foundation of love, is still growing. . . .

Jesus is eternally right. History is replete with the bleached bones of nations that refused to listen to him. May we in the twentieth century hear and follow his words—before it is too late. May we solemnly realize that we shall never be true sons of our heavenly Father until we love our enemies and pray for those who persecute us.

Love is the most durable power in the world. This creative force, so beautifully exemplified in the life of our Christ, is the most potent instrument available in mankind's quest for peace and security.

From Martin Luther King, *Strength to Love* (New York: Collins Publishers, 1977), pp. 47–55. Reprinted by arrangement with The Heirs to the Estate of Martin Luther King Jr., c/o Writer's House as agent for the proprietor. Copyright © 1963 by Martin Luther King Jr., copyright renewed 1991 by Coretta Scott King.

QUESTIONS FOR THOUGHT AND DISCUSSION

1. In the opening paragraph, what two criticisms does King cite of Jesus' command to "love your enemies"? Which of the two is the strongest? Why? What is the most prevalent objection to "loving your enemies" in today's world?

2. Of the three answers King gives to the question of why we should love our enemies, which do you find the most persuasive? Why? Which of the three reasons have you seen "fleshed out"? Describe the situation.

3. What is your reaction to the story of Lincoln and Stanton? What risk was Lincoln taking in choosing Stanton as his Secretary of War? Why do you think he took this risk anyway? Do you know an example of "enemies transformed into friends" by love?

4. What is the ultimate reason for loving our enemies, according to King? Is this reason strictly about private spirituality or does it have wider, societal implications? If so, what are they?

5. King says that loving our enemies is both "our privilege and our obligation." How is it a privilege? Can you give examples? How is it an obligation? To whom is this obligation owed?

6. Read the third to last paragraph. How do you feel when you read King's examples of violence and persecution being met with love? In the modern world, where is such love needed? What would be the result if such love were offered instead of hatred or anger?

7. What did Napoleon say distinguished Jesus' empire from those of Alexander, Caesar, Charlemagne, and himself? Why do you think the power of love endures beyond the power of force?

8. How does Martin Luther King Jr.'s position differ from most activists crusading for justice and reform?

FOUR
SLOTH (ACEDIA)
VERSUS HUNGER FOR
RIGHTEOUSNESS

Sloth is the fourth of the seven deadly sins and—contrary to expectations—the fourth sin of the spirit rather than the first sin of the flesh. Its uniqueness lies in the fact that it is a sin of omission rather than commission, the absence of a positive behavior rather than the presence of a negative one. It is the most distinctively modern of the vices (one that was not on the Greek or Roman lists at all), and also the most religious. Whereas most secular people can go a long way toward understanding pride, envy, anger, avarice, gluttony, and lust without any reference to God, to attempt to do so with sloth changes the original meaning altogether.

Sloth is far more than indolence, physical laziness, or a state of couch-potato lethargy ("Nearer, My Couch, to Thee," as The New York Times headlined it). It is a condition of explicitly spiritual dejection that has given up on the pursuit of God, the true, the good, and the beautiful.

To be clearly understood, sloth must be distinguished from idling—a state of carefree lingering that is often admirable, as in friends lingering over a meal or lovers whiling away the hours in delighted enjoyment. In W. H. Davies's famous lines, "What is this life, if full of care, / We have no time to stand and stare?"

Sloth is far more than indolence, physical laziness, or a state of couch-potato lethargy ("Nearer, My Couch, to Thee," as The New York Times *headlined it).*

149

TO STAND AND STARE (OR WHAT SLOTH ISN'T)

"Relaxing is not sloth. The person who never relaxes is not a saint but a fidget."

—Peter Kreeft

By contrast to idling, sloth is a sluggishness of spirit, feeling, mind, and eventually body that grows from a state of dejection over the worthwhileness of spiritual things. It is a "leanness of the soul," a wasting disease that, if left unchecked, can lead to spiritual and even physical death.

PICTURES AND METAPHORS

Medievals spoke of sloth as "the noonday demon" because it was a kind of ennui that haunts people even at midday when there is not even the excuse of shadows. Captured today in such phrases as listlessness of life, anomie, despondency over meaning, moral burnout, directionless wandering, paralysis of will, and blasé boredom, sloth is the modern melancholy that stems from a hatred of all things spiritual that require effort. Sloth, says Chaucer's Parson, will "endure no hardship nor any penance."

Goethe wrote that sloth is the anvil on which all the sins are fashioned. Before him, Dante blamed sloth for the cowardly shrinking and failure of the soul in the presence of high and arduous enterprise—whether the Israelites who would not go up to win the Promised Land with Moses or the company of Aeneas who refused a share in the founding of the Roman republic.

Although sloth may begin as careless indifference to ideals, its final state is one of despair over the possibility of salvation—ultimately a form of spiritual suicide. Thus commentators have always considered the suicide of Judas worse than his betrayal of Jesus because it signaled his terminal despair at repenting and returning to God.

Although sloth may begin as careless indifference to ideals, its final state is one of despair over the possibility of salvation— ultimately a form of spiritual suicide.

SLOTH'S LOSS

"Then, as the LORD our God commanded us, we set out from Horeb and went toward the hill country of the Amorites through all that vast and dreadful desert that you have seen, and so we reached Kadesh Barnea. Then I said to you, 'You have reached the hill country of the Amorites, which the LORD our God is giving us. See, the LORD your God has given you the land. Go up and take possession of it as the LORD, the God of your fathers, told you. Do not be afraid; do not be discouraged.'

"Then all of you came to me and said, 'Let us send men ahead to spy out the land for us and bring back a report about the route we are to take and the towns we will come to.'

"The idea seemed good to me; so I selected twelve of you, one man from each tribe. They left and went up into the hill country, and came to the Valley of Eshcol and explored it. Taking with them some of the fruit of the land, they brought it down to us and reported, 'It is a good land that the LORD our God is giving us.'

"But you were unwilling to go up; you rebelled against the command of the LORD your God. You grumbled in your tents and said, 'The LORD hates us; so he brought us out of Egypt to deliver us into the hands of the Amorites to destroy us. Where can we go? Our brothers have made us lose heart. They say, 'The people are stronger and taller than we are; the cities are large, with walls up to the sky. We even saw the Anakites there.'

"Then I said to you, 'Do not be terrified; do not be afraid of them. The LORD your God, who is going before you, will fight for you, as he did for you in Egypt, before your very eyes, and in the desert. There you saw how the LORD your God carried you, as a father carries his son, all the way you went until you reached this place.'

"In spite of this, you did not trust in the LORD your God, who went ahead of you on your journey, in fire by night and in a cloud by day, to search out places for you to camp and to show you the way you should go.

"When the LORD heard what you said, he was angry and solemnly swore: 'Not a man of this evil generation shall see the good land I swore to give your forefathers, except Caleb son of Jephunneh. He will see it, and I will give him and his descendants the land he set his feet on, because he followed the LORD wholeheartedly.'"

—Moses, in Deuteronomy 1:19-36

PRACTICAL APPLICATIONS

Sloth is so much the climate of the modern age that it is hard to recognize it as a deadly sin. It is simply the underlying condition of a secular era.

Dante recognized that sloth was peculiarly apt to overcome people in midlife. Under the pressure of the important and the tiring, the middle-aged and old are apt to forget the highest affairs of life and, above all, to ignore spiritual aspirations. "Sloth," as Evelyn Waugh warned, "is not primarily the temptation of the young."

THE BANE OF BOREDOM

"In the United States the difficulties are not a Minotaur or a dragon—not imprisonment, hard labor, death, government harassment, and censorship—but cupidity, boredom, sloppiness, indifference. Not the

> acts of a mighty, all-pervading, repressive government but the failure of a listless public to make use of the freedom that is its birthright."
>
> —Aleksandr Solzhenitsyn, Harvard Commencement address, 1978

Yet, in the modern world, the young are not immune. Theirs is often the reflected attitude of the prevailing art and media. Because art and literature must have subjects "worthy" of exploration and depiction, the trend has been to turn sloth from vice to virtue, holding it forth as a deserving theme in drama, painting, and novels. The irony then of our sloth-infected world is its continued effort to find meaning in its own meaninglessness. The monotonous, uninteresting attitude of sloth is now the "pathos of emptiness" or the "drama of despair."

The irony then of our sloth-infected world is its continued effort to find meaning in its own meaninglessness.

In the popular realm, music is often the conveyer of this cool, aloof, indifference to real joy or real tragedy. The widespread embracing of sloth is perhaps captured best in the pervasive refrain of adolescents: "Whatever."

❧ *Blaise Pascal* ❧

Blaise Pascal (1623–1662) is among the most eminent Christian and Western thinkers—a scientist, mathematician, and Christian apologist. Born in Clermont-Ferrand, France, he was brought up by his father after his mother died when he was four years old. Pascal showed great precociousness from the earliest age, taking part in various mathematical experiments, including those that led to the invention of the barometer and the hydraulic press. He is sometimes also called "the grandfather of the computer" because of his invention of the first calculating machine.

In 1645 Pascal came in contact with the Jansenists, and experienced his "first conversion." They were a slightly maverick, almost semi-Protestant, Catholic community whose convent at Port Royal his sister Jacqueline joined. His second and "definitive conversion" was on November 23, 1654, when he experienced, as he writes, the "God of Abraham, the God of Isaac, the God of Jacob, and not of philosophers and men of science." A record of this deep experience was discovered after his death—he had sewn it into his shirt and had worn it next to him during his final years.

Pascal's greatest work is his Pensées *(thoughts). Never finished, or even begun as a normal book, it is his collected thoughts for a grand vindication of the Christian faith against the influence of the libertines of his day. His style is brilliant, but Pascal's true force comes from the wealth of his personal experience and his philosophical and psychological insights. Incomplete though it is,* Pensées *has become a Western classic and a great Christian apology that has led many searchers to faith in Christ. This reading from the work, an attack on sloth in practice, demonstrates why.*

His style is brilliant, but Pascal's true force comes from the wealth of his personal experience and his philosophical and psychological insights.

PENSÉES

The immortality of the soul is something of such vital importance to us, affecting us so deeply, that one must have lost all feeling not to care about knowing the facts of the matter. All our actions and thoughts must follow such different paths, according to whether there is hope of eternal blessings or not, that the only possible way of acting with sense and judgment is to decide our course in the light of this point, which ought to be our ultimate objective.

Thus our chief interest and chief duty is to seek enlightenment on this subject, on which all our conduct depends. And that is why, amongst those who are not convinced, I make an absolute distinction between those who strive with all their might to learn and those who live without troubling themselves or thinking about it.

I can feel nothing but compassion for those who sincerely lament their doubt, who regard it as the ultimate misfortune, and who, sparing no effort to escape from it, make their search their principal and most serious business.

But as for those who spend their lives without a thought for this final end of life and who, solely because they do not find within themselves the light of conviction, neglect to look elsewhere, and to examine thoroughly whether this opinion is one of those which people accept out of credulous simplicity or one of those which, though obscure in themselves, none the less have a most solid and unshakable foundation: as for them, I view them very differently.

This negligence in a matter where they themselves, their eternity, their all are at stake, fills me more with irritation than pity; it astounds and appalls me; it seems quite monstrous to me. I do not say this prompted by the pious zeal of spiritual devotion. I mean on the contrary that we ought to have this feeling from principles of human interest and self-esteem. For that we need only see what the least enlightened see.

I make an absolute distinction between those who strive with all their might to learn and those who live without troubling themselves or thinking about it.

This negligence in a matter where they themselves, their eternity, their all are at stake, fills me more with irritation than pity; it astounds and appalls me; it seems quite monstrous to me.

One needs no great sublimity of soul to realize that in this life there is no true and solid satisfaction, that all our pleasures are mere vanity, that our afflictions are infinite, and finally that death which threatens us at every moment must in a few years infallibly face us with the inescapable and appalling alternative of being annihilated or wretched throughout eternity.

Nothing could be more real, or more dreadful than that. Let us put on as bold a face as we like: that is the end awaiting the world's most illustrious life. Let us ponder these things, and then say whether it is not beyond doubt that the only good thing in this life is the hope of another life, that we become happy only as we come nearer to it, and that, just as no more unhappiness awaits those who have been quite certain of eternity, so there is no happiness for those who have no inkling of it.

It is therefore quite certainly a great evil to have such doubts, but it is at least an indispensable obligation to seek when one does thus doubt; so the doubter who does not seek is at the same time very unhappy and very wrong. If in addition he feels a calm satisfaction, which he openly professes, and even regards as a reason for joy and vanity, I can find no terms to describe so extravagant a creature.

What can give rise to such feelings? What reason for joy can be found in the expectation of nothing but helpless wretchedness? What reason for vanity in being plunged into impenetrable darkness? And how can such an argument as this occur to a reasonable man?

'I do not know who put me into the world, nor what the world is, nor what I am myself. I am terribly ignorant about everything. I do not know what my body is, or my senses, or my soul, or even that part of me which thinks what I am saying, which reflects about everything and about itself, and does not know itself any better than it knows anything else.

I am terribly ignorant about everything. I do not know what my body is, or my senses, or my soul, or even that part of me which thinks what I am saying, which reflects about everything and about itself, and does not know itself any better than it knows anything else.

'I see the terrifying spaces of the universe hemming me in, and I find myself attached to one corner of this vast expanse without knowing why I have been put in this place rather than that, or why the brief span of life allotted to me should be assigned to one moment rather than another of all the eternity which went before me and all that which will come after me. I see only infinity on every side, hemming me in like an atom or like the shadow of a fleeting instant. All I know is that I must soon die, but what I know least about is this very death which I cannot evade.

'Just as I do not know whence I come, so I do not know whither I am going. All I know is that when I leave this world I shall fall for ever into nothingness or into the hands of a wrathful God, but I do not know which of these two states is to be my eternal lot. Such is my state, full of weakness and uncertainty. And my conclusion from all this is that I must pass my days without a thought of seeking what is to happen to me. Perhaps I might find some enlightenment in my doubts, but I do not want to take the trouble, nor take a step to look for it: and afterwards, as I sneer at those who are striving to this end — (whatever certainty they have should arouse despair rather than vanity) — I will go without fear or foresight to face so momentous an event, and allow myself to be carried off limply to my death, uncertain of my future state for all eternity.'

Who would wish to have as his friend a man who argued like that? Who would choose him from among others as a confidant in his affairs? Who would resort to him in adversity? To what use in life could he possibly be turned? . . .

Nothing is so important to man as his state: nothing more fearful than eternity. Thus the fact that there exist men who are indifferent to the loss of their being and the peril of an eternity of wretchedness is against nature. With everything else they are quite different; they fear the most trifling things, foresee and feel them; and the same man who spends so many days and nights in fury and despair at losing some office or at some imaginary affront to his honor is the very one who knows that he is going to lose everything through death but feels neither anxiety nor emotion. It is a monstrous thing to see one and the same heart at once so sensitive to minor things and so strangely insensitive to the greatest. It is an incomprehensible spell, a supernatural torpor that points to an omnipotent power as its cause.

Nothing is so important to man as his state: nothing more fearful than eternity.

From *Pensées* by Blaise Pascal, translated by A. J. Krailsheimer (Penguin Classics, 1966). Copyright © 1966 by A. J. Krailsheimer. Reproduced by permission of Penguin Books Ltd.

QUESTIONS FOR THOUGHT AND DISCUSSION

1. What is the point of Pascal's opening paragraph? Why do you agree or disagree? How does modern culture measure against Pascal's standard of having "lost all feeling"? What methods do we use today to avoid thinking seriously about "the immortality of the soul"?

2. How does Pascal feel about those who are negligent in matters of eternity? If, as Pascal argues, "human interest" and "self-esteem" ought to naturally provoke consideration of immortality, why is such consideration so lacking in our time?

3. Pascal assumes that most people recognize that there is no "true and solid satisfaction" in this life, that pleasures are "vanity" and afflictions

"infinite." In other words, they know life is not complete in and of itself. Is this sentiment still true today? Why or why not? If not, how does this affect people's thoughts about eternity?

4. What do you think of Pascal's four-paragraph reflection on the vain individual, beginning, "I do not know who put me into the world"? Where have you encountered people with a similar outlook? Which parts of the reflection describe your current or past state of mind? How do you feel in reading this section?

5. What do most secular people you know believe about eternity? Do they acknowledge, as Pascal argues, only two choices: "nothingness" or the wrath of God? On what are their beliefs concerning eternity based?

6. What irony does Pascal highlight in the final paragraph? What modern inventions or institutions contribute to this reversal of fears and priorities? To what does Pascal finally attribute this "monstrous thing"? Why do you agree or disagree?

7. Bringing Pascal's discussion to bear on the modern world, what is the link between secularity (the attitude that the visible world is the only world) and the sloth Pascal describes? What might the antidote be?

❧ *Søren Kierkegaard* ❧

Søren Aabye Kierkegaard (1813–1855) was a leading Christian thinker, modern philosopher, and writer. The son of a wealthy hosier who was a devout Lutheran, he lived almost his entire life in Copenhagen. After a secluded and unhappy childhood, Kierkegaard gave his university years to idleness and amusements. A year later he became engaged to Regina Olsen, but broke it off in a trauma that scarred him for life. From 1843, when he published his first book Either-Or, *until his death at forty-two, he published a series of books that put him in the first rank of modern philosophers.*

Kierkegaard was a profoundly personal thinker who reacted fiercely to both the stuffiness and compromises of the Danish Established Church and to the abstractions of Hegel's fashionable philosophy. Against them both he argued passionately for his own "existential" thinking—viewing human beings as ultimately existing before God.

Kierkegaard has been deeply influential on twentieth-century theologians and philosophers, though his passionately stated positions have often been distorted (for example, his famous rejection of purely speculative systems of thought: "Truth is subjectivity"). His attack on sloth and his "passion for passion" comes through clearly in the following passage.

Kierkegaard was a profoundly personal thinker who reacted fiercely to both the stuffiness and compromises of the Danish Established Church and to the abstractions of Hegel's fashionable philosophy.

ODE TO THE SLUGGARD
The sluggard says, "There is a lion in the road,
　a fierce lion roaming the streets!"
As a door turns on its hinges,
　so a sluggard turns on his bed.
The sluggard buries his hand in the dish;
　he is too lazy to bring it back to his mouth.
The sluggard is wiser in his own eyes
　than seven men who answer discreetly.

—Proverbs 26:13-16

ON THE WICKEDNESS OF THE AGE

Let others complain that the age is wicked; my complaint is that it is wretched, for it lacks passion. Men's thoughts are thin and flimsy like lace, they are themselves pitiable like the lacemakers. The thoughts of their hearts are too paltry to be sinful. For a worm it might be regarded as a sin to harbor such thoughts, but not for a being made in the image of God. Their lusts are dull and sluggish, their passions sleepy. They do their duty, these shopkeeping souls, but they clip the coin a trifle . . . they think that even if the Lord keeps ever so careful a set of books, they may still cheat Him a little. Out upon them! This is the reason my soul always turns back to the Old Testament and to Shakespeare. I feel that those who speak there are at least human beings; they hate, they love, they murder their enemies and curse their descendants throughout all generations, they sin.

Men's thoughts are thin and flimsy like lace, they are themselves pitiable like the lacemakers. The thoughts of their hearts are too paltry to be sinful.

From Søren Kierkegaard, *A Kierkegaard Anthology,* Robert Bretall, ed. (New York: Modern Library, 1959), p. 33.

THE ART OF NOTHINGNESS

"The expression that there is nothing to express, nothing with which to express, nothing from which to express, no power to express, no desire to express, together with the obligation to express."

—Samuel Beckett's artistic creed

QUESTIONS FOR THOUGHT AND DISCUSSION

1. What is Kierkegaard's chief complaint against his age? In light of this reading, how do you think he would define "passion"?

2. What does Kierkegaard mean by "shopkeeping souls"? What is their attitude toward God? How do they differ from the red-blooded human beings in the Bible and Shakespeare?

3. How do the author's comments about the passionless nineteenth century apply to us nearly two centuries later? In what sectors today do you find the most passion? The most sloth? Why do you think this is the case?

4. When have you felt the urge, like Kierkegaard, to shake someone, or a group, from lethargy? What makes this urge so strong?

5. After reading this passage, do you think Kierkegaard would consider sloth a "deadly sin"? Why or why not? How about you?

❧ *Dorothy L. Sayers* ❧

Dorothy Leigh Sayers (1893–1957) was an English scholar, essayist, translator, mystery writer, and Christian apologist. Born in Oxford, she also attended the university and was in the first group of women to be granted a degree. Although a brilliant medievalist, seen later in her translations of Dante, she was also very practical and worked for many years at an advertising agency in London. ("It pays to advertise" was a maxim she coined.)

Sayers is best known for her perennially popular detective novels—most featuring the urbane, aristocratic sleuth Lord Peter Wimsey. She also wrote successful plays for the radio, such as The Man Born to Be King, *and was a*

*widely read essayist and church apologist. Her creativity was always matched by
her sense of humor, her gift of language, and her brilliant intellect. A friend of such
other Christian writers as G. K. Chesterton, C. S. Lewis, and J. R. R. Tolkien, she
was a large, impressive woman with a deep voice who enjoyed composing crossword puzzles and riding motorcycles.*

*It has been said that the older Sayers grew, the more central her faith became
to her life. Her own wry way of saying it was to quote a schoolboy who had written, "And then there was Miss Dorothy Sayers who turned from a life of crime to
join the Church of England." The following passage is from her famous speech-
become-book:* The Other Six Deadly Sins.

NOT WORTH THE TROUBLE

"There are no reasons for going on living, but no more are there any reasons for dying."

—Jacques Rigaut, a writer whose suicide shocked Paris in 1929, the year Samuel Becket
arrived there

"Life is not worth the trouble of leaving it."

—Jacques Rigaut

THE OTHER SIX DEADLY SINS

The sixth Deadly Sin is named by the Church *Acedia* or *Sloth*. In the world it
calls itself Tolerance; but in hell it is called Despair. It is the accomplice of the
other sins and their worst punishment. It is the sin which believes in nothing,
cares for nothing, seeks to know nothing, interferes with nothing, enjoys noth-
ing, loves nothing, hates nothing, finds purpose in nothing, lives for nothing,
and only remains alive because there is nothing it would die for. We have
known it far too well for many years. The only thing perhaps that we have not
known about it is that it is mortal sin. . . .

First, it is one of the favorite tricks of this Sin to dissemble itself under
cover of a whiffling activity of body. We think that if we are busily rushing
about and doing things, we cannot be suffering from Sloth. And besides, violent activity seems to offer an escape from the horrors of Sloth. So the other sins
hasten to provide a cloak for Sloth: Gluttony offers a whirl of dancing, dining,
sports, and dashing very fast from place to place to gape at beauty-spots; which
when we get to them, we defile with vulgarity and waste. Covetousness rakes
us out of bed at an early hour, in order that we may put pep and hustle into

*It is the sin which
believes in nothing, cares
for nothing, seeks to know
nothing, interferes with
nothing, enjoys nothing,
loves nothing, hates
nothing, finds purpose in
nothing, lives for nothing,
and only remains alive
because there is nothing
it would die for.*

our business; Envy sets us to gossip and scandal, to writing cantankerous letters to the papers, and to the unearthing of secrets and the scavenging of dustbins; Wrath provides (very ingeniously) the argument that the only fitting activity in a world so full of evildoers and evil demons is to curse loudly and incessantly. . . .

Let us take particular notice of the empty brain. Here Sloth is in a conspiracy with Envy to prevent people from thinking. Sloth persuades us that stupidity is not our sin, but our misfortune; while Envy at the same time persuades us that intelligence is despicable—a dusty, highbrow, and commercially useless thing.

Let us take particular notice of the empty brain. Here Sloth is in a conspiracy with Envy to prevent people from thinking.

From Dorothy L. Sayers, *The Other Six Deadly Sins* (London: Methuen Ltd, 1943). © 1943 by Dorothy L. Sayers. Reproduced by permission of David Higham Associates Limited.

MIGHT AS WELL LIVE

"Razors pain you;
Rivers are damp;
Acids stain you;
And drugs cause cramp.
Guns aren't lawful;
Nooses give;
Gas smells awful;
You might as well live."

—"Résumé," by Dorothy Parker

QUESTIONS FOR THOUGHT AND DISCUSSION

1. In your own words, how does Sayers depict sloth in the first paragraph? Which characteristic of sloth do you think most is dangerous? Why? Do you agree with Sayers that sloth is the sin that "believes in nothing"? Why is this so?

2. Sloth remains alive, says Sayers, because "there is nothing it would die for." How widespread is this sentiment in the modern world? Where have you observed it? In contrast, where have you seen a willingness to die for a conviction or cause, either in the past or present? To what do you attribute the difference?

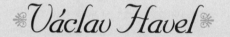

3. How does sloth often disguise itself? How might "violent activity" offer an escape from sloth? Of the various sins which mask sloth, which do you find most tempting? How are such masks perpetuated by institutions in our day?

4. What is the conspiracy between sloth and envy against intelligence? Where have you seen this attack at work? What is the best counter for the celebration of the "empty brain"?

Václav Havel

At the time of this writing, Václav Havel (born 1936) is president of the Czech Republic and one of Europe's foremost playwrights and essayists. Founder and leader of the Charter 77 dissident movement, he was prominent in the Eastern European revolution of 1989 and became the first president of free Czechoslovakia.

Born the son of a civil engineer, Havel was thwarted in gaining higher education for political reasons. Joining a Prague theatre as a stagehand in the 1950s, he worked his way up and became a distinguished playwright. His international stature also derives from his long involvement in the human rights movement and his authorship of many essays on the nature of totalitarianism, including his famous "Open Letter to Dr. Husak." He is a winner of Europe's prestigious Erasmus Award.

Havel was twice sentenced to prison (once for four and one-half years), and while there was allowed to write to his wife, Olga, once a week. He used the occasion for profound reflections on life and modern society. The following is from number 96 in a series of 144 letters written between 1979 and 1983.

ONE REAL QUESTION

"There is but one truly serious philosophical problem, and that is suicide. Judging whether life is worth living amounts to answering the fundamental question of philosophy. . . . I see many people die because they judge that life is not worth living. I see others paradoxically getting killed for the ideas or illusions that

> give them a reason for living (what is called a reason for living is an excellent reason for dying). I therefore conclude that the meaning of life is the most urgent of questions."
> —Albert Camus, *The Myth of Sisyphus*

LETTERS TO OLGA

October 3, 1981

Dear Olga,

In recent years I've met several intelligent and decent people who were very clearly and to my mind, very tragically, marked by their fate: they became bitter, misanthropic world-haters who lost faith in everything. Quite separately, they managed to persuade themselves that people are selfish, evil, and untrustworthy, that it makes no sense to help anyone, to try to achieve anything or rectify anything, that all moral principles, higher aims, and suprapersonal ideals are naively utopian, and that one must accept the world "as it is" — which is to say unalterably bad—and behave accordingly. And that means looking out for no one but oneself and living the rest of one's life as quietly and inconspicuously as possible.

In certain extreme circumstances it is by no means difficult to succumb to this philosophy of life. Nevertheless I think that giving up on life—and this philosophy is an expression of that attitude—is one of the saddest forms of human downfall. Because it is a descent into regions where life really does lose its meaning.

Indeed, it is not the authors of absurd plays or pessimistic poems, nor the suicides, nor people constantly afflicted by anger, boredom, anxiety, and despair, nor the alcoholics and drug addicts, who have, in the deepest sense, lost their grip on the meaning of life and become "nonbelievers": it is people who are apathetic. (By the way, in the last couple of years I've met a lot of eccentrics, miserable and desperate men, adventurers, perverts, Pollyannas, and of course a wide assortment of greater and lesser scoundrels, but not many who are apathetic in the sense I mean. Such men do not remain for long in places like this. Still, some here are making a successful bid to join those ranks—men with a more intellectual bent, or who are "decent men who have tripped up.")

Resignation, like faith, can be deliberate or unpremeditated. If it is deliberate, then the tinge of bad conscience that customarily clings to it requires it to be justified and defended extensively (before whom? why?) by referring to

Quite separately, they managed to persuade themselves that people are selfish, evil, and untrustworthy, that it makes no sense to help anyone, to try to achieve anything or rectify anything, that all moral principles, higher aims, and suprapersonal ideals are naively utopian, and that one must accept the world "as it is"—which is to say unalterably bad—and behave accordingly.

the evil of the world and the incorrigibility of that evil. The important thing to note here, of course, is that it was not the evil of the world that ultimately led the person to give up, but rather his own resignation that led him to the theory about the evil of the world. However "unbelievers" may deny it, the existential choice always comes first, and only then is it followed by the dead-end, pessimistic picture of the world that is meant to justify that choice. And the more resolutely one is determined to say to hell with everything, the more ferociously one clings to apocalyptic theories. To put it even less charitably: "unbelievers" insist on the incorrigible evil of the world so obstinately chiefly to justify committing some of those evils themselves. (Notice that whenever someone starts carrying on about how corrupt everything around him is, it is usually a clear signal that he is preparing to do something rather nasty himself.)

On a certain level, of course, we may observe yet another process: if this "evil world" is described first as something unfortunate but given, as a regrettable status quo, as a "reality" that we have no choice but to come to terms with, then gradually—while the "unbeliever" is learning to live in this evil world, as he grows accustomed to it and establishes himself in it—the reality that was originally regrettable begins, as he conceives it, to change imperceptibly into one that is "not as bad as it could be," certainly better than the eventual state of uncertainty created by "utopian" efforts to transform it, until at last the status quo he once condemned becomes, in essence, an ideal. And thus we arrive at the sad state of affairs wherein the ruthless critic of the world is indiscernibly transformed into its defender, the "uncommitted" theoretician of its immutability becomes an active opponent of changing it, the skeptical outsider becomes a common reactionary.

Today I understand, perhaps better than I ever did before, that one can become embittered. The temptation of Nothingness is enormous and omnipresent, and it has more and more to rest its case on, more to appeal to. Against it, man stands alone, weak and poorly armed, his position worse than ever before in history. And yet I am convinced that there is nothing in this vale of tears that, of itself, can rob man of hope, faith, and the meaning of life. He loses these things only when he himself falters, when he yields to the temptations of Nothingness.

To sum up: I think that resignation, indifference, the hardening of the heart, and laziness of the spirit are dimensions of a genuine "unbelief" and a genuine "loss of meaning." The person who has fallen into that state not only ceases to ask himself what meaning life has, he no longer even spontaneously

Resignation, like faith, can be deliberate or unpremeditated.

The temptation of Nothingness is enormous and omnipresent, and it has more and more to rest its case on, more to appeal to.

responds to the question existentially by living for something—simply because he must, because it won't let him alone, because he is the way he is. The person who has completely lost all sense of the meaning of life is merely vegetating and doesn't mind it; he lives like a parasite and doesn't mind it; he is entirely absorbed in the problem of his own metabolism and essentially nothing beyond that interests him: other people, society, the world, Being— for him they are all simply things to be either consumed or avoided, or turned into a comfortable place to make his bed.

Everything meaningful in life, though it may assume the most dramatic form of questioning and doubting, is distinguished by a certain transcendence of individual human existence—beyond the limits of mere "self-care"— toward other people, toward society, toward the world. Only by looking "outward," by caring for things that, in terms of pure survival, he needn't bother with at all, by constantly asking himself all sorts of questions, and by throwing himself over and over again into the tumult of the world, with the intention of making his voice count—only thus does one really become a person, a creator of the "order of the spirit," a being capable of a miracle: the re-creation of the world. To give up on any form of transcending oneself means, de facto, to give up on one's own human existence and to be contented with belonging to the animal kingdom.

The tragedy of modern man is not that he knows less and less about the meaning of his own life, but that it bothers him less and less.

The tragedy of modern man is not that he knows less and less about the meaning of his own life, but that it bothers him less and less.

When my suffering reached a peak yesterday (I don't mean the pain in my backside, but in my soul) and my decision to write you a letter full of bitter reproaches ripened (for more than two weeks I had not had a single line, from you or anyone else), the good Lord clearly couldn't bear it any longer, he relented and brought down upon my bed a whole armful of correspondence and newspapers. . . . I'm grateful to Ivan for both his letters about physics. I don't completely understand everything on the first reading, but I understand the general sense of his explanation. (I may return to this in my next letter, but for the time being a brief remark: I understand that it is possible to refute the different ways in which something can be explained, and I'm always delighted when it happens. But I don't see how you can refute the conviction that "everything is, somehow," that Being has an order. The realism of that conviction is something so general and vague that it must be utterly immune to criticism! Every proof that Being does not behave as expected can be dismissed by referring to a higher law, inaccessible to us in the same way that our world is inaccessible to two-dimensional beings. And such an assumption can neither be confirmed, nor refuted!)

What can I say about my state? The high temperatures are over, I'm slowly healing; so far, it still hurts a lot; I suffer especially when I have to use my backside. I think it will be sometime yet before I'm completely well.

Greetings to all friends and those close to me.

I kiss you, Vasek

WRITE MORE OFTEN!

WRITE MORE DETAILS!

WRITE MORE!

From *Letters to Olga: June 1979–September 1982* by Václav Havel, translated by Paul Wilson (London: Faber and Faber, 1988, 1990), pp. 235–238. Translation © 1988 by Paul Wilson. © 1983 by Václav Havel. Reprinted by permission of Alfred A. Knopf, Inc.

CONQUERING SLOTH

"One who is slack in his work is brother to one who destroys."

—Proverbs 18:9

"I may lose battles, but no one will ever see me lose minutes, either by over-confidence or sloth."

—Napoleon Bonaparte

QUESTIONS FOR THOUGHT AND DISCUSSION

1. In the first paragraph, Havel describes intelligent people he's met who have been "marked by their fate." What does he mean by this? What traits do they share? Do you recognize this type of person? How would you describe similar people you know?

2. Do you agree with Havel that it is those who are "apathetic" rather than those who are angry, despairing, "alcoholics and drug addicts" who have truly become "nonbelievers" and lost their grip on the meaning of life? How so? What makes the critical difference?

3. What does Havel mean when he says, "the existential choice always comes first"? Why do "unbelievers" cling so obstinately to their belief in

the "incorrigible evil of the world," according to Havel? Where have you seen this connection played out?

4. How is "any form of transcending oneself" crucial to meaning and overcoming sloth? What does complete self-absorption lead to? Why?

5. What does Havel say is the tragedy of modern man? Do you agree? If so, why do you think this is the case? What societal factors of our age contribute to this apathy about eternal things? What forces work against this apathy?

THE COUNTERPOINT TO SLOTH:
Blessed Are Those Who Hunger for Righteousness

The counterpoint to the spiritual lassitude of sloth is the passionate hungering after righteousness that is the soul of seeking. In Jesus' words, "Blessed are those who hunger and thirst for righteousness, for they shall be satisfied."

As Peter Kreeft points out, such hungering is even easier than faith: "No, something even less than faith will do. Faith is finding, but mere seeking overcomes sloth. For seeking becomes finding, and finding becomes joy, and joy overcomes sloth."

HUNGER SATISFIED

Because no one but God is self-sufficient, everything in creation has hunger— whether for food, for meaning, or for love. To hunger and thirst for whatever fulfills is right and appropriate. And the existence of those things which do satisfy has been for many an indication of God's existence and His love for the creation. The Jewish philosopher and convert to Christ, Simone Weil, wrote of a powerful moment on her journey to faith, "The conviction that had come to me was that when one hungers for bread one does not receive stones."

Second only to satisfaction with what is right and true is dissatisfaction with everything less than that. Often, the endless search for inner satisfaction through the wilds of materialism, adrenaline fixes, sex, or false spirituality is the jump-start of the hunger for righteousness (that which is right). It can be a sloth-rousing, active desire that will not rest until it is satisfied.

Because no one but God is self-sufficient, everything in creation has hunger— whether for food, for meaning, or for love. To hunger and thirst for whatever fulfills is right and appropriate.

THE THIRSTY SOUL

O God, you are my God,
    earnestly I seek you;
my soul thirsts for you,
    my body longs for you,

in a dry and weary land
    where there is no water.
I have seen you in the sanctuary and beheld your power and your glory.
Because your love is better than life, my lips will glorify you.
I will praise you as long as I live, and in your name I will lift up my hands.
My soul will be satisfied as with the richest of foods;
    with singing lips my mouth will praise you.
On my bed I remember you;
    I think of you through the watches of the night.
Because you are my help,
    I sing in the shadow of your wings.
My soul clings to you;
    your right hand upholds me.

—Psalm 63:1-8

John Donne (1572–1631) was a great poet as well as a lawyer, minister, and the Dean of St. Paul's Cathedral, London. A distant relative of Sir Thomas More, he was a graduate of Oxford, was widely traveled, and was a popular Court preacher. Donne's early poetry was largely secular; his religious poetry was written in his middle years. Both were vigorous and dramatic, blending passion and argument. The following poem, the most famous of his nineteen "holy sonnets" written around 1609, expresses his intense desire for God in language that is both surprising and feminine.

HOLY SONNET

Batter my heart, three-person'd God, for you
As yet but knock, breathe, shine, and seek to mend;
That I may rise and stand, o'erthrow me, and bend

Your force to break, blow, burn, and make me new.
I, like an usurp'd town to'another due,
Labor to'admit you, but oh, to no end;
Reason, your viceroy in me, me should defend,
But is captiv'd, and proves weak or untrue.
Yet dearly'I love you, and would be lov'd fain,
But am betroth'd unto your enemy;
Divorce me,'untie or break that knot again,
Take me to you, imprison me, for I,
Except you'enthrall me, never shall be free,
Nor ever chaste, except you ravish me.

First published 1633.

QUESTIONS FOR THOUGHT AND DISCUSSION

1. Why do you think John Donne uses such masculine and savage images of passion for God (the ransack of a city, and the ravishing of a woman) and such feminine, receptive images for himself?
2. Do you find these images helpful or not? Which is the most powerful to you?
3. How is Donne's imagery and poetry a counterpoint to sloth? How does it destroy the notion that "hunger for righteousness" is a proper, pious, straight-laced notion? What image of such hunger emerges instead?

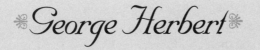

George Herbert (1593–1633) was a poet and Anglican minister. Educated at Trinity College, Cambridge, he was a great orator who served as minister to an obscure country parish instead of pursuing other, more lucrative avenues. His older brother, Lord Herbert of Cherbury, was the forerunner of the Deists, but George Herbert was a man of deep Christian devotion and orthodoxy. He is in the first rank of devotional poets and hymn writers.

Herbert's celebrated poem "Love" has been cherished by many people. It was instrumental, for example, in the conversion of Simone Weil, the French Jewish philosopher whom T. S. Eliot described as "a genius akin to a saint," and Albert Camus, called "the only great spirit of our time." From the age of fourteen onward, Weil had suffered from terrible psychosomatic headaches linked to her sense of universal injustice. When the headaches were at their worst, she would recite the poem and listen to Gregorian music. Slowly, she said later, she moved from a love of the poem's beauty to the intensity of its prayer to the reality of its truth. Finally she felt a presence "more personal, more certain, and more real than that of any human being. . . . Christ himself came down and took possession of me."

Finally she felt a presence "more personal, more certain, and more real than that of any human being. . . . Christ himself came down and took possession of me."

LOVE (III)

Love bade me welcome: yet my soul drew back,
    Guiltie of dust and sinne.
But quick-ey'd Love, observing me grow slack
    From my first entrance in,
Drew nearer to me, sweetly questioning,
    If I lack'd any thing.
A guest, I answer'd, worthy to be here:
    Love said, You shall be he.
I the unkinde, ungratefull? Ah my deare,
    I cannot look on thee.
Love took my hand, and smiling did reply,
    Who made the eyes but I?
Truth Lord, but I have marr'd them: let my shame
    Go where it doth deserve.
And know you not, sayes Love, who bore the blame?
    My deare, then I will serve.
You must sit down, sayes Love, and taste my meat:
    So I did seat and eat.

From George Herbert, *The Poems of George Herbert* (London: Oxford University Press, 1961), p. 180.

QUESTIONS FOR THOUGHT AND DISCUSSION

1. What image of God emerges in the poem? How would you describe Herbert's reaction—as the "I" in the poem—to "Love's" invitation? How might a slothful person have responded instead?

2. What do you find helpful or unhelpful about the metaphor of courtship in Herbert's poem compared to the metaphors of besieging and ravishing in Donne's?

3. In your own experience of the pilgrimage of faith, however short or recent, how much has been the result of your own initiative and how much unmistakably God's?

4. Why do you imagine Herbert's poem was so comforting for Simone Weil? What is the "beauty" of it? The "prayer" of it? The "reality" of it?

FIVE
AVARICE (*AVARITIA*) VERSUS MERCY

Avarice, or greed and covetousness, is the fifth of the seven deadly sins, and the fifth and last of the sins of the spirit—those that are "cold" and "respectable." With the tenth commandment specifically forbidding it ("You shall not covet . . ."), with so much of the teaching of Jesus directed against it (especially in the form of "Mammon"), and with the apostle Paul's blunt verdict "The love of money is the root of all evil," avarice has commonly been reckoned far worse than anger, sloth, gluttony, and lust, and—along with envy—placed second only to pride in seriousness.

Avarice has commonly been reckoned far worse than anger, sloth, gluttony, and lust, and—along with envy—placed second only to pride in seriousness.

SHOW ME THE MONEY!

"Few of us can stand prosperity. Another man's, I mean."

—Mark Twain

"The lack of money is the root of all evil."

—Mark Twain

"To be clever enough to get all that money, you must be stupid enough to want it."

—G. K. Chesterton

"It is preoccupation with possession more than anything else that prevents men from living freely and nobly."

—Bertrand Russell

Avarice is a sin with two components: getting what we do not have and keeping what we do. There are also two confusions in understanding this vice. First, "things" themselves are not the problem. As part of God's creation, things are good in themselves. Avarice only enters the picture when the desire for temporal possessions becomes inordinate and then idolatrous—in other words, when reliance on God's gifts becomes a substitute for relying on God Himself. In the words of Peter Kreeft, "When a creature is made into a god, it becomes a devil."

Avarice is a sin with two components: getting what we do not have and keeping what we do.

The second confusion is equating avarice with miserly stinginess, personified by Ebenezer Scrooge in Charles Dickens's A Christmas Carol. *In this traditional understanding, secret hoarding is the test of avarice, so those who do not hoard are off the hook. What this idea overlooks, however, is that avarice can take different forms in different eras. Thus what was once handled secretly is now paraded publicly—"conspicuous consumption"—but the same spirit of possessing lies behind it.*

The heart of avarice is not the love of possessions but of possessing and therefore of being a possessor. Put differently, counting was the image of traditional avarice, the picture of the miser secretly fondling his gold. Today the shift is toward being counted, such as making the list of the "Forbes fifty" billionaires.

There are also two important observations about real avarice. One is that stinginess and waste are not opposites but two faces of this same deadly sin. As Chaucer's Parson points out, the prodigal son was a waster, whereas Judas was a tightwad (in complaining about Mary Magdalen's "waste" in anointing Jesus). But neither of them was a giver. Judas does not give at all, and the prodigal son wastes rather than gives. Prodigality and illiberality are two sides of the same coin.

There are also two important observations about real avarice. One is that stinginess and waste are not opposites but two faces of this same deadly sin.

The other observation is that avarice is preeminently a secular sin, one that is socially respectable and hard to detect when reinforced by certain cultural trends, as in our own time. Periods of enormous wealth creation, such as the 1980s and 1990s, and such books as Tom Wolfe's Bonfire of the Vanities *have turned the spotlight on the subject from time to time. But discussion of avarice within the world of advanced capitalism is bound to make people somewhat uncomfortable and ambivalent. Witness, for example, the debates about capitalism and its "social engine of greed." Many end up justifying avarice as the necessary fuel for a strong economy.*

It is important to be clear that a critique of greed is not the same as a dismissal of capitalism, let alone an advocacy of the redistribution of wealth. But quite apart from such misunderstandings, it is important to see that there is an illusion in possessing. What do we possess in possessing? Only a transient enjoyment or status that cannot last ("you can't take it with you") and really cannot be passed on to an heir. The <u>pursuit of possessing is therefore a mirage; when pursued obsessively,</u> it is self-defeating. True happiness is a matter of being, not having. Or as George MacDonald wrote, hands can hoard, but "<u>the heart of man cannot hoard.</u>"

    Alexander the Great knew this. He conquered the known world and complained that there were no more worlds to conquer. But he ordered that when he died, his bare hand should hang out of his coffin to show that "you can't take it with you." Like Job, we come into the world naked and will return naked. Not even the most successful people, it has been said, will be accompanied by their lawyers, their accountants, and a Brink's truck.

Calvin and Hobbes by Bill Watterson

GETTING IS BETTER THAN HAVING.

WHO GETS IT?

"Then [Jesus] said to them, 'Watch out! Be on your guard against all kinds of greed; a man's life does not consist in the abundance of his possessions.'

    "And he told them this parable: 'The ground of a certain rich man produced a good crop. He thought to himself, "What shall I do? I have no place to store my crops."

    "'Then he said, "This is what I'll do. I will tear down my barns and build bigger ones, and there I will store all my grain and my goods. And I'll say to myself, 'You have plenty of good things laid up for many years. Take life easy; eat, drink and be merry.'"

    "'But God said to him, "You fool! This very night your life will be demanded from you. Then who will get what you have prepared for yourself?"'"

—Luke 12:15-20

"It's a disgrace to die rich."

—Andrew Carnegie

WHEN YOU *GET* SOMETHING, IT'S NEW AND EXCITING. WHEN YOU *HAVE* SOMETHING, YOU TAKE IT FOR GRANTED AND IT'S BORING.

BUT EVERYTHING YOU *GET* TURNS INTO SOMETHING YOU *HAVE*. | THAT'S WHY YOU ALWAYS NEED TO GET NEW THINGS!

    More sobering still, avarice carries not only an illusion but a judgment—in kind. <u>Those whose passion is the pursuit of possessing become possessed.</u> Midas, whose touch turned everything to gold, asked Bacchus to take his gift away because his gold food was inedible and he needed nourishment. Croesus, the fabulously rich king of Sardis, was captured by the Parthians who, in turn, ordered that molten gold be poured down his throat. As Francis Bacon wrote, "If money be not thy servant, it will be thy master. The covetous man cannot be said to possess wealth, as that may be said to possess him."

I FEEL LIKE I'M IN SOME STOCKHOLDER'S DREAM.

"WASTE AND WANT," THAT'S MY MOTTO.

FREEDOM BY FIRE

"My father used to say, 'Beware of too many possessions. They will end up possessing you.' I'd just like to tell him this morning, 'I'm a free man.'"

    —Malibu resident, after the loss of his home in the fire, November 1993

PICTURES AND METAPHORS

Pictures of avarice are rich and varied. In Dante's Purgatory, *the image is the eyes, bent toward the earth—"Heaven has turned our backs to heaven. . . . Our eyes would never seek the height, / Being bent on earthly matters." In the* Inferno, *the fate of the greedy is worse. Condemned to roll heavy weights that symbolize their toil to accumulate wealth, they become unrecognizable. Seeking to gain the world, they have lost their souls.*

Others picture avarice as spiritual dropsy, or insatiable thirst. The more the covetous seeks to slake his thirst, the more insatiable it grows. Others again portray avarice as a pair of hands, greedily groping to grasp what is beyond reach. For John Bunyan, it is all in a name—with a market town called Love-Gain and such men as Mr. Hold-the-World, Mr. Money-Love, and Mr. Save-All. As such metaphors and names imply, avarice has always been considered a masculine rather than a feminine sin. The avaricious does not give himself to an object or person in a nurturing or strengthening way, as a woman. He wants to have it and hold it in his hands like a man—the profane, secular, masculine sin of the life whose aim is ownership, mastery, domination, and control.

PRACTICAL APPLICATIONS

Avarice is a sin of the spirit that is self-love in a perverted form. It breeds a host of consequences, including loneliness, anxiety, neglect of the poor, waste, crime and injustice, and restless unease.

Mention of the 1980s and The Bonfire of the Vanities *shows how practical and contemporary the consequences of avarice are. Avarice is a sin of the spirit that is self-love in a perverted form. It breeds a host of consequences, including loneliness, anxiety, neglect of the poor, waste, crime and injustice, and restless unease. For Dante, the seven "daughters of Avarice" were treachery, restlessness, fraud, perjury, deceit, inhumanity, and violence. We might even ask how different these are from modern studies of the social consequences of advertising: materialism, irrationality, selfishness, social competitiveness, and sexual preoccupation.*

✺ *Geoffrey Chaucer* ✺

Geoffrey Chaucer (about 1343–1400) was an English poet and public servant, by far the greatest writer of Middle English and one of the finest poets in all litera- ture. Probably born in London, the son of a tavern keeper, he became a page to the wife of the Duke of Clarence and then transferred to the king's household. Taken prisoner in France but ransomed by the king, he traveled extensively on royal ser- vice throughout England and Europe.

On travels to Italy in 1372, Chaucer discovered the works of Dante, Boccaccio, and Petrarch. He was heavily influenced by them as well as the French poets of romantic love. There are no complete copies of some of his earliest works, and his greatest mas- terpiece, The Canterbury Tales, *is unfinished. In it the poet has joined with thirty others to make the annual April pilgrimage to the shrine of the murdered Thomas Becket in Canterbury. Their host at the Tabard Inn promises to come with them to judge who tells the best story along the way. The stories range from chivalrous romances to bawdy locker-room talk, from folk tales to sermons, each fitting the voice of the storyteller.*

The following passage is from the "The Pardoner's Prologue." The pardoner was a well-known medieval figure, a traveling salesperson whose business was selling forgiveness in the form of "indulgences." Here he reveals his fraudulent tricks as well as his own brazen hypocrisy — he preaches primarily against greed while his own motivation is purely avaricious.

THE PARDONER'S PROLOGUE

'My lords,' he said, 'In churches where I preach
I cultivate a haughty kind of speech
And ring it out as roundly as a bell;
I've got it all by heart, the tale I tell.
I have a text, it always is the same
And always has been, since I learnt the game,
Old as the hills and fresher than the grass,
Radix malorum est cupiditas. [Cupidity is the root of all evils.]
  'But first I make pronouncement whence I come,

Show them my bulls in detail and in sum.
And flaunt the papal seal for their inspection
As warrant for my bodily protection,
That none may have the impudence to irk
Or hinder me in Christ's most holy work.
Then I tell stories, as occasion calls,
Showing forth bulls from popes and cardinals,
From patriarchs and bishops; as I do,
I speak some words in Latin—just a few—
To put a saffron tinge upon my preaching
And stir devotion with a spice of teaching.
Then I bring all my long glass bottles out
Cram-full of bones and ragged bits of clout,
Relics they are, at least for such are known.
Then, cased in metal, I've a shoulder-bone,
Belonging to a sheep, a holy Jew's.
"Good men," I say, "take heed, for here is news.
Take but this bone and dip it in a well;
If cow or calf, if sheep or ox should swell
From eating snakes or that a snake has stung,
Take water from that well and wash its tongue,
And it will then recover. Furthermore,
Where there is pox or scab or other sore,
All animals that water at that well
Are cured at once. Take note of what I tell.
If the good man—the owner of the stock—
Goes once a week, before the crow of cock,
Fasting, and takes a draught of water too,
Why then, according to that holy Jew,
He'll find his cattle multiply and sell.

    'And it's a cure for jealousy as well;
For though a man be given to jealous wrath,
Use but this water when you make his broth,
And never again will he mistrust his wife,
Though he knew all about her sinful life,
Though two or three clergy had enjoyed her love. . . .

    'Good men and women, here's a word of warning;
If there is anyone in church this morning

Guilty of sin, so far beyond expression
Horrible, that he dare not make confession,
Or any woman, whether young or old,
That's cuckolded her husband, be she told
That such as she shall have no power or grace
To offer to my relics in this place.
But those who can acquit themselves of blame
Can all come up and offer in God's name,
And I will shrive them by the authority
Committed in this papal bull to me."
    'That trick's been worth a hundred marks a year
Since I became a Pardoner, never fear.
Then, priestlike in my pulpit, with a frown,
I stand, and when the yokels have sat down,
I preach, as you have heard me say before,
And tell a hundred lying mockeries more.
I take great pains, and stretching out my neck
To east and west I crane about and peck
Just like a pigeon sitting on a barn.
My hands and tongue together spin the yarn
And all my antics are a joy to see.
The curse of avarice and cupidity
Is all my sermon, for it frees the pelf.
Out come the pence, and specially for myself,
For my exclusive purpose is to win
And not at all to castigate their sin.
Once dead what matter how their souls may fare?
They can go blackberrying, for all I care! . . .
    'But let me briefly make my purpose plain;
I preach for nothing but for greed of gain
And use the same old text, as bold as brass,
Radix malorum est cupiditas.
And thus I preach against the very vice
I make my living out of—avarice.
And yet however guilty of that sin
Myself, with others I have power to win
Them from it, I can bring them to repent;
But that is not my principal intent.

Covetousness is both the root and stuff
Of all I preach. That ought to be enough.
　'Well, then I give examples thick and fast
From bygone times, old stories from the past.
A yokel mind loves stories from of old,
Being the kind it can repeat and hold.
What! Do you think, as long as I can preach
And get their silver for the things I teach,
That I will live in poverty, from choice?
That's not the counsel of my inner voice!
No! Let me preach and beg from kirk to kirk
And never do an honest job of work,
No, nor make baskets, like St. Paul, to gain
A livelihood. I do not preach in vain.
There's no apostle I would counterfeit;
I mean to have money, wool and cheese and wheat
Though it were given me by the poorest lad
Or poorest village widow, though she had
A string of starving children, all agape.
No, let me drink the liquor of the grape
And keep a jolly wench in every town!
　'But listen, gentlemen; to bring things down
To a conclusion, would you like a tale?
Now as I've drunk a draught of corn-ripe ale,
By God it stands to reason I can strike
On some good story that you all will like.
For though I am a wholly vicious man
Don't think I can't tell moral tales. I can!
Here's one I often preach when out for winning;
Now please be quiet. Here is the beginning.'

TOLL ROAD TO HEAVEN

"Priest, n. A gentleman who claims to own the inside track on the road to Paradise, and wants to charge toll on the same."

—Ambrose Bierce, *The Devil's Dictionary*

QUESTIONS FOR THOUGHT AND DISCUSSION

1. What is the Pardoner's message to his hearers? What authorities does he refer to in order to convince his audience that his message and wares are credible?

2. What canny strategies does the Pardoner use to tap into the root of avarice in his hearers? How real are the "cures" his wares promise? Why do they hold such appeal? Which of the Pardoner's strategies have modern counterparts?

3. Which lines of the poem epitomize the Pardoner's real mission? How much does he care for the true fate of his listener's souls? Could the same be said of any money-making industry or institution in our day? Which ones?

4. Does the bold-faced nature of the Pardoner's greed increase or reduce its impact? Why? What is your response to brazen greed when you encounter it?

5. Looking back over the entire poem, which "promise" of avarice is the most tempting to you? Which is the most unattractive? What strategies do you use to counter the appeal to greed coming your way through modern advertising and commercialism?

☙ Leo Tolstoy ☙

Count Leo Nikolayevich Tolstoy (1828–1910) was a Russian writer whose massive novels War and Peace *and* Anna Karenina *are considered by many to be among the finest ever written. He studied law and oriental languages at Kazan University but never graduated. At twenty-three he joined an artillery regiment and was commissioned as an officer when the Crimean War began in 1854.*

Around this time, Tolstoy began writing and published four books, including an autobiographical trilogy, which were acclaimed by the Russian literary circles of the time. In 1862 he married Sophia Andreyevna Behrs who not only eventually bore him thirteen children but also carried out such duties as copying by hand four drafts of War and Peace. *He settled on his large Volga estate, benevolently overseeing his tenants, and began writing the stories and novels for which he is famed today. In his later years, Tolstoy embraced and promoted a neo-Christian asceticism that led to an eventual rift between him and his family, and also a break with the Russian Orthodox Church, but which made him a world-renowned sage in his own lifetime.*

Writing over an expanse of fifty years, Tolstoy produced stories of all lengths, from brief parables to novellas, many of which are also classics, including the one excerpted below. His prodigious output comes to about ninety volumes of letters, journals, novels, and short stories.

In his later years, Tolstoy embraced and promoted a neo-Christian asceticism that led to an eventual rift between him and his family, and also a break with the Russian Orthodox Church, but which made him a world-renowned sage in his own lifetime.

AHAB'S AVARICE

"Some time later there was an incident involving a vineyard belonging to Naboth the Jezreelite. The vineyard was in Jezreel, close to the palace of Ahab king of Samaria. Ahab said to Naboth, 'Let me have your vineyard to use for a vegetable garden, since it is close to my palace. In exchange I will give you a better vineyard or, if you prefer, I will pay you whatever it is worth.'

"But Naboth replied, 'The LORD forbid that I should give you the inheritance of my fathers.'

"So Ahab went home, sullen and angry. . . . He lay on his bed sulking and refused to eat. . . .

"Jezebel his wife said, 'Is this how you act as king over Israel? Get up and eat! Cheer up. I'll get you the vineyard of Naboth the Jezreelite.'

"So she wrote letters in Ahab's name, placed his seal on them, and sent them to the elders and nobles who lived in Naboth's city with him. In those letters she wrote:

> "'Proclaim a day of fasting and seat Naboth in a prominent place among the people. But seat two scoundrels opposite him and have them testify that he has cursed both God and the king. Then take him out and stone him to death.'
>
> "So the elders and nobles who lived in Naboth's city did as Jezebel directed. . . . As soon as Jezebel heard that Naboth had been stoned to death, she said to Ahab, 'Get up and take possession of the vineyard of Naboth the Jezreelite that he refused to sell you. He is no longer alive, but dead. . . .'
>
> "Then the word of the LORD came to Elijah the Tishbite: 'Go down to meet Ahab king of Israel. . . . Say to him, "This is what the LORD says: Have you not murdered a man and seized his property? . . . In the place where dogs licked up Naboth's blood, dogs will lick up your blood—yes, yours!"'
>
> "Ahab said to Elijah, 'So you have found me, my enemy!'
>
> "'I have found you,' he answered, 'because you have sold yourself to do evil in the eyes of the LORD.'"
>
> —1 Kings 21:1-20

HOW MUCH LAND DOES A MAN NEED?

An elder sister came to visit her younger sister in the country. The elder was married to a tradesman in town, the younger to a peasant in the village. As the sisters sat over their tea talking, the elder began to boast of the advantages of town life: saying how comfortably they lived there, how well they dressed, what fine clothes her children wore, what good things they ate and drank, and how she went to the theatre, promenades, and entertainments.

The younger sister was piqued, and in turn disparaged the life of a tradesman, and stood up for that of a peasant.

"I would not change my way of life for yours," said she. "We may live roughly, but at least we are free from anxiety. You live in better style than we do, but though you often earn more than you need, you are very likely to lose all you have. You know the proverb, 'Loss and gain are brothers twain.' It often happens that people who are wealthy one day are begging their bread the next. Our way is safer. Though a peasant's life is not a fat one, it is a long one. We shall never grow rich, but we shall always have enough to eat."

You know the proverb, 'Loss and gain are brothers twain.'

The elder sister said sneeringly: "Enough? Yes, if you like to share with the pigs and the calves! What do you know of elegance or manners! However much your goodman may slave, you will die as you are living—on a dung heap—and your children the same."

"Well, what of that?" replied the younger. "Of course our work is rough and coarse. But, on the other hand, it is sure, and we need not bow to any one. But you, in your towns, are surrounded by temptations; to-day all may be right, but to-morrow the Evil One may tempt your husband with cards, wine, or women, and all will go to ruin. Don't such things happen often enough?"

Pahóm, the master of the house, was lying on the top of the stove and he listened to the women's chatter.

"It is perfectly true," thought he. "Busy as we are from childhood tilling mother earth, we peasants have no time to let any nonsense settle in our heads. Our only trouble is that we haven't land enough. If I had plenty of land, I shouldn't fear the Devil himself!"

The women finished their tea, chatted a while about dress, and then cleared away the tea-things and lay down to sleep.

But the Devil had been sitting behind the stove and had heard all that was said. He was pleased that the peasant's wife had led her husband into boasting and that he had said that if he had plenty of land he would not fear the Devil himself.

"All right," thought the Devil. "We will have a tussle. I'll give you land enough; and by means of that land I will get you into my power."

II

Close to the village there lived a lady, a small landowner, who had an estate of about three hundred acres. She had always lived on good terms with the peasants until she engaged as her steward an old soldier, who took to burdening the people with fines. However careful Pahóm tried to be, it happened again and again that now a horse of his got among the lady's oats, now a cow strayed into her garden, now his calves found their way into her meadows—and he always had to pay a fine.

Pahóm paid up, but grumbled, and going home in a temper, was rough with his family. All through that summer, Pahóm had much trouble because of this steward, and he was even glad when winter came and the cattle had to be stabled. Though he grudged the fodder when they could no longer graze on the pasture-land, at least he was free from anxiety about them.

In the winter the news got about that the lady was going to sell her land and that the keeper of the inn on the high road was bargaining for it. When the peasants heard this they were very much alarmed.

"Well," thought they, "if the innkeeper gets the land, he will worry us with fines worse than the lady's steward. We all depend on that estate."

So the peasants went on behalf of their Commune and asked the lady not to sell the land to the innkeeper, offering her a better price for it themselves. The lady agreed to let them have it. Then the peasants tried to arrange for the Commune to buy the whole estate, so that it might be held by them all in common. They met twice to discuss it, but could not settle the matter; the Evil One sowed discord among them and they could not agree. So they decided to buy the land individually, each according to his means; and the lady agreed to this plan as she had to the other.

Presently Pahóm heard that a neighbor of his was buying fifty acres, and that the lady had consented to accept one half in cash and to wait a year for the other half. Pahóm felt envious.

"Look at that," thought he, "the land is all being sold, and I shall get none of it." So he spoke to his wife.

"Other people are buying," said he, "and we must also buy twenty acres or so. Life is becoming impossible. That steward is simply crushing us with his fines."

So they put their heads together and considered how they could manage to buy it. They had one hundred rubles laid by. They sold a colt and one half of their bees, hired out one of their sons as a laborer and took his wages in advance, borrowed the rest from a brother-in-law, and so scraped together half the purchase money.

Having done this, Pahóm chose out a farm of forty acres, some of it wooded, and went to the lady to bargain for it. They came to an agreement, and he shook hands with her upon it and paid her a deposit in advance. Then they went to town and signed the deeds; he paying half the price down, and undertaking to pay the remainder within two years.

So now Pahóm had land of his own. He borrowed seed, and sowed it on the land he had bought. The harvest was a good one, and within a year he had managed to pay off his debts both to the lady and to his brother-in-law. So he became a landowner, plowing and sowing his own land, making hay on his own land, cutting his own trees, and feeding his cattle on his own pasture. When he went out to plow his fields, or to look at his growing corn, or at his grass-meadows, his heart would fill with joy. The grass that grew and the flowers that bloomed there seemed to him unlike any that grew elsewhere. Formerly, when he had passed by that land, it had appeared the same as any other land, but now it seemed quite different.

III

So Pahóm was well contented, and everything would have been right if the neighboring peasants would only not have trespassed on his corn-fields and meadows. He appealed to them most civilly, but they still went on: now the Communal herdsmen would let the village cows stray into his meadows, then horses from the night pasture would get among his corn. Pahóm turned them out again and again and forgave their owners, and for a long time he forbore to prosecute any one. But at last he lost patience and complained to the District Court. He knew it was the peasants' want of land, and no evil intent on their part, that caused the trouble, but he thought: "I cannot go on overlooking it or they will destroy all I have. They must be taught a lesson."

So Pahóm was well contented, and everything would have been right if the neighboring peasants would only not have trespassed on his corn-fields and meadows.

So he had them up, gave them one lesson, and then another, and two or three of the peasants were fined. After a time Pahóm's neighbors began to bear him a grudge for this and would now and then let their cattle on to his land on purpose. One peasant even got into Pahóm's wood at night and cut down five young lime trees for their bark. Pahóm passing through the wood one day noticed something white. He came nearer and saw the stripped trunks lying on the ground, and close by stood the stumps where the trees had been. Pahóm was furious.

"If he had only cut one here and there it would have been bad enough," thought Pahóm, "but the rascal has actually cut down a whole clump. If I could only find out who did this, I would pay him out."

He racked his brains as to who it could be. Finally he decided: "It must be Simon—no one else could have done it." So he went to Simon's homestead to have a look round, but he found nothing and only had an angry scene. However, he now felt more certain than ever that Simon had done it, and he lodged a complaint. Simon was summoned. The case was tried, and retried, and at the end of it all Simon was acquitted, there being no evidence against him. Pahóm felt still more aggrieved, and let his anger loose upon the elder and the judges.

"You let thieves grease your palms," said he. "If you were honest folk yourselves you would not let a thief go free."

So Pahóm quarreled with the judges and with his neighbors. Threats to burn his building began to be uttered. So though Pahóm had more land, his place in the Commune was much worse than before.

About this time a rumor got about that many people were moving to new parts.

"There's no need for me to leave my land," thought Pahóm. "But some of the others might leave our village and then there would be more room for us. I would take over their land myself and make my estate a bit bigger. I could then live more at ease. As it is, I am still too cramped to be comfortable."

One day Pahóm was sitting at home when a peasant, passing through the village, happened to call in. He was allowed to stay the night, and supper was given him. Pahóm had a talk with this peasant and asked him where he came from. The stranger answered that he came from beyond the Volga, where he had been working. One word led to another, and the man went on to say that many people were settling in those parts. He told how some people from his village had settled there. They had joined the Commune, and had had twenty-five acres per man granted them. The land was so good, he said, that the rye sown on it grew as high as a horse and so thick that five cuts of a sickle made a sheaf. One peasant, he said, had brought nothing with him but his bare hands, and now he had six horses and two cows of his own.

Pahóm's heart kindled with desire. He thought: "Why should I suffer in this narrow hole, if one can live so well elsewhere? I will sell my land and my homestead here, and with the money I will start afresh over there and get everything new. In this crowded place one is always having trouble. But I must first go and find out all about it myself."

Towards summer he got ready and started. He went down the Volga on a steamer to Samara, then walked another three hundred miles on foot, and at last reached the place. It was just as the stranger had said. The peasants had plenty of land: every man had twenty-five acres of communal land given him for his use, and any one who had money could buy, besides, at two shillings an acre as much good freehold land as he wanted.

Having found out all he wished to know, Pahóm returned home as autumn came on and began selling off his belongings. He sold his land at a profit, sold his homestead and all his cattle, and withdrew from membership of the Commune. He only waited till the spring, and then started with his family for the new settlement.

IV

As soon as Pahóm and his family reached their new abode, he applied for admission into the Commune of a large village. He stood treat to the elders and obtained the necessary documents. Five shares of communal land were given him for his own and his sons' use: that is to say, 125 acres (not all together, but in different fields) besides the use of the communal pasture. Pahóm put up the buildings he needed and bought cattle. Of the communal land alone he had three times as much as at his former home, and the

Pahóm's heart kindled with desire. He thought: "Why should I suffer in this narrow hole, if one can live so well elsewhere?"

land was good cornland. He was ten times better off than he had been. He had plenty of arable land and pasturage and could keep as many head of cattle as he liked.

At first, in the bustle of building and settling down, Pahóm was pleased with it all, but when he got used to it he began to think that even here he had not enough land. The first year, he sowed wheat on his share of the communal land and had a good crop. He wanted to go on sowing wheat but had not enough communal land for the purpose, and what he had already used was not available; for in those parts wheat is only sown on virgin soil or on fallow land. It is sown for one or two years, and then the land lies fallow till it is again overgrown with prairie grass. There were many who wanted such land and there was not enough for all; so that people quarreled about it. Those who were better off wanted it for growing wheat, and those who were poor wanted it to let to dealers, so that they might raise money to pay their taxes. Pahóm wanted to sow more wheat, so he rented land from a dealer for a year. He sowed much wheat and had a fine crop, but the land was too far from the village—the wheat had to be carted more than ten miles. After a time Pahóm noticed that some peasant dealers were living on separate farms and were growing wealthy, and he thought: "If I were to buy some freehold land and have a homestead on it, it would be a different thing altogether. Then it would all be nice and compact."

At first, in the bustle of building and settling down, Pahóm was pleased with it all, but when he got used to it he began to think that even here he had not enough land.

The question of buying freehold land recurred to him again and again.

He went on in the same way for three years, renting land and sowing wheat. The seasons turned out well and the crops were good, so that he began to lay money by. He might have gone on living contentedly, but he grew tired of having to rent other people's land every year and having to scramble for it. Wherever there was good land to be had, the peasants would rush for it and it was taken up at once, so that unless you were sharp about it you got none. It happened in the third year that he and a dealer together rented a piece of pasture land from some peasants, and they had already plowed it up, when there was some dispute and the peasants went to law about it, and things fell out so that the labor was all lost.

"If it were my own land," thought Pahóm, "I should be independent, and there would not be all this unpleasantness."

So Pahóm began looking out for land which he could buy, and he came across a peasant who had bought thirteen hundred acres but having got into difficulties was willing to sell again cheap. Pahóm bargained and haggled with him, and at last they settled the price at 1,500 rubles, part in cash and part to be paid later. They had all but clinched the matter when a passing dealer happened to stop at Pahóm's one day to get a feed for his horses. He drank tea with Pahóm and they had a talk. The dealer said that he was just returning from the land of the Bashk'rs, far away, where he had bought thirteen thousand acres of land, all for 1,000 rubles. Pahóm questioned him further, and the tradesman said: "All one need do is to make friends with the chiefs. I gave away about one hundred rubles worth of silk robes and carpets, besides a case of tea, and I gave wine to those who would drink it; and I got the land for less than a penny an acre."

And he showed Pahóm the title-deeds, saying: "The land lies near a river, and the whole prairie is virgin soil."

Pahóm plied him with questions, and the tradesman said: "There is more land there than you could cover if you walked a year, and it all belongs to the Bashk'rs. They are as simple as sheep, and land can be got almost for nothing."

"There now," thought Pahóm, "with my one thousand rubles, why should I get only thirteen hundred acres, and saddle myself with a debt besides? If I take it out there, I can get more than ten times as much for the money."

V

Pahóm inquired how to get to the place, and as soon as the tradesman had left him, he prepared to go there himself. He left his wife to look after the homestead and started on his journey, taking his man with him. They stopped at a town on their way and bought a case of tea, some wine, and other presents, as the tradesman had advised. On and on they went until they had gone more than three hundred miles, and on the seventh day they came to a place where the Bashk'rs had pitched their tents. It was all just as the tradesman had said. The people lived on the steppes, by a river, in felt-covered tents. They neither tilled the ground nor ate bread. Their cattle and horses grazed in herds on the steppe. The colts were tethered behind the tents, and the mares were driven to them twice a day. The mares were milked and from the milk kumiss was made. It was the women who prepared kumiss, and they also made cheese. As far as the men were concerned, drinking kumiss and tea, eating mutton, and playing on their pipes, was all they cared about. They were all stout and merry, and all the summer long they never thought of doing

"There now," thought Pahóm, "with my one thousand rubles, why should I get only thirteen hundred acres, and saddle myself with a debt besides? If I take it out there, I can get more than ten times as much for the money."

any work. They were quite ignorant, and knew no Russian, but were good-natured enough.

As soon as they saw Pahóm, they came out of their tents and gathered round their visitor. An interpreter was found, and Pahóm told them he had come about some land. The Bashk'rs seemed very glad; they took Pahóm and led him into one of the best tents, where they made him sit on some down cushions placed on a carpet, while they sat round him. They gave him some tea and kumiss and had a sheep killed, and gave him mutton to eat. Pahóm took presents out of his cart and distributed them among the Bashk'rs and divided the tea amongst them. The Bashk'rs were delighted. They talked a great deal among themselves and then told the interpreter to translate.

"They wish to tell you," said the interpreter, "that they like you and that it is our custom to do all we can to please a guest and to repay him for his gifts. You have given us presents, now tell us which of the things we possess please you best, that we may present them to you."

"What pleases me best here," answered Pahóm, "is your land. Our land is crowded and the soil is exhausted, but you have plenty of land and it is good land. I never saw the like of it."

The interpreter translated. The Bashk'rs talked among themselves for a while. Pahóm could not understand what they were saying but saw that they were much amused and that they shouted and laughed. Then they were silent and looked at Pahóm while the interpreter said: "They wish me to tell you that in return for your presents they will gladly give you as much land as you want. You have only to point it out with your hand and it is yours."

"What pleases me best here," answered Pahóm, "is your land. Our land is crowded and the soil is exhausted, but you have plenty of land and it is good land. I never saw the like of it."

The Bashk'rs talked again for a while and began to dispute. Pahóm asked what they were disputing about, and the interpreter told him that some of them thought they ought to ask their Chief about the land and not act in his absence, while others thought there was no need to wait for his return.

VI

While the Bashk'rs were disputing, a man in a large fox-fur cap appeared on the scene. They all became silent and rose to their feet. The interpreter said, "This is our Chief himself."

Pahóm immediately fetched the best dressing-gown and five pounds of tea and offered these to the Chief. The Chief accepted them and seated himself in the place of honor. The Bashk'rs at once began telling him something. The Chief listened for a while, then made a sign with his head for them to be silent, and addressing himself to Pahóm, said in Russian: "Well, let it be so. Choose whatever piece of land you like; we have plenty of it."

"How can I take as much as I like?" thought Pahóm. "I must get a deed to make it secure, or else they may say, 'It is yours' and afterwards may take it away again."

"Thank you for your kind words," he said aloud. "You have much land, and I only want a little. But I should like to be sure which bit is mine. Could it not be measured and made over to me? Life and death are in God's hands. You good people give it to me, but your children might wish to take it away again."

"You are quite right," said the Chief. "We will make it over to you."

"I heard that a dealer had been here," continued Pahóm, "and that you gave him a little land, too, and signed title-deeds to that effect. I should like to have it done in the same way."

The Chief understood.

"Yes," replied he, "that can be done quite easily. We have a scribe, and we will go to town with you and have the deed properly sealed."

"And what will be the price?" asked Pahóm.

"Our price is always the same: one thousand rubles a day."

Pahóm did not understand.

"A day? What measure is that? How many acres would that be?"

"We do not know how to reckon it out," said the Chief. "We sell it by the day. As much as you can go round on your feet in a day is yours, and the price is one thousand rubles a day."

Pahóm was surprised.

"But in a day you can get round a large tract of land," he said.

The Chief laughed.

"It will all be yours!" said he. "But there is one condition: if you don't return on the same day to the spot whence you started, your money is lost."

"But how am I to mark the way that I have gone?"

"Why, we shall go to any spot you like and stay there. You must start from that spot and make your round, taking a spade with you. Wherever you think necessary, make a mark. At every turning, dig a hole and pile up the turf; then afterwards we will go round with a plow from hole to hole. You may make as large a circuit as you please, but before the sun sets you must return to the place you started from. All the land you cover will be yours."

"You may make as large a circuit as you please, but before the sun sets you must return to the place you started from. All the land you cover will be yours."

Pahóm was delighted. It was decided to start early next morning. They talked a while, and after drinking some more kumiss and eating some more mutton, they had tea again, and then the night came on. They gave Pahóm a feather-bed to sleep on, and the Bashk'rs dispersed for the night, promising to assemble the next morning at daybreak and ride out before sunrise to the appointed spot.

VII

Pahóm lay on the feather-bed, but could not sleep. He kept thinking about the land.

"What a large tract I will mark off!" thought he. "I can easily do thirty-five miles in a day. The days are long now, and within a circuit of thirty-five miles what a lot of land there will be! I will sell the poorer land or let it to peasants, but I'll pick out the best and farm it. I will buy two ox-teams, and hire two more laborers. About a hundred and fifty acres shall be plow-land, and I will pasture cattle on the rest."

Pahóm lay awake all night, and dozed off only just before dawn. Hardly were his eyes closed when he had a dream. He thought he was lying in that same tent and heard somebody chuckling outside. He wondered who it could be, and rose and went out, and he saw the Bashk'r Chief sitting in front of the tent holding his sides and rolling about with laughter. Going nearer to the Chief, Pahóm asked, "What are you laughing at?" But he saw that it was no longer the Chief, but the dealer who had recently stopped at his house and had told him about the land. Just as Pahóm was going to ask, "Have you been here long?" he saw that it was not the dealer, but the peasant who had come up from the Volga, long ago, to Pahóm's old home. Then he saw that it was not the peasant either, but the Devil himself with hoofs and horns, sitting there and chuckling, and before him lay a man barefoot, prostrate on the ground, with only trousers and a shirt on. And Pahóm dreamt that he looked more attentively to see what sort of a man it was that was lying there, and he saw that the man was dead and that it was himself! He awoke horror-struck.

"What things one does dream," thought he.

Looking round he saw through the open door that the dawn was breaking.

"It's time to wake them up," thought he. "We ought to be starting."

He got up, roused his man (who was sleeping in his cart), bade him harness, and went to call the Bashk'rs.

"It's time to go to the steppe to measure the land," he said.

The Bashk'rs rose and assembled, and the Chief came too. Then they began drinking kumiss again, and offered Pahóm some tea, but he would not wait.

"If we are to go, let us go. It is high time," said he.

VIII

The Bashk'rs got ready and they all started: some mounted on horses, and some in carts. Pahóm drove in his own small cart with his servant and took a spade with him. When they reached the steppe, the morning red was beginning to kindle. They ascended a hillock (called by the Bashk'rs a *shikhan*) and dismounting from their carts and their horses, gathered in one spot. The Chief came up to Pahóm and, stretching out his arm towards the plain, "See," said he, "all this, as far as your eye can reach, is ours. You may have any part of it you like."

Pahóm's eyes glistened: it was all virgin soil, as flat as the palm of your hand, as black as the seed of a poppy, and in the hollows different kinds of grasses grew breast high.

The Chief took off his fox-fur cap, placed it on the ground and said:

"This will be the mark. Start from here, and return here again. All the land you go round shall be yours."

Pahóm took out his money and put it on the cap. Then he took off his outer coat, remaining in his sleeveless under-coat. He unfastened his girdle and tied it tight below his stomach, put a little bag of bread into the breast of his coat, and tying a flask of water to his girdle, he drew up the tops of his boots, took the spade from his man, and stood ready to start. He considered for some moments which way he had better go—it was tempting everywhere.

"No matter," he concluded, "I will go towards the rising sun."

"I must lose no time," he thought, "and it is easier walking while it is still cool."

The sun's rays had hardly flashed above the horizon, before Pahóm, carrying the spade over his shoulder, went down into the steppe.

Pahóm started walking neither slowly nor quickly. After having gone a thousand yards he stopped, dug a hole, and placed pieces of turf one on another to make it more visible. Then he went on, and now that he had walked off his stiffness he quickened his pace. After a while he dug another hole.

Pahóm looked back. The hillock could be distinctly seen in the sunlight, with the people on it, and the glittering tires of the cart-wheels. At a rough

Pahóm's eyes glistened: it was all virgin soil, as flat as the palm of your hand, as black as the seed of a poppy, and in the hollows different kinds of grasses grew breast high.

guess Pahóm concluded that he had walked three miles. It was growing warmer; he took off his under-coat, flung it across his shoulder, and went on again. It had grown quite warm now; he looked at the sun, it was time to think of breakfast.

"The first shift is done, but there are four in a day, and it is too soon yet to turn. But I will just take off my boots," said he to himself.

He sat down, took off his boots, stuck them into his girdle, and went on. It was easy walking now.

"I will go on for another three miles," thought he, "and then turn to the left. This spot is so fine that it would be a pity to lose it. The further one goes, the better the land seems."

He went straight on for a while, and when he looked round, the hillock was scarcely visible and the people on it looked like black ants, and he could just see something glistening there in the sun.

"Ah," thought Pahóm, "I have gone far enough in this direction, it is time to turn. Besides I am in a regular sweat, and very thirsty."

He stopped, dug a large hole, and heaped up pieces of turf. Next he untied his flask, had a drink, and then turned sharply to the left. He went on and on; the grass was high, and it was very hot.

Pahóm began to grow tired; he looked at the sun and saw that it was noon.

"Well," he thought, "I must have a rest."

He sat down and ate some bread and drank some water, but he did not lie down, thinking that if he did he might fall asleep. After sitting a little while, he went on again. At first he walked easily: the food had strengthened him, but it had become terribly hot and he felt sleepy, still he went on, thinking: "An hour to suffer, a life-time to live."

He went a long way in this direction also and was about to turn to the left again, when he perceived a damp hollow. "It would be a pity to leave that out," he thought. "Flax would do well there." So he went on past the hollow, and dug a hole on the other side of it before he turned the corner. Pahóm looked towards the hillock. The heat made the air hazy: it seemed to be quivering, and through the haze the people on the hillock could scarcely be seen.

He looked at the sun: it was nearly half-way to the horizon, and he had not yet done two miles of the third side of the square. He was still ten miles from the goal.

"Ah!" thought Pahóm, "I have made the sides too long; I must make this one shorter." And he went along the third side, stepping faster. He looked at the sun: it was nearly half-way to the horizon, and he had not yet done two miles of the third side of the square. He was still ten miles from the goal.

"No," he thought, "though it will make my land lopsided, I must hurry back in a straight line now. I might go too far, and as it is I have a great deal of land."

So Pahóm hurriedly dug a hole and turned straight towards the hillock.

IX

Pahóm went straight towards the hillock, but he now walked with difficulty. He was done up with the heat, his bare feet were cut and bruised, and his legs began to fail. He longed to rest, but it was impossible if he meant to get back before sunset. The sun waits for no man, and it was sinking lower and lower.

"Oh dear," he thought, "if only I have not blundered trying for too much! What if I am too late?"

He looked towards the hillock and at the sun. He was still far from his goal, and the sun was already near the rim.

Pahóm walked on and on; it was very hard walking but he went quicker and quicker. He pressed on but was still far from the place. He began running, threw away his coat, his boots, his flask, and his cap, and kept only the spade which he used as a support.

"What shall I do?" he thought again. "I have grasped too much and ruined the whole affair. I can't get there before the sun sets."

And this fear made him still more breathless. Pahóm went on running, his soaking shirt and trousers stuck to him and his mouth was parched. His breast was working like a blacksmith's bellows, his heart was beating like a hammer, and his legs were giving way as if they did not belong to him. Pahóm was seized with terror lest he should die of the strain.

Though afraid of death, he could not stop. "After having run all that way, they will call me a fool if I stop now," thought he. And he ran on and on, and drew near and heard the Bashk'rs yelling and shouting to him, and their cries inflamed his heart still more. He gathered his last strength and ran on.

The sun was close to the rim, and cloaked in mist looked large, and red as blood. Now, yes now, it was about to set! The sun was quite low, but he was also quite near his aim. Pahóm could already see the people on the hillock waving their arms to hurry him up. He could see the fox-fur cap on the ground and the money on it, and the Chief sitting on the ground holding his sides. And Pahóm remembered his dream.

"There is plenty of land," thought he, "but will God let me live on it? I have lost my life, I have lost my life! I shall never reach that spot!"

"There is plenty of land," thought he, "but will God let me live on it? I have lost my life, I have lost my life! I shall never reach that spot!"

Pahóm looked at the sun, which had reached the earth: one side of it had already disappeared. With all his remaining strength he rushed on, bending his body forward so that his legs could hardly follow fast enough to keep him from falling. Just as he reached the hillock it suddenly grew dark. He looked up—the sun had already set! He gave a cry. "All my labor has been in vain," thought he and was about to stop, but he heard the Bashk'rs still shouting and remembered that though to him, from below, the sun seemed to have set, they on the hillock could still see it. He took a long breath and ran up the hillock. It was still light there. He reached the top and saw the cap. Before it sat the Chief laughing and holding his sides. Again Pahóm remembered his dream, and he uttered a cry: his legs gave way beneath him, he fell forward and reached the cap with his hands.

"Ah, that's a fine fellow!" exclaimed the Chief. "He has gained much land!"

Pahóm's servant came running up and tried to raise him, but he saw that blood was flowing from his mouth. Pahóm was dead!

The Bashk'rs clicked their tongues to show their pity.

His servant picked up the spade and dug a grave long enough for Pahóm to lie in and buried him in it. Six feet from his head to his heels was all he needed.

His servant picked up the spade and dug a grave long enough for Pahóm to lie in and buried him in it. Six feet from his head to his heels was all he needed.

Leo Tolstoy, "How Much Land Does a Man Need?" 1886. Translated by Louise and Aylmer Maude.

ALL THAT DOESN'T GLITTER . . .

"Those who have seen the exhibition of Tutankhamen's treasures must in the end find something ghastly in it. We think of the body of the king sealed with his riches for all those centuries in a dark and airless chamber. When it is opened, his body has decomposed, but the gold and the alabaster have kept their substance and form, and glitter as brightly as ever. What is absent from them is the king himself. They tell us of his majesty—in other words, of his status—but they tell us nothing of the man. They are relics of a civilization in which, under the sway of its cosmology and beliefs, the king was as depersonalized and dehumanized as his subjects. We look back at the treasures; with all their brilliance and art they are decadent and meaningless. We think again of the king among his treasures—an object only, buried among other objects. It was they that survived. Perhaps we have gone to the exhibition in such large numbers because we are looking at something we can understand: at the contents of a tomb from which, when the stone was rolled away, it was the objects and not the man that rose again, in which the man had become the most lifeless of all the objects. If we look straightforwardly at our societies now, how can we deny that this is an image of us?"

—Henry Fairlie, *The Seven Deadly Sins Today*

QUESTIONS FOR THOUGHT AND DISCUSSION

1. What criteria do the two sisters use to judge each others' lives? By which of these criteria—or another—do you tend to evaluate your life?

2. What is Pahóm's response to the women's chatter? What does the Devil decide to do when he hears Pahóm boasting?

3. How does Pahóm change when he becomes a landowner? What is the common theme in his reactions to the ensuing news of various new and better lands?

4. What is the Bashk'rs' "one thousand rubles a day" policy? What is the real test of the policy?

5. What dream does Pahóm have the night before his journey? What is the dream's warning? How does Pahóm excuse it?

6. Why does Pahóm die in his pursuit of the land? How much land does it take to bury him?

7. What is the heart of avarice as Tolstoy describes it? How does it grow so naturally that it is difficult to detect or challenge? What might have checked the growing avarice in Pahóm?

8. What do your own ambitions and life goals look like in the light of Tolstoy's parable?

Langdon Gilkey

Langdon Brown Gilkey (born 1919) is a theologian and author of such well-read theological works as Reaping the Whirlwind. *Before he began his distinguished academic career at the University of Chicago Divinity School, he went to China as a young man and taught at Yenching University, near Beijing. During World War II he was rounded up by the invading Japanese and put in an internment camp for two-and-a-half years, along with a motley assortment of other foreigners working in China. The* Shantung Compound *is based on the journal he kept.*

The Japanese internment camp lay somewhere in between ordinary, routine life and the dire extremity of a Nazi concentration camp. With more than two thousand people from dozens of nations crammed into the space of a block, and with no maintenance staff, no machinery, no running water, and no central heating, the social and political problems of running the camp were titanic. The compound, incidentally, was where Henry Luce, founder of Time, *was born earlier, and where Eric Liddell, the doctor, missionary, and hero of* Chariots of Fire, *died during internment.*

How do people survive when their props are taken away? How do they sustain their principles and traditions under pressure? The results are sometimes surprising, sometimes shocking. But as this incident shows, the camp was a miniature society that brought human virtues and vices into sharp focus—including avarice.

> How do people survive when their props are taken away? How do they sustain their principles and traditions under pressure?

SHANTUNG COMPOUND

> The future stretched on as endless and dreary as the snow-covered flatlands beyond the barbed wire on the walls of the compound.

By the beginning of the winter of 1944–1945, food from the parcels had long since vanished, and the cuts in our supplies were growing ever more drastic. Winter on the plains of North China is biting cold—such as one might expect in Detroit or Chicago. We were issued very little coal dust with which to heat our rooms. Morale in the camp was at its all-time low. The future stretched on as endless and dreary as the snow-covered flatlands beyond the barbed wire on the walls of the compound.

Then suddenly, without warning, one cold January day the most wonderful thing imaginable happened. Some internees who happened to be near the great front gate saw it swing open as usual. The familiar donkey carts that carried our supplies came plodding in through the snow. But what they saw in those carts, they found hard to believe. Piled high, box on box, were seemingly endless numbers of Red Cross parcels! Word spread swiftly around the camp. In a twinkling, a huge crowd had gathered. Everyone was laughing and crying at once. We all looked on in disbelief as cartload after cartload kept coming through the gate. In utter amazement, tears streaming down our faces, we counted fourteen of those carts, each one carrying well over a hundred parcels!

"Why, they're the same parcels!" someone said. "See there's the label—AMERICAN RED CROSS—but there are many, many more than before!"

"I just heard from a committeeman that there's no covering letter for these parcels, no indication as to who is to get them."

"Then *who* are they for?"

This question, "Who is to get them?" ran like wildfire among us. Quite naturally, the first reactions had been generally that the Americans were in luck again. But, when more and more carts kept coming in the gate, notions as to who would be given them became confused. The Americans, counting the carts as they went by, began to speculate happily on this windfall.

"My God," exclaimed one in a loud voice, "I figure there must be at least fifteen hundred parcels there—wow! Why, that's seven to eight parcels for each American! I don't even know where I'll put all that stuff!"

But other thoughts were going through other minds as the significance of the quantity struck home: "Why, fifteen hundred is just about the number of people in the camp! Could it be that we British are going to get a parcel, too? Could they be for *everybody* this time?"

As this question swept through the assembled crowd—which, by now, was comprised of the entire camp—it collided head-on with the exultation of the Americans. Frowns replaced looks of amazed wonder, angry mutterings succeeded the early shouts of joy.

"Damn it, you limey," one outraged Yankee voice cried out, "that's American stuff, and you lousy spongers aren't going to get a bit of it. Why doesn't *your* Red Cross take care of *you?*"

The answer was a snort of disgust.

"Well, you Americans *are* a bunch of bloody buggers! You want everything for yourselves, don't you? If it's your property, no one else is to have a look in, is that the idea?"

And so it went. The parcels were piled up in a great heap in the church building awaiting word from *some* authority as to how all this wonderful wealth was to be distributed. A heavy guard was posted to watch over them. Every row of rooms and every dorm where Americans lived with other nationals began to stew in bitter disputes. In those where no Americans lived, there was general gloomy agreement that while Americans might be rich, they were certainly neither very human nor very trustworthy; for when the chips were down, they wanted to be sure they got theirs—and who cared about the other fellow.

Two days later the Japanese authorities posted a notice which seemed to settle the issue to everyone's apparent satisfaction. The commandant, after stating that he was acting according to official instructions, proclaimed that the parcels were to be distributed to the entire camp the next day at 10 A.M. Every American was to receive one and one-half parcels; every other internee, one parcel. This ingenious distribution was possible because there were 1,550 parcels for a camp of 1,450 persons, 200 of whom were Americans.

I was elated. I regarded this as a master stroke of statesmanship in a touchy situation. It looked as though the whole camp would be well fed by this arrangement. At the same time, the super patriots among the Americans would be appeased because they were getting substantially more than did the "damn furriners."

It is impossible to set down the joy and excitement that gripped the camp that night. It was as though everyone were living through every Christmas Eve of his lifetime all rolled into one.

What a heaven of goodies awaited each child with a parcel of his own! What blessed security was promised to every father and mother with three, possibly four, parcels for their family, enough surely to last through the spring, whatever might happen to our camp supplies! The dreary remnant of winter and the stark uncertainty of the days ahead seemed no longer impossible to contemplate as each internee savored the prospect of rich food and tried vainly to quiet his excited children who were already pleading to get in line for the great distribution.

Universal good will flooded the camp; enthusiasm for American generosity was expressed on every hand. Our morale and our sense of

The parcels were piled up in a great heap in the church building awaiting word from some *authority as to how all this wonderful wealth was to be distributed.*

What a heaven of goodies awaited each child with a parcel of his own! What blessed security was promised to every father and mother with three, possibly four, parcels for their family, enough surely to last through the spring, whatever might happen to our camp supplies!

community had climbed swiftly from an all-time low to an all-time high. As Bruce, the sardonic Scotsman in our dorm, said, "I almost feel tonight that I might be able to love other people—and that for me, brother, is a very rare feeling indeed!"

The next morning, long before the appointed hour, the camp in festive mood lined up for the parcels. Then suddenly the bottom dropped out of everything. Just before ten, a guard strode past and hammered up an official-looking notice on the board.

Those at the head of the line crowded around at once to see what the announcement said. They came away looking black as thunder. I made my way up to the bulletin board, peering over the heads of the crowd to read the words. As I approached, an Englishman was turning away. "The bloody bastards!" I heard him say. "What the bloody hell am I going to tell my kids?" An awful heart-sinking prescience told me what the notice said—and I wasn't wrong.

The notice contained one short but pregnant sentence:

DUE TO PROTESTS FROM THE AMERICAN COMMUNITY, THE PARCELS WILL
NOT BE DISTRIBUTED TODAY AS ANNOUNCED.
THE COMMANDANT

When we tried to find out what had happened, we were told that seven young Americans had gone to see the commandant about the matter. They had demanded that he produce his authorization to distribute American Red Cross parcels to internees who were not American citizens. Since there was no such proof, the seven insisted that these parcels be turned over at once to the American community, the rightful owners, for them to do with as they saw fit.

One may, I think, legitimately surmise that the Japanese official was caught completely off guard by this strong and reasoned appeal to what is a peculiarly Western sense of ownership. From his own cultural background he could conjure up no ready defense against it. The commandant had apparently acted solely on the basis of his own moral judgment in announcing the distribution to all internees, and had no higher authority with which to back up this judgment. In this case, surely, it would have been better for all concerned had he used some of the customary military inflexibility. Had he merely told the delegation to get out, the camp would have been spared much bitterness and the Americans much later humiliation. But he wavered, promising he would refer the whole question to the arbitration of Tokyo. Then he canceled the distribution.

Through the action of these seven men, the American community found itself in the unenviable position of preventing the distribution of life-giving parcels to their hungry fellows.

Through the action of these seven men, the American community found itself in the unenviable position of preventing the distribution of life-giving parcels to their hungry fellows. Apparently we were content to let them go hungry so long as we got our seven and one-half parcels.

The inevitable result was that all the bitter arguments of the two days previous broke out more strongly than before. Men who, like the Englishman I overheard, had to explain to the expectant children that "the Americans had taken away Santa," were not inclined to feel lightly about this. The Americans, finding themselves bitterly accused of a selfishness and greed which they had not explicitly encouraged, were not inclined to admit their own fault nor that of their countrymen, especially to enraged foreigners. With that pathetic but automatic defense mechanism almost every man develops with nationals of another country, Americans hotly defended whatever their countrymen had done long before they found out either what it was or what they themselves really thought about it.

There followed about ten days of delay, while we all waited for word from Tokyo. This hiatus provided the opportunity for all the hostility, jealousy, and national pride of 1,450 hungry, exasperated, and anxious people to accumulate and to boil over. Where there had been only arguments before, now there were fist fights. In one row, an American boy and a British boy got in a scuffle over the matter. When the fathers discovered this battle between erstwhile best friends, they at first chastised the youths. But when they learned what the fight was about, they themselves came to blows. Others had to step in and separate this pathetic but furious pair who had been neighbors and friends for a year and a half.

It was the same story all over. A community where everyone had long forgotten whether a man was American or British, white, Negro, Jew, Parsee, or Indian, had suddenly disintegrated into a brawling, bitterly divided collection of hostile national groups. Ironically, our wondrous Christmas gift had brought in its wake the exact opposite of peace on earth. The massive mounds of life-giving parcels lay inert in the center of the camp, while gusts of human conflict and ill will swirled turbulently around them.

A community where everyone had long forgotten whether a man was American or British, white, Negro, Jew, Parsee, or Indian, had suddenly disintegrated into a brawling, bitterly divided collection of hostile national groups. Ironically, our wondrous Christmas gift had brought in its wake the exact opposite of peace on earth.

For the first time, I felt fundamentally humiliated at being an American. The British in our dorm were too courteous to be openly nasty—they knew how most of our group there deplored this—but their silence spoke volumes.

The experience of the Red Cross parcels vividly revealed to me aspects of human communal life of which I had been formerly unaware. A day or so later as I was staring moodily at that heap of magnificent parcels, pondering the irony of our suddenly brawling society, I came to see that wealth is by no means an unmitigated blessing to its community. It does not, as may often be supposed, serve to feed and comfort those who are lucky enough to possess it, while leaving unaffected and unconcerned others in the community who are not so fortunate. Wealth is a dynamic force that can too easily become demonic—for if it does not do great good, it can do great harm.

The arrival of those parcels represented for our camp an accretion of sheer wealth almost of incomprehensible scope. It was as if, I thought, our small community had been whisked overnight from the living standard of a thirteenth-century village to that of modern affluent industrial society. Now we had food to keep us all from hunger through the spring.

And yet, the introduction of this wealth—the central factor in material progress—was in fact the occasion for an increase in bitterness and conflict such as we had never known before. Staring at those symbols of our material advance, I suddenly realized that Western culture's dream of material progress as the answer to every ill was no more than a dream. Here was evidence before my eyes that wealth and progress can have demonic consequences if misused.

Had this food simply been used for the good of the whole community, it would have been an unmitigated blessing in the life of every one of us. But the moment it threatened to become the hoarded property of a select few, it became at once destructive rather than creative, dividing us from one another and destroying every vestige of communal unity and morale.

Staring at those symbols of our material advance, I suddenly realized that Western culture's dream of material progress as the answer to every ill was no more than a dream.

I realized that this was no mere matter of angry words and irate looks. It was just the kind of issue which men were willing to fight over. Seeing the guards now patrolling the streets, I was glad they were there. Had there been no Japanese guns guaranteeing order in the camp, we might easily have faced real civil strife. Thus might our community have destroyed itself over this issue.

I suddenly saw, as never so clearly before, the really dynamic factors in social conflict: how wealth compounded with greed and injustice leads inevitably to strife, and how such strife can threaten to kill the social organism. Correspondingly, it became evident that the only answer was not less wealth or material goods, but the development of moral character that might lead to sharing and so provide the sole foundation for social peace. It is the moral or immoral use of wealth, not its mere accumulation, it seemed to me, that determines whether it will play a creative or destructive role in any society. The American claim for all the parcels, and its devastating effects on our social fabric, had taught me at last the true significance of moral character in any human community, and I would never forget it.

QUESTIONS FOR THOUGHT AND DISCUSSION

1. How does the author describe the mood in the camp prior to the arrival of the parcels? How does the ongoing sense of deprivation affect avarice?

2. What was the initial response of the internees to seeing the truck-loads of parcels arrive? What is the first question that begins the escalation of greed?

3. What allotment did the Japanese decide on for dispersing the parcels? How would you have adjudicated over the distribution of the parcels?

4. What would have been your response to the seven American "complainers"? What reasons would you have given to the disappointed internees?

5. How did Gilkey feel, being an American, during the incident and its aftermath?

6. What does Gilkey conclude about the mixed blessing of wealth? In the end, what does he see as the "only answer" to social conflict based on greed? Where have you seen moral character or the lack of it determine the outcome of a conflict over wealth?

7. What lessons do you take away from this story?

THE COUNTERPOINT TO AVARICE:

Blessed Are Those Who Are Merciful

The sin of avarice centers on a double greed: to get what we do not have and keep what we do. The counterpoint to the former is contentment and to the latter is generosity, both of which are at the heart of mercy.

Whereas greed seeks less than justice for others, mercy seeks more—its character is to give beyond reason, beyond justice, beyond expectation. As Shakespeare's Portia says in The Merchant of Venice, "The quality of mercy is not strained."

Whereas greed seeks less than justice for others, mercy seeks more—its character is to give beyond reason, beyond justice, beyond expectation.

SPENDERS WEEPERS, GIVERS KEEPERS

"What I kept, I lost; what I spent, I had; what I gave, I have."

—Old Epitaph

Put differently, avarice can trigger further sins, both of commission (such as fraud, treachery, and violence) and omission (such as indifference to one's neighbor's need). The medievals summarized such sins of omission simply as "insensitivity to mercy."

Mercy is not just the absence of avarice, but the presence of generosity. More than just "not being greedy," it is proactive in giving—not simply giving up wealth but giving out to the needy. As William F. May wrote, "The true opposite of the tight-fistedness of avarice is not the empty-handedness of death, but the open-handedness of love."

"The true opposite of the tight-fistedness of avarice is not the empty-handedness of death, but the open-handedness of love."

—William F. May

MERCY TO THE MERCILESS

Mercy, as Jesus describes it, is no respecter of persons; rather, it reaches its highest form when offered to those who least deserve it—our enemies and those who persecute us unjustly. "And if you do good to those who are good to you," asks Jesus, "what credit is that to you? . . . But love your enemies and do good to them."

Mercy loves both friends and enemies and actively does good to both. And God himself is the model, who "causes his sun to rise on the evil and the good, and sends rain on the righteous and the unrighteous."

❋ *Victor Hugo* ❋

Victor Hugo was introduced in part 2 on envy. The following passage is also from Les Misérables, *and takes place prior to the passage discussed earlier. It describes the near-miraculous act of mercy by the bishop, which becomes the turning point in Jean Valjean's life. Valjean, having been given warm hospitality by the bishop, steals his silver. When arrested by the gendarmes, he faces the grim prospect of a second and even longer prison sentence. Truly, his life must have seemed over.*

THE BISHOP AT WORK

The next day at sunrise, Monseigneur Bienvenu was walking in the garden. Madame Magloire ran toward him quite beside herself.

"Monseigneur, Monseigneur," she cried, "does Your Lordship know where the silver basket is?"

"Yes," said the bishop.

"God be praised!" she said. "I did not know what had become of it."

The bishop had just found the basket on a flower bed. He gave it to Madame Magloire and said, "Here it is."

"Yes," she said, "but there's nothing in it. Where's the silver?"

"Ah!" said the bishop. "It's the silver then that troubles you. I don't know where that is."

"Good heavens! It's stolen. That man who came last night stole it!"

And in the twinkling of an eye, with all the agility of her age, Madame Magloire ran to the oratory, went into the alcove, and came back to the bishop. The bishop was bending with some sadness over a *cochlearia des Guillons*, which the basket had broken in falling. At Madame Magloire's cry he looked up.

"Monseigneur, the man has gone! The silver is stolen!"

While she was uttering this exclamation, her eyes fell on a corner of the garden where she saw traces of the escape. A capstone of the wall had been dislodged.

"See, that is where he got out; he jumped into Cochefilet Lane. The wretch! He stole our silver!"

The bishop was silent for a moment, then raising his serious eyes, he said mildly to Madame Magloire, "Now first, did this silver belong to us?"

Madame Magloire was speechless. After a moment the bishop continued, "Madame Magloire, for a long time I have wrongfully been withholding this silver. It belonged to the poor. Who was this man? A poor man, quite clearly."

"Alas! alas!" returned Madame Magloire. "It's not on my account or Mademoiselle's; it is all the same to us. But it's for you, Monseigneur. What is Monsieur going to eat with now?"

The bishop looked at her with amazement. "But don't we have any pewter cutlery?"

Madame Magloire shrugged her shoulders. "Pewter smells."

"Well, then, iron."

Madame Magloire grimaced.

"Iron has a taste."

"Well, then," said the bishop, "wooden implements."

In a few minutes he was breakfasting at the table where Jean Valjean sat the night before. While breakfasting Monseigneur Bienvenu pleasantly remarked to his sister who said nothing, and Madame Magloire, who was grumbling to herself, that there was really no need even of a wooden spoon or fork to dip a piece of bread into a cup of milk.

"Was there ever such an idea?" said Madame Magloire to herself, as she went back and forth: "To take in a man like that, and to give him a bed at his side; and yet what a blessing he did nothing but steal! Oh, good Lord! It gives me the chills just to think of it!"

As the brother and sister were rising from the table there was a knock at the door.

"Come in," said the bishop.

The door opened. A strange, fierce group appeared on the threshold. Three men were holding a fourth by the collar. The three men were gendarmes; the fourth Jean Valjean.

A brigadier of gendarmes, who appeared to head the group, was near the door. He advanced toward the bishop, giving a military salute.

The bishop was silent for a moment, then raising his serious eyes, he said mildly to Madame Magloire, "Now first, did this silver belong to us?"

"Monseigneur," he said—

At this word Jean Valjean, who was sullen and seemed entirely dejected, raised his head with a stupefied air. "Monseigneur!" he murmured. "Then it is not the curé!"

"Silence!" said a gendarme. "It is his lordship, the bishop."

In the meantime Monseigneur Bienvenu had approached as quickly as his great age permitted: "Ah, there you are!" he said, looking at Jean Valjean. "I'm glad to see you. But I gave you the candlesticks, too, which are silver like the rest and would bring two hundred francs. Why didn't you take them along with your cutlery?"

Jean Valjean opened his eyes and looked at the bishop with an expression no human tongue could describe.

Jean Valjean opened his eyes and looked at the bishop with an expression no human tongue could describe.

"Monseigneur," said the brigadier, "then what this man said was true? We met him. He was acting like a fugitive, and we arrested him in order to find out. He had this silver."

"And he told you," interrupted the bishop, with a smile, "that it had been given to him by a good old priest at whose house he had slept. I see it all. And you brought him back here? It's all a mistake."

"If that's so," said the brigadier, "we can let him go."

"Please do," replied the bishop.

The gendarmes released Jean Valjean, who shrank back.

"Is it true they're letting me go?" he muttered, as if talking in his sleep.

"Yes! You can go. Don't you understand?" said a gendarme.

"My friend," said the bishop, "before you go away, here are your candlesticks; take them."

He went to the mantelpiece, took the two candlesticks, and handed them to Jean Valjean. The two women observed without a word, gesture, or look that could disturb the bishop.

He went to the mantelpiece, took the two candlesticks, and handed them to Jean Valjean. The two women observed without a word, gesture, or look that could disturb the bishop.

Jean Valjean was trembling all over. He took the two candlesticks distractedly, with a bewildered expression.

"Now," said the bishop, "go in peace. By the way, my friend, when you come again, you needn't come through the garden. You can always come and go by the front door. It is only closed with a latch, day or night." Then turning to the gendarmes, he said, "Messieurs, you may go." The gendarmes left.

Jean Valjean felt like a man about to faint.

The bishop approached him and said, in a low voice, "Do not forget, ever, that you have promised me to use this silver to become an honest man."

Jean Valjean, who had no recollection of any such promise, stood dumbfounded. The bishop had stressed these words as he spoke them. He continued, solemnly, "Jean Valjean, my brother, you no longer belong to evil, but to good. It is your soul I am buying for you. I withdraw it from dark thoughts and from the spirit of perdition, and I give it to God!"

He continued, solemnly, "Jean Valjean, my brother, you no longer belong to evil, but to good. It is your soul I am buying for you. I withdraw it from dark thoughts and from the spirit of perdition, and I give it to God!"

QUESTIONS FOR THOUGHT AND DISCUSSION

1. When do you think the bishop first realizes that Valjean has stolen the silver? When does Madame Magloire realize it?

2. How does the bishop respond to Madame Magloire's exclamation, "He stole our silver!" How might you have responded?

3. What particularly offends Madame Magloire about Valjean's action? What did she expect from him instead?

4. Who did Valjean assume would answer the bishop's door? How do you think he felt when he realized it was the bishop himself, now seeing him under arrest by the gendarmes? What do you think he expected the bishop to say?

5. What are the bishop's actual words to Valjean? What do you think were Jean Valjean's inner emotions at that moment? How do his physical reactions, expressions, and words reveal what he was feeling?

6. How does the bishop increase the intensity of his act of mercy? How does he take advantage of Valjean's bewilderment to spur him on to reform himself? Was this manipulative or just wise? Did the bishop, as he suggests, truly "buy back" Valjean's soul from evil and give it to God? How?

7. Have you ever witnessed any comparable act of stunning mercy? What were your emotions at the time?

SIX

GLUTTONY *(GULA)* VERSUS COURAGE UNDER SUFFERING AND PERSECUTION

Gluttony, or self-indulgence, is the sixth of the seven deadly sins and the first of the two sins of the flesh, which are "warm" but "disreputable." It is often treated as the least serious of the seven sins. Just as avarice idolizes possession and lust sex, so gluttony idolizes food. It lifts it out of its place and distorts both food and eating. Thus, unlike a gourmet who enjoys and appreciates food, a traditional glutton enjoys eating, almost regardless of its taste, beauty, or the company shared. Whereas the gourmet savors, the traditional glutton devours. Gluttons "make pigs of themselves" by reducing all food to the level of slop.

Gluttons "make pigs of themselves" by reducing all food to the level of slop.

THE LAST HURRAH

"But see, there is joy and revelry,
slaughtering of cattle and killing of sheep,
eating of meat and drinking of wine!
'Let us eat and drink,' you say,
'for tomorrow we die!'"

—Isaiah 22:13

Thus the distinctiveness of the "warm" sin of gluttony is twofold: First, gluttons abuse something essential to our human survival and, second, the spiritual penalties of gluttony are the lightest of the seven deadly sins while the physical penalties are the swiftest and heaviest.

Yet two things block us modern people from taking traditional gluttony seriously. One is our association of gluttony with the hedonistic decadence of ancient Rome—epitomized by Trimalchio's lavish banquets in Petronius' Satyricon with their groaning tables, appalling manners, and disgusting vomitariums. (One Roman senator had slaves walking backward in front of him to hold his paunch.) The other blockage is our modern self-congratulation on our disapproval of obesity and our newfound dedication to health, fitness, and dieting. Our gods, it seems, are not our bellies but our flat abdominal muscles (or in the fitness slang, our "washboard abs").

For reasons such as these, gluttony is often treated as a relatively harmless overindulgence in whatever we long for.

For reasons such as these, gluttony is often treated as a relatively harmless overindulgence in whatever we long for. Ironically, the word "sinful" is playfully applied to eating dessert more readily than to any other behavior or attitude in contemporary English.

THE OTHER THREE SINS

"If there are 7 deadly sins, then here's 8, 9, & 10."

—1993 ad for Denny's Restaurants'
"Truly Delectable" Desserts (Chills 'n Thrills, Peanut Butter Binge,
and Chocolate Challenge)

Because even Thomas Aquinas agreed that gluttony is the least serious sin, jokes about Christian proneness to gluttony abound. In one Italian story, a recent and fairly spiritual pope arrived at the gates of heaven. St. Peter stood aside to allow his successor to let himself in with his own keys. After much hunting and rummaging through his pockets, however, the new arrival was embarrassed to find himself still locked out—he had brought the keys to the Vatican wine cellar by mistake.

Dedicated to the gratification of appetite, gluttony grows from and leads to a terrible emptiness that—no matter how much we stuff ourselves—is never satisfied.

But both the origins and consequences of gluttony are more serious than that. Dedicated to the gratification of appetite, gluttony grows from and leads to a terrible emptiness that—no matter how much we stuff ourselves—is never satisfied. People overeat to compensate for emotional emptiness, but the overeating never compensates. The belly is stuffed, but the heart is hollow. Like all addictions, gluttony deceives. "We are what we eat" becomes our condemnation.

THE INTERNATIONAL CONSUMER

"Gluttony ransacks, as it were, Noah's ark for food, only to feed the riot of one meal."

—Sir Thomas Overbury

"Strange, therefore, it is, that for the stomach, which is scarce a span long, there should be provided so many furnaces and ovens, huge fires, and an army of cooks, cellars swimming with wine, and granaries sweating with corn; and that into one belly should enter the vintage of many nations, the spoils of distant provinces, and the shell-fishes of several seas."

— Jeremy Taylor

"Gluttony in all its forms is sinful in that it represents a degree of self-love which is self-destructive."

— Karl Menninger

In the medieval view, there were five ways of sinning by gluttony — eating and drinking too soon, too expensively, too much, too eagerly, and with too much fuss. All are symptoms of a philosophy of life that is finally materialist, and hedonistic, captured in the motto, "Let us eat and drink, for tomorrow we die." Thus, as modern ethicists point out, modern gluttony is not observed only in bulging midriffs, high blood pressures, poisoned livers, bottle-noses, and bad breath. It can also be traced in the fanatical modern devotion to dieting, health foods, and drug taking. In a society in which cookbooks outsell the Bible by something like ten to one, food and diets have been given a time and place that are gluttonous.

Thus in our modern society gluttony is not entirely straightforward. We need to remember the distinction C. S. Lewis makes between "the gluttony of excess" and "the gluttony of delicacy" — for medievals, the latter is the fifth aspect of the gluttony that is eating "with too much fuss."

Today, when the gluttony of delicacy outweighs the more traditional gluttony of excess, we must appreciate the difference between the two. The gluttony of excess is tied to a culture of scarcity just as the gluttony of delicacy is tied to a culture of abundance. The reason is that in a culture of scarcity food was for most people the only accessible luxury. Luxuries such as gold, silks, and land, for example, required money, but hard work or luck in (say) hunting brought food and wine within reach. For most of the West, the shift from scarcity to abundance happened in the nineteenth century. It was paralleled by an accompanying shift from the gluttony of excess to the gluttony of delicacy. As modern people, we may not admire indulgence and obesity, but we have a thousand polite words to cover our fussing over food.

The gluttony of delicacy is unquestionably our principal Western problem with food. Where food was once simply a matter of human sustenance, enjoyment, and sharing, it is now laden with myriad forms of "food guilt." How was it produced (on pesticide-ridden factory farms by exploited factory farmhands)? How is it

In a society in which cookbooks outsell the Bible by something like ten to one, food and diets have been given a time and place that are gluttonous.

Kudzu
by Doug Marlette

Kudzu by Doug Marlette. By permission of Doug Marlette.

marketed (in non-biodegradable garbage-creating containers)? What will be its consequences (depleted resources/increased heart attacks/thickened midriffs and hips)? As noted earlier, the word sinful is more likely to be used of dessert today than of any evil thought or act.

SOOOOO BAD!

"Sindulgence."

—Advertising slogan for Bailey's Irish Cream Liqueur, 1999

One writer notes, "It's not unusual at all to hear a woman wail, 'I was so bad today,' only to follow this dramatic statement with a seemingly tame admission like 'I ate two doughnuts and a bag of Cheetos.'" The traditional moral categories of "good" and "bad" are applied less often to "what comes out of" a person, as in words or deeds, than to "what goes in." And even then, it's not the overuse or fussiness about food that is negatively categorized, as in the medieval view, but simply the food itself.

BLESSED ARE THE BEAUTIFUL?

"If you look at advertising and current events in the print and other media—for example, as you encounter them in supermarket checkouts, newsstands, and bookstores or on television and radio—you might think that the most unfortunate people in the world today are the fat, the misshapen, the bald, the ugly, the old, and those not relentlessly engaged in romance, sex, and fashionably equipped physical activities.

"The sad truth is that many people around us, and especially people in their teens and young adulthood, drift into a life in which being thin and correctly shaped, having 'glorious' hair, appearing youthful, and so forth, are the only terms of blessedness or woe for their existence. It is all they know."

—Dallas Willard, *The Divine Conspiracy*

Though the modern tragedy of eating disorders is utterly distinct from the gluttony of delicacy, there is a link. The myth of the "perfectly thin female" that feeds the gluttony of delicacy is one factor—though not necessarily the primary one—in eating disorders, which are today nearly epidemic on college campuses. (Some campuses estimate that one in ten to one in five of their female students have had an eating disorder.) Though binge eating and bulimia account for part of the problem, anorexia nervosa is by far the most prevalent disorder, now affecting five to seven percent of America's twelve million undergraduates (mostly women). First launched into public awareness by the death of singer Karen Carpenter from complications of the disease, anorexia is best described as a pathological fear of weight gain leading to extreme weight loss. The approximate recovery time for anorexia sufferers is seven years, and the death rate twenty percent—the highest of any mental disorder.

The tragedy of such illnesses is perhaps the predictable outcome of a culture preoccupied with external image—and food as a means of controlling it. The weekly Weight Watchers weigh-in has replaced the Catholic confessional as the prototypical act of self-disclosure. Obsession with various forms of non-eating is trendy, but just as gluttonous as obsession with eating—especially to Christian believers whose anticipated joy in a heavenly banquet will surely be oblivious to whether the bread has butter or margarine on it and the milk is 98 percent fat-free.

Obsession with various forms of non-eating is trendy, but just as gluttonous as obsession with eating—especially to Christian believers whose anticipated joy in a heavenly banquet will surely be oblivious to whether the bread has butter or margarine on it and the milk is 98 percent fat-free.

❊ *Petronius/Time Magazine* ❊

Gaius Petronius (died A.D. *66) is a Latin writer who was described by Tacitus as* arbiter elegantiae *(judge of taste) at the court of Nero. He is the author of* The Satyricon, *a fragmentary manuscript considered one of the first examples of the novel form. It is also a classic study of gluttony, giving a vivid, sardonic picture of first century Roman luxuries and decadence. Later, Petronius reportedly committed suicide to escape being put to death by the cruel and tyrannical Nero.*

Trimalchio, the central figure in Petronius' Satyricon, is a flaky, vulgar multimillionaire who gives a colossal and extravagant banquet. More recently The Satyricon *was portrayed in Federico Fellini's famous 1969 film of the same name. But few people realize that Trimalchio was the prototype of F. Scott Fitzgerald's earlier work,* The Great Gatsby *(1925), which was originally titled* Trimalchio's Banquet. *The 1972 article from* Time *magazine, which follows the excerpt from* The Satyricon, *is a reminder that the traditional style of gluttony has not altogether disappeared.*

DRUNKARD'S DEAD END

"If a man has a stubborn and rebellious son who does not obey his father and mother and will not listen to them when they discipline him, his father and mother shall take hold of him and bring him to the elders at the gate of his town. They shall say to the elders, 'This son of ours is stubborn and rebellious. He will not obey us. He is a profligate and a drunkard.' Then all the men of his town shall stone him to death. You must purge the evil from among you. All Israel will hear of it and be afraid."

—Deuteronomy 21:18-21

THE SATYRICON

This was the sort of chatter flying around when Trimalchio came in, dabbed his forehead and washed his hands in perfume. There was a very short pause, then he said:

'Excuse me, dear people, my inside has not been answering the call for several days now. The doctors are puzzled. But some pomegranate rind and resin in vinegar has done me good. But I hope now it will be back on its good behavior. Otherwise my stomach rumbles like a bull. So if any of you wants to go out, there's no need for him to be embarrassed. None of us was born solid. I think there's nothing so tormenting as holding yourself in. This is the one thing even God Almighty can't object to. Yes, laugh, Fortunata, but you generally keep me up all night with this sort of thing.

'Anyway, I don't object to people doing what suits them even in the middle of dinner—and the doctors forbid you to hold yourself in. Even if it's a longer business, everything is there just outside—water, bowls, and all the other little comforts. Believe me, if the wind goes to your brain it starts flooding your whole body too. I've known lots of people die from this because they wouldn't be honest with themselves.'

We thanked him for being so generous and considerate and promptly proceeded to bury our amusement in our glasses. Up to this point, we'd not realized we were only half-way up the hill, as you might say.

The orchestra played, the tables were cleared, and then three white pigs were brought into the dining room, all decked out in muzzles and bells. The first, the master of ceremonies announced, was two years old, the second three, and the third six. I was under the impression that some acrobats were on their way in and the pigs were going to do some tricks, the way they do in street shows. But Trimalchio dispelled this impression by asking:

'Which of these would you like for the next course? Any clodhopper can do you a barnyard cock or a stew and trifles like that, but my cooks are used to boiling whole calves.'

He immediately sent for the chef and without waiting for us to choose he told him to kill the oldest pig.

We thanked him for being so generous and considerate and promptly proceeded to bury our amusement in our glasses. Up to this point, we'd not realized we were only half-way up the hill, as you might say.

THE IMPORTANCE OF BEING GREEDY

In Downey, Calif. a man in his early 20s went through the prime-ribs line seven times at Marmac's, a restaurant that provides an unlimited amount of roast beef for only $3.50. If the evening was a total loss for Marmac's, it was for the customer too. He wound up in a hospital, having his stomach pumped out. But less than a week later he was back in the beef line at the same restaurant.

The Downey episode is just one of many similar instances of gluttony that occur daily across the U.S. in an ever-increasing number of "all-you-can-eat" restaurants. Apart from regulars, like the dainty little old lady who routinely gobbles 20 pieces of fried chicken (for only $1.55) on each visit to Shakey's Pizza Parlor in Los Angeles, gluttons have only their appetites in common and are difficult to identify at a glance. Manager Edward White of Manhattan's Stockholm Restaurant (unlimited smorgasbord for $6.95) still shudders when he remembers the tall, beautifully groomed woman who ravaged his 85-dish buffet. With exquisite technique but total nondiscrimination, she forked slabs of roast beef onto heaps of shrimp, added globs of Swedish meatballs and salted herring, then ladled a quart or so of Russian dressing over the mess. "It looked like an exploding volcano," says White, "and she repeated three or four times." On her next visit, some customers, sickened by the sight of the orgy, began to complain, and White politely told the woman she was welcome no longer.

Considerably easier to detect was the mob of high school kids who descended on a Howard Johnson's restaurant in Spring Valley, N.Y. They arrived on chicken night (unlimited amount for $1.69) and devoured 360 pieces of chicken (about 90 lbs.), along with salad and rolls, before vanishing into the night. Another easy-to-spot glutton was the "gigantic man" who waddled into a Sir George's Smorgasbord House branch in the San Fernando Valley. He opened with 2 lbs. of salad, then reduced a chicken to rubble, inhaled two plates of roast beef, and washed it all down with milk. Then he thoughtfully wiped his plate clean with half a loaf of bread, paid his $2.50 check and left (inexplicably, he passed up dessert). Jack LaFever, a vice president of Sir George, while denying that the huge customer was responsible, reports that most of the restaurants in the chain have since stopped advertising its all-you-can-eat come-on. "The policy remains the same," he says, "but we don't plug it any more."

The supreme challenge to gluttons is posed by the $10 Fiesta dinner

The Downey episode is just one of many similar instances of gluttony that occur daily across the U.S. in an ever-increasing number of "all-you-can-eat" restaurants.

offered by the Club El Bianco on Chicago's Southwest Side. The three to four-hour Super Bowl of gluttony begins with appetizers (bean salad, salami, and pepperoni) and a vast antipasto tray, continues with soup, tossed salad, stuffed peppers, ribs, eggplant parmigiana, veal scaloppini, chicken cacciatore, and piles of pasta. Dessert includes pastries, fruit, and cookies, followed by a nut cart. If anyone complains that he is still hungry, Manager Peter Bianco Jr. has a secret weapon that few could stomach: a huge submarine sandwich topped by a "Champion" trophy. "Nobody's finished the whole thing yet," says Bianco. "If anyone really has, he hasn't lived to talk about it."

Most restaurateurs suffer silently under a gourmand's assault, but they all frown on one particular variant, the Takeout Artist. At the Stockholm, for example, Manager White caught one soberly dressed couple making off with 4 lbs. of shrimp in a concealed plastic bag after they finished dining. When White intercepted them, both complained angrily—and the woman dumped the smuggled shrimp on the floor at his feet. A pair of California countercul-turists astounded the manager of a Shakey's Pizza Parlor with the huge amounts of food they were putting away—until he found an excuse to open their guitar case and found 200 pieces of chicken stashed inside.

Still, the all-you-can-eat theme keeps spreading, and profits keep rolling in. Explains Larry Ellman, whose 37-unit Steak and Brew chain offers unlimited amounts of salad, drinks, and bread with a modestly priced entrée. "The person who eats too much is a fantastic advertisement for us, because he'll tell other people about his great buy." Fifteen Steak and Brew establishments are on the drawing boards, and further expansion seems to be limited only by the output of world agriculture. "We've never run out of food," boasts Robert Gladstone, manager of one of the Steak and Brews. "We let them eat as long as they want to."

A pair of California counterculturists astounded the manager of a Shakey's Pizza Parlor with the huge amounts of food they were putting away—until he found an excuse to open their guitar case and found 200 pieces of chicken stashed inside.

QUESTIONS FOR THOUGHT AND DISCUSSION

1. In *The Satyricon*, what does Trimalchio mean by "going out," "holding yourself in"? What is the appeal of straightforward gluttony—unpleasant as it may seem to us?

2. Have you ever felt full to the point of sickness? In your experience, what usually motivates overeating?

3. What are the similarities and contrasts between Petronius' description of Roman gluttony and America's all-you-can-eat greed for food two thousand years later?

4. How are you affected when you read the descriptions of the various gluttons' "food crusades" in the *Time* article? Why is it harder to feel the same repulsion toward the earlier "reputable" sins of the spirit (pride, envy, anger, sloth, and avarice)?

5. If the *amount* of food offered at a party or dinner was once considered a sign of wealth and status, what dimension of food serves the same function today?

❧ C. S. Lewis ❧

C. S. Lewis was introduced earlier in part 1 on pride. The passage below is from his famous book The Screwtape Letters. *It is a study in temptation that takes the form of a correspondence to a junior devil, Wormwood, from his uncle and senior devil, Screwtape.*

THE SCREWTAPE LETTERS

MY DEAR WORMWOOD,

The contemptuous way in which you spoke of gluttony as a means of catching souls, in your last letter, only shows your ignorance. One of the great achievements of the last hundred years has been to deaden the human conscience on that subject, so that by now you will hardly find a sermon preached or a conscience troubled about it in the whole length and breadth of Europe.

One of the great achievements of the last hundred years has been to deaden the human conscience on that subject, so that by now you will hardly find a sermon preached or a conscience troubled about it in the whole length and breadth of Europe.

This has largely been effected by concentrating all our efforts on gluttony of Delicacy, not gluttony of Excess. Your patient's mother, as I learn from the dossier and you might have learned from Glubose, is a good example. She would be astonished—one day, I hope, *will* be—to learn that her whole life is enslaved to this kind of sensuality, which is quite concealed from her by the fact that the quantities involved are small.

But what do quantities matter, provided we can use a human belly and palate to produce querulousness, impatience, uncharitableness, and self-concern? Glubose has this old woman well in hand. She is a positive terror to hostesses and servants. She is always turning from what has been offered her to say with a demure little sigh and a smile "Oh please, please . . . *all* I want is a cup of tea, weak but not too weak, and the teeniest weeniest bit of really crisp toast."

You see? Because what she wants is smaller and less costly than what has been set before her, she never recognizes as gluttony her determination to get what she wants, however troublesome it may be to others. At the very moment of indulging her appetite she believes that she is practicing temperance. In a crowded restaurant she gives a little scream at the plate which some over-worked waitress has set before her and says, "Oh, that's far, far too much! Take it away and bring me about a quarter of it." If challenged, she would say she was doing this to avoid waste; in reality she does it because the particular shade of delicacy to which we have enslaved her is offended by the sight of more food than she happens to want.

If challenged, she would say she was doing this to avoid waste; in reality she does it because the particular shade of delicacy to which we have enslaved her is offended by the sight of more food than she happens to want.

The real value of the quiet, unobtrusive work which Glubose has been doing for years on this old woman can be gauged by the way in which her belly now dominates her whole life. The woman is in what may be called the "All-I-want" state of mind. *All* she wants is a cup of tea properly made, or an egg properly boiled, or a slice of bread properly toasted. But she never finds any servant or any friend who can do these simple things "properly"—because her "properly" conceals an insatiable demand for the exact, and almost impossible, palatal pleasures which she imagines she remembers from the past; a past described by her as "the days when you could get good servants" but known to us as the days when her senses were more easily pleased and she had pleasures of other kinds which made her less dependent on those of the table. Meanwhile, the daily disappointment produces daily ill temper: cooks give notice and friendships are cooled. If ever the Enemy introduces into her mind a faint suspicion that she is too interested in food, Glubose counters it by suggesting to her that she doesn't mind what she eats herself but "does like to have things nice for her boy." In fact, of course, her greed has been one of the chief sources of his domestic discomfort for many years.

Now your patient is his mother's son. While working your hardest, quite rightly, on other fronts, you must not neglect a little quiet infiltration in respect of gluttony. Being a male, he is not so likely to be caught by the "*All* I want" camouflage. Males are best turned into gluttons with the help of their vanity. They ought to be made to think themselves very knowing about food, to pique themselves on having found the only restaurant in the town where steaks are really "properly" cooked. What begins as vanity can then be gradually turned into habit. But, however you approach it, the great thing is to bring him into the state in which the denial of any one indulgence—it matters not which, champagne or tea, sole colbert or cigarettes—"puts him out," for then his charity, justice, and obedience are all at your mercy.

What begins as vanity can then be gradually turned into habit.

Mere excess in food is much less valuable than delicacy. Its chief use is as a kind of artillery preparation for attacks on chastity. On that, as on every other subject, keep your man in a condition of false spirituality. Never let him notice the medical aspect. Keep him wondering what pride or lack of faith has delivered him into your hands when a simple inquiry into what he has been eating or drinking for the last twenty-four hours would show him whence your ammunition comes and thus enable him by a very little abstinence to imperil your lines of communication. If he *must* think of the medical side of chastity, feed him the grand lie which we have made the English humans believe, that physical exercise in excess and consequent fatigue are specially favorable to this virtue. How they can believe this, in face of the notorious lustfulness of sailors and soldiers, may well be asked. But we used the schoolmasters to put the story about—men who were really interested in chastity as an excuse for games and therefore recommended games as an aid to chastity. But this whole business is too large to deal with at the tail end of a letter,

Your affectionate uncle

SCREWTAPE

Mere excess in food is much less valuable than delicacy.

QUESTIONS FOR THOUGHT AND DISCUSSION

1. What is the difference between the gluttony of excess and that of delicacy? Why is the second form so difficult to recognize as gluttony?
2. What negative traits does the gluttony of delicacy produce in a person? What is the underlying self-centered basis of it? Ironically, what does this kind of gluttony perceive itself to be?
3. What does Lewis mean by the "All-I-want" state of mind, described by Screwtape? Where does vanity enter into the gluttony of delicacy? What purpose can it eventually serve for Wormwood?
4. Where have you seen the "denial of any one indulgence" put someone out? How do you feel when you can't have a particular food, drink, or other indulgence that you're used to or have been "craving"? How might you view this tendency in light of this passage by Lewis?
5. How would you describe modern Western society when it comes to the gluttony of excess? Of delicacy? What factors have contributed to gluttony becoming "fashionable"?

❧ *Henry Fairlie* ❧

Henry Fairlie was introduced earlier in part 2 on envy. His passage below, as so often with Fairlie, is a brilliant characterization of gluttony in the modern age.

THE GLUTTONY OF OUR AGE

An invitation to dinner has, in many cases, become a hazard. What used to be a sociable occasion has been turned into a form of solitude.

An invitation to dinner has, in many cases, become a hazard. What used to be a sociable occasion has been turned into a form of solitude. The hostess or host—for when they take up cooking as a fine art, men are the worst offenders—will hardly be with their guests. They will be in the kitchen. But that is not all. The guests in turn are hardly permitted to be with each other. As each course is brought to the table, it must be tasted, discussed, each ingredient told, the method of preparation recounted at length, praised, vaunted: literally *ad nauseam*, which is not the effect that good eating is meant to produce, except in some distant cultures. All other conversation is merely an entr'acte as the real drama unfolds with each dish. This is no less a form of solitude than that of the glutton at his trough. All companionship is destroyed. The guests might as well have stayed at home and read *The Art of French Cooking*, or watched Julia Child whip up a soufflé on television. At least they would not have had to applaud her. . . .

It may be agreed that our obsession with eating is one of the most wide-spread expressions of idolatry in our age, but we usually think of gluttony as so unsightly and bloated that few of us today may seem guilty of it. On the one hand, there are the dieters and calorie counters; on the other, the addicts of health foods. No one now seems able to rise in the morning and go out to meet the world without stepping on the bathroom scales. These may seem to reflect a self-denying abstemiousness, but there is Gluttony in all of them. (Fastidiousness in eating is regarded in theology as just as much a fault of the sin as excess in it.) Each of them shows an inordinate interest in eating, even though it may appear to be in not eating. They make their own fetish of eating, no less than the glutton with whom we are more familiar. They are just as obsessed with their food, even if their attention is fixed only on a raw carrot and a prune; and their refrigerators and their larders tell, not merely of the time, but of the energy and the anxiety that they give to the most natural of functions.

It is worth watching the obsessive dieters. They are constantly going to their refrigerators, perhaps more than anyone else, even when it is not yet time for their rations, counting what is there, making sure that not one item is missing of what has become so precious to them. They gaze on the morsels, fondle them, even rearrange them, each in its sack, all lovingly known and enumerated. From hour to hour they return to make an inventory. When *in extremis*, they count the spinach leaves. But at last the bell rings. It is mealtime. Salivating like Pavlov's dogs, they scurry to the kitchen table with a stick of celery, a radish, a spoonful of cottage cheese, and a dried apricot for dessert. Watch them as they eat. They devour their delicacies just as the conventional glutton sucks up his bouillabaisse. Their eyes also are fixed on their plates.

They occupy the rest of their days by reading and thinking about food. There must be some new regimen that they should be following, one more impurity that has been discovered in the endive. Whether they are eating or not, their minds are on their food and what their food is doing to their bodies. (Their obsession with it is destroying their minds, but that does not bother them.) What is there to say about six segments of orange on a bed of dandelion leaves, one may ask, but one should not underestimate the inventiveness

It is worth watching the obsessive dieters. They are constantly going to their refrigerators, perhaps more than anyone else, even when it is not yet time for their rations, counting what is there, making sure that not one item is missing of what has become so precious to them.

of an absorbing interest. From so unpromising a beginning, an entire discourse will be developed on the relative dangers and benefits of cyanocobalamin, thiamin, pantothenic acid, riboflavin, glucose, dextrose, dextro-glucose, sucrose, galactose, melibiose, hemoglobin, lecithoprotein, cytoglobin, and (for it must not be forgotten) phosphoaminolipide. There is neither time nor need to talk of anything else. The interest is gluttonous and, as with all forms of Gluttony, the end is solitude. For none of the activity needs a companion. The driving motive of the dieter is again an inordinate self-love.

This is no less true of the addicts of health foods, as they exclaim at the wholesomeness of a sassafras nut or hymn ecstatically the savor of a sunflower seed. They also may not seem to be gluttons in the common sense, yet their interest in their eating is again a form of Gluttony. It is disproportionate and unnatural. There is a great deal of the fastidiousness of self-love in it. A creaturely thing is magnified beyond its actual significance and made some kind of expression of oneself.

A creaturely thing is magnified beyond its actual significance and made some kind of expression of oneself.

One of the pleasures of food, as even theology admits, is that it offers occasions for social intercourse. But it is precisely this that is refused by the dieters and addicts of health foods. Eating is their one staple of interest and conversation. By giving to food a false value, they also rob it of its real value. In contrast to them and to the more familiar glutton, the gourmet thinks and talks very little about his food, except at the moment of preparation or appreciation. At the gourmet's table one notices the food, expresses a brief appreciation of the savor, and expands about other things. . . .

Labia mea Domine . . . is the prayer of the gluttonous in purgatory: "O Lord, open thou my lips, and my mouth shall show forth Thy praise." The appropriateness of the prayer is that it reminds them that the mouth was made for other things than eating and drinking. When we let Gluttony grow in us, it is these other things that we forget. Dante makes a telling leap from our everyday Gluttony to Adam's and Eve's eating of the apple. . . .

The Gluttony of our own age—including the drug takers with their "uppers" and "downers," and the inordinate interest of the dieters in what they eat—has at least a part of its cause, perhaps even the main part, in the boredom of our societies. When there is so much to do, when so much is spread before us for our titillation, surely we should not be bored. Yet it is all so dissatisfying, with neither purpose nor deep reward. Gluttony is a grievous sin, according to theology, if it induces us to find all our contentment in the gratifying of our appetites. But this is today almost all that our societies offer us, the only strenuousness of activity to which we are excited. We are left with a hollow at our core, a sinking feeling in our spirits from day to day, and we resort to the device of the glutton in his private life, one which is well known to the psychiatrist in the patient who overeats as a compensation for some emotional lack. We will fill and stuff our emptiness, even if it is only by chewing ravenously on a raw carrot. We are becoming a breed of junkies. If our societies are founded on Avarice, the state to which they reduce us is Gluttony. With the sin already in us, we do not stir ourselves to resist.

Gluttony is a grievous sin, according to theology, if it induces us to find all our contentment in the gratifying of our appetites.

QUESTIONS FOR THOUGHT AND DISCUSSION

1. How does Henry Fairlie see modern dieters' and health freaks' fastidiousness about food as a form of gluttony? Do you agree? If so, what makes these activities gluttonous?

2. What factors make gluttony a kind of solitude? What examples does Fairlie give of this solitude both in social dining and in dieting?

3. How does preoccupation with food affect the life of the mind?

4. What examples have you encountered, in your circles or in the media and entertainment world, of food being "magnified beyond its actual significance"? Of it being turned into some type of "expression of oneself"?

5. What connection does Fairlie make between gluttony and sloth? Why do you think people see food as an answer to personal emptiness?

✳ *Frederick Buechner* ✳

Frederick Buechner is a Presbyterian minister turned author, and former School Minister at Phillips Exeter Academy. His first novel, A Long Day's Dying, *was published in 1950 to a warm reception from both critics and readers.* Godric—*his story of a medieval saint—was nominated for the 1981 Nobel Prize in literature. To date, he has produced close to thirty works, both fiction and nonfiction, including novels, essays, sermons, and memoirs.*

Buechner's writing is celebrated for its poetic eloquence, depth of imagination, and accent on the ordinary as a window to the divine. In the tradition of Augustine's Confessions, *he urges his readers to be "theologians of autobiography," seeing in the particulars of their everyday lives—as he struggles to see in his own—a glimpse of God's love amid an often ambiguous and darkened world. The death of his father by suicide when he was just ten years old is a recurring touchstone in Buechner's writing and personal journey to God, which he traces in his autobiographical trio:* The Sacred Journey *(1982),* Now and Then *(1983), and* Telling Secrets *(1991).*

In the passage below from Telling Secrets, *Buechner describes his painful confrontation with his daughter's anorexia. He does not tell her story, "It is only hers to tell," but his own, one of obsession and fear that eventually led to personal freedom and a palpable sense of God's presence, "holding his breath, loving her, loving us all." (As mentioned earlier, it should be emphasized that the disease of anorexia has no direct connection to the gluttony of delicacy; rather, our culture of the latter that is obsessed with weight and body image is one sad factor in the epidemic of the former.)*

MORE TO LIFE THAN WHAT'S FOR DINNER

"It was like a competition to see who could eat the least. At dinner they would say, 'All I had today was an apple,' or 'I haven't had anything.' It was surreal."

— College sorority president describing dinner in the house

"I can tell a girl that what matters is what's going on in her head and heart. But when she turns on the TV, she sees that what matters is how you look."

— Sociologist Tony Mann

"I finally realized I didn't want to keep living like that. There's more to worry about in life than what's for dinner."

— Laura Mislevy, recovered anorexic

"In my mind, anorexics ate a leaf of lettuce a day and were stick thin. That wasn't me."
—Sara Hunnicutt, commenting on her anorexia when she was 5'1' and 90 pounds

"I was terrified of fat the way other people are afraid of lions or guns."
—Lisa Arndt, anorexia sufferer

THE DWARVES IN THE STABLE

One November morning in 1936 when I was ten years old, my father got up early, put on a pair of gray slacks and a maroon sweater, opened the door to look in briefly on my younger brother and me, who were playing a game in our room, and then went down into the garage where he turned on the engine of the family Chevy and sat down on the running board to wait for the exhaust to kill him. Except for a memorial service for his Princeton class the next spring, by which time we had moved away to another part of the world altogether, there was no funeral because on both my mother's side and my father's there was no church connection of any kind and funerals were simply not part of the tradition. He was cremated, his ashes buried in a cemetery in Brooklyn, and I have no idea who if anybody was present. I know only that my mother, brother, and I were not.

There was no funeral to mark his death and put a period at the end of the sentence that had been his life, and as far as I can remember, once he had died my mother, brother, and I rarely talked about him much ever again, either to each other or to anybody else. It made my mother too sad to talk about him, and since there was already more than enough sadness to go round, my brother and I avoided the subject with her as she avoided for her own reasons also with us. Once in a while she would bring it up but only in very oblique ways. I remember her saying things like "You're going to have to be big boys now" and "Now things are going to be different for all of us," and to me, "You're the man of the family now," with that one little three-letter adverb freighted with more grief and anger and guilt and God knows what all else than it could possibly bear. . . .

Don't talk, don't trust, don't feel is supposed to be the unwritten law of families that for one reason or another have gone out of whack, and certainly it was our law. We never talked about what had happened. We didn't trust the world with our secret, hardly even trusted each other with it. And as far as my ten-year-old self was concerned anyway, the only feeling I can remember

It made my mother too sad to talk about him, and since there was already more than enough sadness to go round, my brother and I avoided the subject with her as she avoided for her own reasons also with us.

from that distant time was the blessed relief of coming out of the dark and unmentionable sadness of my father's life and death into fragrance and greenness and light. . . .

Don't talk, don't trust, don't feel is supposed to be the unwritten law of families that for one reason or another have gone out of whack, and certainly it was our law.

In the mid 1970s, as a father of three teenage children and a husband of some twenty years standing by then, I would have said that my hearing was pretty good, that I could hear not only what my wife and children were saying but lots of things they weren't saying too. I would have said that I saw fairly well what was going on inside our house and what was going on inside me. I would also have said if anybody had asked me that our family was a close and happy one—that we had our troubles like everybody else but that we loved each other and respected each other and understood each other better than most. And in a hundred ways, praise God, I believe I was right. I believe that is the way it was. But in certain other ways, I came to learn, I was as deaf as my mother was with her little gold purse full of hearing aids none of which really ever worked very well, and though I did not shut my eyes when I talked to people the way she did, I shut them without knowing it to a whole dimension of the life that my wife and I and our children were living together on a green hillside in Vermont during those years.

There are two pieces of stained glass that sit propped up in one of the windows in the room where I write—a room paneled in old barn siding gone silvery gray with maybe as much as two centuries of weathering and full of a great many books, many of them considerably older than that which I've collected over the years and try to keep oiled and repaired because books are my passion, not only writing them and every once in a while even reading them but just having them and moving them around and feeling the comfort of their serene presence. One of those pieces of stained glass, which I think I asked somebody to give me one Christmas, shows the Cowardly Lion from *The Wizard of Oz* with his feet bound with rope and his face streaming with tears as a few of the Winged Monkeys who have bound him hover around in the background. The other is a diptych that somebody gave me once and that always causes me a twinge of embarrassment when I notice it because it seems a little too complacently religious. On one of its panels are written the words "May the blessing of God crown this house" and on the other "Fortunate is he whose work is blessed and whose household is prospered by the Lord."

I have never given either the lion or the diptych much thought as they've sat there year after year gathering dust, but I happened to notice them as I was preparing these pages and decided they might well serve as a kind of epigraph for this part of the story I'm telling. The Cowardly Lion is me, of course—crying, tied up, afraid. I am crying because at the time I'm speaking of, some fifteen years ago, a lot of sad and scary things were going on in our house that I felt helpless either to understand or to do anything about. Yet despite its rather self-satisfied religiosity, I believe the diptych is telling a truth about that time too. . . .

The other half of the diptych's message—"whose household is prospered by the Lord"—was full of irony. Whether because of the Lord or good luck or the state of the stock market, we were a prosperous family in more ways than just economic, but for all the good our prosperity did us when the chips were down, we might as well have been paupers.

What happened was that one of our daughters began to stop eating. There was nothing scary about it at first. It was just the sort of thing any girl who thought she'd be prettier if she lost a few pounds might do—nothing for breakfast, maybe a carrot or a Diet Coke for lunch, for supper perhaps a little salad with low calorie dressing. But then, as months went by, it did become scary. Anorexia nervosa is the name of the sickness she was suffering from, needless to say, and the best understanding of it that I have been able to arrive at goes something like this. Young people crave to be free and independent. They crave also to be taken care of and safe. The dark magic of anorexia is that it satisfies both of these cravings at once. By not eating, you take your stand against the world that is telling you what to do and who to be. And by not eating you also make your body so much smaller, lighter, weaker that in effect it becomes a child's body again and the world flocks to your rescue. This double victory is so great that apparently not even self-destruction seems too high a price to pay.

Be that as it may, she got more and more thin, of course, till she began to have the skull-like face and fleshless arms and legs of a victim of Buchenwald, and at the same time the Cowardly Lion got more and more afraid and sad, felt more and more helpless. No rational argument, no dire medical warning, no pleading or cajolery or bribery would make this young woman he loved eat normally again but only seemed to strengthen her determination not to, this young woman on whose life his own in so many ways depended. He could not solve her problem because he was of course himself part of her problem. She remained very much the same person she had always been—creative, loving, funny, bright as a star—but she was more afraid of gaining weight than she was afraid of death itself because that was what it came to finally. Three years were about as long as the sickness lasted in its most intense form with some moments when it looked as though

The Cowardly Lion is me, of course—crying, tied up, afraid. I am crying because at the time I'm speaking of, some fifteen years ago, a lot of sad and scary things were going on in our house that I felt helpless either to understand or to do anything about.

By not eating, you take your stand against the world that is telling you what to do and who to be. And by not eating you also make your body so much smaller, lighter, weaker that in effect it becomes a child's body again and the world flocks to your rescue. This double victory is so great that apparently not even self-destruction seems too high a price to pay.

things were getting better and some moments when it was hard to imagine they could get any worse. Then finally, when she had to be hospitalized, a doctor called one morning to say that unless they started feeding her against her will, she would die. It was as clear-cut as that. Tears ran down the Cowardly Lion's face as he stood with the telephone at his ear. His paws were tied. The bat-winged monkeys hovered.

I will not try to tell my daughter's story for two reasons. One is that it is not mine to tell but hers. The other is that of course I do not know her story, not the real story, the inside story, of what it was like for her. For the same reasons I will not try to tell what it was like for my wife or our other two children, each of whom in her own way was involved in that story. I can tell only my part in it, what happened to me, and even there I can't be sure I have it right because in many ways it is happening still. The fearsome blessing of that hard time continues to work itself out in my life in the same way we're told the universe is still hurtling through outer space under the impact of the great cosmic explosion that brought it into being in the first place. I think grace sometimes explodes into our lives like that—sending our pain, terror, astonishment hurtling through inner space until by grace they become Orion, Cassiopeia, Polaris to give us our bearings, to bring us into something like full being at last.

My anorectic daughter was in danger of starving to death, and without knowing it, so was I. I wasn't living my own life any more because I was so caught up in hers. If in refusing to eat she was mad as a hatter, I was if anything madder still because whereas in some sense she knew what she was doing to herself, I knew nothing at all about what I was doing to myself. She had given up food. I had virtually given up doing anything in the way of feeding myself humanly. To be at peace is to have peace inside yourself more or less in spite of what is going on outside yourself. In that sense I had no peace at all. If on one particular day she took it into her head to have a slice of toast, say, with her dietetic supper, I was in seventh heaven. If on some other day she decided to have no supper at all, I was in hell.

I choose the term *hell* with some care. Hell is where there is no light but only darkness, and I was so caught up in my fear for her life, which had become in a way my life too, that none of the usual sources of light worked any more, and light was what I was starving for. I had the companionship of my wife and two other children. I read books. I played tennis and walked in the woods. I saw friends and went to the movies. But even in the midst of such times as that I remained so locked inside myself that I was not really present

The fearsome blessing of that hard time continues to work itself out in my life in the same way we're told the universe is still hurtling through outer space under the impact of the great cosmic explosion that brought it into being in the first place.

in them at all. Toward the end of C. S. Lewis's *The Last Battle* there is a scene where a group of dwarves sit huddled together in a tight little knot thinking that they are in a pitch black, malodorous stable when the truth of it is that they are out in the midst of an endless grassy countryside as green as Vermont with the sun shining and blue sky overhead. The huge golden lion, Aslan himself, stands nearby with all the other dwarves "kneeling in a circle around his forepaws" as Lewis writes, "and burying their hands and faces in his mane as he stooped his great head to touch them with his tongue." When Aslan offers the dwarves food, they think it is offal. When he offers them wine, they take it for ditch water. "Perfect love casteth out fear," John writes, (1 John 4:18), and the other side of that is that fear like mine casteth out love, even God's love. The love I had for my daughter was lost in the anxiety I had for my daughter.

The only way I knew to be a father was to take care of her, as my father had been unable to take care of me, to move heaven and earth if necessary to make her well, and of course I couldn't do that. I didn't have either the wisdom or the power to make her well. None of us has the power to change other human beings like that, and it would be a terrible power if we did, the power to violate the humanity of others even for their own good. The psychiatrists we consulted told me I couldn't cure her. The best thing I could do for her was to stop trying to do anything. I think in my heart I knew they were right, but it didn't stop the madness of my desperate meddling, it didn't stop the madness of my trying. Everything I could think to do or say only stiffened her resolve to be free from, among other things, me. Her not eating was a symbolic way of striking out for that freedom. The only way she would ever be well again was if and when she freely chose to be. The best I could do as her father was to stand back and give her that freedom even at the risk of her using it to choose for death instead of life. . . .

How easy it is to write such words and how impossible it was to live them. What saved the day for my daughter was that when she finally had to be hospitalized in order to keep her alive, it happened about three thousand miles away from me. I was not there to protect her, to make her decisions, to manipulate events on her behalf, and the result was that she had to face those events on her own. There was no one to shield her from those events and their consequences in all their inexorability. In the form of doctors, nurses, social workers, the judge who determined that she was a

The love I had for my daughter was lost in the anxiety I had for my daughter.

danger to her own life and thus could be legally hospitalized against her will, society stepped in. Those men and women were not haggard, dithering, lovesick as I was. They were realistic, tough, conscientious, and in those ways, though they would never have put it in such terms themselves, loved her in a sense that I believe is closer to what Jesus meant by love than what I had been doing.

God loves in something like their way, I think. The power that created the universe and spun the dragonfly's wing and is beyond all other powers holds back, in love, from overpowering us. I have never felt God's presence more strongly than when my wife and I visited that distant hospital where our daughter was. Walking down the corridor to the room that had her name taped to the door, I felt that presence surrounding me like air—God in his very stillness, holding his breath, loving her, loving us all, the only way he can without destroying us. One night we went to compline in an Episcopal cathedral, and in the coolness and near emptiness of that great vaulted place, in the remoteness of the choir's voices chanting plainsong, in the grayness of the stone, I felt it again—the passionate restraint and hush of God.

The power that created the universe and spun the dragonfly's wing and is beyond all other powers holds back, in love, from overpowering us.

Little by little the young woman I loved began to get well, emerging out of the shadows finally as strong and sane and wise as anybody I know, and little by little as I watched her healing happen, I began to see how much I was in need of healing and getting well myself. Like Lewis's dwarves, for a long time I had sat huddled in the dark of a stable of my own making. It was only now that I started to suspect the presence of the green countryside, the golden lion in whose image and likeness even cowardly lions are made.

From Frederick Buechner, *Telling Secrets.* © 1991 by Frederick Buechner. Reprinted by permission of HarperCollins Publishers, Inc.

QUESTIONS FOR THOUGHT AND DISCUSSION

1. In your own words, describe the family's reaction to the death of Frederick Buechner's father. How did this experience teach him to deal with later crises in his life? What "messages" from your parents have influenced the way you handle crises?

2. How did Buechner feel when his mother said, "You're the man of the family now"? How might this have contributed to the role he sought to play during his daughter's struggle with anorexia?

3. How does Buechner describe his family in the mid-1970s? How well did he believe he knew and "heard" them? How did his daughter's illness take him by surprise?

4. What images are portrayed on the two pieces of stained glass in Buechner's writing room? How does he now see these images as descriptions of the difficult time he describes in this piece?

5. What is the "best understanding" Buechner is able to glean of his daughter's sickness, anorexia nervosa? Have you or someone you know suffered from an eating disorder? How would you describe the emotional plea behind the disease?

6. What role does food take on in anorexia? In other eating disorders? Why do you think food is a particularly easy "substance" to use in acting out or covering up underlying emotional problems? Why do you think it's particularly prevalent on college campuses?

7. What is the journey of Buechner's response to his daughter's illness? When and how does he feel the "presence of God" in the midst of it? What personal lessons does he take away as a father from this wrenching experience?

8. How, if at all, do you think the gluttony of excess or the gluttony of delicacy in Western culture fosters the spread of eating disorders, especially among young women? What images of women does such a culture find acceptable and desirable? What images does it reject? What's inherently wrong with this value system?

THE COUNTERPOINT TO GLUTTONY:

Blessed Are Those Who Are Persecuted for Righteousness' Sake

The traditional counterpoint to gluttony—both the gluttony of excess and the gluttony of delicacy—is courage under suffering and persecution. Although at first it may seem a far stretch, the dedication, discipline, and patience required to undergo hardship with courage is a powerful opposite to the self-indulgence or finickiness of gluttony.

Although at first it may seem a far stretch, the dedication, discipline, and patience required to undergo hardship with courage is a powerful opposite to the self-indulgence or finickiness of gluttony.

As Jesus states in the beatitude, "Blessed are those who are persecuted for righteousness' sake, for theirs is the kingdom of heaven." Whereas gluttony is a form of indiscipline and self-pampering, courage under suffering is discipline and contentment raised to the level of self-sacrifice.

The counterpoint is poignant on another level. Gluttony is a form of seeking that consumes in order to find, yet ends in losing. Courage under suffering and persecution is a form of being consumed that seems to lose, yet ends in finding. The contrasts are worth pondering.

ENDURING REWARDS

"Consider it pure joy, my brothers, whenever you face trials of many kinds, because you know that the testing of your faith develops perseverance. Perseverance must finish its work so that you may be mature and complete, not lacking anything."

—James 1:2-4

"Since you have kept my command to endure patiently, I will also keep you from the hour of trial that is going to come upon the whole world to test those who live on the earth."

—Revelation 3:10

✳ *Thomas à Kempis* ✳

Thomas à Kempis was introduced earlier in part 1 on pride. The passage below, from The Imitation of Christ, *is a clear example of traditional Christian teaching on patience and discipline under suffering.*

OF PATIENT SUFFERING OF INJURIES AND WRONGS AND WHO IS TRULY PATIENT

My son, what is it you say? Why do you thus complain? Cease, cease, complain no more. Consider My Passion and the passion of My saints, and you will see well that what you suffer for Me is very little. You have not yet suffered to the shedding of your blood, and surely you have suffered little in comparison with those who have suffered so many great things from Me in time past, and those who have been so strongly tempted, so grievously troubled, and in so many ways put to the test. It behooves you, therefore, to remember the great, serious things others have suffered for Me, so that you may the more lightly bear your little grief. And if they do not seem little to you, take care that your impatience is not the cause. Nevertheless, whether they are little or great, study always to bear them patiently, if you can, without begrudging or complaining. The better you dispose yourself to suffer them, the more wisely you act, and the more merit will you have, and because of your good disposition and your good will, your burden will be lighter.

You will never say: I cannot suffer this thing from such a person, nor is it expected of me to suffer it. He has done me great wrong, and accused me of things I never thought; but from another man I am willing to suffer for what I thought. Such kind of utterance is not good, for it does not consider the virtue of patience, or by whom patience shall be crowned; rather, it considers the persons and the offenses done.

And so, he is not truly patient who will suffer only as much as he pleases, or from whom he pleases. A truly patient man gives no heed from whom he suffers, whether from his superior or from his equal or from someone below him, or whether he is a good and a holy man, or an evil and an unworthy man.

The better you dispose yourself to suffer them, the more wisely you act, and the more merit will you have, and because of your good disposition and your good will, your burden will be lighter.

But whenever any adversity or wrong befalls him, whatever it be, no matter from whom it comes or how often it comes, he takes all faithfully from the hand of God, and accounts it as a rich gift and a great benefit, for he knows that there is nothing a man can suffer for God that goes without great merit.

Be ready for battle, therefore, if you would have victory. Without battle you cannot come to the crown of patience, and if you will not suffer, you refuse to be crowned. Wherefore, if you desire to be crowned, resist strongly and suffer patiently, for without labor no man can come to rest, and without battle no man can come to victory.

O Lord Jesus, make possible to me by grace what is impossible to me by nature. You know well that I can suffer little, and that I am soon cast down by a little adversity. Wherefore, I beseech You that hereafter I may love and desire trouble and adversity for Your Name; truly, to suffer and to be troubled for You is very good and profitable for the health of my soul.

From *The Imitation of Christ* by Thomas à Kempis. Copyright © 1955 by Doubleday, a division of Random House, Inc. Used by permission of Doubleday, a division of Random House, Inc.

QUESTIONS FOR THOUGHT AND DISCUSSION

1. Why does Thomas à Kempis advise his readers to bear suffering with patience, "without begrudging or complaining"?
2. What is the problem with being willing to suffer "only as much as [you] please, or from whom [you] please"?
3. Do you agree with the author's belief that a person cannot undergo suffering with such patience "by nature"? If so, what is the necessary power for such endurance?
4. Why is patience in suffering the antithesis to gluttony?
5. Have you ever found suffering to be "good and profitable" for the health of your soul, as the passage suggests? How so?
6. In a culture of convenience, suffering is absurdly unfashionable. Living in the modern world, what do you think of Thomas à Kempis's advice?

John of the Cross

John of the Cross, born Juan de Yepes y Álvarez (1542–1591), was a mystic, a writer, and the joint founder of a branch of the Carmelite monastic order. Born in Spain to a poor family of noble origin, he became a Carmelite monk in 1563. He studied theology at Salamanca University and was ordained a priest in 1567. Dissatisfied with the laxity of his fellow Carmelites, he initiated reform with the help of Teresa of Avila.

For much of the rest of his life, John was caught up in bitter disputes between the different branches of the Carmelite order. Refusing to compromise his convictions, he underwent severe suffering—including imprisonment, banishment, and several illnesses—and died before he was fifty. He was canonized by the Roman Catholic Church in 1726.

John's writings combine the sensitivity of a poet with the sharpness of a theologian and the profundity of a mystic. His deeply mystical works, mostly written from prison, speak of the purging of the soul through "the night of the senses." The highest purification of all is the transformation into union with God, described in this passage as being consumed by a living flame. Men and women consume and are consumed by many things, some of which only shrink and debase them. But the ultimate consumption—and the grand counterpoint to gluttony—is a human being ablaze with the glory of God as if consumed with divine fire.

ON THE DIVINE LIGHT

For the sake of further clarity in this matter, we ought to note that this purgative and loving knowledge or divine light we are speaking of has the same effect on a soul that fire has on a log of wood. The soul is purged and prepared for union with the divine light just as the wood is prepared for transformation into the fire. Fire, when applied to wood, first dehumidifies it, dispelling all moisture and making it give off any water it contains. Then it gradually turns the wood black, makes it dark and ugly, and even causes it to emit a bad odor. By drying out the wood, the fire brings to light and expels all those ugly and dark accidents which are contrary to fire. Finally, by heating and enkindling

Men and women consume and are consumed by many things, some of which only shrink and debase them. But the ultimate consumption—and the grand counterpoint to gluttony—is a human being ablaze with the glory of God as if consumed with divine fire.

it from without, the fire transforms the wood into itself and makes it as beautiful as it is itself. Once transformed, the wood no longer has any activity or passivity of its own, except for its weight and its quantity which is denser than the fire. For it possesses the properties and performs the actions of fire: it is dry and it dries; it is hot and it gives off heat; it is brilliant and it illumines; and it is also light, much lighter than before. It is the fire that produces all these properties in the wood.

Similarly, we should philosophize about this divine, loving fire of contemplation. Before transforming the soul, it purges it of all contrary qualities. It produces blackness and darkness and brings to the fore the soul's ugliness; thus the soul seems worse than before and unsightly and abominable. This divine purge stirs up all the foul and vicious humors of which the soul was never before aware; never did it realize there was so much evil in itself, since these humors were so deeply rooted. And now that they may be expelled and annihilated they are brought to light and seen clearly through the illumination of this dark light of divine contemplation. Although the soul is no worse than before, neither in itself nor in its relationship with God, it feels undoubtedly so bad as to be not only unworthy that God should see it but deserving of his abhorrence; in fact, it feels that God now does abhor it.

This divine purge stirs up all the foul and vicious humors of which the soul was never before aware; never did it realize there was so much evil in itself, since these humors were so deeply rooted.

John of the Cross, 1583–1584.

QUESTIONS FOR THOUGHT AND DISCUSSION

1. What steps are involved in fire consuming a piece of wood? How do these steps parallel a soul being consumed by God's divine love?

2. How does the author view his own soul in the various stages of "purging"?

3. What are the contrasts between consuming food in gluttony and being consumed by God's love as in fire?

4. What is the difference between the consuming John of the Cross describes and modern talk of being "consumed" by a passion for a sport, a person, or a hobby?

Lust, or licentiousness, is the seventh and last of the seven deadly sins and the second of the two sins of the flesh, which are "warm" but "disreputable." Its distinctiveness lies in the fact that almost all mankind (the word mankind being more accurate here than humankind) knows something about this sin from experience—and knows that they know.

Indeed, lust is often so exaggerated that all by itself it is treated as tantamount to "vice" and "immorality." This was the reason Dorothy Sayers entitled her book The Other Six Deadly Sins.

Lust is not the most serious sin. It is far lower on the totem pole than pride, and it is a sin of the flesh, not the spirit—though, needless to say, sins of the flesh can corrupt the spirit. But it is certainly the juiciest and most popular sin. Even Thomas Aquinas commented that lust is "about the greatest of pleasures, and these absorb the mind more than any others." Not surprisingly, modern advertisers have capitalized openly on lust, sometimes with an explicitness that would have been unthinkable a generation ago. It is important, therefore, to state without coyness or hypocrisy just why lust is a deadly sin.

Lust is not the most serious sin. It is far lower on the totem pole than pride, and it is a sin of the flesh, not the spirit— though, needless to say, sins of the flesh can corrupt the spirit. But it is certainly the juiciest and most popular sin. Even Thomas Aquinas commented that lust is "about the greatest of pleasures, and these absorb the mind more than any others."

THE WORD NEVER HEARD

"By a hideous irony, our shirking reprobation of that sin [lust] has made us too delicate so much as to name it, so that we have come to use for it the words which were made to cover the whole range of human corruption. A man

239

may be greedy and selfish; spiteful, cruel, jealous, and unjust; violent and brutal; grasping, unscrupulous, and a liar; stubborn and arrogant; stupid, morose, and dead to every noble instinct—and still we are ready to say of him that he is not an immoral man."

—Dorothy Sayers

MUST WE LUST?

"Lust isn't a sin, it's a necessity, for with lust as our guide we imagine our bodies moving the way our bodies were meant to move."

—From "Act I: LUST (I think I love you—Who are you, anyway?),"
a lavish 12-page ad by Nike in *People* magazine, 1993

Lust is often formally dissected in terms of such components as promiscuity, pornography, adultery, incest, seduction, prostitution, rape, and unnatural vice. But at its heart, lust is an idolizing of sex in the sense of an unethical and unrestrained expression of the sexual impulse. It happens even in proper sexual relations when the object of sexual desire is not the sexual partner but rather the pleasure or services that the partner can provide.

Like food, sex is of course good in the biblical understanding. But at certain times in the Christian past, its goodness has been severely undervalued, chiefly because of a dualism inherited from the Greeks who saw the mind as positive and the body as negative. From this warped viewpoint, we worship with our minds and sin with our bodies. (Or as comedian Jonathan Winters put it, "God is in my mind, but the Devil is in my pants.") From the biblical point of view, however, the challenge is quite the opposite: We worship God with our bodies as well as our minds and hearts, and we sin above all with our minds, not our bodies.

From the biblical point of view, however, the challenge is quite the opposite: we worship God with our bodies as well as our minds and hearts, and we sin above all with our minds, not our bodies.

At the same time, in modern culture the place of sex is greatly exaggerated—not only through the overheated claims of the sexual revolution but through the omnipresent equation of sex and advertising. Happiness, runs the "Grand Modern Lie," depends upon being forever sexually attractive and fulfilled. The cult of sexual pleasure and physical beauty has therefore been made integral to identity, clothing, lifestyle, and status in our sex-obsessed popular culture. Yet this blatant sexiness of magazine covers, romance novels, and most movies and television shows is always fantasy sexuality, and therefore feeds the other sins of anger (growing out of frustration), and often envy.

At the same time, sexuality has been freed from its former ties to procreation, setting the stage for the isolation and exaggeration of the sexual impulse. This movement reaches its climax in the advocates of sexual mysticism who regard sexual intercourse as the ultimate revelatory breakthrough between human beings—as if lovemaking were the equivalent of Mt. Sinai or the resurrection. D. H. Lawrence, for example, reaches for the comparison in Lady Chatterly's Lover *when he parodied Psalm 24 in talking of sex: "Let the King of Glory enter in."*

There are many important implications of the sexual revolution. One is that if the double standard of the "male chauvinist" past has gone, lust is no longer a masculine preserve. Sexual equality means that the lust that was sauce for the gander is now sauce for the goose, too. Another is the reminder that marriage does not solve the problem of lust. Lust in marriage is more subtle than lust outside marriage. Well short of marital rape, lust may be present in marriage when life is so absorbed elsewhere or love is so absent elsewhere that lovemaking is routine rather than expressive, purely physical and one-dimensional rather than total.

Mention of the sexual revolution also carries a caution. Dorothy Sayers stressed that people fall into the sin of lust for two main reasons. One is through "sheer exuberance of animal spirits." The other, which is far harder to address, is when "men and women may turn to lust in sheer boredom and discontent." Indeed, she says, "The mournful and medical aspect of twentieth-century pornography and promiscuity strongly suggests that we have reached one of those periods of spiritual depression, where people go to bed because they have nothing better to do."

Many evils have traditionally been ascribed to lust. But the two main pangs of lust are dehumanization and self-deception. All modern sex has been dehumanized, Henry Fairlie notes, by the scientific "animalization" of modern sexual manuals. But on top of that, lust essentially "uses" and dehumanizes another (still a problem of which women are more often victims than men). But the users deceive themselves, too. Lust-driven seduction without personal engagement ends only in the void of empty-armedness and an even deeper longing.

In what is traditionally called the Sermon on the Mount, Jesus stressed this inner destructiveness of lust. He directed His words to those who thought themselves sexually upright because they did not strictly violate the commandment, but would nevertheless follow a woman with their eyes. In contrast, Jesus emphasized that the mere fact that one does not commit adultery with a certain man or woman does not mean that one's relation to that person in the domain of sexuality is as it should be or that one is truly pure sexually. It is not just a matter of the act of the body, but the thoughts of the heart and mind.

Many evils have traditionally been ascribed to lust. But the two main pangs of lust are dehumanization and self-deception.

DEAD AT DAWN

"Love has meaning only insofar as it includes the idea of its continuance. . . . But Lust dies at the next dawn, and when it returns in the evening, to search where it may, it is with its own past erased. Love wants to enjoy in other ways the human being whom it has enjoyed in bed; it looks forward to having breakfast. But in the morning Lust is always furtive. It dresses as mechanically as it undressed and heads straight for the door, to return to its own solitude."

—Henry Fairlie, *The Seven Deadly Sins Today*

Lust claims that love without sex is impossible and that sex without love still satisfies. But both claims are wrong. Paradoxically, the profligate is more frustrated than fulfilled. Or as the Talmud puts it straightforwardly, "There is a small organ which when constantly fed is hungry but when deprived is full."

Expressed more positively, the biblical view of sexual intercourse is that it is not only procreative but expressive. It is the ultimate expression of intimacy, of complete and unconditional unveiling, of which two human beings are capable. As such, it is an act that is misleading and damaging outside marriage, the only setting that is totally self-giving.

UNVEILING LOVE

My lover thrust his hand through the latch-opening;
　　my heart began to pound for him.
I arose to open for my lover,
　　and my hands dripped with myrrh,
my fingers with flowing myrrh,
　　on the handles of the lock.
I opened for my lover,
　　but my lover had left; he was gone.
　　My heart sank at his departure.
I looked for him but did not find him.
　　I called him but he did not answer.
The watchmen found me
　　as they made their rounds in the city.
They beat me, they bruised me;
　　they took away my cloak,
　　those watchmen of the walls!
O daughters of Jerusalem, I charge you—
　　if you find my lover,
what will you tell him?
　　Tell him I am faint with love.

Place me like a seal over your heart,
  like a seal on your arm;
for love is as strong as death,
  its jealousy unyielding as the grave.
It burns like blazing fire,
  like a mighty flame.
Many waters cannot quench love;
  rivers cannot wash it away.
If one were to give
all the wealth of his house for love,
it would be utterly scorned.

           —Song of Songs 5:4-8; 8:6-7

Lust is therefore sexual activity whose ultimate expressive purpose is violated for the sake of immediate sexual pleasure. The satisfaction of psychological or bodily desires supersedes the power of lovemaking to give and receive love. The surface words and deeds may profess love, but they mask the self-love by which they are really driven.

Lust is therefore sexual activity whose ultimate expressive purpose is violated for the sake of immediate sexual pleasure.

LUST'S BITTER AFTERTASTE

"In the course of time, Amnon son of David fell in love with Tamar, the beautiful sister of Absalom son of David.

"Amnon became frustrated to the point of illness on account of his sister Tamar, for she was a virgin, and it seemed impossible for him to do anything to her. Now Amnon had a friend named Jonadab son of Shimeah, David's brother. Jonadab was a very shrewd man. He asked Amnon, 'Why do you, the king's son, look so haggard morning after morning? Won't you tell me?'

"Amnon said to him, 'I'm in love with Tamar, my brother Absalom's sister.'

"'Go to bed and pretend to be ill,' Jonadab said. 'When your father comes to see you, say to him, "I would like my sister Tamar to come and give me something to eat. Let her prepare the food in my sight so that I may watch her and then eat it from her hand."'

"So Amnon lay down and pretended to be ill. When the king came to see him, Amnon said to him, 'I would like my sister Tamar to come and make some special bread in my sight, so I may eat from her hand.'

"David sent word to Tamar at the palace: 'Go to the house of your brother Amnon and prepare some food for him.' So Tamar went to the house of her brother Amnon, who was lying down. She took some dough, kneaded it, made the bread in his sight and baked it. Then she took the pan and served him the bread, but he refused to eat.

"'Send everyone out of here,' Amnon said. So everyone left him. Then Amnon said to Tamar, 'Bring the food here into my bedroom so that I may eat from your hand.' And Tamar took the bread she had prepared and brought it to her brother Amnon in his bedroom. But when she took it to him to eat, he grabbed her and said, 'Come to bed with me, my sister.'

"'Don't, my brother!' she said to him. 'Don't force me. Such a thing should not be done in Israel! Don't do this wicked thing. What about me? Where could I get rid of my disgrace? And what about you? You would be like one of the wicked fools in Israel. Please speak to the king; he will not keep me from being married to you.' But he refused to listen to her, and since he was stronger than she, he raped her.

"Then Amnon hated her with intense hatred. In fact, he hated her more than he had loved her. Amnon said to her, 'Get up and get out!'

"'No!' she said to him. 'Sending me away would be a greater wrong than what you have already done to me.'

"But he refused to listen to her. He called his personal servant and said, 'Get this woman out of here and bolt the door after her.' So his servant put her out and bolted the door after her. She was wearing a richly ornamented robe, for this was the kind of garment the virgin daughters of the king wore. Tamar put ashes on her head and tore the ornamented robe she was wearing. She put her hand on her head and went away, weeping aloud as she went."

—2 Samuel 13:1-19

Molière, the pen name of Jean Baptiste Poquelin (1622–1673), was a French comic playwright. Born in Paris and educated by the Jesuits, he founded a theatre company in 1643 and obtained the patronage of Philippe d'Orléans, eventually organizing a regular theatre before King Louis XIV. From 1659 on, he produced at least one major dramatic achievement each year, such as Tartuffe *(1664) and* Le Misanthrope *(1666). He died in Paris after acting in his own last play.*

Molière's unsparing ridicule was brought to bear on courtiers, clergy, physicians, and even his fellow dramatists. Fortunately for him, Molière was the royal favorite and shielded by the king. But several of his plays were banned for many years. At the insistence of the clergy, he was denied holy burial. But he remains unrivaled as a comic portrayer of human character and a debunker of hypocrisy and vice.

Needless to say, the legendary figure of Don Juan, the young nobleman of Seville, is the epitome of the profligate. Mozart's opera Don Giovanni *(1787) is the most famous form of the Don Juan story. George Bernard Shaw's* Man and Superman *is a successful English version. But Molière's* Don Juan *perfectly captures the obsessive and unscrupulous pursuer of women and aptly prefigures the playboy Don Juan of the modern sexual revolution.*

Molière's Don Juan perfectly captures the obsessive and unscrupulous pursuer of women and aptly prefigures the Playboy Don Juan of the modern sexual revolution.

PRESIDENTIAL UNDRESSING

"[He] gave me the full Bill Clinton. . . . It was this look, it's the way he flirts with women. When it was time to shake my hand, the smile disappeared, the rest of the crowd disappeared and we shared an intense but brief sexual exchange. He undressed me with his eyes."

—Monica Lewinsky in Andrew Morton's *Monica's Story*, 1999

DON JUAN, OR THE FEAST WITH THE STATUE

SGANARELLE: Oh! Good Heavens! I know my Don Juan to my finger-tips: your heart is the greatest rover in the world; it is pleased to run from one bondage to another and does not love to rest in one place.

DON JUAN: Now, tell me, do you not think I am right in acting in such a manner?

SGANARELLE: Ah! Monsieur.

DON JUAN: What? Speak.

SGANARELLE: Undoubtedly you are right, if you have a mind to it; there is no gain saying that. But if you were not inclined to it, it might, perhaps, be another matter.

DON JUAN: I give you leave to speak and to tell me your feelings.

SGANARELLE: In that case, Monsieur, I will tell you frankly I do not approve of your goings on, and I think it a very base thing to make love on all sides as you do.

DON JUAN: What! Would you have a man bind himself to remain with the first object that attracts him, renounce everything for her, and be blind to every one else? A pretty thing to pique oneself on the empty honor of being faithful, to bury oneself for ever in one passion and to be dead from one's youth to all other beauties that may captivate!

I may be engaged, but the love I have for one fair one does not compel my heart to act with injustice towards others; I have eyes to see the merit of them all, and to pay to each the homage and tribute nature demands from us.

No, no: constancy is fit only for fools; every beautiful woman has a right to charm. The advantage of being the first to be loved ought not to rob others of the just pretensions they all have to our hearts.

For my part, beauty delights me wherever I find it, and I readily yield to the sweet tyranny which it exercises. I may be engaged, but the love I have for one fair one does not compel my heart to act with injustice towards others; I have eyes to see the merit of them all, and to pay to each the homage and tribute nature demands from us. However it may be, I cannot refuse my heart to any lovely creature I see; and, as soon as a pretty face asks me, had I ten thousand hearts I would give them all.

First beginnings, besides, have indescribable charms, and all the pleasure of love consists in variety. It is an extreme delight to reduce, by a hundred wiles, the heart of a young beauty; to see the gradual progress we make from day to day; to combat, by raptures, tears, and sighs the innocent modesty of a heart which can hardly surrender itself; to force, inch by inch, through all the little obstacles which she throws in our way; to overcome the scruples upon which she prides herself; and to lead her gently whither we have a mind to bring her.

But as soon as she is mastered, there is nothing left to be said or to be desired; all the charm of the passion is at an end, and we should fall asleep in the tranquillity of such a love unless some new object came to awaken our desires, and to present to our heart the fascinating charms of a conquest still to make: in short there is nothing so agreeable as to triumph over the resistance of a fair maiden, and, in this matter, I am as ambitious as conquerors who fly perpetually from one victor to another, and who cannot endure to set bounds to their wishes. There is nothing which can restrain the impetuosity of my desires. I find I have a heart capable of loving the whole world, and, like Alexander, I could wish for other worlds that I might extend my amorous conquests.

From *The Plays of Molière*, Volume IV, A. R. Waller, trans. (Edinburgh: John Grant, 1826), pp. 149, 151.

THE GREATEST LOVER

"A philanderer is a man who is strongly attracted by women. He flirts with them, falls half in love with them, makes them fall in love with him, but will not commit himself to any permanent relation with them, and often retreats at the last moment if his suit is successful—loves them but loves himself more—is too cautious, too fastidious, ever to give himself away."

—George Bernard Shaw, *The Philanderer*

"The greatest lover has made love not to a thousand different women, but to one woman a thousand different ways."

—French proverb

QUESTIONS FOR THOUGHT AND DISCUSSION

1. Why do you think Sganarelle describes Don Juan's various affairs as running "from one bondage to another"?

2. What other words or phrases in Don Juan's monologue paint his affairs in terms of compulsion or powerlessness to choose otherwise? What do you think of this way of understanding sexually promiscuous behavior?

3. How does Don Juan view the idea of faithfulness and devotion to one woman? How does he use the terms of justice and injustice to make his behavior seem more legitimate?

4. How do you feel when you read Don Juan's description of the gradual seduction of a young woman in the paragraph starting "First beginnings"? What happens to his amorous feelings after the "conquest"? How is this description a contradiction of the way he has portrayed his romances earlier?

5. Does Don Juan truly have a heart "capable of loving the whole world," as he suggests? Why or why not?

6. What are the similarities between Don Juan's philosophy of love and modern attitudes following the sexual revolution? Where do the differences lie?

7. What are the fallacies of Don Juan's philosophy?

D. H. Lawrence

David Herbert Lawrence (1885–1930) was an English novelist, poet, short story writer, and essayist. Born in Eastwood, Nottinghamshire, the son of a miner, he later became a school teacher. After the success of his first novel, however, he decided to make a living by writing.

D. H. Lawrence is known for his controversial but deeply idealistic views about sexual relations and his interest in primitive religions and native mysticism. Sex, he believed, was a cure for our human maladjustment to modern industrial society. His best known novels, Sons and Lovers (1913), Women in Love (1921), and Lady Chatterly's Lover (1928), are all a powerful rebellion against what he saw as Anglo-Saxon puritanism. He was therefore involved in some of the most famous censorship cases of the twentieth century. But he is still regarded by many as the greatest modern English novelist. Incurably restless, Lawrence lived in Italy, Germany, Ceylon, Australia, New Zealand, Tahiti, France, and Mexico, and even dreamed of an artists' colony in Taos, New Mexico.

Sex, he believed, was a cure for our human maladjustment to modern industrial society.

The following reading is from his novel The Rainbow (1915), also prosecuted for obscenity. It describes the role of lust in the breakdown of the relationship of an engaged couple, Skrebensky and Ursula. Significantly, the couple are engaged (rather than a "one night stand"), the destructive lust is the woman's, and her final reflections on the destructiveness are profoundly theological. Lust, it suggests, is a form of idolatry that tries to usurp God's place and shape the sexual partner in its own image—with inevitably destructive consequences.

TEMPTING VIRTUE

"Those stupid moralists who preach about improving people hardly succeed with one in a thousand, while tempting virtue into the wildest and most unbridled fornication is the easiest thing in the world. And what fun it is! What would life be worth if immorality with all its variants didn't exist?"

—Alfred Nobel, *Nemesis*

THE RAINBOW

The days went by unmarked, in a full, almost strenuous enjoyment of one's own physique. Skrebensky was one among the others, till evening came, and he took her for himself. She was allowed a great deal of freedom and was treated with a good deal of respect, as a girl on the eve of marriage, about to depart for another continent.

The trouble began at evening. Then a yearning for something unknown came over her, a passion for something she knew not what. She would walk the foreshore alone after dusk, expecting, expecting something, as if she had gone to a rendezvous. The salt, bitter passion of the sea, its indifference to the earth, its swinging, definite motion, its strength, its attack, and its salt burning, seemed to provoke her to a pitch of madness, tantalizing her with vast suggestions of fulfillment. And then, for personification, would come Skrebensky, Skrebensky, whom she knew, whom she was fond of, who was attractive, but whose soul could not contain her in its waves of strength, nor his breast compel her in burning, salty passion.

One evening they went out after dinner, across the low golf links to the dunes and the sea. The sky had small, faint stars, all was still and faintly dark. They walked together in silence, then plowed, laboring, through the heavy loose sand of the gap between the dunes. They went in silence under the even, faint darkness, in the darker shadow of the sandhills.

Suddenly, cresting the heavy, sandy pass, Ursula lifted her head, and shrank back, momentarily frightened. There was a great whiteness confronting her, the moon was incandescent as a round furnace door, out of which came the high blast of moonlight, over the seaward half of the world, a dazzling, terrifying glare of white light. They shrank back for a moment into shadow, uttering a cry. He felt his chest laid bare, where the secret was heavily hidden. He felt himself fusing down to nothingness, like a bead that rapidly disappears in an incandescent flame.

"How wonderful!" cried Ursula, in low, calling tones. "How wonderful!"

And she went forward, plunging into it. He followed behind. She too seemed to melt into the glare, towards the moon.

There was a great whiteness confronting her, the moon was incandescent as a round furnace door, out of which came the high blast of moonlight, over the seaward half of the world, a dazzling, terrifying glare of white light.

The sands were as ground silver, the sea moved in solid brightness, coming towards them, and she went to meet the advance of the flashing, buoyant water. She gave her breast to the moon, her belly to the flashing, heaving water. He stood behind, encompassed, a shadow ever dissolving.

She stood on the edge of the water, at the edge of the solid, flashing body of the sea, and the wave rushed over her feet.

"I want to go," she cried, in a strong, dominant voice. "I want to go."

He saw the moonlight on her face, so she was like metal, he heard her ringing, metallic voice, like the voice of a harpy to him.

She prowled, ranging on the edge of the water like a possessed creature, and he followed her. He saw the froth of the wave followed by the hard, bright water swirl over her feet and her ankles, she swung out her arms, to balance, he expected every moment to see her walk into the sea, dressed as she was, and be carried swimming out.

But she turned, she walked to him.

"I want to go," she cried again, in the high, hard voice, like the scream of gulls. "Where?" he asked.

"I don't know."

And she seized hold of his arm, held him fast, as if captive, and walked him a little way by the edge of the dazzling, dazing water.

Then there in the great flare of light, she clinched hold of him, hard, as if suddenly she had the strength of destruction, she fastened her arms round him and tightened him in her grip, whilst her mouth sought his in a hard, rending, ever-increasing kiss, till his body was powerless in her grip, his heart melted in fear from the fierce, beaked, harpy's kiss. The water washed again over their feet, but she took no notice. She seemed unaware, she seemed to be pressing in her beaked mouth till she had the heart of him. Then, at last, she drew away and looked at him—looked at him. He knew what she wanted. He took her by the hand and led her across the foreshore back to the sandhills. She went silently. He felt as if the ordeal of proof was upon him, for life or death. He led her to a dark hollow.

"No, here," she said, going out to the slope full under the moonshine. She lay motionless, with wide-open eyes looking at the moon. He came direct to her, without preliminaries. She held him pinned down at the chest, awful. The fight, the struggle for consummation was terrible. It lasted till it was agony to his soul, till he succumbed, till he gave way as if dead, and lay with his face buried, partly in her hair, partly in the sand, motionless, as if he would be motionless now for ever, hidden away in the dark, buried, only buried, he only wanted to be buried in the goodly darkness, only that, and no more.

He seemed to swoon. It was a long time before he came to himself. He was aware of an unusual motion of her breast. He looked up. Her face lay like an image in the moonlight, the eyes wide open, rigid. But out of the eyes, slowly, there rolled a tear that glittered in the moonlight as it ran down her cheek.

But out of the eyes, slowly, there rolled a tear that glittered in the moonlight as it ran down her cheek.

He felt as if the knife were being pushed into his already dead body. With head strained back, he watched, drawn tense, for some minutes, watched the unaltering, rigid face like metal in the moonlight, the fixed, unseeing eyes, in which slowly the water gathered, shook with glittering moonlight, then surcharged, brimmed over and ran trickling, a tear with its burden of moonlight, into the darkness, to fall in the sand.

He drew gradually away as if afraid, drew away—she did not move. He glanced at her—she lay the same. Could he break away. He turned, saw the open foreshore, clear in front of him, and he plunged away, on and on, ever further from the horrible figure that lay stretched in the moonlight on the sands with the tears gathering and traveling on the motionless, eternal face.

He felt, if ever he must see her again, his bones must be broken, his body crushed, obliterated for ever. And as yet, he had the love of his own living body. He wandered on a long, long way, till his brain grew dark and he was unconscious with weariness. Then he curled in the deepest darkness he could find, under the sea-grass, and lay there without consciousness.

She broke from her tense cramp of agony gradually, though each movement was a goad of heavy pain. Gradually, she lifted her dead body from the sands, and rose at last. There was now no moon for her, no sea. All had passed away. She trailed her dead body to the house, to her room, where she lay down inert.

Morning brought her a new access of superficial life. But all within her was cold, dead, inert. Skrebensky appeared at breakfast. He was white and obliterated. They did not look at each other nor speak to each other. Apart from the ordinary, trivial talk of civil people, they were separate, they did not speak of what was between them during the remaining two days of their stay. They were like two dead people who dare not recognize, dare not see each other.

Then she packed her bag and put on her things. There were several guests leaving together, for the same train. He would have no opportunity to speak to her.

He tapped at her bedroom door at the last minute. She stood with her umbrella in her hand. He closed the door. He did not know what to say.

"Have you done with me?" he asked her at length, lifting his head.

"It isn't me," she said. "You have done with me—we have done with each other."

He looked at her, at the closed face, which he thought so cruel. And he knew he could never touch her again. His will was broken, he was seared, but he clung to the life of his body.

"Well, what have I done?" he asked, in a rather querulous voice.

"I don't know," she said, in the same, dull, feelingless voice. "It is finished. It had been a failure."

He was silent. The words still burned his bowels.

"Is it my fault?" he said, looking up at length, challenging the last stroke.

"You couldn't—" she began. But she broke down.

He turned away, afraid to hear more. She began to gather her bag, her handkerchief, her umbrella. She must be gone now. He was waiting for her to be gone.

At length the carriage came and she drove away with the rest. When she was out of sight, a great relief came over him, a pleasant banality. In an instant, everything was obliterated. He was childishly amiable and companionable all the day long. He was astonished that life could be so nice. It was better than it had been before. What a simple thing it was to be rid of her!

They were like two dead people who dare not recognize, dare not see each other.

How friendly and simple everything felt to him. What false thing had she been forcing on him?

But at night he dared not be alone. His room-mate had gone, and the hours of darkness were an agony to him. He watched the window in suffering and terror. When would this horrible darkness be lifted off him? Setting all his nerves, he endured it. He went to sleep with the dawn.

He never thought of her. Only his terror of the hours of night grew on him, obsessed like a mania. He slept fitfully, with constant wakings of anguish. The fear wore away the core of him.

His plan was, to sit up very late: to drink in company until one or half past one in the morning; then he would get three hours of sleep, of oblivion. It was light by five o'clock. But he was shocked almost to madness if he opened his eyes on the darkness.

In the daytime he was all right, always occupied with the thing of the moment, adhering to the trivial present, which seemed to him ample and satisfying. No matter how little and futile his occupations were, he gave himself to them entirely, and felt normal and fulfilled. He was always active, cheerful, gay, charming, trivial. Only he dreaded the darkness and silence of his own bedroom, when the darkness should challenge him upon his own soul. That he could not bear, as he could not bear to think about Ursula. He had no soul, no background. He never thought of Ursula, not once, he gave her no sign. She was the darkness, the challenge, the horror. He turned to immediate things. He wanted to marry quickly, to screen himself from the darkness, the challenge of his own soul. He would marry his Colonel's daughter. Quickly, without hesitation, pursued by his obsession for activity, he wrote to this girl, telling her his engagement was broken—it had been a temporary infatuation which he less than anyone else could understand now it was over—and could he see his very dear friend soon. He would not be happy till he had an answer.

Only he dreaded the darkness and silence of his own bedroom, when the darkness should challenge him upon his own soul.

He received a rather surprised reply from the girl, but she would be glad to see him. She was living with her aunt. He went down to her at once, and proposed to her the first evening. He was accepted. The marriage took place quietly within fourteen days' time. Ursula was not notified of the event. In another week, Skrebensky sailed with his new wife to India. . . .

Very far off was her old experience—Skrebensky, her parting with him—very far off. Some things were real; those first glamorous weeks. Before, these had seemed like hallucination. Now they seemed like common reality. The rest was unreal. She knew that Skrebensky had never become finally real. In the weeks of passionate ecstasy he had been with her in her desire, she had created him for the time being. But in the end he had failed and broken down.

Strange, what a void separated him and her. She liked him now, as she liked a memory, some bygone self. He was something of the past, finite. He was that which is known. She felt a poignant affection for him, as for that which is past. But, when she looked with her face forward, he was not. Nay, when she looked ahead, into the undiscovered land before her, what was there she could recognize but a fresh glow of light and inscrutable trees going up from the earth like smoke. It was the unknown, the unexplored, the undiscovered upon whose shore she had landed, alone, after crossing the void, the darkness which washed the New World and the Old.

There would be no child: she was glad. If there had been a child, it would have made little difference, however. She would have kept the child and herself, she would not have gone to Skrebensky. Anton belonged to the past.

There came the cablegram from Skrebensky: "I am married." An old pain and anger and contempt stirred in her. Did he belong so utterly to the cast-off past? She repudiated him. He was as he was. It was good that he was as he was. Who was she to have a man according to her own desire? It was not for her to create, but to recognize a man created by God. The man should come from the Infinite and she should hail him. She was glad she could not create her man. She was glad she had nothing to do with his creation. She was glad that this lay within the scope of that vaster power in which she rested at last. The man would come out of Eternity to which she herself belonged.

Nay, when she looked ahead, into the undiscovered land before her, what was there she could recognize but a fresh glow of light and inscrutable trees going up from the earth like smoke.

LEAD US INTO . . .

"Snow, even in the city, reminded him of skiing, which he had given up. His wife didn't ski. In his bachelor days, he had associated his ski vacations with romantic encounters. Single girls who skied were not averse to speed, or to other physical risks. He'd once met a Dutch girl in Klosters. She was too tall for the bed at the Chesa Grischuna, where (in the athleticism of their lovemaking) she'd broken her right big toe against the headboard and couldn't ski for the rest of her holiday. He had escaped that relationship with only minor injuries.

"He'd suffered more lasting scars from an adventure in Aspen, of which (despite the passage of time) he was enduringly fond. She was a German girl who drank Absolut, straight out of the freezer, while she overheated herself in his shower at the Hotel Jerome. She'd made an unheard-of deal with room service: they brought her the frosted fifth of vodka—a full bottle—and a frozen shot glass. She offered him an icy swallow, but his hand was wet, the shot glass was slippery, and he dropped the small, heavy glass in the steamy shower. He promptly stepped on it, cutting his foot.

"Then *he* was the one who couldn't ski. The stitches, in the ball of his left foot, made him limp on his heel. But while the German girl skied, he happily anticipated her daily arrival in his room at the Jerome. She was admirably consistent: she would begin by ordering the frosty bottle, which was always full, and the ice-cold shot glass. He still dreamed about her reddened skin, smelling of the pine-scented soap from the shower. Usually her hair was wet; he couldn't recall its true color.

"She was traveling with her parents—and with her kid sister, with whom she shared a room. She had to have dinner with her family every evening. If she ever spent the night with him, her sister would have ratted to her parents, but their late-afternoon liaisons were all that he could have hoped for.

"One afternoon, in the passion of the moment, the shot glass rolled under the bed. The German girl proposed that they sip the half-frozen vodka from each other's bellybutton. His navel was disappointingly shallow. In the waning light, as the room grew colder, his bed got wet. As he remembered it, the girl's bellybutton was as deep as a well. He never spilled—he drank every drop.

"Now, as the newfallen snow blanketed Manhattan, he remembered the German girl's navel—and her other exciting parts. From the kitchen freezer of his apartment, he poured himself a shot glass of Absolut. He kept the bottle and the shot glass in the rear of the freezer, behind the frozen fish sticks and the frozen peas and corn, the Popsicles that the children liked, and his wife's homemade tomato sauce.

"One chilly swallow of the vodka, and the snow that was falling on Lexington Avenue could have been falling on Aspen—dotting the heads and shoulders of the tired skiers returning to the Hotel Jerome.

"He never regretted that his wife didn't ski, or that she wore socks to bed and would have slapped him if he'd ever poured half-frozen vodka in her navel. He loved family life. The risks of skiing, and romantic encounters, no longer tempted him. Now, even when it snowed, the Absolut sufficed."

—Advertisement for Absolut Vodka, in *New York Times Magazine*, August 1998

QUESTIONS FOR THOUGHT AND DISCUSSION

1. In the middle of the second paragraph, Lawrence writes, "And then, for personification, would come Skrebensky . . ." What is the significance of this line? What does it indicate about the priority of the individual person in fulfilling one's lust?

2. The third paragraph sets up what might otherwise be a scene of romance. What are the chief differences between genuine romance and the lustful encounter that follows this setup?

3. How do Ursula and Skrebensky react to the light of the moon? Why this reaction? What does the line, "He felt his chest laid bare" suggest? Can you think of modern examples of the connection between lust and darkness?

4. What words in the text suggest obsession on Ursula's part? Lawrence describes her as being "like metal," with a "high, hard voice." What do such images of harshness suggest about the nature of lust? In contrast, what images might be used to describe affectionate love?

5. Does the tear on Ursula's cheek following the sexual encounter surprise you? Why or why not? What might she be feeling in that moment? What might Skrebensky be feeling that causes him to run away from her?

6. How do the two respond to each other at breakfast the next morning? Why did being "together" the night before actually create infinite distance between them?

7. After Ursula's departure, how does Skrebensky react? How does he try to escape from his pain?

8. As Ursula reflects on the encounter, she observes, "Skrebensky had never become finally real." What does she mean by this? What is the connection between unreal images and lust?

9. Have you ever been infatuated by an "image" of a person rather than the actual person? Why is this tendency so powerful? Can you find examples in which contemporary society encourages this practice? Why is it destructive?

10. How does Ursula's lust differ from Don Juan's in the earlier reading? How are the consequences similar or different?

11. In what ways do Ursula's theological reflections in the last paragraph throw light on the nature of lust?

12. In the box, "Lead Us Into . . . ," what is the strategy of the advertisement for Absolut Vodka? Why do you think it's written in "story" form? What evaluation of lust and illicit sex does it leave with the reader?

❧ *Ernesto Cardenal* ❧

Ernesto Martinez Cardenal (born 1925) is a Nicaraguan poet, writer, ordained Roman Catholic priest, and former Minister of Culture in Nicaragua. Born in Granada, Nicaragua, he attended the University of Mexico, followed by graduate studies at Columbia University in New York.

Cardenal is the author of many volumes of poetry and the winner of several literary prizes, including the Christopher Book Award in 1972. Cardenal's poems are characterized by their strongly blended feelings of love, political passion, and social criticism. Following his conversion to Christ in 1956, he studied under Thomas Merton in Kentucky and became both a priest and an advocate of nonviolence. In the 1980s, Pope John Paul II reprimanded Cardenal for promoting a liberation theology that diverged from Christian orthodoxy. But for all the controversy Cardenal has roused, he is a major Spanish-speaking poet and an incisive critic of modern life.

The following poem on Marilyn Monroe throws light on a very different side of lust—the prototypical modern "sex goddess" caught up in the vortex of such forces as consumption, celebrity worship, voyeurism, and fantasy. Hollywood, Marilyn Monroe herself observed, is the place where "they'll pay you a thousand dollars for a kiss and fifty cents for your soul."

WHITE HOUSE ASPIRIN

"I don't know about you, Harold, but if I don't have a woman every three days, I get these terrible headaches. How about you?"

—President John F. Kennedy to Britain's prime minister, Harold Macmillan, during their first meeting. (Macmillan had been married to the same woman for forty-five years.)

A PRAYER FOR MARILYN MONROE

Lord accept this girl
called Marilyn Monroe throughout the world
though that was not her name
(but you know her real name, that of the orphan raped at nine

the shopgirl who tried to kill herself when aged sixteen)
who now goes into your presence without make-up
without her Press Agent
without her photographs or signing autographs
lonely as an astronaut facing the darkness of outer space.
When a girl she dreamed she was naked in a church
(according to *Time*)
standing in front of a prostrate multitude, heads to the ground,
and had to walk on tiptoes to avoid the heads.
You know our dreams better than all psychiatrists.
    Church, house or cave all represent the safety of the womb but also something more . . .
    The heads are admirers, so much is clear (that the mass of heads in the darkness below the beam of the screen)
    but the temple isn't the studios of 20th-Century Fox.
    The temple, of marble and gold, is the temple of her body in which the Son of Man stands whip in hand driving out the money-changers of a 20th-Century Fox who made your house of prayer a den of thieves.
    Lord, in this world
contaminated equally by radioactivity and sin,
surely you will not blame a shopgirl
who (like any other shopgirl) dreamed of being a star.
And her dream became a 'reality' (Technicolour reality).
All she did was follow the script we gave her,
that of our own lives, but it was meaningless.
Forgive her, Lord, and likewise all of us
for this our 20th Century
and the Mammoth Super-Production in whose making we all shared.
She was hungry for love and we offered her tranquilizers.
For the sadness of our not being saints
they recommended psychoanalysis.
Remember, Lord, her increasing terror of the camera
and hatred of make-up (yet insistence on being newly made-up
for every scene) and how the terror grew.
Like any other shopgirl she dreamed
of being a star.
And her life was as unreal as a dream an analyst reads and files.
Her romances were kisses with closed eyes

You know our dreams better than all psychiatrists.

Lord, in this world contaminated equally by radioactivity and sin, surely you will not blame a shopgirl who (like any other shopgirl) dreamed of being a star.

which when the eyes are opened

are seen to have been played out beneath the spotlights

but the spotlights have gone out,

and the two walls of the room (it was a set) are taken down while the

Director moves away notebook in hand,

the scene being safely canned.

Or like a cruise on a yacht, a kiss in Singapore, a dance in Rio;

a reception in the mansion of the Duke and Duchess of Windsor

viewed in the sad tawdriness of a cheap apartment.

The film ended without a final kiss.

They found her dead in bed, hand on the phone

And the detectives knew not whom she was about to call.

It was as

though someone had dialed the only friendly voice and heard a pre-

recorded tape just saying 'WRONG NUMBER'

or like someone wounded by gangsters, who reaches out towards a dis-

connected phone.

Lord, whomsoever

it may have been that she was going to call

but did not (and perhaps it was not one at all

or Someone not named in the Los Angeles directory)

Lord, answer the phone.

Lord, whomsoever it may have been that she was going to call but did not (and perhaps it was not one at all or Someone not named in the Los Angeles directory) Lord, answer the phone.

From Ernesto Cardenal, *Apocalypse and Other Poems.* Copyright © 1977 by Ernesto Cardenal and Robert Pring-Mill. Reprinted by permission of New Directions Publishing Corporation.

THE PARTY OF JESUS

"Blessed are the physically repulsive,
Blessed are those who smell bad,
The twisted, misshapen, deformed,
The too big, too little, too loud,
The bald, the fat, and the old—
For they are all riotously celebrated in the party of Jesus."

—Dallas Willard, *The Divine Conspiracy*

QUESTIONS FOR THOUGHT AND DISCUSSION

1. Why do you think Cardenal includes these phrases in his poem: "that was not her real name"? "The orphan raped at nine"? And "the shopgirl who tried to kill herself"? How do such facts contrast to the Hollywood image of Marilyn Monroe?

2. What do you think about the parallel Cardenal makes between Monroe's body (taken over by 20th-Century Fox) and the temple from which Christ drove the money-changers? Where does this analogy place the blame for the tragedy of Monroe's life? Do you agree or disagree?

3. Which paragraph is the most striking for you? What does it convey about the role lust played in making Monroe's career?

4. Cardenal refers to Monroe's use of drugs. Alcohol and drugs are known to be prominent in today's sexually oriented businesses, such as the topless dancing industry. Why do you think this is the case? How might the lust inherent in such businesses contribute to the need to "numb" oneself?

5. What are your emotions when you read the poem? How far does it capture the pathos and tragedy of the modern sex-goddess and the tangle of motivations surrounding such a person? What is the irony of the public image of such women, including Marilyn Monroe?

6. To what extent is the public responsible for a tragedy like Marilyn Monroe's?

THE COUNTERPOINT TO LUST:
Blessed Are the Pure in Heart

The counterpoint to lust is purity of heart. Whereas lust is unethical and unrestrained, purity of heart is the ethical and disciplined devotion of the heart. Whereas lust blinds and dissipates our strength, purity of heart is both clear-sighted and a concentrated focusing of strength.

> *Whereas lust blinds and dissipates our strength, purity of heart is both clear-sighted and a concentrated focusing of strength.*

"Pure" means true, authentic, simple, wholly itself, and therefore, cleansed. In Søren Kierkegaard's famous sentence, "Purity of heart is to will one thing." Thus to love God with a love that is pure, clear, simple, undiluted, and total is the counterpoint to lust and the idolatry of sexual pleasure that accompanies it.

But such a strenuous ideal of an untarnished heart can crush us with disillusionment if it is not accompanied by grace and forgiveness. Jesus upset all expectations here, including those of moralistic believers of all ages. He offers forgiveness and restoration to those caught in sexual sin. As William F. May noted, "The ancient Hebrew circumcised the penis; he did not amputate it. Jesus forgave the adulterous woman; he did not stone her."

PURE HEARTS ONLY

"Who may ascend the hill of the LORD?
Who may stand in his holy place?
He who has clean hands and a pure heart,
who does not lift up his soul to an idol
or swear by what is false."

—Psalm 24:3-4

❈ *Augustine* ❈

Augustine (A.D. 354–430) was an orator, philosopher, theologian, bishop, and writer. He is often celebrated as the finest thinker in the two-thousand-year history of the Church of Christ. Born in North Africa in what is now Algeria, he was the son of a pagan father and a devout Christian mother, Monica. From the time of his first visit to Carthage at age sixteen, he pursued the career of an orator while delving into various philosophies and religions (such as Manicheism and Neo-Platonism) and pursuing the fruits of a lax lifestyle (which included a mistress and a bastard son).

In A.D. 385, in a villa outside Rome, he experienced one of the most dramatic conversions in Christian history. On being baptized, Augustine turned his passionate heart and formidable mind to the service of Christ. In the process he became the last major thinker of the ancient world, the first of the Middle Ages, and the vital forerunner of the Reformation. His two greatest classics are The City of God, written to answer Roman critics who blamed Christians for the fall of Rome, and his spiritual autobiography Confessions.

This reading from his Confessions gives us his mature, autobiographical account of his losing battle with lust as a young man.

TURNER'S TOP TEN

The Ten Commandments are "a little out of date. If you're only going to have ten rules, I don't know if [prohibiting] adultery should be one of them."

—Television mogul Ted Turner, speech to the National Family Planning and Reproductive Health Association

"One of the most telling things about contemporary human beings is that they cannot find a reason for not committing adultery. Yet intimacy is a spiritual hunger of the human soul, and we cannot escape it."

—Dallas Willard, *The Divine Conspiracy*

CONFESSIONS

I must now carry my thoughts back to the abominable things I did in those days, the sins of the flesh which defiled my soul. I do this, my God, not because I love those sins, but so that I may love you. For love of your love I shall retrace my wicked ways. The memory is bitter, but it will help me to savor your sweetness, the sweetness that does not deceive but brings real joy and never fails. For love of your love I shall retrieve myself from the havoc of disruption which tore me to pieces when I turned away from you, whom alone I should have sought, and lost myself instead on many a different quest. For as I grew to manhood I was inflamed with desire for a surfeit of hell's pleasures. Foolhardy as I was, I ran wild with lust that was manifold and rank. In your eyes my beauty vanished and I was foul to the core, yet I was pleased with my own condition and anxious to be pleasing in the eyes of men.

The memory is bitter, but it will help me to savor your sweetness, the sweetness that does not deceive but brings real joy and never fails.

2

I cared for nothing but to love and be loved. But my love went beyond the affection of one mind for another, beyond the arc of the bright beam of friendship. Bodily desire, like a morass, and adolescent sex welling up within me exuded mists which clouded over and obscured my heart, so that I could not distinguish the clear light of true love from the murk of lust. Love and lust together seethed within me. In my tender youth they swept me away over the precipice of my body's appetites and plunged me in the whirlpool of sin. More and more I angered you, unawares. For I had been deafened by the clank of my chains, the fetters of the death which was my due to punish the pride in my soul. I strayed still farther from you and you did not restrain me. I was tossed and spilled, floundering in the broiling sea of my fornication, and you said no word. How long it was before I learned that you were my true joy! You were silent then, and I went on my way, farther and farther from you, proud in my distress and restless in fatigue, sowing more and more seeds whose only crop was grief.

Was there no one to lull my distress, to turn the fleeting beauty of these new-found attractions to good purpose and set up a goal for their charms, so that the high tide of my youth might have rolled in upon the shore of marriage? The surge might have been calmed and contented by the procreation of children, which is the purpose of marriage, as your law prescribes, O Lord. By this means you form the offspring of our fallen nature, and with a gentle hand you prune back the thorns that have no place in your paradise. For your almighty power is not far from us, even when we are far from you. Or, again, I might have listened more attentively to your voice from the clouds saying of those who marry that they will *meet with outward distress, but I leave you your freedom;* that *a man does well to abstain from all commerce with women,* and that *he who is unmarried is concerned with God's claim, asking how he is to please God; whereas the married man is concerned with the world's claim, asking how he is to please his wife.* These were the words to which I should have listened with more care, and if I had made myself a *eunuch for love of the kingdom of heaven,* I should have awaited your embrace with all the greater joy.

But, instead, I was in a ferment of wickedness. I deserted you and allowed myself to be carried away by the sweep of the tide. I broke all your lawful bounds and did not escape your lash. For what man can escape it? You were always present, angry and merciful at once, strewing the pangs of bitterness over all my lawless pleasures to lead me on to look for others unallied with pain. You meant me to find them nowhere but in yourself, O Lord, for you teach us by inflicting pain, you smite so that you may heal, and you kill us so that we may not die away from you. Where was I then and how far was I banished from the bliss of your house in that sixteenth year of my life? This was the age at which the frenzy gripped me and I surrendered myself entirely to lust, which your law forbids but human hearts are not ashamed to sanction. My family made no effort to save me from my fall by marriage. Their only concern was that I should learn how to make a good speech and how to persuade others by my words.

These were the words to which I should have listened with more care, and if I had made myself a eunuch for love of the kingdom of heaven, I should have awaited your embrace with all the greater joy.

3

. . . In the meanwhile, during my sixteenth year, the narrow means of my family obliged me to leave school and live idly at home with my parents. The brambles of lust grew high above my head and there was no one to root them out, certainly not my father. One day at the public baths he saw the signs of active virility coming to life in me and this was enough to make him relish the thought of having grandchildren. He was happy to tell my mother about it, for his happiness was due to the intoxication which causes the world to forget you, its Creator, and to love the things you have created instead of loving you, because the world is drunk with the invisible wine of its own perverted, earthbound will. But in my mother's heart you had already begun to build your temple and laid the foundations of your holy dwelling, while my father was still a catechumen and a new one at that. So, in her piety, she became alarmed and apprehensive, and although I had not yet been baptized, she began to dread that I might follow in the crooked path of those who do not keep their eyes on you but turn their backs instead. . . .

Nothing deserves to be despised more than vice; yet I gave in more and more to vice simply in order not to be despised. If I had not sinned enough

Nothing deserves to be despised more than vice; yet I gave in more and more to vice simply in order not to be despised.

to rival other sinners, I used to pretend that I had done things I had not done at all, because I was afraid that innocence would be taken for cowardice and chastity for weakness. These were the companions with whom I walked the streets of Babylon. I wallowed in its mire as if it were made of spices and precious ointments, and to fix me all the faster in the very depths of sin the unseen enemy trod me underfoot and enticed me to himself, because I was an easy prey for his seductions. For even my mother, who by now had escaped from the center of Babylon, though she still loitered in its outskirts, did not act upon what she had heard about me from her husband with the same earnestness as she had advised me about chastity. She saw that I was already infected with a disease that would become dangerous later on, but if the growth of my passions could not be cut back to the quick, she did not think it right to restrict them to the bounds of married love. This was because she was afraid that the bonds of marriage might be a hindrance to my hopes for the future—not of course the hope of the life to come, which she reposed in you, but my hopes of success at my studies. Both my parents were unduly eager for me to learn, my father because he gave next to no thought to you and only shallow thought to me, and my mother because she thought that the usual course of study would certainly not hinder me, but would even help me, in my approach to you. To the best of my memory this is how I construe the characters of my parents. Furthermore, I was given a free rein to amuse myself beyond the strict limits of discipline, so that I lost myself in many kinds of evil ways, in all of which a pall of darkness hung between me and the bright light of your truth, my God. What malice proceeded from my pampered heart!

10

Can anyone unravel this twisted tangle of knots? I shudder to look at it or think of such abomination. I long instead for innocence and justice, graceful and splendid in eyes whose sight is undefiled. My longing fills me and yet it cannot cloy. With them is certain peace and life that cannot be disturbed. The man who enters their domain goes to *share the joy of his Lord.* He shall know no fear and shall lack no good. In him that is goodness itself he shall find his own best way of life. But I deserted you, my God. In my youth I wandered away, too far from your sustaining hand, and created of myself a barren waste.

In my youth I wandered away, too far from your sustaining hand, and created of myself a barren waste.

ADULTERY BY ANY OTHER NAME . . .

"I made a covenant with my eyes not to look lustfully at a girl."

—Job 31:1

There is no such thing as "committing adultery with the right woman, at the right time, and in the right way, for it is . . . simply wrong."

—Aristotle

"With eyes full of adultery, they never stop sinning; they seduce the unstable; they are experts in greed—an accursed brood!"

—2 Peter 2:14

"Just as the thief is the person who would steal if circumstances were right, so the adulterer is the one who would have wrongful sex if the circumstances were right. Usually that means if he or she could be sure it would not be found out. This is what Jesus calls 'adultery in the heart.'"

—Dallas Willard, *The Divine Conspiracy*

QUESTIONS FOR THOUGHT AND DISCUSSION

1. In the opening paragraph, Augustine describes God's love as "the sweetness that does not deceive." In contrast, how does lust deceive?

2. Augustine says his anxiousness "to be pleasing in the eyes of men" contributed to his lust problem. He was fearful of admitting "innocence" or "chastity." How have things changed or stayed the same for young people today? How can parents help to counter these concerns?

3. What is the true, positive desire Augustine felt at the time of his life he describes? What were the specific consequences of trying to meet that desire through lustful encounters?

4. In hindsight, what does Augustine see as the two ways his lust may have been remedied? What do you think of each of these suggestions—how would they have countered or not countered his lust?

5. Augustine describes feelings of "bitterness" and "pain" in his various affairs, emotions often reserved for women who have been "used" by such encounters. Is he just more sensitive than most men, or do the emotional consequences of lust fall on both men and women? Why do you hold the position you do?

6. What role does Augustine see God playing in his youthful restlessness and searching? What does he now long for, instead of the fleeting rewards of lust?

7. Overall, what do you think of Augustine's evaluation, mature and given from the perspective of faith, of his earlier period of promiscuity?

William F. May

William F. May (born 1927) is the Cary M. Maguire Professor of Ethics at Southern Methodist University in Dallas, Texas. Born in Chicago, Illinois, he is a graduate of the universities of Princeton and Yale. A former president of the American Academy of Religion and a founding fellow of the Hastings Center, he has taught at Smith College, Indiana University, and Georgetown University.

Much of May's work has been on the ethics of death and dying, including his book, The Patient's Ordeal *(1991). His latest work is* The Beleaguered Rulers; The Public Obligations of the Professional. *The following passage comes from an earlier and more general work,* A Catalogue of Sins. *It is one of the most illuminating contemporary books on sin and sins.*

DIVAS AND DAFFODILS

"Jesus took time in his teaching to point out the natural beauty of every human being. He calls attention to how the most glamorous person you know ('Solomon in all his splendor') is not as ravishingly beautiful as a simple field flower. Just place a daffodil side-by-side with anyone at the president's inaugural ball or at the motion-picture Academy Awards, and you will see. But the abundant life of the kingdom flowing through us makes us of greater natural beauty than the plants."

—Dallas Willard, *The Divine Conspiracy*

FALSE WORSHIP: IMPURITY OF HEART

When Gulliver was washed ashore in the land of the Lilliputians, the king sent two investigators to examine his person and report items of a threatening nature that might be used by the giant against his captors. In going through Gulliver's pockets the investigators came across three articles of particular interest. They described one as a great carpet, large enough to cover the floor in the royal hall. What they had discovered, of course, was Gulliver's handkerchief. The second, they said, was a mighty engine with poles distended from it the size of the palisades before the king's court. What they had found, in this case, was Gulliver's comb. But the third item was the most baffling of all. In a further recess of Gulliver's clothing they reported another great engine that made a noise like a waterfall and had an invisible partition which prevented them from examining the monstrous figures on its face. It was, of course, Gulliver's watch. But in writing their report to the king, the investigators said that it was either a strange animal Gulliver had brought with him from his own country, or his god—because he consulted it so often.

Swift, of course, is satirizing one of the gods of modern men—mechanical time—but he is also describing what the real god of a man is: whatever in his life he consults most often. John Calvin once observed that man is distinguished from all other creatures by the fact that he does not live without a religion. Man is an incorrigible god-maker, a creature given to worship and adoration. Another way of putting the same thing is to say that he is a manufacturer of idols. Man does not rid himself of religion when he sins; quite the contrary, he reeks of it. He denies God by falling under the spell of the world or one of its powers. . . .

Men deny God by turning away from him toward some creaturely power, whether it is the glitter of gold, the fertility of the soil, the excitement of a career, the fascination of a woman, or the claim of a great public cause. Man not only lives in the world, he magnifies the world; he takes something out of its place and glorifies it. . . .

IMPURITY OF HEART

The objective and the subjective aspects of the problem of idolatry are best linked together in the prophetic-priestly term Kierkegaard used in his essay on monotheism: impurity of heart. Purity of heart is not a sexual term. It refers primarily to single-mindedness, wholeness, integrity, or unity of heart. Impurity of heart, correspondingly, means a heart divided in its allegiances—double-minded, as it were.

In a further recess of Gulliver's clothing they reported another great engine that made a noise like a waterfall and had an invisible partition which prevented them from examining the monstrous figures on its face. It was, of course, Gulliver's watch.

Men deny God by turning away from him toward some creaturely power, whether it is the glitter of gold, the fertility of the soil, the excitement of a career, the fascination of a woman, or the claim of a great public cause.

The objective basis for purity of heart is monotheism. The prophets and priests called for purity of heart because God is one—therefore, the heart should be purely his. "Hear, O Israel: the Lord our God is one Lord." This declarative sentence is the objective basis for the negative and positive imperatives: "Thou shalt have no other gods before me," and "Thou shalt love the Lord thy God with all thine heart, and with all thy soul and with all thy might."

Kierkegaard defined the subjective correlate of this monotheism in the simplest of terms, by appeal to the letter of James: "Purify your hearts, you men of double mind" (James 4:8). If the world were composed of a plurality of divine powers, then it would be wrong to love God with wholeness of heart. The heart ought to be shared tactfully with all the good powers that be. Men ought to live appreciatively in relationship to a full host of deities. If God is one, however, then the heart belongs to him alone. In idolatry, the soul forsakes the integrity of its heart before the one God by glutting itself with other powers and glories that vie for its attention. It is guilty of the sin of impurity of heart.

OF BEDROOMS AND BOARDROOMS

"The Church is uncommonly vocal about the subject of bedrooms and so singularly silent on the subject of boardrooms."

—Dorothy L. Sayers

QUESTIONS FOR THOUGHT AND DISCUSSION

1. What do you think of Swift's definition of man's god as "whatever in his life he consults most often"? What do modern advertising and commercialism encourage our "gods" to be? By Swift's definition, what might others say your god is?

2. According to John Calvin, how does the nature of men and women make them prone to be idolators? What does May mean by the odd statement that humans "reek" of religion when they sin?

3. Which, if any, of the common idols May mentions in the paragraph beginning "Men deny God" surprise you? What are other, more subtle idols in your circles? Among the teenagers you know? In Western culture at large?

4. What does Kierkegaard mean by purity of heart? By impurity of heart? What is the connection between purity of heart and monotheism? What power do we ascribe to those things to which our hearts are bonded in competition with God?

5. Why, when William F. May says that purity of heart is not a sexual term, is it the counterpoint to lust? Why is lust a form of idolatry?

CONCLUSION:
FIVE REMINDERS

The benefits of exploring the vices and virtues should be obvious by now. But there are also dangers, the main one being the risk of spiritual hypochondria. As one tends to take on new illnesses when studying a medical or psychological textbook, so with these readings. There is a risk that once we recognize the intricate subtleties of the vices, we imagine that we suffer from them all and that our condition is incurable. The result is depression rather than growth. We therefore need to conclude this study with a series of constructive reminders that help us to keep our perspective and balance.

There is a risk that once we recognize the intricate subtleties of the vices, we imagine that we suffer from them all and that our condition is incurable.

REMINDER ONE:
Remember the Place of Discipline— Training Ourselves to Do What We Cannot Ordinarily Do

Regardless of where our root sins may lie, or the virtues we seek to cultivate as counterpoints, no real change can occur without discipline. Discipline is the training we undertake in order to do what we cannot do by ordinary, direct effort. Whether it be playing the piano, running a marathon, or blessing our enemies, we undergo training so that we can do what *needs to be done* when *it needs to be done.*

Whether it be playing the piano, running a marathon, or blessing our enemies, we undergo training so that we can do what needs to be done when it needs to be done.

271

In the following passage, Aristotle sets forth his understanding of the way virtues are cultivated. The full development of the virtues in us, he says, comes by practicing them to the point where they become habit. Habit in this sense is as vital to spiritual growth as practice is to playing golf or the violin.

Yet Aristotle is only half right. In his stress on habit, he leaves out the supernatural element in spiritual formation. The two are not opposed. Rather, they work in cooperation. Deep, lasting cultivation of the virtues takes place as our human efforts are joined with the supernatural work of the Spirit to move and change us. Central to the process is grace, which allows for shortcomings and fresh beginnings.

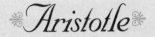

Aristotle

Aristotle (384–322 B.C.) was one of the world's greatest and most influential thinkers. Born in Stageira, Macedon, he studied in Athens under Plato. When Plato died, he returned to Macedon to become the tutor of the young Alexander the Great. When Alexander succeeded his father Philip to the throne in 335, Aristotle returned to Athens where he founded his own school, the Lyceum, and attracted a large number of scholars. After Alexander's death in 323, a strong anti-Macedonian reaction took place in Athens and Aristotle fled to Chalcis. He died there a few months later, in 322.

The range of Aristotle's thinking was remarkable. He explored, discovered, argued, and taught in fields as diverse as logic, metaphysics, theology, history, politics, aesthetics, ethics, psychology, anatomy, biology, zoology, botany, astronomy, and the ancient equivalents of physics and chemistry. If Plato's ideas were influential in such schools as Platonism and to such thinkers as Augustine, Aristotle's influence has been enormous too—for example, on Thomas Aquinas, and thus on all medieval Christendom.

Aristotle's Ethics is one of his two most famous works, along with Politics. The title, in Greek, should really be translated "Matters to Do with Character" and the central concern is "the morally good person." Passages such as the following were widely discussed in the eighteenth century. One Aristotelian theme *that has put its stamp on America is his insistence that character is a combination of two elements: the* right *and the* routine*—hence Alexis de Tocqueville's celebrated phrase about the "habits of the heart," and Nietzsche's about "a long obedience in the same direction."*

MORAL GOODNESS

Moral virtues, like crafts, are acquired by practice and habituation.

Virtue, then, is of two kinds, intellectual and moral. Intellectual virtue owes both its inception and its growth chiefly to instruction, and for this very reason needs time and experience. Moral goodness, on the other hand, is the result of habit, from which it has actually got its name, being a slight modification of the word *ethos.* This fact makes it obvious that none of the moral virtues is engendered in us by nature, since nothing that is what it is by nature can be made to behave differently by habituation. For instance, a stone, which has a natural tendency downwards, cannot be habituated to rise, however often you try to train it by throwing it into the air; nor can you train fire to burn downwards; nor can anything else that has any other natural tendency be trained to depart from it. The moral virtues, then, are engendered in us neither *by* nor *contrary to* nature; we are constituted by nature to receive them, but their full development in us is due to habit.

Again, of all those faculties with which nature endows us we first acquire the potentialities, and only later effect their actualization. (This is evident in the case of the senses. It was not from repeated acts of seeing or hearing that we acquired the senses but the other way round: we had these senses before we used them; we did not acquire them as the result of using them.)

But the virtues we do acquire by first exercising them, just as happens in the arts. Anything that we have to learn to do we learn by the actual doing of it: people become builders by building and instrumentalists by playing instruments. Similarly we become just by performing just acts, temperate by performing temperate ones, brave by performing brave ones. This view is supported by what happens in city-states. Legislators make their citizens good by habituation; this is the intention of every legislator, and those who do not carry it out fail of their object. This is what makes the difference between a good constitution and a bad one.

Virtue, then, is of two kinds, intellectual and moral.

Again, the causes or means that bring about any form of excellence are the same as those that destroy it, and similarly with art; for it is as a result of playing the harp that people become good and bad harpists. The same principle applies to builders and all other craftsmen. Men will become good builders as a result of building well, and bad ones as a result of building badly. Otherwise there would be no need of anyone to teach them: they would all be born either good or bad. Now this holds good also of the virtues. It is the way that we behave in our dealings with other people that makes us just or unjust, and the way that we behave in the face of danger, accustoming ourselves to be timid or confident, that makes us brave or cowardly. . . . So it is a matter of no little importance what sort of habits we form from the earliest age—it makes a vast difference, or rather all the difference in the world.

Excerpt from Aristotle, *The Nicomachean Ethics*, trans. J. A. K. Thompson (London: Allen & Unwin, 1976), book 2. Reprinted by permission of Unwin Hyman of HarperCollins Publishers Ltd.

QUESTIONS FOR THOUGHT AND DISCUSSION

1. What two types of virtue does Aristotle identify? How are each attained?
2. What contrast does Aristotle make between "faculties of nature" and virtues in the ways they are acquired and used? What art or skill have you learned by doing? Describe the process you followed.
3. Do you agree with Aristotle that we become just "by performing just acts" and brave "by performing brave ones"? Can you give an example of "obtaining virtue by doing" from your own life or the life of someone close to you?
4. Why is repeating a task not enough to ensure doing it well? What else is necessary? How does this principle apply to developing the virtues? To eliminating the vices?
5. Aristotle's notion of virtue as habit, or learned second nature, is the opposite of such modern notions as spontaneity and self-expression. What practical and social differences do you see flowing out of such differences?
6. What sort of education and training is needed to form character and virtue into a habit?

REMINDER TWO:
Remember Deception— Our Utility Sin That Assists All Other Sinning

THE SILENT CONTRACT OF TRUTH

"A lie may be defined as an attempt to deceive without the other's consent. This definition assumes that there is a 'silent contract among men to speak the truth.'"

—Abraham Heschel, *A Passion for Truth*

Whatever sins we include in the list of deadly sins, and however seriously we rate them, there is one sin that serves them all—deception. As Adlai Stevenson quipped with deadly seriousness, "A lie is an abomination to the Lord and a very present help in trouble." Unfortunately, however, we not only deceive each other but we deceive ourselves. Deception is therefore a companion sin to the seven deadly sins. Although it pursues no purpose of its own, it serves to soften or disguise the others. For example, boasting is deceit in the service of pride; slander is deceit in the service of envy; insincerity is deceit in the service of lust.

In the long run, however, it simply will not work. Damage control for sin is simply not possible.

Unfortunately, however, we not only deceive each other but we deceive ourselves.

DEADLY DECEIT

"Early the next morning Joshua had Israel come forward by tribes, and Judah was taken. The clans of Judah came forward, and he took the Zerahites. He had the clan of the Zerahites come forward by families, and Zimri was taken. Joshua had his family come forward man by man, and Achan son of Carmi, the son of Zimri, the son of Zerah, of the tribe of Judah, was taken.

"Then Joshua said to Achan, 'My son, give glory to the LORD, the God of Israel, and give him the praise. Tell me what you have done; do not hide it from me.'

"Achan replied, 'It is true! I have sinned against the LORD, the God of Israel. This is what I have done: When I saw in the plunder a beautiful robe from Babylonia, two hundred shekels of silver and a wedge of gold weighing fifty shekels, I coveted them and took them. They are hidden in the ground inside my tent, with the silver underneath.'

"So Joshua sent messengers, and they ran to the tent, and there it was, hidden in his tent, with the silver underneath. They took the things from the tent, brought them to Joshua and all the Israelites and spread them out before the LORD. Then Joshua, together with all Israel, took Achan son of Zerah, the silver, the robe, the gold wedge, his sons and daughters, his cattle, donkeys and sheep, his tent and all that he had, to the Valley of Achor. "Joshua said, 'Why have you brought this trouble on us? The LORD will bring trouble on you today.'

Then all Israel stoned him, and after they had stoned the rest, they burned them. Over Achan they heaped up a large pile of rocks, which remains to this day. Then the LORD turned from his fierce anger. Therefore that place has been called the Valley of Achor ever since."

—Joshua 7:16-26

Samuel Johnson

Samuel Johnson (1709–1784), known simply as Dr. Johnson, was an English lexicographer, essayist, poet, and moralist—the major literary figure of the second half of the eighteenth century. Born in Lichfield, Staffordshire, he was educated at Oxford University and then went to London as a journalist.

For eight years, starting in 1747, he worked on his massive Dictionary of the English Language. He also started a moralistic periodical, The Rambler. A founding member of the Literary Club, he produced an important edition of Shakespeare. Yet, in many ways, Johnson's reputation as a man and a conversationalist outweighs his literary reputation—partly due to Boswell's Life of Samuel Johnson, written after their famous hiking tour of the Hebrides when Johnson was sixty-four.

Johnson was evidently somewhat slovenly in person, abrupt in manner, and plagued by hypochondria and melancholy. But he was also kind, generous, sociable, and a man of deep Christian faith. The book of his collected prayers is particularly moving. The passage below is from his ethical writings. It shows his acute insight into our human capacity for self-deception.

'HONESTY LITE'

"When you say that you agree to a thing in principle, you mean that you have not the slightest intention of carrying it out in practice."

—Otto von Bismarck

SELF-DECEPTION

One sophism by which men persuade themselves that they have those virtues which they really want, is formed by the substitution of single acts for habits. A miser who once relieved a friend from the danger of a prison, suffers his imagination to dwell for ever upon his own heroick generosity; he yields his heart up to indignation at those who are blind to merit, or insensible to misery, and who can please themselves with the enjoyment of that wealth, which they never permit others to partake. From any censures of the world, or reproaches of his conscience, he has an appeal to action and to knowledge; and though his whole life is a course of rapacity and avarice, he concludes himself to be tender and liberal, because he has once performed an act of liberality and tenderness.

As a glass which magnifies objects by the approach of one end to the eye, lessens them by the application of the other, so vices are extenuated by the inversion of that fallacy, by which virtues are augmented. Those faults which we cannot conceal from our own notice, are considered, however frequent, not as habitual corruptions, or settled practices, but as casual failures, and single lapses. A man who has, from year to year, set his country to sale, either for the gratification of his ambition or resentment, confesses that the heat of party now and then betrays the severest virtue to measures that cannot be seriously defended. He that spends his days and nights in riot and debauchery, owns that his passions oftentimes overpower his resolution. But each comforts himself that his faults are not without precedent, for the best and the wisest men have given way to the violence of sudden temptations.

There are men who always confound the praise of goodness with the practice, and who believe themselves mild and moderate, charitable and faithful, because they have exerted their eloquence in commendation of mildness, fidelity,

One sophism by which men persuade themselves that they have those virtues which they really want, is formed by the substitution of single acts for habits.

and other virtues. This is an error almost universal among those that converse much with dependents, with such whose fear or interest disposes them to a seeming reverence for any declamation, however enthusiastick, and submission to any boast, however arrogant. Having none to recall their attention to their lives, they rate themselves by the goodness of their opinions, and forget how much more easily men may shew their virtue in their talk than in their actions.

The tribe is likewise very numerous of those who regulate their lives, not by the standard of religion, but the measure of other men's virtue; who lull their own remorse with the remembrance of crimes more atrocious than their own, and seem to believe that they are not bad while another can be found worse.

For escaping these and a thousand other deceits, many expedients have been proposed. Some have recommended the frequent consultation of a wise friend, admitted to intimacy, and encouraged to sincerity. But this appears a remedy by no means adapted to general use: for in order to secure the virtue of one, it presupposes more virtue in two than will generally be found. In the first, such a desire of rectitude and amendment, as may incline him to hear his own accusation from the mouth of him whom he esteems, and by whom, therefore, he will always hope that his faults are not discovered; and in the second such zeal and honesty, as will make him content for his friend's advantage to lose his kindness.

A long life may be passed without finding a friend in whose understanding and virtue we can equally confide, and whose opinion we can value at once for its justness and sincerity. A weak man, however honest, is not qualified to judge. A man of the world, however penetrating, is not fit to counsel. Friends are often chosen for similitude of manners, and therefore each palliates the other's failings, because they are his own. Friends are tender and unwilling to give pain, or they are interested, and fearful to offend.

These objections have inclined others to advise, that he who would know himself, should consult his enemies, remember the reproaches that are vented to his face, and listen for the censures that are uttered in private. For his great business is to know his faults, and those malignity will discover, and resentment will reveal. But this precept may be often frustrated; for it seldom happens that rivals or opponents are suffered to come near enough to know our conduct with so much exactness as that conscience should allow and reflect the accusation. The charge of an enemy is often totally false, and commonly so mingled with falsehood, that the mind takes advantage from the failure of one part to discredit the rest, and never suffers any disturbance afterward from such partial reports.

Yet it seems that enemies have been always found by experience the most

Friends are often chosen for similitude of manners, and therefore each palliates the other's failings, because they are his own.

faithful monitors; for adversity has ever been considered as the state in which a man most easily becomes acquainted with himself, and this effect it must produce by withdrawing flatterers, whose business it is to hide our weaknesses from us, or by giving loose to malice, and licence to reproach; or at least by cutting of those pleasures which called us away from meditation on our conduct, and repressing that pride which too easily persuades us, that we merit whatever we enjoy.

Part of these benefits it is in every man's power to procure himself, by assigning proper portions of his life to the examination of the rest, and by putting himself frequently in such a situation by retirement and abstraction, as may weaken the influence of external objects. By this practice he may obtain the solitude of adversity without its melancholy, its instructions without its censures, and its sensibility without its perturbations.

As reprinted in *Vice and Virtue in Everyday Life: Introductory Readings in Ethics*, eds. Christina and Fred Sommers (New York: Harcourt Brace Jovanovich, 1989), pp. 339–342.

THE TRUTH TEST OF FRIENDSHIP

"Although it is vastly disagreeable to be accused of faults yet no person ought to be offended when such accusations are delivered in the spirit of friendship."

—Abigail Smith (Adams) to John Adams in a letter asking him to be her "second conscience" by pointing out her faults

"It was a letter from you telling me of my faults, which first established and I believe immovably, in my mind, the persuasion and feeling of your being my real friend."

—William Wilberforce to businessman Samuel Roberts, on what had won his friendship, 1817

QUESTIONS FOR THOUGHT AND DISCUSSION

1. What is the form of sophism, or rationalization, that Johnson describes in the first paragraph? Why is it particularly powerful as a form of deception? Where have you seen it used? Has this sort of claim to virtue ever played a part in your own life? How so?

2. How does the technique of deception in the second paragraph differ from the first? What method does it use to exaggerate one's virtues?

3. Of the second and third strategies for deceiving oneself, which do you find the most tempting?

4. Johnson points out the inadequacies of human forms of moral account-ability, yet we all need some accountability. What form have you found best for helping you see your own self-deception?

5. Deception of anyone is ultimately attempted deception of God. Why do we ever try anything so foolish, let alone wrong?

REMINDER THREE:
Remember the Danger of Moralism—Our Ugly Counterfeit of Virtue

Anyone who takes right and wrong seriously is bound to be tempted by moralism: the harsh-faced attitude that responds to sin by removing all grace from the equation, reducing all of life to one dimension—the moral—and rationalizing its own sense of superiority in judgment of others. Closely related to legalism and Pharisaism, moralism has been described as an abiding curse of Americans because of the distortions of the Puritan heritage. At a time when Christians recoil from the headlong flight away from Christendom taken by modern culture, too many in the church instinctively resort to moralism in both private and public responses to what they deplore.

Closely related to legalism and Pharisaism, moralism has been described as an abiding curse of Americans because of the distortions of the Puritan heritage.

ALL GLASS HOUSES

"At dawn [Jesus] appeared again in the temple courts, where all the people gathered around him, and he sat down to teach them. The teachers of the law and the Pharisees brought in a woman caught in adultery. "They made her stand before the group and said to Jesus, 'Teacher, this woman was caught in the act of adultery. In the Law, Moses commanded us to stone such women. Now what do you say?' They were using this question as a trap, in order to have a basis for accusing him.

"But Jesus bent down and started to write on the ground with his finger. "When they kept on questioning him, he straightened up and said to them, 'If any one of you is without sin, let him be the first to throw a stone at her.' Again he stooped down and wrote on the ground.

"At this, those who heard began to go away one at a time, the older ones first, until only Jesus was left, with the woman still standing there. Jesus straightened up and asked her, 'Woman, where are they? Has no one condemned you?'

"'No one, sir,' she said. 'Then neither do I condemn you,' Jesus declared. 'Go now and leave your life of sin.'"

—John 8:2-11

Langdon Gilkey

*Langdon Gilkey was introduced in part 3 on avarice. The following passage comes from the same book—*Shantung Compound*—and illustrates the danger of moralism that too often turns attempted stands for truth, meant to be positive, into unattractive and counterproductive attitudes. The fact is, moralism doesn't serve justice as it pretends to. It serves the moralist's own ends by rationalizing his or her self-claimed superiority. It is sobering to remember that Jesus always took the side of the despised sinner against the moralistic champions of law.*

It is sobering to remember that Jesus always took the side of the despised sinner against the moralistic champions of law.

SHANTUNG COMPOUND

Legalism was, however, the most prevalent failing of the conservative missionary, and its distressing effects were felt by most of the community. By legalism, I mean the practice, exemplified by Baker, of judging one's own actions and those of everyone else, by a rigid set of prescribed and usually trivial "do's and don'ts." The saddest example had to do with our monthly cigarette ration.

Each internee was permitted to buy at the canteen a certain rationed number of cigarettes, enough for the light smoker but woefully inadequate for the pack-a-day man. Consequently, many of the heavier smokers were always trying to get nonsmokers to let them purchase an extra lot of cigarettes with their ration cards. Since most of the missionaries did not use tobacco, they seemed fair game. Probably over half of them offered their cards good-humoredly and made no issue of it. But a significant number of the conservative ones refused, saying, "I would never allow cigarettes to be registered on my canteen card." Apparently they feared that this would act as a "demerit" to be held against them at some later balancing of the celestial books. Most laymen naturally felt that this was pretty narrow and, as they put it, ". . . no more than we might expect from the ruddy missionaries." But on the whole not much comment was made.

When, however, sixteen packs of American cigarettes arrived in each of the Red Cross parcels, a complex moral problem was presented to the pious. What were they to do with them? Certainly their rigid law against smoking demanded that they should destroy these cigarettes — especially when they had refused to lend out their ration cards because smoking was sinful.

On the other hand, it was very tempting not to destroy their cigarettes. Lucrative deals were now possible, since heavy smokers offered tins of milk, butter, and meat in exchange for a pack or two. Was a man not justified in trading them so that his children might have more to eat? Apparently the missionaries decided that he was. Almost all who had refused to lend out their ration cards before now exchanged their sixteen packs for the immense wealth of tins of milk or meat. To the cynical observer it almost seemed that to these pious associating themselves with smoking was not a sin if a profit was involved!

On our cooking shift was a most pleasant, open, kind fundamentalist named Smithfield. He was a red-haired fellow, hard working, cheerful, and an excellent ballplayer. One day a fellow on our shift pressed him about how he dealt with the seemingly clear contradiction involved in the selling of cigarettes.

To the cynical observer it almost seemed that to these pious associating themselves with smoking was not a sin if a profit was involved!

"Look, Smithfield, if smoking is sinful, then how can you encourage it by trading cigarettes? And if fags aren't really so bad — which you seem certainly to believe by trading them — then why don't you guys admit it, and let others use your cards to get an extra ration? You can't have your milk and your virtue both, you know!

"You know what I think? I think you don't feel they're really wrong at all. Would you be a 'pusher' of opium for milk as you now are of cigarettes? Of course you wouldn't! No, you guys just talk a lot about cigarettes and those other vices because, by avoiding them, you've found a fairly painless way of being pious. You don't really take your moral talk seriously at all, Smithfield!"

Smithfield, though an intelligent man, never saw any contradiction at all in what he did.

"I don't want them on my card because to use tobacco is sinful," he stated confidently, "and I'm not going to touch sin if I can help it. And as for the trading — I sold them for milk because my kids need milk. Isn't that reason enough?"

I couldn't help thinking that Smithfield's sharp questioner had been on the right track. It boiled down to how seriously the missionaries took their own moral code. Filled with all manner of relatively petty "do's and don't's," that code seemed too trivial to bear the weight of righteousness which they sought to pump into it. What had happened, I decided, was that somehow in the development of the Protestant ethic, the magnificent goal of serving God within the world had been perverted or lost in the shuffle.

Instead of bringing love and service into the world through his calling and his family life, the Protestant began to try to keep himself "holy"
in spite of the world. As he began to accept more and more of the world's
fundamental values of property, security, and prestige, inevitably the "holiness" he sought in the world became more and more trivial. He ended by
concentrating only on avoiding the vices which might prevent him from
being respectable.

After all, to love your neighbor within the everyday world is a risky and
explosive thing to do. It might upset firm property rights, the barriers of class
and race, and cast doubt on the sanctity and righteousness of war and violence!
No class moving upward in society can easily afford love as their goal! But in
"holiness" they can combine moral fervor with social expediency. The "holy
man," properly defined by prudent churchmen, could be propertied and prestigious as well as being a pious pillar of the church.

Through some such development, I thought, Protestantism has produced a degenerate moralism, a kind of legalism of life's petty vices that
would be boring and pathetic did it not have such a terrible hold on so
many hundreds of otherwise good-hearted people. For many of them being
a good Christian appeared to mean almost exclusively keeping one's life free
from such vices as smoking, gambling, drinking, swearing, card playing,
dancing, and movies.

So much are these legal requirements of purity the working criteria by
which they judge themselves and their neighbors ("He can't be a Christian,
he cusses") that multitudes of Christians feel they can, amid all the ambigu-
ities of life, exactly determine the status of a man's immortal soul by his
attitude to these vices. In this way, those of the legalist mentality would sooner
attend the White Citizens' Council than be seen in a bar; they would think
it better to be involved in an aggressive war than in a game of cards; they
would rather be caught underpaying their help than be heard to swear. To hear
the clergy of this persuasion preach, one would gather that, in a segregated,
militaristic and, in many respects, economically unjust American society, they
have come close to bringing in Utopia when they have succeeded in barring
the legal sale of liquor!

I learned from this experience that the fault in this Protestant ethic was
not that these legalistic missionaries were too moral. Rather, it was that many
of them were not free of their law to be moral enough. Their legalism prevented them from being as creative as the sincerity of their faith should have

*After all, to love your
neighbor within the
everyday world is a risky
and explosive thing to do.
It might upset firm
property rights, the
barriers of class and race,
and cast doubt on the
sanctity and righteousness
of war and violence!*

made them. Everyone in camp—missionary and layman, Catholic and Protestant—failed in some way or another to live up to his own ideals and did things he did not wish to do and felt he ought not to do. It was not of this common human predicament that I was thinking. What I felt especially weak in these Protestants was their false standard of religious and ethical judgment that frustrated their own desire to function morally within the community, for this standard judged the self and others by criteria which were both arbitrary and irrelevant. In the end, it left the self feeling righteous and smug when the real and deadly moral issues of camp life had not yet even been raised, much less resolved.

It had long been evident that our community was faced with moral problems deep enough to threaten its very existence. And yet a significantly large group of Christian leaders was concerned exclusively with moral issues and vices not connected with these deeper problems of our life. For this reason their very moral intensity tended to make both themselves and the serious morality which they represented seem to be a socially irrelevant segment of life rather than the creative force they might have been. The constructive moral forces in our life were only weakened and the cynical forces strengthened when missionaries judged honest, hard-working, and generally self-sacrificing men as "weak"—and even went so far as to warn their young people not to associate with them!—because they smoked or swore.

I learned from this experience that the fault in this Protestant ethic was not that these legalistic missionaries were too moral. Rather, it was that many of them were not free of their law to be moral enough.

"If *that* is morality, then I want none of it," said a man on our shift disgusted with this narrowness. Serious religion in this way became separated from serious morality, with the result that both religion and morality—and the community in which both existed—were immeasurably debilitated.

The most pathetic outcome of this legalism, however, was the barrier it created between the self-consciously pious and the other human beings around them. Almost inevitably the conservative Protestant would find himself disapproving, rejecting, and so withdrawing from those who did not heed his own fairly rigid rules of personal behavior.

Once I watched with fascinated horror this process of rejection and withdrawal take place when a nice young British fundamentalist named Taylor joined our cooking shift. Taylor wanted with all his heart to get along with the men there, to be warm and friendly to them, as he knew a Christian should be. All went well for the first few hours or so; no one told a dirty joke or otherwise made life difficult for Taylor. But then when we were ladling out the stew for lunch, a few drops of the thick, hot liquid fell on Neal's hand. Tom Neal was an ex-sailor of great physical strength and brass-bound integrity. Naturally this British tar made the air blue with his curses as he tried to get the burning stew off his hand. When the pain was over, as it was in a minute or so, he relaxed and returned to his usual bantering, cheerful ways.

But something was now different. Taylor hadn't *said* a word, nor had he moved a muscle. But he looked as if he had frozen inside, as if he had felt an uprush of uncontrollable disapproval. That feeling, like all deep feelings, projected itself outward, communicating itself silently to everyone around. An intangible gulf had appeared from nowhere, as real as the stew both were ladling out of the cauldron. Of course Neal felt it, and looked up closely and searchingly into Taylor's withdrawn and unhappy eyes. With surprising insight he said, "Hey, boy, them words of mine can't hurt you! Come and help me get this stew to the service line."

Taylor tried to smile; he hated himself for his reaction. But he felt immensely uncomfortable and spent the rest of his time with us on the shift spiritually isolated and alone. He was happy, so he told me one day, only when he was with the other "Christian folk."

Not a few missionaries seemed to exult in their code, using it, one was tempted to believe, as an instrument of pride against their neighbors, as a means of disapproving of the other person and so of elevating themselves spiritually in their own eyes—and, they were sure, in the eyes of God as well. But others were victims of their own law, in "bondage" to it, as St. Paul says. Though they wanted to accept their fellow men, their whole legal understanding of religion prevented this, forcing on them willy-nilly this sense of disapproval, this unwilled rejection, and this hated, inevitable barrier. Such men were not hypocrites—as others often felt who found themselves judged by these unknown laws. They didn't *want* to judge others—they couldn't help it.

It was ironic that these Protestants here described seemed to incarnate even more than their monastic brothers the very view of Christianity they repeatedly deplored, namely, a Christianity which removed itself from men to seek salvation away from the actual life of real people. In their frantic effort to escape the fleshly vices and so to be "holy," many fell unwittingly into the far more crippling sins of the spirit, such as pride, rejection, and lovelessness. This, I continue to feel, has been the greatest tragedy of Protestant life.

SAINTLY SOLDIERS?

"A fellow can't get into this war unless he has a certificate of all the virtues, signed by a majority of the freeholders in his precinct, and is pronounced pious by his pastor. Why, if the best fighters in my old company were spaded out of a half-hundred Southern battlefields, their lives restored and their youth renewed, they would be contumeliously rejected at the recruiting station for moral unfitness to stop Spanish bullets! They were a bad lot in an incalculable number of ingenious ways; but they could everlastingly lick ten times their weight of the churchly dudes and psalming eligibles of this degenerate day. Pah! a soldier should be able to quaff great bumpers of brandy, swear good mouth-filling oaths and play a famous game of cards to win his comrade's monthly wage. He should know how to loot a farm, sack a town, and harry the thrifty civilian generally, 'without regard to political affiliations.'"

—Ambrose Bierce, attacking overt religiosity during the Spanish-American War

QUESTIONS FOR THOUGHT AND DISCUSSION

1. What lay behind the conservative missionaries' refusal to let the smokers use their cards to buy an extra ration of cigarettes? How does the line beginning, "I would never allow" give away this underlying attitude?

2. How did the missionaries' attitudes change when the opportunity arose to swap cigarettes for milk and meat? How was this difference interpreted by the "cynical observer"?

3. What do you think of the argument posed to Smithfield about the inherent contradiction of his behavior? Was the questioner right? What "fairly painless way of being pious" do modern Christians embrace? Which ones do you embrace?

4. How would you respond to Gilkey's critique that believers have traded "love and service" of the world for the goal of keeping one's self "untouched" by the world? Why is this a perversion of Jesus' teachings?

5. How did the "legalism of life's petty vices" of the Protestants in the camp actually work against displays of true goodness and morality?

6. What does the example of Taylor and Tom Neal say about moralism's tendency to create barriers? Where have you seen this take place in your circles? Why is the reaction often to form "ghettoes" of people who think like we do?

7. The specific forms of moralism mentioned by Gilkey have changed in the fifty years since the camp. What are today's equivalents? How can we stand for moral concerns without falling into the trap of moralism?

REMINDER FOUR:

Remember That Differences Make a Difference — Our Unwelcome Insistence in a Day of Pluralism

There are simply too many conflicting claims about what is right and wrong and why. So who cares? The result, at best, is a form of fuzzy goodwill that pretends that if differences exist, they don't matter.

One of the great pitfalls of talking about right and wrong in a pluralistic society is indifference. There are simply too many conflicting claims about what is right and wrong and why. So who cares? The result, at best, is a form of fuzzy goodwill that pretends that if differences exist, they don't matter. From the perspective of the Bible, by contrast, all ideas have consequences—especially if written—and differences make a big difference.

AN INFINITE DIFFERENCE

"I am astonished that you are so quickly deserting the one who called you by the grace of Christ and are turning to a different gospel—which is really no gospel at all. Evidently some people are throwing you into confusion and are trying to pervert the gospel of Christ. But even if we or an angel from heaven should preach a gospel other than the one we preached to you, let him be eternally condemned! As we have already said, so now I say again: If anybody is preaching to you a gospel other than what you accepted, let him be eternally condemned!

"Am I now trying to win the approval of men, or of God? Or am I trying to please men? If I were still trying to please men, I would not be a servant of Christ. I want you to know, brothers, that the gospel I preached is not something that man made up."

—Galatians 1:6-11

C. S. Lewis

C. S. Lewis was introduced earlier in part 1 on pride. The first of these two passages is from his Mere Christianity, *and the second from* The Weight of Glory. *They are clear examples of his view that, because the individual outweighs history and human institutions, no thought or act is so small that it does not have eternal significance. Whereas Zen Buddhists believe that "man is a stone thrown in a pond who causes no ripples," the biblical view is that human ripples go on forever. Modern indifference to differences is therefore disastrous. Differences always make a difference—perhaps even the difference between heaven and hell.*

WHO CAN STAND IT?

"I am thoroughly convinced that God will let everyone into heaven who, in his considered opinion, can stand it. But 'standing it' may prove to be a more difficult matter than those who take their view of heaven from popular movies or popular preaching may think. The fires in heaven may be hotter than those in the other place."

—Dallas Willard, *The Divine Conspiracy*

CHRISTIAN BEHAVIOUR

We are now getting to the point at which different beliefs about the universe lead to different behavior. And it would seem, at first sight, very sensible to stop before we got there, and just carry on with those parts of morality that all sensible people agree about. But can we? Remember that religion involves a series of statements about facts, which must be either true or false. If they are true, one set of conclusions will follow about the right sailing of the human fleet: if they are false, quite a different set. For example, let us go back to the man who says that a thing cannot be wrong unless it hurts some other human being. He quite understands that he must not damage the other ships in the convoy, but he honestly thinks that what he does to his own ship is simply his own business. But does it not make a great difference whether his ship is his own property or not? Does it not make a great difference whether I am, so to speak, the landlord of my own mind and body, or only a tenant, responsible to the real

If somebody else made me, for his own purposes, then I shall have a lot of duties which I should not have if I simply belonged to myself.

landlord? If somebody else made me, for his own purposes, then I shall have a lot of duties which I should not have if I simply belonged to myself.

Again, Christianity asserts that every individual human being is going to live for ever, and this must be either true or false. Now there are a good many things which would not be worth bothering about if I were going to live only seventy years, but which I had better bother about very seriously if I am going to live for ever. Perhaps my bad temper or my jealousy are gradually getting worse — so gradually that the increase in seventy years will not be very noticeable. But it might be absolute hell in a million years: in fact, if Christianity is true, Hell is the precisely correct technical term for what it would be. And immortality makes this other difference, which, by the by, has a connection with the difference between totalitarianism and democracy. If individuals live only seventy years, then a state, or a nation, or a civilization, which may last for a thousand years, is more important than an individual. But if Christianity is true, then the individual is not only more important but incomparably more important, for he is everlasting and the life of a state or a civilization, compared with his, is only a moment.

From C. S. Lewis, *Mere Christianity.* Copyright © 1942 by C. S. Lewis Pte. Ltd. Extracts reprinted by permission.

THE WEIGHT OF GLORY

Meanwhile the cross comes before the crown and tomorrow is a Monday morning. . . . That being so, it may be asked what practical use there is in the speculations which I have been indulging. I can think of at least one such use. It may be possible for each to think too much of his own potential glory hereafter; it is hardly possible for him to think too often or too deeply about that of his neighbor. The load, or weight, or burden of my neighbor's glory should be laid daily on my back, a load so heavy that only humility can carry it, and the backs of the proud will be broken. It is a serious thing to live in a society of possible gods and goddesses, to remember that the dullest and most uninteresting person you talk to may one day be a creature which, if you saw it now, you would be strongly tempted to worship, or else a horror and a corruption such as you now meet, if at all, only in a nightmare. All day long we are, in some degree, helping each other to one or other of these destinations. It is in the light of these overwhelming possibilities, it is with the awe and the circumspection proper to them, that we should conduct all our dealings with one another, all friendships, all loves, all play, all politics. There are no *ordinary* people. You have never talked to a mere mortal. Nations, cultures, arts, civilization—these are mortal, and their life is to ours as the life of a gnat. But it is immortals whom we joke with, work with, marry, snub, and exploit— immortal horrors or everlasting splendors. This does not mean that we are to be perpetually solemn. We must play. But our merriment must be of that kind (and it is, in fact, the merriest kind) which exists between people who have, from the outset, taken each other seriously—no flippancy, no superiority, no presumption. And our charity must be a real and costly love, with deep feeling for the sins in spite of which we love the sinner—no mere tolerance or indulgence which parodies love as flippancy parodies merriment. Next to the Blessed Sacrament itself, your neighbor is the holiest object presented to your senses. If he is your Christian neighbor he is holy in almost the same way, for in him also Christ *vere latitat*—the glorifier and the glorified, Glory Himself, is truly hidden.

If he is your Christian neighbor he is holy in almost the same way, for in him also Christ vere latitat—*the glorifier and the glorified, Glory Himself, is truly hidden.*

QUESTIONS FOR THOUGHT AND DISCUSSION

1. In the passage from *Mere Christianity,* what defense does Lewis give for exploring differences in beliefs rather than just similarities?
2. What difference do the facts make in the two areas Lewis mentions: whether humans are "landlords" of their own minds and bodies or merely "tenants"? Whether humans will live forever?
3. In what other areas do, or should, beliefs about the universe lead to different behavior? In the context of Lewis's essay, how would you answer the person who argues that "what is true for you may not be true for me"?
4. In the excerpt from *The Weight of Glory,* what does Lewis mean by the statement, "There are no *ordinary* people"? How should this realization influence our daily behavior?
5. In light of his observations about humans, how does Lewis view "toleration"—the most prized "virtue" in modern Western culture? Why is it a slight to "real and costly love"?

REMINDER FIVE:

Remember Demonstration— Virtue Embodied in Action

"Preach the gospel constantly," said St. Francis of Assisi, "and if necessary, use words." In a study like this, it is necessary to use words—to read, to discuss, to ask questions, and to provide feedback. Yet here at the end, it should be emphasized that all of these words hold little value unless translated into action.

Our culture is a noisy one. Newspapers, magazines, billboards, and talk shows flood our lives with words—words to entertain, words to sell, words to persuade—and all too often many of us become cynical. We hunger for something deeper and truer, something beyond suspicion.

The biblical writer James said that faith not demonstrated by works is a non-living faith. It can breathe life into no one because it has no life itself. In the same vein, Jesus said, "No good tree bears bad fruit, nor does a bad tree bear good fruit. Each tree is recognized by its fruit." Thus, wordless actions are the clearest and truest witness of the inward reality. They are both the natural outflow of the heart and the demonstration of real heart change.

Yet caution is also appropriate. Actions can be imposters. To practice "deeds of righteousness" in order to be revered by men pollutes the act. Jesus reserved His harshest words for the teachers of the law: "You are like whitewashed tombs, which look beautiful on the outside but on the insider are full of dead men's bones and everything unclean." Therefore, an outward expression of goodness cannot substitute for a lack of inward reality. Hollowness will eventually be exposed. The inward reality of the heart must rather overflow into true and good actions. It is thus that the gospel is most powerfully proclaimed—without words.

"Preach the gospel constantly," said St. Francis of Assisi, "and if necessary, use words."

Yet caution is also appropriate. Actions can be imposters. To practice "deeds of righteousness" in order to be revered by men pollutes the act.

FAITH INDEED

"Let your light shine before men, that they may see your good deeds and praise your Father in heaven."
—Matthew 5:16

"Live such good lives among the pagans that, though they accuse you of doing wrong, they may see your good deeds and glorify God on the day he visits us."

—1 Peter 2:12

"What good is it, my brothers, if a man claims to have faith but has no deeds? Can such faith save him? Suppose a brother or sister is without clothes and daily food. If one of you says to him, 'Go, I wish you well; keep warm and well fed,' but does nothing about his physical needs, what good is it? In the same way, faith by itself, if it is not accompanied by action, is dead."

—James 2:14-17

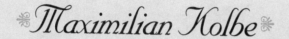

Maximilian Kolbe

Maximilian Kolbe was born near Lodz, Poland in 1894. As a child, he suffered from tuberculosis and was frail in health most of his life. At the age of thirteen he joined the Order of St. Francis and eventually studied at Gregorian University in Rome. Ordained a priest in the Roman Catholic Church in 1918, Kolbe was arrested by the Gestapo in 1939 and again in 1941 for his anti-Nazi publications. Following the second arrest, he was imprisoned in Auschwitz, where he gave his life for condemned prisoner Franciszek Gajowniczek. Following two weeks of starvation, Kolbe eventually died of a lethal carbolic acid injection. He was canonized by Pope John Paul II on October 10, 1982.

The excerpts that follow are from Ian MacMillan's novel Orbit of Darkness, in which he retells the story of Kolbe's sacrifice and its startling effect on the camp at Auschwitz. When one prisoner refused to come forward to confess an offense, the camp commander ordered ten prisoners, randomly chosen, to die of starvation for the grievance. Though Kolbe was not one of the ten, he spontaneously offered to take the place of Gajowniczek, whom he knew had a wife and child awaiting his release. Kolbe was allowed to make what the guards considered an absurd gesture. The reprieved prisoner Gajowniczek did survive Auschwitz to eventually return to his family.

In an age of wordy debates about ethics—what is really good and how it can be known—MacMillan's account reminds us of what one good and wordless action can accomplish.

LOVE'S PINNACLE

"Greater love has no one than this, that he lay down his life for his friends."

—John 15:13

"Maximilian did not die, but 'gave his life . . . for his brother.'"

—Pope John Paul II, in his homily at the canonization of Maximilian Kolbe

---

ORBIT OF DARKNESS

AUSCHWITZ—Penal Block 11

July 30, 1941

Just inside the doorway to the Block of Death the ten men are ordered to strip. Scharführer Hubert Pfoch observes the men taking off their filthy striped uniforms, their muddy clogs, and the alert one, the insane priest who volunteered for this, dropping his spectacles on the pile of dirty clothes. The strange story of his act preceded his arrival by two minutes; Pfoch is intrigued by it because it would be so much easier for the man to simply throw himself at the electric fence, as so many others have done. . . .

The guards have heard the story of the demented holy man, and now, at the base of the stairway, they engage in an exchange of wit: he suffers from indigestion and sees this as a cure; he never liked our food, poor man; he'll do anything to get out of work. . . .

The inmates' bodies have a strange, phosphorescent pallor in the darkness, so that they appear as a collection of walking ghosts with dark pits for eyes. Then he sees the priest, standing in the middle of the room looking back at Pfoch. His face is steady and composed, and his eyes, under the dark eyebrows that nearly join above the bridge of his nose, assess Pfoch with a kind of contemplative objectivity, nothing else. Pfoch smiles at him and snorts derisively before he slams the heavy door and turns to the patch of dusty light at the base of the stairwell. He feels a nervous intensity in his flesh—when he was a child he always felt a strange sensation of littleness, or primeval shame, in the presence of any priest. But he passes the feeling off—if anything it is exhilaration, or perhaps hunger. "Well," he whispers, "it is nearly time to eat."

The inmates' bodies have a strange, phosphorescent pallor in the darkness, so that they appear as a collection of walking ghosts with dark pits for eyes. Then he sees the priest, standing in the middle of the room looking back at Pfoch.

August 4, 1941

The two guards position themselves as far from the oak doors of the starvation cells as they can. The older guard, Thomas Guerber, sits in a creaky wooden chair smoking a cigarette. Jurgen Vierck, the younger of the two, begins to whistle softly, and Guerber sighs with lazy irritation and says, "Stop that."

"I'm sorry," Vierck says. He is hardly aware of what he had whistled and realizes now that it is one of those hymns that leak incessantly through the doors of the starvation cells. The sound seems to be in the walls, circulating in the bricks, because the ten men in the adjoining cell, further on in their punishment, have risen from their moribund lassitude and are listening in and singing and praying along with the group the priest leads. Hour by hour, there is the faint sound of singing, and then, fainter, the sound of mumbling voices, led by the mad priest. Vierck sometimes listens, and is convinced that he can hear nothing, but then feels it coming from all directions like the whispers of the dead. . . .

He pauses, listening to the wall. Then he says, "Do you know what they say about that man in there?" Guerber raises his eyebrows with fatigued question. "They say he's been giving his food away for months. They say that the guards and Kapos gave him the worst jobs, and he did them all and gave away his food." Vierck sees no reaction on Guerber's face. "I wonder if he's—" But Vierck isn't sure what he was about to say.

August 5, 1941

"I've come to see the saint," the tall officer booms amiably. Jurgen Vierck rises, assuming that the man must be of higher rank. Vierck now recognizes him as a Scharführer from the deputy commandant's staff.

"Which saint are you referring to, sir?" Vierck asks.

"The priest—the one who volunteered for this duty," the Scharführer says, drawing something from his tunic. It is a piece of cheese wrapped in a book page.

"With submission, sir, but we are not permitted to feed the men in the starvation cells."

"I know, I know," the man says with a kind of good-natured petulance. "I've come to perform a test. Open the cell."

Vierck reasons that because the man is higher in rank, he has to obey. He leads the tall Scharführer down the hall to the cell. . . .

Vierck unlocks the door. When the hinges groan, the men inside stir slowly. The expressions on their faces bear little of the wild hope of the previous days. One man is dead, curled up in a fetal position in one corner.

"Priest!" the man says, "would you like a bite of cheese?"

One man rises quickly and approaches the Scharführer in a half-crawl, and gasps out, "Please, I beg you, please, water! Please!" Another man comes out with a cracked laugh. . . .

"Priest," the Scharführer says. The other men are now more alert, muttering softly to one another, all with their eyes on the block of cheese encased in the book page. The priest slowly stands up and looks at the Scharführer, who stares back for a moment, thinking. "I see what they mean about your eyes," he says. "I've brought you some cheese. Would you like it?"

Vierck sees a sudden twinge of shocked desire in the priest's face, but then the expression vanishes, leaving him staring with that peculiar objectivity Vierck has seen before. He is so composed that Vierck imagines him observing the Scharführer as if he were for some reason mildly interesting.

Vierck sees a sudden twinge of shocked desire in the priest's face, but then the expression vanishes, leaving him staring with that peculiar objectivity Vierck has seen before.

"Here," the Scharführer says, "take it."

"Please give it to these men," the priest says.

"I want to give it to you."

"Thank you, no. I have food." And then the priest turns and goes to his place and sits down.

"We must leave," Vierck says.

"Last opportunity," the Scharführer croons seductively. The priest does not respond. Then the Scharführer laughs and walks out.

Back near the stairwell, he pauses and says, "Did you see his face? I got to him. He's human after all." He looks back down the hall. "The way I heard it the little shit had the whole camp wrapped around his finger."

"Who said that?"

"The word got round—that this man had somehow made this part of the camp grind to a halt or something, just by volunteering."

"No. The inmates have something for him, though."

"What about you?"

"I—" Vierck suddenly feels nervous.

"He gets to you, too, then. That's what I was talking about."

August 9, 1941

Dieter Nehring sees the young soldier coming across the hard dirt between two buildings.

"Sturmmann Jurgen Vierck."

"Ah, yes. What can I do for you?"

"Regarding the matter of the priest—"

"Still alive, is he?"

"Yes," Vierck says, and then he smiles, but the smile has an obsequious, conspiratorial look to it. "I think it is time to do away with him." Nehring studies the man's eyes—in them he sees a strange, haunted look, as if he is aware of something threatening behind him.

"Why?"

"His effect on the men."

"What men?"

It is apparent that Vierck knows he is being in effect cross-examined. Nehring has heard of this effect, too—men who claim that his gaze leaves a rash on the skin, men who claim that they feel intense pressure upon entering the starvation cell.

"I wish to be transferred, sir," Vierck says.

"Why?"

The man laughs again, this time with an apparent frustration at Nehring's failure to see the obvious. "I looked into things," Vierck says to the wall next to Nehring. "He hasn't eaten, certainly, in nine days, but it is apparent that he hasn't eaten in many weeks, perhaps in months. It is apparent—"

"Stop it," Nehring says. "It's *you* he affects. No, no. You will see this through. He will starve to death as ordered. You will be there on the last day."

"He is a preternatural being."

Nehring looks at him, trying to contain his anger. "A what? Are you out of your mind?"

"I think he is a preternatural being. His eyes—"

"Shut up!" Nehring shouts. He looks around. Prisoners and Kapos are looking in his direction. When he looks at them, they quickly look away. "This is disgusting," he whispers. "Come to your senses—these religious freaks and their sunny dispositions are nothing but self-sacrificial idiots, can't you see that?"

"I wish to be—"

"No. I will not have soldiers of the Reich turning into whining babies over something as foolish as this. You stay at your post. You will leave him to starve as ordered, do you hear?"

"Yes, sir." Now Vierck's expression seems distant, and he has the resigned look of a condemned man. Nehring's inner fury turns into a kind of sympathetic perplexity.

"In a day or so I am going to take you into the cell and show you a foul-smelling corpse and there will be nothing in his eyes, understand?"

"Yes, sir. . . . "

"A priest," he says, "and look what he's done to you." Then he understands why this has become a problem in the first place. "He's made self-sacrifice a virtue, and by doing that he's fogging our certainty, don't you see? He's using himself as an example to make men out of vermin. Don't you see it in these prisoners' eyes?" Vierck thinks, nods slowly. "Now they all walk around acting as if there's some sort of virtue in martyrdom, and all because of this one little man." Vierck seems unconvinced. "Listen," Nehring says, "it's late in the afternoon. Go and eat something—I've found that this has a healthy effect myself, whenever something troubles me. Go and eat something, and in a while you'll feel fine."

"Yes, sir."

August 13, 1941

"No prisoners, Kapos, no one shall come out," Nehring says. He looks down at the rumpled corpse of Sturmmann Vierck. Kassler was the first to get to him and pulled his hand off the wire with a broom. Near the fence stands a nervous Kapo, who alerted Kassler.

"This was an accident," Nehring says to Guerber.

"Yes, Oberst."

"You," Nehring says to Kassler. "I want you to go to the river tomorrow—I want you to inform the German Kapos that anyone mentioning that priest's name shall be beaten to death, understand? Leave all the other Kapos out of this. Only the Germans—Krott, and so on."

"Yes, Oberst."

"In addition, I want them to watch for people helping each other or for people giving food away—it is obvious that this lessens their own ability to work, self-sacrificial benevolence notwithstanding. When these acts are observed both parties shall be beaten to death, do you understand?"

"Yes, Oberst."

"All this good-heartedness is making these people smug, and I want no more of it. Tomorrow we'll see how the priest can handle a little carbolic acid."

August 15, 1941

Prisoners are removing the priest's corpse from the penal block. Thomas Guerber watches as the men maneuver the wooden litter down the steps, one man at the priest's head, holding the handles of the litter up at his shoulders so that the corpse will remain level. Small groups of men have gathered at points between the penal block and the crematorium so that they will be able to see him as he passes. . . .

Just beyond the steps he sees that boy who has spent the past two weeks sitting by the cell window. The boy watches the corpse pass with a wide-eyed stare and then takes his cap off. Guerber is aware that other men nearby are also furtively taking off their caps, strictly forbidden, but unnoticed because

"All this good-heartedness is making these people smug, and I want no more of it. Tomorrow we'll see how the priest can handle a little carbolic acid."

the guards present are looking at the strangely clean, almost bright corpse rocking slightly in the wooden trough. . . .

The boy stumbles back out of the way of the priest's litter, his cap still in his hands. Other men nearby watch the priest pass and put their caps back on. Two Kapos emerge from the block, and one of them stops on the stairs and watches the boy. Then he lunges off the steps toward him and slaps him on the head. He raises his hand to hit the boy again.

"You!" Guerber yells. The Kapo stops. "Let him alone—can't you see he's off his head?" The Kapo backs away. The boy puts his cap back on his head, and Guerber looks at him briefly. He thinks, why on earth is he at this place?

"Well," he says, "go on, but be more careful." The boy runs off, and Guerber suddenly feels vaguely embarrassed at the ridiculousness of address-ing the boy, and at the absurdity of intervening on his behalf.

He turns to the penal block steps, and Kassler emerges. He comes down the steps to Guerber and says, "The little man lasted more than two weeks."

"Yes."

"I lost a bet," he says and twists his face into a look of tragic perplexity. Then he laughs and says, "I guessed at eleven days. . . ."

Then Guerber is left standing at the base of the steps. He watches the heavy smoke coming from the crematorium chimney.

Excerpts from *Orbit of Darkness*, © 1991 by Ian MacMillan, reprinted by permission of Harcourt Inc.

QUESTIONS FOR THOUGHT AND DISCUSSION

1. In the excerpt dated July 30, why is Pfoch intrigued by the story of the priest trading places with the condemned man? What does he assume is the priest's motive? What do you think lies behind the guards' jokes about the priest's actions?

2. How does Pfoch feel when the priest's eyes meet his? To what does he attribute it?

3. In the August 4 excerpt, where do the starvation cell guards position themselves? Why? In the last paragraph, what do Vierck's words to Guerber convey about his developing thoughts regarding the priest?

4. On August 5, the Scharführer decides to "test" the priest with a piece of cheese. What is he really testing? What would "failing the test" look like?

5. How does the priest respond to the offer of cheese? What does the priest mean when he says, "I have food"? Why does the Scharführer think he's "gotten to" the priest? Why do you agree or disagree?

6. What has the Scharführer heard about the priest's effect on the camp? How does Vierck's response to the Scharführer's inquiry give him away? How would you describe the effect the priest is having on Vierck?

7. In the excerpt from August 9, what is the reason Vierck gives for wanting to "do away" with the priest? Do you believe him? If not, what do you think is the real reason?

8. By this time, what has Vierck concluded about the priest? What, if any, effect do Nehring's counter-arguments have on him? What do Nehring's attacks on the priest suggest about his own state of mind? How is the priest "fogging (his) certainty"?

9. On August 13, Vierck's body is found. Why has he, the guard, thrown himself on the electric fence? How does Nehring react to the incident? What has been the effect of the priest's example on the behavior of the other prisoners? Why do you think this change rattles Nehring so severely?

10. As you read the August 15 excerpt, how do you feel? What strikes you about the reaction of the prisoners to the priest's death? What is the significance of Guerber's intervening on behalf of the boy who sat by the priest's cell? How would you sum up the overall effect of the priest's sacrificial act on the camp? When have you seen a sacrificial act deeply change an individual or a community? What is the place of wordless action in making ethical stands?

❦ Corrie ten Boom ❦

Corrie ten Boom was born in Haarlem, Holland in 1892. The second daughter of a watchmaker, she became the first woman in Holland to qualify for the profession. During World War II, she and her sister Betsie served time in the German concentration camp at Ravensbruck for the crime of hiding persecuted Jews. She survived to tell the story in her best-selling book, The Hiding Place.

After the war, Corrie ten Boom founded a rehabilitation home in Holland for survivors of the Holocaust and was honored in 1968 by the state of Israel for her efforts on behalf of the Jews. She was invited to plant a tree in the Avenue of the Righteous Gentiles where Otto Schindler is also recognized.

Until the age of eighty-five, Corrie ten Boom traveled and spoke extensively, visiting over sixty countries and working for forgiveness and reconciliation between former enemies. The story that follows took place during one such trip to Munich two years after the war ended. It is a moving testimony of the power and grace of virtue embodied in action.

LOVE YOUR ENEMY

It was in a church in Munich that I saw him—a balding, heavyset man in a gray overcoat, a brown felt hat clutched between his hands. People were filing out of the basement room where I had just spoken, moving along the rows of wooden chairs to the door at the rear. It was 1947 and I had come from Holland to defeated Germany with the message that God forgives.

It was the truth they needed most to hear in that bitter, bombed-out land, and I gave them my favorite mental picture. Maybe because the sea is never far from a Hollander's mind, I liked to think that that's where forgiven sins were thrown. "When we confess our sins," I said, "God casts them into the deepest ocean, gone forever. And even though I cannot find a Scripture for it, I believe God then places a sign out there that says, NO FISHING ALLOWED."

The solemn faces stared back at me, not quite daring to believe. There were never questions after a talk in Germany in 1947. People stood up in silence, in silence collected their wraps, in silence left the room.

And that's when I saw him, working his way forward against the others. One moment I saw the overcoat and the brown hat; the next, a blue uniform and a visored cap with its skull and crossbones. It came back with a rush: the huge room with its harsh overhead lights; the pathetic pile of dresses and shoes in the center of the floor; the shame of walking naked past this man. I could see my sister's frail form ahead of me, ribs sharp beneath the parchment skin. *Betsie, how thin you were!*

The place was Ravensbruck and the man who was making his way forward had been a guard—one of the most cruel guards.

Now he was in front of me, hand thrust out: "A fine message, Fraulein! How good it is to know that, as you say, all our sins are at the bottom of the sea!"

"When we confess our sins," I said, "God casts them into the deepest ocean, gone forever. And even though I cannot find a Scripture for it, I believe God then places a sign out there that says, NO FISHING ALLOWED."

The place was Ravensbruck and the man who was making his way forward had been a guard—one of the most cruel guards.

And I, who had spoken so glibly of forgiveness, fumbled in my pocket-book rather than take that hand. He would not remember me, of course—how could he remember one prisoner among those thousands of women?

But I remembered him and the leather crop swinging from his belt. I was face-to-face with one of my captors and my blood seemed to freeze.

"You mentioned Ravensbruck in your talk," he was saying. "I was a guard there." No, he did not remember me.

"But since that time," he went on, "I have become a Christian. I know that God has forgiven me for the cruel things I did there, but I would like to hear it from your lips as well. Fraulein,"—again the hand came out—"will you forgive me?"

And I stood there—I whose sins had again and again to be forgiven—and could not forgive. Betsie had died in that place—could he erase her slow terrible death simply for the asking?

It could not have been many seconds that he stood there—hand held out—but to me it seemed hours as I wrestled with the most difficult thing I had ever had to do.

It could not have been many seconds that he stood there—hand held out—but to me it seemed hours as I wrestled with the most difficult thing I had ever had to do.

For I had to do it—I knew that. The message that God forgives has a prior condition: that we forgive those who have injured us. "If you do not forgive men their trespasses," Jesus says, "neither will your Father in heaven forgive your trespasses."

I knew it not only as a commandment of God, but as a daily experience. Since the end of the war I had had a home in Holland for victims of Nazi brutality. Those who were able to forgive their former enemies were able also to return to the outside world and rebuild their lives, no matter what the physical scars. Those who nursed their bitterness remained invalids. It was as simple and as horrible as that.

And still I stood there with the coldness clutching my heart. But forgiveness is not an emotion—I knew that too. Forgiveness is an act of the will, and the will can function regardless of the temperature of the heart. "Jesus, help me!" I prayed silently. "I can lift my hand. I can do that much. You supply the feeling."

The current started in my shoulder, raced down my arm, sprang into our joined hands. And then this healing warmth seemed to flood my whole being, bringing tears to my eyes.

And so woodenly, mechanically, I thrust my hand into the one stretched out to me. And as I did, an incredible thing took place. The current started in my shoulder, raced down my arm, sprang into our joined hands. And then this healing warmth seemed to flood my whole being, bringing tears to my eyes.

"I forgive you, brother!" I cried. "With all my heart."

For a long moment we grasped each other's hands, the former guard and the former prisoner. I had never known God's love so intensely as I did then. But even so, I realized it was not my love. I had tried, and did not have the power. It was the power of the Holy Spirit as recorded in Romans 5:5, ". . . because the love of God is shed abroad in our hearts by the Holy Ghost which is given unto us."

"I'm Still Learning to Forgive" by Corrie ten Boom. Excerpted with permission from *Guideposts* magazine, copyright © 1972 Guideposts Associates, Inc, Carmel, NY.

QUESTIONS FOR THOUGHT AND DISCUSSION

1. What do you think it would have been like to carry the message of God's forgiveness to Germany in 1947, especially as a former concentration camp prisoner?

2. How do you think Corrie ten Boom felt when she first recognized the man who was coming toward her as the former Ravensbruck guard?

3. The former guard says, "How good it is to know that, as you say, all our sins are at the bottom of the sea." If you had been in ten Boom's place at that moment, what thoughts might you have had? What impact would it have had on you to realize the guard did not remember you?

4. The guard asks Corrie ten Boom to forgive him personally, putting out his hand. What justifications might you have given yourself for refusing to take this man's hand? How would the fact that your sister had died under his treatment have come into play?

5. Why did Corrie ten Boom know she had no choice but to forgive? How had she seen the power of forgiveness among Nazi victims in her Holland home?

6. Do you agree that "forgiveness is not an emotion"? Have you ever experienced forgiveness as an "act of the will"? How did this understanding enable Corrie ten Boom to make the first move toward forgiving the guard?

7. What happened in the moment that Corrie ten Boom thrust out her hand to meet the hand of the man? Where did she later realize the power to forgive had come from?

8. Who do you think was changed most deeply by this encounter? When have you been changed by the act of forgiveness?

9. How would this story have been different if Corrie ten Boom had refused to shake the guard's hand? How would her refusal have affected the man? Affected her? In light of this story, why do you think the biblical writer James says, "Faith without works is dead"?

10. As you think back over all the readings, how important do you believe an understanding of the virtues and vices to be to our shared public life? In your own life? How will your life be different as a result of what you've studied? How does the truth of forgiveness—both God's forgiveness of us, and our forgiveness of others, as demonstrated in this final reading—inform our understanding of the virtues and the vices?

For Further Reading

For those who desire to read further on the subject of the seven deadly sins, the following is a short list of books that are both helpful and accessible.

Henry Fairlie, *The Seven Deadly Sins Today* (Washington, D.C.: New Republic Books and New York: Simon and Schuster, 1978).

Peter Kreeft, *Back to Virtue* (San Francisco: Ignatius Press, 1992).

C. S. Lewis, *Mere Christianity* (New York: Macmillan, 1952).

Solomon Schimmel, *The Seven Deadly Sins* (New York: Free Press, 1992).

Christina and Fred Sommers, *Vice and Virtue in Everyday Life: Introductory Readings in Ethics* (San Diego: Harcourt Brace Jovanovich, 1989).

Angus Wilson, W. H. Auden, et al., *The Seven Deadly Sins* (New York: William Morrow, 1992).

READER'S GUIDE

Using This Book in a Discussion Group

The following reader's discussion guide offers a format for leading eight ninety-minute discussions of *Steering Through Chaos*. Ideally, participants will read about three selections from the book before each group meeting. However, it's possible (though somewhat more difficult) for people to participate even if they have not had time to read the material beforehand.

The goals of this discussion group are to help participants:

- Understand what ethics is about
- Understand what each of the seven deadly sins is, and be able to recognize it in themselves, others, and society
- Understand the virtues that are the great opposites of the deadly vices
- Face evil in their own hearts
- Commit themselves to move from talking about good to taking action to pursue good in their lives

The eight group sessions break down as follows. The readings selected for group discussion are in ( ). In addition to the main readings marked here, you will sometimes discuss the short quotations in the gray boxes that are scattered throughout the book.

1. Overview and Pride, part 1 (Coles, Lewis)
2. Pride, part 2 (Milton, Golding, Taylor)
3. Envy (Plutarch, Hawthorne, Shaffer, Wesley)
4. Anger (Plutarch, Weir, Gordon, King)
5. Sloth (Pascal, Kierkegaard, Havel, Herbert)
6. Avarice (Tolstoy, Gilkey, Hugo)
7. Gluttony and Lust (Lewis, Lawrence, May)
8. Reminders One (Aristotle), Two (Johnson), Three (Gilkey), and Five (MacMillan)

If you have time for an extra session at the end, you may want to discuss what each of you plans to do over the next six months with what you've discussed. Ideas for this ninth session can be found on page 340 of this guide.

The Leader's Role

You don't need any special background in order to lead this discussion group effectively. The readings in this book include background information about the writers and their ideas. This discussion guide offers help in small group leadership. The format of the group will be discussion, not lecture, so you will not be expected to teach or answer questions. Any background you have (in history, philosophy, ethics, and so on) will enrich the group, but your knowledge will not be the group's focus.

Your role is:
- To begin and end the meeting on time
- To introduce each reading
- To ask people to read aloud key portions of each reading
- To keep the group moving from reading to reading at a reasonable pace
- To select the questions that are most important for the group to discuss
- To ask questions
- To listen closely to answers and ask follow-up questions as appropriate
- To express your opinions at appropriate moments
- To set a tone of respect and free exchange of ideas
- To make sure that everyone who wants to speak gets adequate air time
- To help the group keep track of the big picture that the readings are sketching

Beginning and ending on time is a way of respecting participants. Latecomers won't mind if you start without them, and doing so rewards those who come on time. Likewise, even if you're in the middle of a great discussion, people will thank you if you cut it off when the time is up. Those who need to leave can do so and, if your host permits, others can stay and continue the conversation informally.

Each reading is preceded by a brief introduction about the author and the context. As you come to each reading, begin by summarizing this introduction in a few sentences. Then, ask someone to read aloud a portion of the reading that relates to the first question you want to ask. (This guide will suggest portions to be read aloud.) Reading aloud and asking questions will set the rhythm of the discussion. Reading aloud refreshes everyone's memory and involves people who may not have read the material ahead of time. It is especially effective with drama, such as Milton's *Paradise Lost* in part 1 or Shaffer's *Amadeus* in part 2. Assign the roles of Satan in *Paradise Lost* and Salieri in *Amadeus* to people who can read with feeling. (However, be aware that some people are uncomfortable reading aloud. You may want to ask people ahead of time how they feel about doing so.)

After twenty to thirty minutes, summarize the discussion about that reading and introduce the next one.

Most groups function better with two cofacilitators rather than with one. It's helpful to take turns guiding discussions on the different readings, or to let one person guide the discussion while the other keeps track of the time.

The Group's Emphasis

Some groups emphasize the sharing of personal experiences and feelings. Many don't challenge people to think deeply. This series addresses whole people, the understanding as well as the feeling parts of them. Your task is to help the group think, understand, and draw conclusions together. However, the conversation will not be banter about airy notions. The questions are designed to be practical. The issues raised are relevant to the nitty-gritty lives of each person in your group. Ideally, people will leave each meeting with new thoughts about what they do all day: conduct business, raise children, vote for lawmakers, relate to neighbors, spend money. And you may be surprised at how emotional these thoughtful discussions become as people's hearts are pierced with new perspectives on their lives.

Each session is designed to take about ninety minutes. During that time you will discuss three or four readings from *Steering Through Chaos*. That means you will spend just twenty to thirty minutes on each reading. Therefore, you won't have time to discuss all the questions about each reading. You won't be able to have an exhaustive discussion about any of them. Instead, you'll draw out the main points of each reading so that group members can follow the inner logic that flows through the progression of readings. You don't want to take time and become bogged down in one reading because if you did, you would lose the thread of the big picture. In any given session, each person is likely to find at least one of the readings personally meaningful. It is always better to cut off a good discussion than to drag it out until it dies.

This reader's discussion guide will point out the questions for each reading that will be most helpful for group discussion. This guidance is meant to simplify your job. Nevertheless, you are still the group leader, so if you think your group will benefit most from questions other than those suggested here, then follow your intuition. Instead of the pointed questions that follow each reading, you may prefer to use open-ended questions, such as, "What is your perspective, feeling, or reaction to this reading?"

Guiding the Discussion

Most groups depend heavily on the leader in the beginning. The leader asks a question, and someone answers. The leader asks another question, and someone answers. People direct their responses to the leader. However, an effective leader nudges participants toward talking to each other. The leader plays referee and timekeeper so that the group stays on track.

One tool for nudging people to talk to each other is the follow-up question. For instance, one type of follow-up question invites others' input: "What do some of the rest of you think about Terry's view?" Other kinds of follow-up questions include:
- Rephrasing the question
- Probing gently for more information ("Can you say more about that?")
- Asking for clarification ("So are you saying that . . .?")
- Summarizing a portion of the discussion

You will probably want to summarize (or ask someone else to do so) at the end of your discussion of each reading. This will help people keep track of where each reading fits into the big picture.

Maintain eye contact with all participants, particularly those on your immediate left and right, so that everyone feels included in the discussion. It's a good idea to arrange the room in a circle before the meeting so that people will be able to see each other's faces.

Avoid answering your own questions. Allow silence, especially when people are looking at the readings to refresh their memories. If people seem not to understand your question, it's best to rephrase it, rather than answering it.

Also, avoid commenting on each participant's response. Instead, ask a follow-up question to draw out others' comments.

Encourage participants to ask questions about one another's comments. Your ultimate goal is to foster a lively discussion among participants about the point under discussion. However, if you sense that the conversation is drifting off the main point of the reading, summarize the comments that have been made and move on to a new question that builds toward the focus of the reading.

Dealing with Talkative and Quiet People

In any discussion group, some people are naturally more talkative than others. While it's desirable for everyone to participate aloud, it's not essential for this group. One of the ground rules (see pagees 310 and 315) is that everyone is welcome to speak, but no one is obliged to speak. There are several reasons why a person might be quiet during the meeting, and you'll want to assess which reasons apply to each of your quiet people. Reasons for quietness include the following:

- A person may be overwhelmed by the material and not be following the discussion. This person needs you to listen to his or her concerns outside the group meeting.
- A person may be processing the discussion internally. Some people prefer to digest ideas and feelings inside and speak only when they have thought through what they want to say. By contrast, other people think out loud. They often don't know what they think until it comes out of their mouths. It's possible that both the talkative and the quiet people are getting what they need in your group. Don't assume that silence equals nonparticipation.
- A person may strongly disagree with what is being said but may be uncomfortable with overt conflict. There are ways of handling covert conflict that strengthen the group. See page 310.
- A person may want to speak but feel intimidated in group settings. It's usually best to draw such people out in conversation outside the formal discussion, but not to call attention to them during the meeting.

This is not an exhaustive list of reasons for quietness. The important thing is to gauge each person individually and ask yourself, "What might this person need?"

With people who seem to talk too much, it's less important to consider why they're talking and more important to assess their effect on the group. Are the quieter people getting something out of what the talker is saying? Or are they wishing they were somewhere else? If you think someone's talking is excessive, there are several subtle ways to discourage it. You can sit next to the person rather than face him. You can avoid making eye contact or nodding, because these are signals that the speaker should continue. In extreme cases, you can take the person aside after the meeting and enlist his help in drawing out the quieter group members.

Above all, as a leader, take care that you are not the group member who talks too much. Keep the group focused on the readings, not on you. Resist the temptation to fill silence with your observations. Silence can be productive if people are thinking.

Disagreement and Conflict

In a discussion group of this kind, disagreement is good. *Tough-minded discussion* occurs when one person's ideas, conclusions, or opinions are incompatible with another's, and the two seek a deeper understanding of truth or wisdom together. Views are aired openly, and everyone has a chance to evaluate the merits of each position. Someone might even change his or her mind.

Debate occurs when people's ideas, conclusions, or opinions are incompatible; each person argues for his or her position; and a winner is declared. Debate is not necessarily bad in a group either. People may feel strongly that they are right and someone else is wrong. A strenuous defense of one's position is fair play.

Some ground rules can make tough-minded discussion and debate constructive:

- Genuine disagreement is an achievement because it enables people to learn. We assume that a disagreement is valuable until proven otherwise.
- Deepening our understanding of truth or wisdom is more important in this group than winning an argument.
- Respect is important in this group. The merits of a position may be debated, but persons may not be attacked.
- If people feel attacked, they will say so respectfully, and the group will assess the situation together.

Many people fear all forms of conflict, including discussion and debate. If you have group members who are uncomfortable with conflict in the group, you may want to have a discussion about constructive conflict. Explain that, while quarreling is unproductive, disagreement is not. Emphasize that *concurrence-seeking* is less productive than tough-minded discussion. Concurrence-seeking happens when group members inhibit discussion in order to avoid disagreement. Concurrence-seeking can lead to "groupthink," in which everyone feels obliged to think alike and people cease to think for themselves.

A certain amount of concurrence-seeking is natural in a group of people who don't know each other well. However, the more you can draw covert conflict out into the open, the less likely people are to withdraw from the group because of unvoiced dissatisfaction. If you sense people simmering but not speaking, the best course may be to give a short speech about the value of healthy disagreement and to state some ground rules for controversy.

THE BIG PICTURE

Because you'll cover a lot of ground in each group session, you'll find it helpful to keep in mind the book's "big picture." Each reading contains many more interesting ideas than you'll have time to discuss, but you can help the group get the most out of its study if you keep bringing people back to these themes:

- The cardinal virtues and the deadly vices offer us a moral compass by which we can steer through the chaos of modern society.
- Ethics deals first of all with what kind of person I am to be, and only then with what I should do in given instances. Ethics is not primarily about solving problems ("Is it wrong to watch R-rated movies?"), but about becoming a good human being and a good society of human beings.
- Being comes before doing, but doing is more important than talking. It's important to *do* what is right, not merely to *know* what is right.
- Grace enables us to become good, not just to talk about what is good.
- In order to become good, we need grace plus effort.
- Personal and social ethics are both important. I must consider the kind of person I want to be in my relationships with family, friends, colleagues, employees, fellow citizens, and neighbors across the globe. I must also consider the kinds of laws, customs, and leaders that encourage individuals and groups to be just and good.
- We needn't blush to use categories like good and evil. The ethical tradition of the West has both a high view of human nature and a deeply realistic view of the presence and power of evil. That is, it has a high view of what humans were created to be and of the good both individuals and society can do. At the same time, it takes seriously the deep evil of which both individuals and societies are capable. This idea of our potential for both great good and great evil contrasts starkly with the modern notion that wrongdoers are merely sick psychologically rather than tainted with evil. At the same time, it contrasts with the modern indifference to becoming good (as opposed to "fulfilled" or "happy").
- The seven deadly sins are the root sins from which all others grow. Each deadly sin stems from a disordering of love—defective love, excessive love of the wrong thing, and so on.

- The seven virtues in this book come from the Beatitudes in Jesus' Sermon on the Mount. They are not antidotes or curatives, but superb opposites. They summarize the delight of the supernatural virtue of God's kingdom. Citizens of God's kingdom seek to cultivate these virtues. They express the perfect ordering of love.

This book contains two introductory readings. We will discuss the one (Coles) that establishes one of the themes of the book: Being and doing good are worth far more than intellectualizing about good.

We will then discuss each deadly vice in turn. The Western tradition regards the five sins of the spirit (pride, envy, anger, sloth, avarice) as more serious than the two sins of the flesh (gluttony, lust). The sins of the spirit are considered more respectable in most societies, but in fact they are the more destructive failures of love. Hence, we will spend two sessions on pride (because it's the worst sin); one each on envy, anger, sloth, and avarice; one session on gluttony and lust together; and one session on the reminders.

This book closes with five reminders. All are important, but we will discuss four: the need for discipline in becoming good, the dangers of self-deception and moralism, and (as in the introduction) the importance of doing, not just talking.

A final, optional session is available for groups who want to discuss how to put into practice what they've learned.

In the end, participants should be able to identify each deadly sin and life-giving virtue as expressed in society, in others and, most importantly, in themselves.

SESSION 1

Unless yours is an ongoing group, people will usually treat the first meeting as an opportunity to decide whether they want to participate. They will decide what they think about one another, the material, and the discussion format. Therefore, you'll want to do a few extra things in the first meeting that will help people feel comfortable with each other, have a sense of where the group is going, and become excited enough about the group to return.

Perhaps the best way to break the ice in a new group is to share a meal. Plan a simple enough meal that the focus will be on conversation. Schedule the meal so that people don't feel rushed as they eat, yet you still have ninety minutes for a full discussion session. You'll want the full ninety minutes in order to give people a realistic taste of what the group will be like. If sharing a full meal is impractical, consider planning a two-hour session in which the first half-hour is devoted to light refreshments and informal chatting.

Overview and Introductions   (20 minutes)

When the food is set aside and the group gathers formally, welcome everyone. Then take ten minutes to give people an overview of what to expect. Explain:

- What the *Trinity Forum Study Series* is: It makes the forum curricula available to study groups. It helps thoughtful people examine the foundational issues through which faith acts upon the public good of modern society. It is Christian in commitment, but open to all who are interested in its vision. Issues are discussed in the context of faith and the sweep of Western civilization.
- The theme of this particular study: You might read it aloud from page 7.
- The goals of this study: See page 305.
- The big picture of this study: See pages 312–313. A two- or three-minute summary of this will be plenty.
- The format of the group: Your discussions will take about ninety minutes. In each session, you will cover three or four readings from the book. Ideally, everyone will have read the readings ahead of time, but it is possible to participate without having done so. As the leader, you'll select questions for each reading that you think are

most helpful for the group to discuss. Your goal is an open give-and-take, and you will not be lecturing. Differing opinions are welcome.

- Ground rules: See the list on page 310.
- Logistics: Tell people anything they need to know about the location and schedule of the meetings. Explain that the group will finish promptly at the official ending time. That is the "soft" ending. However, if the host permits, you can also set a "hard" ending time thirty, sixty, or more minutes later. In that case, people are free to stay after the soft ending and talk informally until the hard ending time. (Setting a hard ending is a courtesy to the host if you are meeting in a home.)

Here is a list of suggested ground rules for your group. You may want to add to this list the ones about disagreement, page 310:

- Leadership: The leader is not an expert or an authority, merely a facilitator and fellow-seeker. All in the group are teachers, all are students.
- Confidentiality: All discussion is free, frank, and *off-the-record.* Nothing will be repeated outside the group without permission.
- Voluntary Participation: Everyone is free to speak; no one is required to take part. The only exception will be in the final session, when everyone will be asked to share two or three things he or she has found helpful or striking.
- Non-denominational, non-partisan spirit: Many people have strong beliefs and allegiances, both denominational and political. However, the desire here is to go deeper, so it will be important to transcend political advocacy and denominational differences. The book comes from the perspective of what C. S. Lewis called "mere Christianity," and reflects no particular denomination. Participants are welcome to express their own views and even to disagree with the readings.
- Punctuality: In order to get to all of the readings, the leader will keep the discussion moving. The formal meeting will begin and end on time.

If participants don't already know each other, go around the group and have each person introduce himself or herself briefly. You'll go first to model the length and type of response you're looking for. That is, if your answer is one sentence, the others will usually give one sentence. If you take one minute, or three minutes, others will follow suit. The same is true for the content of your answer: If you tell what you do for a living and who is in your family, others will do the same. If you want answers that are a bit more revealing or interesting, you can ask people to tell one thing about themselves that has nothing to do with their job or their family relationships.

Introduction   (10 minutes)

Pages 8–11 introduce the material by answering two questions: Why is it worthwhile to study ethics? And why, if we're going to study ethics, should we focus on the vices and virtues of the Western tradition? Much of the argument deals with failings in the ways modern society thinks about ethics. It would be a good idea for you to go over these failings briefly:

- Much of the current interest in ethics is simply fashionable and transient.
- Much of it aims more at avoiding being caught or sued than at doing right.
- Much of it emphasizes social ethics at the expense of individual virtue.
- It reflects shallow views of human nature—our capacity for good and our propensity for evil.
- It stumbles over our culture's belief that there are no absolute rights and wrongs.
- It ignores the problems of a "permissive," "transgressive," and "remissive" society.
- It ignores the virtues and vices, which are the most profound and influential ethical tradition in the West.

You might pause to let people respond to these claims about our culture. For instance, do participants agree that people they know are more concerned with not getting caught than with doing the right thing? Does everyone understand what "a high view of human nature" means? You might want to quickly clarify the words "permissive," "transgressive," and "remissive." *Permissive* means people seem to believe nothing is absolutely wrong and so everything is permitted. *Transgressive* means that breaking the rules is seen as a virtue. *Remissive* means standards are in an ever-accelerating slide.

The section, "Why 'Sins' and Why 'Seven'?" contains some of the themes of the study, so part of it is worth reading aloud. In the paragraph that begins "From then on . . . ," have someone start reading aloud with "Also, as Chaucer's Parson says. . . ." The key point here is that the seven deadly sins are not an exhaustive list of sins, but are the root of all other sins. As you study the seven over the next several weeks, you may want to think about how they give rise to all other sins that plague you.

Then have several people read aloud from the paragraph that begins "A number of other introductory points . . ." to the end of the introduction. Take a few moments to point out the themes that will run through your study: Each vice is a disordering of love, the sins of the spirit are more serious than those of the flesh, and the vices/sins are paired with the virtues/beatitudes. Invite the group to look over the summary list of vices and virtues to see where their discussion will go during the coming weeks. Point out features that may spark people's interest: Sloth, for example, is not what most people think.

If it seems helpful, you can add a few words about why it's valuable to explore ethics in a group. One of the writers you'll encounter in your study is the Greek philosopher Aristotle. Toward the end of his book *Ethics,* he makes some intriguing observations on how friendship helps people become good. First, when people are friends, they aim together at whatever they consider to be good, whether that's golfing well or loving God and neighbor well. Second, friends model for us what to do and be. Our friends' pride or humility rubs off on us as we learn from their example. Third, friends hold up a mirror to us so that we can see what we're really like. And fourth, they draw us to appreciate both their similarities and their otherness. Learning to appreciate their otherness forces us to deal with pride (Am I better than my friend?), envy (Is my friend better off than I am?), anger (What happens when my friend doesn't want to do something my way?), and so on. Your group can do all of these things for each other.

Finally, you may want to warn your group about what can happen when people study the vices. Strong emotions sometimes surface. A person may recognize her envy for the first time and be deeply ashamed. Someone may get angry at the suggestion that his pride is a problem. Some people find all seven deadly sins lurking in their hearts and despair ever changing. So much conviction all at once can make people feel hopeless. A few attitudes can help make this process constructive rather than discouraging. First, applaud people for recognizing their own faults. Assure them that they are not beyond hope: God is in the business of helping them change. If someone confesses sin, the appropriate response is to assure him of God's forgiveness. Second, treat expressions of emotion (sorrow, anger, and so on) with respect, and ask people to show respect for the group in the way they express strong emotions. Third, cultivate humor. Pride makes us want to believe, and want others to believe, that we are blameless. Humility recognizes that none of us is blameless. Nothing takes the air out of our pride better than a little humor.

Robert Coles   (15 minutes)

The main point of this introductory reading is that doing good is more important than talking about it. This is a helpful point with which to begin an extended discussion of vice and virtue. You are going to do a lot of talking about goodness and badness, but as this big-shot psychiatrist learned from an illiterate woman and a child, talk is cheap.

Have someone read aloud the first paragraph of this reading. Discuss question 1. Read aloud the rest of the reading. Discuss question 4.

Invite the group to keep Ruby Bridges in mind as they discuss the rest of the book.

Introduction to Pride   (10 minutes)

Each of the vices is introduced in a few pages. Have someone read aloud the first paragraph of the introduction to pride. Raise some questions that the group will be equipped to answer by the end of their study:

- Why is pride the worst of the seven deadly sins?
- How is pride a component of each of the other sins?
- Why is pride classed as a sin of the spirit?
- Why is it said that pride comes from the Devil, rather than the world or the flesh?
- Is it true that most of us are unaware of our pride?

The introduction goes on to contrast pride with self-respect. Read aloud the three paragraphs that begin "Against both these changes . . . ," "Seen this way . . . ," and "In most other views. . . ." Ask the group how pride is different from self-respect. What's wrong with pride?

Each of the introductions to the various vices includes practical ways in which the vice is expressed in individuals and in groups. Draw attention to these in the paragraph that begins "But this is only. . . ." Read aloud Dorothy Sayers' comment on pride: "The devilish strategy of Pride is that it attacks us, not in our weakest points, but in our strongest. It is preeminently the sin of the noble mind."

Ask the group to read the last two paragraphs on their own. Then ask, "What's the connection between pride and discontent?"

C. S. Lewis   (30 minutes)

Summarize in a few sentences who C. S. Lewis was. This reading comes from his book *Mere Christianity* and was originally a radio address.

Ask participants to read the first paragraph to themselves and share the statement that strikes them most deeply.

Ask people to reflect on Lewis's test question in the third paragraph under "The Great Sin": "How much do I dislike it when other people snub me, or refuse to take any notice of me, or shove their oar in, or patronize me, or show off?" Allow a minute of silence for people to think about this. Then ask, "What do you think of this question as a measure of pride?"

Read aloud the fourth paragraph and discuss question 3. Invite people to assess how competitive they are and whether they think their competitiveness reflects pride.

Read aloud the two paragraphs that begin "In God you come up . . ." and "That raises a terrible question." What test does Lewis offer for detecting pride in religious people? What do you think of his test?

Ask people to read Lewis's three misunderstandings of pride and to state each one simply. How is pride different from enjoyment of praise, or the love and admiration of someone? Why is it inaccurate to think our pride offends God's pride?

Conclude with question 9. In this first meeting of your group, people may not yet feel comfortable disclosing their temptations to pride. That's okay. Let the question hang in the air as people leave. You can raise the likelihood that people will be honest with themselves if you speak honestly about what tempts you to pride.

Ask participants to read Milton, Golding, and Taylor for next time. Also, send them off with some encouragement: Discussing sin is not meant to weigh them down, but to spur them on to a better course.

SESSION 2

Session 1 introduced the deadliest of the deadly sins: pride. Session 2 continues with three more readings on that topic. It might be helpful to begin by inviting people to recap what they discussed about pride in session 1. If necessary, prompt with a few questions: According to C. S. Lewis, why is pride a completely anti-God state of mind? Why do we so dislike pride in others? Why is pride classed as a sin of the spirit?

Two of the readings in this session deal with pride; the third discusses its opposite: humility. You will probably spend most of your time on the first two.

John Milton   (30 minutes)

Summarize the biographical information about Milton in a few sentences. *Paradise Lost* is Milton's epic poem about how Adam and Eve fell into sin. Many readers feel the most interesting character in the story is the villain, Satan. You've already heard from Lewis that pride comes from the Devil; Milton's depiction makes clear why that's the case.

The excerpt picks up the story after Satan and his fellow rebel angels have fought against God, and God has thrown them all out of heaven and into hell. To capture the drama of this scene, ask for two readers who will read with feeling. The first reader is the narrator; he or she reads from the beginning of the excerpt to the end of the paragraph ("Who durst defy th' Omnipotent to arms."). The second reader plays Satan in a coldly arrogant tone, reading from "Is this the region . . ." to the end of the excerpt. Before they begin, ask the rest of the group to follow along, underlining statements that express Satan's pride.

Note the connection between envy and pride in lines 9–11: Satan decided to deceive Eve ("the mother of mankind") because of his prideful envy of God and desire to take revenge on God. How was Satan's envy of God (his desire to rob God of God's happiness) related to his pride?

In the narrator's section, how does Milton describe Satan's pride?

In Satan's speech, what statements express pride?

Discuss questions 3 through 5 until you run out of time for this reading. Be sure to let the group discuss what they think about Satan: Does he seem strong or arrogant? Horrifying or heroic? Would he make a good corporate CEO?

William Golding   (40 minutes)

Summarize the first three paragraphs of the introduction to this reading, and read aloud the fourth. The theme of this reading is "the invisible line between calling and drivenness, vision and *hubris*, enterprise and egotism." This applies equally to the pride of religious people, business people, parents who push their children, or anyone bent on achieving something.

In the interest of time, you may want to quickly summarize answers to questions 1 through 3 and devote your discussion to questions 4, 5, 6, 8, and 10. The master builder tries to convince Jocelin that his project is impossible, a defiance of physical laws. He tells Jocelin to look down and contemplate how far the building—and his reputation—will fall when the project fails. He appeals to the Dean's humility, his sense of limitedness as a finite human being. "Pride goes before a fall," he seems to say. Jocelin imagines the devasting fall and almost gives in to the fear of failure. But the very appeal to human finitude inflames his pride. Read aloud the nine paragraphs from "Jocelin's eyes were shut" through "'Roger, I tell you the thing can be done.'" How does Jocelin deal with the suggestion that he has to live within human limits, the limits of physical reality? What is prideful about this attitude?

Discuss question 4. Read aloud the paragraph that begins "'You tried to frighten me. . . .'" Discuss question 5. Read aloud the three paragraphs that begin "'Now I'll tell you . . .'" and end with "'. . . a new thing comes.'" Discuss question 6.

Read the final line, spoken by the master builder. He sees Jocelin's ambition not as a response to God's call, but as a proud, diabolical drivenness. How do you see it? What marks the difference?

Discuss question 10.

If you have time, ask some summary questions about pride: What have you learned about pride from the readings? Why is it the worst sin?

Jeremy Taylor   (10 minutes)

After each set of readings about a vice, the book contains a couple of readings about the virtue that is the vice's superb opposite. Take a few minutes to go over the section entitled, "The Counterpoint to Pride" (page 60). Ask, how does false humility actually reflect pride? How does true humility show "realism about ourselves plus trust in God"?

The readings on humility are left largely for participants to read on their own. Take just a few minutes to look at Jeremy Taylor's guidelines for practicing humility, written 350 years ago. Read aloud numbers 1, 3, 4, 6, 7, 10, 11, 13, and 15. For each guideline, ask the group to put it into modern English terms. Then ask them to explain why it would or wouldn't work for cultivating humility.

In closing, ask participants to read the introduction to part 2 on envy, and the readings by Plutarch, Hawthorne, Shaffer, and Wesley. You might also invite them to try practicing Taylor's guidelines for a week and let the group know how it goes.

SESSION 3

Begin by asking whether anyone tried practicing Jeremy Taylor's guidelines for humility. If anyone did, invite that person to tell the group what he or she learned from the experience.

This session deals with envy, the feeling of horror at someone else's success or superiority and the desire to bring that person down. Envy is pride's Siamese twin: If we pridefully believe we need to be number one at all times, then we are bound to be horrified when someone else is, has, or appears to have more than we. The introduction contrasts envy with emulation and jealousy. Ask the group to read the relevant paragraphs and explain how envy is different from emulation (paragraphs 2 and 3) and jealousy (paragraphs 4 and 5).

From paragraph 6, read aloud the statement, "envy is a vice of proximity." Why are we more prone to envy people close to us than those who are very different?

Read aloud the paragraph that begins "Fourth, envy is often petty. . . ." The point there about hatred is valuable.

Plutarch   (20 minutes)

Summarize the introduction to this reading. You may also want to refer to the box on pages 81–82 entitled "Ostracism," which explains the custom. Plutarch's account of Aristides the Just illustrates envy on a public level. It tells how the Athenian masses came to envy Aristides so much that they had him exiled. It illustrates how envy can work in a democracy.

Plutarch presents Aristides as possibly wealthy and certainly just in his political dealings. In the first paragraph of the reading, Plutarch comments that it was usually men of "great houses" whose station exposed them to envy. In the fourth paragraph, though, he says Aristides was envied primarily for his reputation as the Just. Read aloud the fourth paragraph ("Aristides, therefore, had at first . . ."). Discuss questions 3 and 4. Read aloud the last paragraph and discuss question 5.

Discuss question 7.

Nathaniel Hawthorne (20 minutes)

Summarize the first two paragraphs of the introduction and read aloud the third. As the reading from Plutarch illustrated public envy, this excerpt from *The Scarlet Letter* illustrates private envy at its last stage: revenge. Chillingworth has chosen to respond to his wife's infidelity by devoting his life to bringing down the man who committed adultery with her.

Read the first paragraph of the excerpt and discuss question 1. Read the next paragraph and discuss question 3. Read the last paragraph and discuss questions 5 and 6.

Peter Shaffer (40 minutes)

Shaffer's *Amadeus* is a study in professional envy. Beyond that, it raises the question of whether God is unjust to endow people with unequal abilities. Perhaps it is not Aristides who should be exiled for being nobler than his fellows. Perhaps God is the one who should be banished for making Aristides so noble and Mozart so talented. Perhaps we should blame God for the limitations that wound our pride. After all, it's bad enough to be limited as all humans are, but to have our noses rubbed in it when we find ourselves more limited than someone else is a terrible thing!

Most participants will have seen the film *Amadeus,* if not the play. However, it may be helpful to set up the context of the two scenes excerpted here. In the first scene, Salieri has manipulated Mozart's wife into giving him the original and only drafts of the compositions Mozart has been working on. He has used Mozart's financial dependence to extort these scores, and envy has nearly driven him to blackmail Mozart's wife into sleeping with him, purely for revenge. Yet reading the musical scores only increases Salieri's envy.

The second scene is the very end of the play. Salieri has been up all night confessing to the audience the crimes to which envy has driven him. As dawn breaks, he performs his final acts of defiance against God.

Ask for someone to read Salieri's lines with gusto. (Ask someone who will not be embarrassed about garbling the Italian words.) Have someone else read the stage directions. Read the first scene, then discuss as much of questions 1 through 6 as you can in about twenty minutes. Then read the second scene and discuss questions 7 through 9.

Question 9 is personal. However, it may be easier for people to discuss their Salieri-like rivalries than their kinship with Hawthorne's Chillingsworth or Plutarch's common people. Still, you can broaden the question by inviting people to talk about their temptations to envy public figures or rivals for someone's affection. Be aware that this discussion could unearth intense feelings.

John Wesley   (10 minutes)

If you have time, take a few minutes to look at John Wesley's "Committed Body Rules." These rules were established in 1752 for the earliest Methodist groups. They are designed to address one of the expressions of envy in a community: gossip. Ask one or more of these questions: Which of these rules stands out to you most? Which do you think would be the most difficult to follow? How would your circle be different if each person committed to following these six rules?

In closing, ask participants to read the introduction to part 3 on anger, and the readings by Plutarch, Weir, Gordon, and King. You might also invite them to try practicing Wesley's rules for a week and let the group know how it goes.

SESSION 4

It will be important to go over some of the key points in the introduction to anger in part 3. Participants will come to this discussion with some preconceptions about anger that need to be put on the table. On the one hand, some people have grown up with the notion that all anger is bad and should be suppressed; one should be nice at all times. In reaction against this incorrect notion is the pop psychological belief that anger is just an emotion, that emotions are neither good nor bad, and that suppressing any emotion is unhealthy. The introduction makes clear that anger is sometimes sinful, sometimes necessary, and often a mixture. Suppressing an emotion (in the sense of pretending it's not there) does not prevent its negative consequences anymore than denying one's pride or envy will prevent him or her from causing harm. It is possible, however, to *govern* one's emotions without suppressing them.

To introduce the session, then, first contrast the sin of anger with mere emotion and with justifiable outrage. Then go over the five typical features of the sin: the contribution of the will, the wrongness of the motive, the excess and disorderliness of the expression, the desire for revenge, and the easy descent into contempt. You can use these five features as a grid by which to assess the three examples of anger in Alexander the Great (Plutarch), AIDS activist David Feinberg (Weir), and novelist Mary Gordon (her own account). In what ways does each of these people cross the line from feeling an emotion to committing a deadly sin? What harm does their anger do?

All three of these readings deal with hot anger. It may be important, therefore, to underscore the fifth feature of sinful anger: its easy slide into cold contempt. The attitude that someone is beneath our respect is a poisonous brew of anger and pride.

Plutarch   (15 minutes)

In order to have time for the fourth reading in this session, you'll need to spend just a brief time on Plutarch. Summarize the background to this reading (from its introduction) and the reading's first eight paragraphs. Alexander and his men are drunk at dinner, and Clitus, who once saved Alexander's life, is angry because Alexander has begun to treat his Greek comrades like Persian subjects. Clitus's outrage is partly justifiable (he is correct that he deserves more respect from Alexander than he has been getting lately), but his expression is disorderly. Not surprisingly, Alexander is provoked. Read aloud the four paragraphs beginning "But Clitus for all this. . . ." Evaluate Alexander's anger: Is its motive right or wrong? Is its expression excessive? Disorderly? In what way is his will involved? What role does revenge play? This is a fairly straightforward incidence of drunken anger, so there probably won't be much debate. You might draw attention to the fact that Aristophanes had hidden Alexander's sword before the argument began—what does that say about Aristophanes's previous experience of his master?

Now read the last three paragraphs, which describe the advice Alexander gets after his rage turns to remorse. Discuss question 7. Plutarch takes a fairly typical display of drunken rage and shows how rationalizing such behavior ("It was fate!" or "You're the boss; you can do what you like!") makes it even deadlier. Note especially how Anaxarchus feeds Alexander's pride and encourages him to view everyone but himself with contempt. How will this affect his ability to control his anger in the future?

John Weir   (30 minutes)

John Weir writes about "anger politics" not as an outsider but as one who has traveled well down that road and seen its dead end. He and David Feinberg have been members of ACT UP, the now-defunct gay rights organization that was fueled by anger over the AIDS crisis. Now Feinberg is dead, and Weir reflects on what he has learned from his closest friend's life and death.

In the first paragraph, Weir mentions a tenet of ACT UP ideology: AIDS patients were not merely dying, they were being "killed by government neglect." Where do you hear anger politics in that assertion? How are such words intended to affect the public? What other emotive phrases have you heard used in anger politics?

Begin reading aloud from the last sentence of the third paragraph: "He used irony to distance himself from pain. . . ." Read that sentence and the next two paragraphs. End with, "The group's miscalculation is that feelings alone, directly and powerfully expressed, can change things." What was the place of rage in the psychology of homosexual activists? In what other group activism have you seen anger play a similar defining role?

Discuss question 5. When you talk about crossing the line into deadly sin, keep in mind the five typical features of the sin. Think about political causes you support as well as those you oppose or to which you are indifferent.

Read aloud the paragraph that begins "Like David. . . ." Discuss question 6.

In the paragraph that begins "It isn't poetry . . ." read from "He was angry about dying" to the end of the paragraph. Discuss question 8. What's the connection between such anger and selfishness?

Mary Gordon   (30 minutes)

Many participants may find it hard to identify with a general who murders his comrade in a drunken rage or with an AIDS activist. But most of us can recognize ourselves in Gordon's account of losing it at her family.

Read aloud the first paragraph and discuss question 1. Read the second paragraph and discuss question 2. Read the fourth paragraph and discuss question 3. Discuss questions 4, 5, and 8 to the degree that you have time.

Martin Luther King Jr.   (15 minutes)

The utter opposite of exploding or seething with rage toward those who harm us is loving our enemies. It's easy to dismiss platitudes about love, but King knew what it was to have enemies. He was stalked by them, jailed by them, and eventually murdered by one of them. Yet instead of feeding the all-too-legitimate rage of black Americans, he called them—all of us—to a higher way of responding to injustice. The contrast between King and Feinberg is sobering.

Read the first paragraph and discuss question 1. Read the fourth through the sixth paragraphs and discuss question 2. Read the paragraphs that begin "We must hasten to say . . ." and "My friends, we have followed. . . ." Discuss question 4. As a strategy for a successful personal life, whose strategy is more practical: David Feinberg's or Martin Luther King's? What about as a strategy for changing society?

To close, invite participants to summarize what they've learned about anger from this discussion. Ask them to read Pascal, Kierkegaard, Havel, and Herbert for your next session. Also, encourage them to notice how they deal with anger during the coming week and to report what they learn when you next meet.

SESSION 5

Most Americans equate sloth with laziness or even recreation. You may want to begin your discussion by reading aloud the definitions in the introduction to sloth in part 4: "spiritual dejection that has given up on the pursuit of God, the true, the good, and the beautiful" (paragraph 2); "a sluggishness of spirit, feeling, mind, and eventually body that grows from a state of dejection over the worthwhileness of spiritual things" (paragraph 4); "despondency over meaning, moral burnout . . . paralysis of will . . . hatred of all things spiritual that require effort" (paragraph 5). This last line raises the question of whether some spiritual things require effort or whether grace eliminates the need for discipline, tough choices, and persistence in the face of obstacles. Put this way, the answer seems obvious, but one can find believers in effortless spirituality today among Christians, Jews, and New Age adherents of all stripes.

The section "Practical Applications" mentions middle-aged worldweariness, youthful despair, and the exaltation of meaninglessness that is hip in art and music. Keep these and other manifestations of sloth in mind as you discuss the readings.

Blaise Pascal   (30 minutes)

For Pascal, sloth is not caring whether or not one will cease to exist at death. The immortality of the soul is the ultimate spiritual issue, and not caring about it is the ultimate spiritual laziness. This definition will bewilder many people today and perhaps some in your group.

Question 1 is the crucial one here. Many modern people are so far from Pascal's view of the world that his opening sentence in this reading would mean nothing to them. They feel deeply about many things, but the immortality of the soul is not one of them. The average neuroscientist will tell you that what Pascal called a soul is really a complex pattern of electrochemical reactions in a human brain. And while caring for one's soul attracts enough interest to produce best-selling books, these books often teach how to have a loving and happy soul now and say nothing about planning for the day after one's heart stops beating. It will be important to ask participants whether and why the soul's immortality matters to them.

You may also have time for questions 3 and 5 (read aloud the fifth through the seventh paragraphs, beginning with "This negligence . . ."), but be sure to read Pascal's final paragraph and discuss questions 6 and 7.

Søren Kierkegaard (20 minutes)

Kierkegaard defines sloth in a way more moderns could grasp: Sloth is the lack of passion. The romantics among us are much in favor of passion—passion for art, nature, sexual pleasure, books, food, or even social causes. Kierkegaard might have ranked such people above the "shopkeeping souls" he decries in this reading. Passion for something is better than passion for nothing. The next question is, "What things most deserve our passion?"

But begin with questions 1 through 3, and address the question, "Passionate about what?" if you have time.

Václav Havel (30 minutes)

Havel speaks to the peculiarly modern form of sloth: deliberate apathy about any meaning in life higher than one's own survival. Havel might say the "shopkeeping souls" whom Kierkegaard bemoaned suffered from unpremeditated resignation— they had given up on life's meaning without ever having thought about it. Even worse, Havel observed deliberately resigned people who have thought about it. They may have spent a short or long period as persons with ideals, as believers in something, but they have become disillusioned and given up. Moreover, they defend the wisdom of their resignation as stoutly as any true believer.

Read the first paragraph and discuss question 1. Read the third paragraph up to the parentheses and discuss question 2. Read the two paragraphs that begin "To sum up . . ." and "Everything meaningful in life . . ." and discuss question 4.

The sentence, "The tragedy of modern man . . ." has become a famous line because it so well defines modern sloth. Read it and discuss question 5.

George Herbert (10 minutes)

You can conclude your discussion in one of two ways. Participants may want to talk about their own struggles with sloth (it's easier to admit to sloth or anger than to admit pride or envy). Or they may want to talk about the opposite of sloth: the hunger for spiritual reality regardless of cost. If so, take a few minutes to look at Herbert's poem, "Love," and discuss question 1.

For next time, ask participants to read Tolstoy, Gilkey, and Hugo in part 5 and to be aware of the forces in their worlds that tempt them to sloth.

SESSION 6

have probably found in each session that people bring to the discussion pre-
ceptions about each deadly sin that need to be addressed. Pride is easily
confused with self-respect. Anger is misunderstood in light of the pop-psych
doctrine that emotions are never good or bad, but simply happen. In the same
way, avarice is obscured by decades of rhetoric about the virtues and/or evils
of capitalism. One set of voices condemns corporations for seeking profits above
the welfare of their workers, other people, and the environment. Another set
of voices sees rampant materialism and consumption as the engine of a happy,
healthy economy. Each group views the other with a certain contempt.

For the first group, avarice is a terrible, hideous sin of which *other* people (rich
people, corporate executives, stockholders, politicians) are guilty. The second group,
weary of such accusations, tunes out any suggestion that their relationship with
possessions might be sinful. You could say a little about this war of rhetoric at the
beginning of your discussion so that people can look at the readings with fresh eyes.

The fact is, it is nearly impossible for anyone in our society—welfare recip-
ient, factory worker, or business manager—to avoid the temptation to avarice.
Children know themselves to be consumers long before they think about being citizens. Advertising—the systematic stimulation of material desire—is a legitimate
business expense and a ubiquitous presence. Whether that is a social problem
would be an interesting topic for discussion.

The introduction to avarice explains that the desire for temporal possessions
becomes a problem when it "becomes inordinate and then idolatrous—in other
words, when reliance on God's gifts becomes a substitute for relying on God
Himself." When enjoyment of things becomes worship of things, then it is sinful.

Few people would admit to "worshiping" things. Your task in the readings,
then, will be to identify signs of possession-worship in the characters of
Tolstoy's fictional story and Gilkey's true story. If participants can see how those
characters worship things, then they can more easily see how they themselves
do so. Put simply, the avaricious person loves things and uses people. The generous or merciful person (as stunningly portrayed in the excerpt from Hugo's
Les Misérables) uses things and loves people. The theme of Tolstoy's story is
that to love things more than people is foolish: It will ruin your life. The theme
of Gilkey's story is that to love things more than people is destructive: It will
ruin your society. Hugo's story illustrates how loving people more than things
enriches both the individual and the community.

Leo Tolstoy   (35 minutes)

This story is too long to read aloud in its entirety. If people have read it ahead of time, you may not have to read much in the group because the story is memorable. If necessary, summarize the first section, then take turns reading aloud paragraphs of section II until you've read all of it. Read also the first two paragraphs of section III. Discuss question 3.

Summarize the rest of section III and the first three paragraphs of section IV. Read aloud the paragraph under section IV that begins "He went on in the same way . . . ," as well as the next short paragraph. Summarize the rest of section IV, section V, and the first half of section VI. Then in section VI, read from "'Our price is always the same . . .'" through "if you don't return on the same day to the spot whece you started, your money is lost." Discuss question 4.

Summarize section VII. In section VIII, read from "'I will go on for another three miles . . .'" through "he looked at the sun and saw that it was noon." In section IX, read from "'What shall I do?'" through the end of the paragraph that begins "Though afraid of death, he could not stop." Then read the ending as Pahóm dies and his servant buries him. Ask the group, "What is the meaning of the story's title? Why does Pahóm die in his pursuit of land?" Discuss also questions 7 and 8.

Langdon Gilkey   (35 minutes)

Make the point that Shantung Compound was a miniature society in which most of the dynamics of larger societies could be seen in sharp focus. Summarize the situation at the beginning of the story. Read aloud the paragraph that begins "This question, 'Who is to get them?'. . ." Discuss question 2.

Direct people to the paragraph that begins "Two days later . . ." and ask question 3. Look at the paragraph that begins "When we tried to find out . . ." and discuss question 4. Read aloud the paragraphs that begin "The experience of the Red Cross parcels . . . ," "And yet, the introduction of this wealth . . . ," and "Had this food. . . ." Read the first half of the paragraph that begins, "I suddenly saw. . . ." Discuss questions 6 and 7.

Victor Hugo (20 minutes)

Avarice grows from a world view of scarcity. The avaricious person usually believes he has insufficient resources and must acquire more in order to have "enough." At the very best, he believes he has just enough to satisfy his desires (and so can consume with abandon). He does not believe he has enough to share with others. Life is about acquiring and consuming in order not to feel deprived.

The bishop in Hugo's novel has a very different view of the world. He believes in a generous God who has provided him with more than enough for his needs. He does not find his life's meaning in acquiring, consuming, and avoiding deprivation. He finds meaning in giving and loving. His is a world view of abundance.

Most participants are probably familiar with this story because of the musical based on the book. For those who are not, you might briefly explain that Jean Valjean did forced labor on a galley ship for many years as punishment for theft. He has just been freed at the end of his sentence, but he has nothing and is everywhere spurned as a convict. On a rainy night he has been given hospitality by a man whom he thinks is an ordinary priest. He has repaid the kindness by stealing the priest's silver cutlery.

Read three paragraphs from the exchange between the bishop and Madame Magloire, beginning with "'See, that is where he got out.'" Next, read from the paragraph that begins "In the meantime . . ." to the end. Discuss questions 3 through 7 with as much time as you have. Or you could simply ask, "In what ways would you like to resemble the bishop? What would that require?"

You'll deal with both of the sins of the flesh next time. Ask the group to read the introduction to gluttony and the Lewis reading in part 6, as well as the introduction to lust, the Lawrence reading in part 7, and the William F. May reading under purity of heart.

SESSION 7

The sins of the flesh—gluttony and lust—involve excessive love for two normal physical pleasures: food and sex. As avarice worships possession, so gluttony worships food and lust worships sex. To worship something is to ascribe ultimate value to it, to see it as the source of one's life. All of us depend on food for physical survival, but while the spiritual person thanks God as the provider of food, the glutton treats food as god. He turns to food for spiritual and emotional fulfillment—to avoid anxiety, sadness, or meaninglessness. The glutton has a "relationship" with food: Food is his friend or his enemy. This relationship seems more important than relationships with real people, so gluttony interferes with love. Food is often on the glutton's mind, driving out other thoughts.

These characteristics of gluttony resemble what modern experts in substance abuse call *addiction*. One can have a gluttonous attachment to almost any pleasure: food, dieting, alcohol, painkillers, mood-enhancing drugs, television, video games, sports, exercise, mystery novels, skiing. That which relaxes the mind or strengthens the body in moderation becomes corrupt when done (as the introduction to gluttony puts it) "too soon, too expensively, too much, too eagerly, [or] with too much fuss." Your discussion will focus on food, but you can welcome people to bring up other pleasures they are tempted to idolize.

C. S. Lewis   (20 minutes)

As the introduction points out, our modern obsession with thinness has made the gluttony of excess less common than the "gluttony of delicacy." This is what Lewis's senior devil, Screwtape, describes in this reading. To get at what Lewis means by "gluttony of delicacy," read aloud the last sentence of the first paragraph ("She would be astonished . . ."), all of the second paragraph ("But what do quantities matter . . . "), and the first few sentences of the third. Discuss question 2.

Read the last few sentences of the fifth paragraph, starting with, "But, however you approach it. . . ." Discuss question 4. If people have trouble seeing their own attachments to indulgences, ask them how they react when they miss their favorite television program, sport (watching it or playing it), coffee, or health routine. Some people have trouble seeing any gluttony in their lives because self-indulgence is treated as a virtue in our culture as long as one doesn't grow fat or lose the ability to work long, hard hours.

If you have time, look back at what the introduction says about dieting. Ask the group how one can tell when dieting is appropriate and when it becomes gluttony of delicacy.

D. H. Lawrence   (40 minutes)

Before you turn to the excerpt from Lawrence's novel, spend a little time on the introduction to lust. In the paragraph that begins "Lust is often formally dissected . . . ," read the last two sentences: "But at its heart, lust is an idolizing of sex. . . ." Read also the paragraph that begins "Many evils have traditionally. . . ." These will set the stage for your discussion of Lawrence. As participants examine the excerpt from *The Rainbow*, ask them to assess Ursula's behavior in light of these comments about lust. Two of the intriguing aspects of this excerpt are that the destructive lust is the woman's and the couple are engaged.

Read aloud the second paragraph and discuss question 1. How does this paragraph show that the object of Ursula's desire is not Skrebensky?

Read the eight short paragraphs beginning with "'I want to go,' she cried, in a strong, dominant voice." Discuss question 4. Read the paragraph that begins, "Morning brought her . . ." and discuss question 6. Why has this sexual escapade on a moonlit beach not left the couple feeling fulfilled?

Read the paragraph that begins "Very far off . . ." and the one after it. What phrases show Ursula dehumanizing Skrebensky? Discuss question 9. Read the last paragraph and discuss question 11.

William F. May   (30 minutes)

The opposite of worshiping food or sex or anything else is worshiping God with a pure heart. Read the last few sentences of the first paragraph of this reading and the first sentence of the second paragraph. Discuss question 2. Read the rest of the second paragraph and discuss question 3. Read the third paragraph and discuss question 4. Read the next paragraph and discuss questions 5 and 6.

You have now looked at all of the seven deadly sins. Session 8 will address four of the six "reminders" in the final section of the book. These are things to keep in mind as you pursue virtue in your own lives. Ask the group to read Aristotle (Reminder One), Johnson (Reminder Two), Gilkey (Reminder Three) and MacMillan (Reminder Five).

SESSION 8

If only learning *about* the deadly sins were enough. However, the point of all this talking is to do something constructive with what you've learned. Read aloud the opening paragraph of the "Five Reminders" section to explain the purpose of these reminders.

You will be skimming quickly through four readings in order to have time for the last portion of this meeting, entitled "Closing Thoughts." The omitted questions on these readings would be worthy of an additional session if you so choose, but the "Closing Thoughts" section is important if this is your last meeting. Alternatively, the optional session 9 page 340 would be another way to bring closure to the group.

Reminder One: Discipline   (15 minutes)

The first reminder deals with the role of practice in cultivating the virtues. Some Christians feel that discussion of discipline undermines the primacy of the Holy Spirit in transforming us. The introduction to this reminder explains that discipline works in partnership with the Spirit.

Read aloud the thesis of the reading from Aristotle's *Ethics:* "Moral virtues, like crafts, are acquired by practice and habituation." Then read aloud the third paragraph: "But the virtues we do acquire. . . ." Discuss question 3. In the fourth paragraph, read the sentence that begins "Men will become good builders . . ." and the sentence that follows it. Discuss question 4. The point here is that the sheer number of relationships we have had is no guarantee that our pride and anger are decreasing. On the contrary, unless we "build well"— that is, consciously practice humility and forgiveness—we will continue to behave destructively in relationship after relationship.

Discuss questions 5 and 6 if you have time (that is, if you have scheduled an extra meeting).

Reminder Two: Deception   (20 minutes)

The second reminder is to watch for our habit of deception. As the "companion sin to the seven deadly sins . . . it serves to soften or disguise the others." Uprooting envy or avarice will be impossible as long as we're lying to ourselves and others about our envy and avarice. This issue is so central that it's worth plenty of time to discuss it.

In the first paragraph of the Johnson reading, Johnson describes the first way in which we deceive ourselves about ourselves: substitution of single acts for habits. Ask participants to read the first paragraph and discuss question 1.

The second paragraph describes the mirror image of the first: Instead of viewing a single (good) act as demonstration of our character, we view a single (bad) act as an exception to our character's general rule. Ask participants what examples of this they have seen.

Read aloud the first sentence of the third paragraph. It describes the third form of self-deception. Ask participants which of the three forms they find most tempting:

- Viewing a single good act as evidence of a habit
- Viewing a single bad act as an exception
- Praising a virtue rather than practicing it

Johnson points out the weaknesses of both friends and enemies in holding us accountable. He advocates cultivating a habit of self-examination. Nonetheless, because we all have blindspots, some feedback from others provides a useful companion to self-examination. Discuss questions 4 and 5 if you have extra time (if you have scheduled an extra session).

Reminder Three: Moralism   (20 minutes)

If you have time for only three readings in this session, skip this one so that you can end with Reminder Five. However, because moralism is so common among Christians, it deserves at least a brief discussion. Moralism is a form of self-deception. The moralist selects a narrow list of vices in order to rationalize his or her self-claimed superiority. It is a form of spiritual pride. The Gilkey reading describes how missionaries in the internment camp focused on smoking and other petty sins of the flesh (gambling, drinking, swearing) so that they wouldn't have to face their own besetting sins: pride and lovelessness.

Summarize the situation with the cigarette rations that sets up this reading. Read aloud the conversation between Smithfield and the other man on his shift—the four paragraphs beginning with "'Look, Smithfield. . . .'" Discuss question 3. Read the two paragraphs beginning with "Instead of bringing love and service . . ." and discuss question 4. Read the paragraph that begins "It had long been evident . . ." and discuss question 5.

Discuss question 7 if you have time.

Reminder Five: Demonstration   (15 minutes)

The account of Maximilian Kolbe from Ian MacMillan's novel takes your group back to where you started with Robert Cole's account of Ruby Bridges. Like Bridges, Kolbe is a person who enacts the gospel in a situation that would paralyze those of us who are more accustomed to talk. It is easy to make a show of virtue when the stakes are low, but in the face of violent malevolence, people respond according to what is in their hearts. You needn't spend a lot of time going through the questions on the MacMillan reading. Simply summarize what Kolbe did (see the second paragraph of the reading's introduction) and ask, "What was it about Kolbe that affected so many people?" To spark people's memories, you can read aloud portions of the reading. For example, read from "Vierck unlocks the door" through "'We must leave,' Vierck says." Read also the paragraph that begins "'A priest,' he says, 'and look what he's done to you'" at the end of the August 9 entry.

Closing Thoughts   (20 minutes)

To close your session, go around the room and let each person respond to this question: "What key thoughts, ideas, and comments struck you personally during our study over the past eight weeks? What stands out to you?" Think carefully ahead of time who you will ask to answer this question first, because that person's answer will set the tone for the other responses. Choose someone who you think is reflective and has been taking the readings to heart.

Thank everyone for participating. Some light refreshments and informal time to talk would be a fitting way to end the meeting.

SESSION 9 (OPTIONAL)

Some groups may want some extended time to contemplate what participants want to do with what they have learned and areas of their lives in which they want to take action. Other groups may prefer to have those conversations as couples at home or informally outside the group. Whether you choose to have a formal session 9, informal conversations, or private reflection, here are some questions to consider:

- How important is character to you in our shared public life? In your family? At your work? In other areas of your life?
- What evidence of the seven deadly vices do you see in your own life?
- What action can you take to uproot those vices from your heart and replace them with the habits of the seven virtues? What is one habit you can focus on?

AUTHOR

Os Guinness is a Senior Fellow at The Trinity Forum in McLean, Virginia. Born in China and educated in England, he is a graduate of Oxford University. He is the author or editor of numerous books, including *The Call, The American Hour, Invitation to the Classics,* and *Time for Truth.*